BEACH BOYS ARCHEOLOGY
VOLUME 8

BEACH BOYS AND BRIAN WILSON JOURNALS

BEACH BOYS JOURNALS AND BRIAN WILSON SESSIONS

FOREWORD

JOURNALS PART 1 (1961-67)

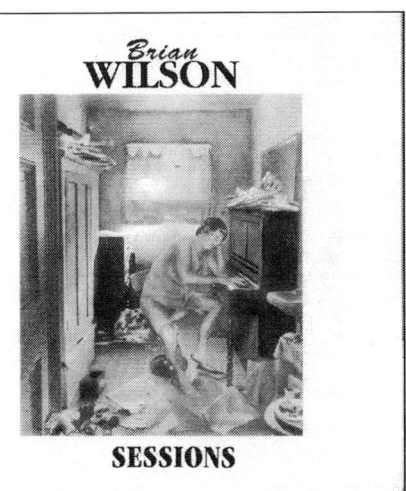

JOURNALS PART 2 (1968-88)

Brian WILSON SESSIONS

EARLY IN THEIR EVOLUTION, bootlegs were vinyl discs in plain white cardboard sleeves with either an ink stamp on the cover or a copied black and white sheet inserted between the cover and the plastic seal. They were produced in some of the actual pressing plants that were producing legitimate records and issued in very limited numbers. The Beach Boys even had a handful of bootleg discs produced from various entrepreneurs, some of whom were general bootleggers and others who were actual fans of the band. The book *Bootleg!* offers a very interesting if not fully accurate history of the records and the people who produced them.

Jump ahead 25 years or so and CDs are all the rage. The bootleg had come a long way from the mediocre sound quality tapes that had been previously used. Some discs were issued with deluxe color covers which made it hard to tell from legitimate releases. Computers made it easier to work on the audio quality and the graphic design of the covers.

The bootleg industry had learned a lot about bootleg collectors and their appetites. Which brings us to The Beach Boys Journals, at that time the most ambitious to-date effort to package a bootleg for Beach Boys fans. The creators clearly intended to amass the rare and unreleased versions of songs...including tracks that were released on the first Capitol Box Set. Maybe the goal was a supplement to the original LPs (or CD reissues).

What made the collection truly remarkable (besides the creation of what was essentially a 23-disc set split into three parts) was the packaging. Each set came with a pressed tin case (which ironically was too small to hold the book and CDs together...oops) and a 64 page 12" x 12" book in color and black and white.

Supposedly, only 1000 of the sets were created. Many times, collectors got copies or "burns" of the discs, which certainly came without the collector books. So here is your opportunity to have replications of the books (in a slightly smaller size but more convenient format). The information and articles reprinted in the booklets come from a variety of sources. Some of it is still accurate and some has since been proven to be incomplete. It still offers an interesting insight into both the band and the release that at the time was revolutionary in many aspects.

These days, most people can download the content of these and other boots, and huge amounts of other unreleased audio, and store it on their computers without ever seeing or needing the graphics. But in those days, the included graphics were part of the same and part of the experience for fans. Here's a chance to see some of the rare and limited materials that previously made their way into fans hands and collections. Enjoy.

BEACH BOYS JOURNALS AND BRIAN WILSON SESSIONS

JOURNALS PART 1

JOURNALS PART 2 (1968-88)

SESSIONS

BEACH BOYS JOURNALS PART 1

JOURNALS PART 1 (1961-67)

BEACH BOYS JOURNALS PART 1

BEACH BOYS JOURNALS PART 1

COMPUTER ENHANCED - DIGITALLY REMASTERED

JOURNALS PART 1 (1961 - 67)

DISC ONE
1. SURFIN'
2. PUNCHLINE
3. THEIR HEARTS WERE FULL OF SPRING
4. LAND AHOY
5. LAND AHOY
6. LAND AHOY
7. CINDY OH CINDY
8. SURFIN' USA
9. LITTLE SURFER GIRL
10. IN MY ROOM
11. THE BAKER MAN
12. OUR CAR CLUB
13. THE ROCKIN' SURFER
14. BE TRUE TO YOUR SCHOOL
15. I DO
16. IN MY ROOM
17. HUSHABYE
18. WENDY
19. I GET AROUND
20. I GET AROUND
21. DON'T BACK DOWN
22. ALL SUMMER LONG
23. LITTLE HONDA
24. WHEN I GROW UP (TO BE A MAN)
25. I'M SO YOUNG
26. ALL DRESSED UP FOR SCHOOL
27. DANCE DANCE DANCE
28. DANCE DANCE DANCE (RADIO SPOTS)
29. HI, THIS IS THE BEACH BOYS'
30. K.O.M.A.
31. BRIAN
32. K.A.Y.A.
33. K.D.W.B.
34. K.E.W.B.
35. MURRAY THE 'K'
36. WHERE'S YOUR I.D.?
37. THE BEACH BOYS SHOW
38. HAPPY BIRTHDAY TO YOU
39. HONDA '55
TOTAL CD TIME 62.20

DISC TWO
1. PLEASE LET ME WONDER
2. PLEASE LET ME WONDER
3. PLEASE LET ME WONDER
4. PLEASE LET ME WONDER
5. PLEASE LET ME WONDER
6. DO YOU WANNA DANCE
7. DO YOU WANNA DANCE
8. IN THE BACK OF MY MIND (INSTR)
9. GOOD TO MY BABY
10. GOOD TO MY BABY
11. I'M SO YOUNG
12. HELP ME RONDA
13. BRIAN & MURRY WILSON (PART 1)
14. BRIAN & MURRY WILSON (PART 2)
15. BRIAN & MURRY WILSON (PART 3)
16. BRIAN & MURRY WILSON (PART 4)
17. HELP ME RONDA
18. HELP ME RHONDA
19. MONKEY'S UNCLE
20. LET HIM RUN WILD
TOTAL CD TIME 69.19

DISC THREE
1. CALIFORNIA GIRLS
2. CALIFORNIA GIRLS
3. GRADUATION DAY
4. THE LITTLE GIRL I ONCE KNEW
5. THE LITTLE GIRL I ONCE KNEW
6. TROMBONE DIXIE
7. WOULDN'T IT BE NICE
8. WOULDN'T IT BE NICE
9. WOULDN'T IT BE NICE
10. WOULDN'T IT BE NICE
11. WOULDN'T IT BE NICE
12. YOU STILL BELIEVE IN ME
13. YOU STILL BELIEVE IN ME
14. HANG ON TO YOUR EGO
15. HANG ON TO YOUR EGO
16. HANG ON TO YOUR EGO
17. HANG ON TO YOUR EGO
18. I JUST WASN'T MADE FOR THESE TIMES
TOTAL CD TIME 71.00

DISC FOUR
1. I'M WAITING FOR THE DAY
2. GOD ONLY KNOWS
3. GOD ONLY KNOWS
4. GOD ONLY KNOWS
5. I'M WAITING FOR THE DAY
6. I JUST WASN'T MADE FOR THESE TIMES
7. STUDIO CHAT
8. DON'T TALK (PUT YOUR HEAD ON MY SHOULDER)
9. DON'T TALK (PUT YOUR HEAD ON MY SHOULDER)
10. DON'T TALK (PUT YOUR HEAD ON MY SHOULDER)
11. HEROES & VILLAINS
12. HEROES & VILLAINS
13. GOOD VIBRATIONS
14. GOOD VIBRATIONS
15. GOOD VIBRATIONS
16. GOOD VIBRATIONS
17. GOOD VIBRATIONS
18. GOOD VIBRATIONS
19. GOOD VIBRATIONS
20. GOOD VIBRATIONS
21. GOOD VIBRATIONS
22. GOOD VIBRATIONS
23. DO YOU LIKE WORMS
24. DO YOU LIKE WORMS
TOTAL CD TIME 63.13

DISC FIVE
1. INTRO
2. OUR PRAYER
3. OUR PRAYER
4. HEROES AND VILLAINS
5. HEROES & VILLAINS
6. HEROES & VILLAINS
7. HEROES & VILLAINS
8. HEROES & VILLAINS
9. HEROES & VILLAINS
10. HEROES & VILLAINS
11. HEROES & VILLAINS
12. DO YOU LIKE WORMS
13. DO YOU LIKE WORMS
14. GOOD VIBRATIONS
15. WONDERFUL
16. WONDERFUL
17. CHILD IS FATHER OF THE MAN
18. CHILD IS FATHER OF THE MAN
19. CABINESSENCE
20. CABINESSENCE
21. CABINESSENCE 'THE ELEMENTS' (EARTH)
22. VEGA-TABLES / I'M IN GREAT SHAPE (WIND)
23. VEGA-TABLES / I'M IN GREAT SHAPE (WIND)
24. WIND CHIMES (FIRE)
25. MRS. O'LEARY'S COW (WATER)
26. COOL COOL WATER
27. I'D LOVE TO SAY DADA
28. SURF'S UP
29. SURF'S UP
30. THE OLD MASTER PAINTER / YOU ARE MY SUNSHINE (BONUS TRACKS)
31. HOLIDAYS
32. BARNYARD
33. TONES
TOTAL CD TIME 74.07

DISC SIX
1. SURF'S UP
2. SURF'S UP
3. MEDLEY - THE OLD MASTER PAINTER / YOU ARE MY SUNSHINE
4. 'SMILE' RADIO ADVERT
5. TONES
6. TONES
7. TONES
8. YOU'RE WELCOME
9. SHE'S GOIN' BALD
10. WITH ME TONIGHT
11. GOD ONLY KNOWS
12. CALIFORNIA GIRLS
13. SURFER GIRL
14. SURFER GIRL
15. YOU'RE SO GOOD TO ME
16. THE LETTER
17. HELP ME RHONDA
18. HEROES & VILLAINS
19. THEIR HEARTS WERE FULL OF SPRING
20. WITH A LITTLE HELP FROM MY FRIENDS
21. THE LETTER
22. I WAS MADE TO LOVE HER
23. CAN'T WAIT TOO LONG
24. CAN'T WAIT TOO LONG
25. CAN'T WAIT TOO LONG
TOTAL CD TIME 58.34

DISC SEVEN
1. CARL WILSON / INTRO
2. WHAT I'D SAY
3. INTRO
4. SURFIN' USA
5. SURFER GIRL
6. HUSHABYE
7. BE TRUE TO YOUR SCHOOL
8. DON'T WORRY BABY
9. INTERVIEW
10. FUN FUN FUN
11. LONG TALL TEXAN
12. IN MY ROOM
13. GRADUATION DAY
14. PAPA-OOM-MOW-MOW
15. INTRODUCTION TO THE BAND
16. LITTLE DEUCE COUPE
17. SURFER GIRL
18. MONSTER MASH
19. LOUIE, LOUIE
20. SURFIN' USA
21. DON'T WORRY BABY
22. I GET AROUND
23. JOHNNY B. GOODE
24. INTRODUCTION
25. LITTLE DEUCE COUPE
26. IN MY ROOM
27. BE TRUE TO YOUR SCHOOL
28. SURFER GIRL
29. KFWB THEME
30. CLOSING CREDITS
TOTAL CD TIME 66.19

DISC EIGHT
1. RUBY BABY
2. PREAMBLE
3. YOU'VE GOT TO HIDE YOUR LOVE AWAY
4. YOU'VE GOT TO HIDE YOUR LOVE AWAY
5. TICKET TO RIDE
6. PREAMBLE
7. RIOT IN CELL BLOCK NO. 9
8. RIOT IN CELL BLOCK NO. 9
9. LAUGH AT ME
10. ONE KISS LED TO ANOTHER
11. ONE KISS LED TO ANOTHER
12. (PREAMBLE / JOKE)
13. MOUNTAIN OF LOVE
14. MOUNTAIN OF LOVE
15. MOUNTAIN OF LOVE
16. MOUNTAIN OF LOVE
17. CALIFORNIA GIRLS
18. I GET AROUND
19. I GET AROUND
20. POISON IVY / LITTLE DEUCE COUPE
21. HELP ME RHONDA
22. I GET AROUND
23. MEDLEY - SURFIN' SAFARI / FUN FUN FUN / SHUT DOWN / LITTLE DEUCE COUPE / SURFIN' USA
24. INTRO
25. SURFER GIRL
26. PAPA-OOM-MOW-MOW
27. INTRO
28. YOU'RE SO GOOD TO ME
29. YOU'RE SO GOOD TO ME
30. INTRO
31. YOU'VE GOT TO HIDE YOUR LOVE AWAY
32. INTRO
33. GOOD VIBRATIONS
34. INTRO
35. CALIFORNIA GIRLS
36. INTRO
37. SLOOP JOHN B
38. WOULDN'T IT BE NICE
39. INTRO
40. GOD ONLY KNOWS
41. HEROES & VILLAINS
42. ALL I WANNA DO
TOTAL CD TIME 73.47

Brother records

THE 2 'JOURNALS' BOX SETS (WITH A TOTAL OF 16 CD'S) CONTAIN ALL YOU NEED AS A BEACH BOYS COLLECTOR. NEARLY HALF OF THE TRACKS IN BOTH BOX SETS HAVE **NEVER** APPEARED ON CD BEFORE. MANY RECORDINGS APPEAR HERE FOR THE FIRST TIME EVER. EITHER MASTER TAPES WERE USED OR EXTENSIVE COMPUTER ENHANCEMENT (INCLUDING DE-CLICKING) WAS USED TO ENSURE THE BEST POSSIBLE SOUND QUALITY EVER AVAILABLE. IF YOU HAVE ALL THE STANDARD ALBUM ISSUES THESE 2 BOXES PROVIDE YOU WITH ALL THE OTHER TRACKS EVER ISSUED. AMONGST THE NUMEROUS RARE GEMS ON THIS 8 CD SET WE HAVE ALL THE OUTTAKES, REJECTS & REHEARSALS FROM PARTY', 'PET SOUNDS', 'CONCERT' & MANY RECORDINGS WHICH HAVE NEVER SURFACED BEFORE NOW FOR 'SMILE' FANS THIS IS THE **ULTIMATE**. ALL PREVIOUS ISSUES OF THIS MUSICAL TREASURE HAVE USED POOR (SOUND) TAPES TO COMPILE A VERSION OF 'SMILE' WHICH ALWAYS PREVENTED YOU FROM MAKING YOUR OWN MIX OF THE ALBUM VIA YOUR PROGRAMMABLE CD PLAYERS. WHICH WE HAVE DONE ! YOU CAN SELECT THE VERSION / MIX YOU WANT, SIT BACK & ENJOY ! ANY PREVIOUS ISSUES OF 'SMILE' YOU MAY HAVE BOUGHT ARE NOW REDUNDANT AS WE HAVE BEEN ABLE TO USE TAPES MADE DIRECT FROM THE MASTER TO CREATE THE BEST SOUND QUALITY VERSION EVER ! WE'VE ALSO INCLUDED ALL THE TRACKS ISSUED ON BOTH THE U.S. & AUSTRALIAN 'RARITIES' LP'S, PLUS ALL THE 'BONUS TRACKS' WHICH WERE PREVIOUSLY SCATTERED OVER SOME 13 CD'S ARE COLLECTED TOGETHER HERE IN CHRONOLOGICAL ORDER TO CREATE A 'CD HISTORY' OF THE BAND. A 68 PAGE FULL COLOR BOOK IS ALSO INCLUDED WHICH FEATURES RARE PHOTOS, INTERVIEWS, DISCOGRAPHIES & EVERY CD HAS EXHAUSTIVE LINER NOTES DETAILING THE UNIQUE FEATURES OF ALL TRACKS IN THE SET.

NUMBER ____ OF LIMITED EDITION OF 1,000 COPIES

BEACH BOYS JOURNALS PART 1

The Beach Boys' early line-up: left to right, Dennis, David Marks, Carl, Mike Love and Brian.

BEACH BOYS JOURNALS PART 1

COMPUTER ENHANCED - DIGITALLY REMASTERED

JOURNALS PART 1 VOL.1 (1961 - 64)

CD - 09

THIS 16 CD ANTHOLOGY OF THE BEACH BOYS STARTS WITH THE EARLIEST AVAILABLE RECORDING IN 1961 AND PROGRESSES THROUGH MANY RARE & UNRELEASED TRACKS, WHILE ALL ALONG, INSERTING THE VARIOUS 'BONUS' TRACKS WHICH HAVE BEEN SCATTERED OVER ALL THE VARIOUS RE-ISSUES & BOX SETS OVER THE PAST 10 YEARS OR SO. AS WITH ALL THE CD'S IN THIS SET, WE'VE ARRANGED THE TRACKS CHRONOLOGICALLY SO AS TO 'MAKE SENSE' WHEN YOU LISTEN TO THIS SET, WHICH WE'RE SURE YOU **WILL** DO OVER AND OVER.

#	SONGTITLE	TIME	SONGWRITERS	RECORDING DATE	COMMENTS
1.	SURFIN'	1.34	B.WILSON-M.LOVE	Sept '61	(REHEARSAL)
2.	PUNCHLINE	1.52	BRIAN WILSON	Jan 2 '62	(FINAL MIX) (INSTRUMENTAL)
3.	THEIR HEARTS WERE FULL OF SPRING	2.36	BOBBY TROUP	April '62	(DEMO)
4.	LAND AHOY	1.51	BRIAN WILSON	Sep 6 '62	VOCAL OVER-DUB #1 (TAKE 4)
5.	LAND AHOY	1.45	BRIAN WILSON	Sep 6 '62	VOCAL OVER-DUB #1 (TAKE 5)
6.	LAND AHOY	1.40	BRIAN WILSON	Sep 6 '62	(FINAL MIX) 'SURFIN' SAFARI', OUTTAKE, VERSE WAS RECYCLED INTO 'CHERRY CHERRY COUPE' IN 1963
7.	CINDY OH CINDY	2.10	B.BARONS-B.LONG	Sep 13 '62	(FINAL MIX) MURRY WILSON'S COMMENT ON INTRO. '56 HIT FOR EDDIE FISHER
8.	SURFIN' USA	1.48	CHUCK BERRY-B.WILSON	Early '63	(DEMO)
9.	LITTLE SURFER GIRL	0.33	BRIAN WILSON	Early '63	(EXCERPT)
10.	IN MY ROOM	2.36	B.WILSON-G.USHER	Early '63	(DEMO)
11.	THE BAKER MAN	2.37	BRIAN WILSON	March 7 '63	(FINAL MIX) INSPIRED BY THE OLYMPICS' 'HULLY GULLY'
12.	OUR CAR CLUB	2.15	B.WILSON-M.LOVE	July 16 '63	INSTRUMENTAL BACKING TRACK
13.	THE ROCKIN' SURFER	1.38	TRAD. ARR. B.WILSON	July 16 '63	(ALTERNATE VERSION) MUCH FASTER & DRASTICALLY DIFFERENT ARRANGEMENT
14.	BE TRUE TO YOUR SCHOOL	2.10	BRIAN WILSON	Sep. '63	45 VERSION, COMPLETELY DIFFERENT TO THE ALBUM TAKE WITH BACKING VOCALS BY 'THE HONEYS' (FEAT. MARILYN ROVELL LATER MRS. BRIAN WILSON)
15.	I DO	2.10	BRIAN WILSON	Nov 11 '63	(FINAL MIX) VERSES ARE A RE-WRITE OF 'COUNTY FAIR'.
16.	IN MY ROOM	2.19	B.WILSON-G.USHER	March 3 '64	(FINAL MIX) (GERMAN VERSION) CAPITOL'S IDEA A-LA THE BEATLES
17.	HUSHABYE	2.42	D.POMUS-M.SCHUMAN	April '64	('SEPARATED' MIX) VOCALS & INST. COMPLETELY SEPARATE.
18.	WENDY	2.26	BRIAN WILSON	April '64	('SEPARATED' MIX)
19.	I GET AROUND	2.18	BRIAN WILSON	April 16 '64	(INSTRUMENTAL) BACKING TRACK
20.	I GET AROUND	2.21	BRIAN WILSON	April 16 '64	(ALTERNATE VOCALS)
21.	DON'T BACK DOWN	1.40	BRIAN WILSON	April 29 '64	(ALTERNATE VERSION) COMPLETELY DIFFERENT TO THE 'ALL SUMMER LONG' ALBUM.
22.	ALL SUMMER LONG	2.14	BRIAN WILSON	May 7 '64	('SEPARATED' MIX)
23.	LITTLE HONDA	2.13	B.WILSON-M.LOVE	June 23 '64	(ALTERNATE VERSION) DIFF. LYRICS, LEAD & BACKING VOCALS BUT SAME BACKING TRACK
24.	WHEN I GROW UP (TO BE A MAN)	2.20	BRIAN WILSON	Aug 10 '64	('SEPARATED' MIX) VOCALS & INST. COMPLETELY SEPARATE
25.	I'M SO YOUNG	2.28	W.H.TYRUS JNR.	Sep 9 '64	(ALTERNATE VERSION) COMPLETELY DIFF. TO 'TODAY' LP
26.	ALL DRESSED UP FOR SCHOOL	2.24	BRIAN WILSON	Sep 16 '64	(FINAL MIX) LYRICS A BIT RISQUE FOR 1964, VERSE RECYCLED FOR 'I JUST GOT MY PAY' & 'MARCELLA'
27.	DANCE DANCE DANCE	2.03	B.WILSON-C.WILSON	Sep '64	(ALTERNATE VERSION) DIFFERENT LYRICS (& BACKING VOCALS). THE BEACH BOYS THEMSELVES PLAY THE INSTRUMENTS ON THIS VERSION.
28.	DANCE DANCE DANCE (RADIO SPOTS)	2.13	B.WILSON-C.WILSON	Oct 9 '64	INSTRUMENTAL BACKING TRACK (TAKE 17)
29.	'HI, THIS IS THE BEACH BOYS'	0.10		Circa late '64	(PROMO) EACH MEMBER SAYS 1 WORD (TO FORM SENTENCE)
30.	K.O.M.A.	0.10		Circa late '64	STATION I.D. PROMO (SUNG)
31.	BRIAN	0.15		Circa late '64	SPOKEN MESSAGE TO DISC JOCKEYS ('DANCE, DANCE, DANCE' THANK-YOU)
32.	K.A.Y.A.	0.10		Circa late '64	STATION I.D. PROMO (SUNG)
33.	K.D.W.B.	0.10		Circa late '64	MIKE'S THANK YOU (SPOKEN PROMO)
34.	K.E.W.B.	0.20		Circa late '64	STATION I.D. PROMO (SUNG)
35.	MURRAY 'THE K'	0.10		Circa late '64	(SUNG) PROMO
36.	'WHERE'S YOUR I.D.?'	0.10		Circa late '64	MINI-COMEDY SKETCH (SPOKEN PROMO)
37.	'THE BEACH BOYS SHOW'	0.22		Circa late '64	(SUNG) PROMO
38.	HAPPY BIRTHDAY TO YOU	0.54	HILL-HILL	Circa late '64	SUNG TO THE 'FOUR FRESHMEN' (CHECK THE LYRICS)
39.	HONDA '55	1.58	BRIAN WILSON	Circa late '64	(VOCAL SESSION) FOR A RADIO / TV ADVERTISEMENT

TOTAL CD TIME 62.20

Brother records

BEACH BOYS JOURNALS PART 1

Brian, Mike, Dennis, Carl, David

BEACH BOYS JOURNALS PART 1

BEACH BOYS JOURNALS PART 1

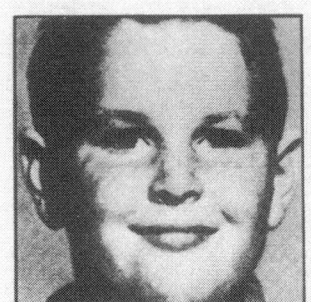

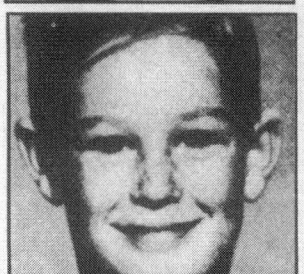

BEACH BOYS JOURNALS PART 1

COMPUTER ENHANCED - DIGITALLY REMASTERED

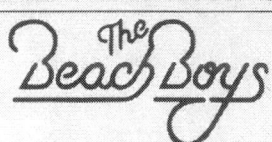

JOURNALS PART 1 VOL.2 (1965)

CD-10

OUR SECOND EXCURSION INTO STUDIO OUTTAKES & RARITIES OFFERS (MOST SIGNIFICANTLY) THE AUDIO FOR THE **ACTUAL** SESSION WHICH CONTAINS THE INFAMOUS CONFRONTATION BETWEEN BRIAN & (FATHER) MURRY WILSON WHICH (FOR THE **FIRST** TIME) WE'VE SEPARATED INTO 4 PARTS SO AS TO MAKE IT EASIER TO GET TO A PARTICULAR SECTION, (EG. THE CLIMAX OF THE 'DISCUSSION') WHEN MURRY WALKS OUT & STATES THAT HE (& THE WILSON BROTHERS' MOTHER) WILL NEVER AGAIN ATTEND A BEACH BOYS RECORDING SESSION. A PROMISE WHICH MURRY KEPT UNTIL THE SESSION FOR THE FINAL CAPITOL SINGLE 'BREAKAWAY' IN 1969. MURRY ALSO CO-WROTE THE SONG UNDER THE GUISE OF R. DUNBAR.

#	SONGTITLE	TIME	SONGWRITERS	RECORDING DATE	COMMENTS
1.	PLEASE LET ME WONDER	1.32	B.WILSON-M.LOVE	Jan 7 '65	(VOCAL OVERDUB) TAKE 1A
2.	PLEASE LET ME WONDER	0.59	B.WILSON-M.LOVE	Jan 7 '65	(VOCAL OVERDUB) TAKE 2A
3.	PLEASE LET ME WONDER	2.44	B.WILSON-M.LOVE	Jan 7 '65	(VOCAL OVERDUB) TAKE 3A
4.	PLEASE LET ME WONDER	0.37	B.WILSON-M.LOVE	Jan 7 '65	(VOCAL OVERDUB) TAKE 4A
5.	PLEASE LET ME WONDER	3.20	B.WILSON-M.LOVE	Jan 7 '65	(VOCAL OVERDUB) TAKE 5A
6.	DO YOU WANNA DANCE	0.53	BOBBY FREEMAN	Jan 11 '65	(VOCALS ONLY)
7.	DO YOU WANNA DANCE	3.05	BOBBY FREEMAN	Jan 11 '65	(ALTERNATE VOCALS) TAKE 2A
8.	IN THE BACK OF MY MIND	2.16	BRIAN WILSON	Jan 13 '65	(INSTRMENTAL)
9.	GOOD TO MY BABY	2.26	BRIAN WILSON	Jan 19 '65	(INSTRUMENTAL)
10.	GOOD TO MY BABY	2.29	BRIAN WILSON	Jan 19 '65	(STEREO MIX) UNRELEASED (FINAL VERSION)
11.	I'M SO YOUNG	2.41	W.H.TYRUS JNR.	Jan 19 '65	(STEREO MIX) UNRELEASED (FINAL VERSION)
12.	HELP ME RONDA	11.17	BRIAN WILSON	Jan 19 '65	('LP VERSION') SESSION
13.	BRIAN & MURRY WILSON #1	12.24	(INCORPORATING 'HELP ME RONDA') B.WILSON	Jan 19 '65	THIS WAS THE ACTUAL CONFRONTATION BETWEEN BRIAN WILSON & HIS FATHER AS PORTRAYED IN THE TELE-MOVIE
14.	BRIAN & MURRY WILSON #2	6.58	" " "	Jan 19 '65	" " "
15.	BRIAN & MURRY WILSON #3	4.23	" " "	Jan 19 '65	" " "
16.	BRIAN & MURRY WILSON #4	4.01	" " "	Jan 19 '65	
17.	HELP ME RONDA	3.18	BRIAN WILSON	Jan 19 '65	(STEREO MIX) UNRELEASED (FINAL VERSION)
18.	HELP ME RHONDA	2.55	BRIAN WILSON	Feb 24 '65	(45 VERSION) INSTRUMENTAL BACKING TRACK
19.	MONKEY'S UNCLE	2.32	R.SHERMAN-R.SHERMAN	Feb '65	(FEAT. ANNETTE FUNICELLO) 45 ISSUED FROM THE FILM 'THE GIRLS ON THE BEACH' WHICH FEATURED A GUEST APPEARANCE BY THE BEACH BOYS PERFORMING THIS TRACK.
20.	LET HIM RUN WILD	2.17	BRIAN WILSON	Mar 30 '65	(ALTERNATE VERSION)

TOTAL CD TIME 69.19

Brother records

BEACH BOYS JOURNALS PART 1

Top right (left to right): Annie, Carol (Dennis' first wife), Dennis, and David Anderle (with head in hand). Bottom left, Annie is standing behind Carl. Annie's brother, Billy Hinsche, is standing behind the Wilson brothers' cousin, Steve Korthof. Bottom right, Chuck Britz, Carl, and Bruce. The photos were taken in January and February of 1967.

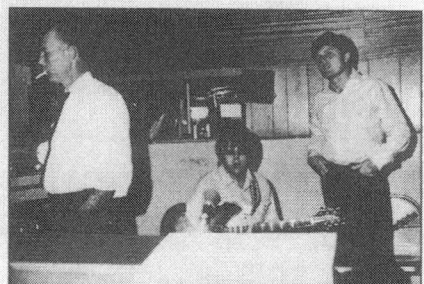

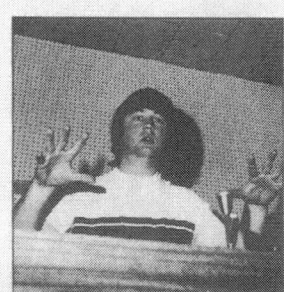

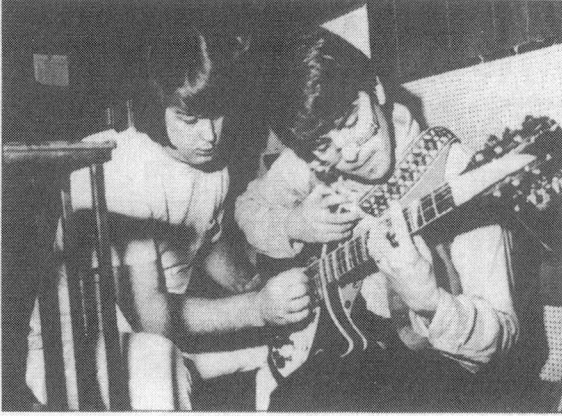

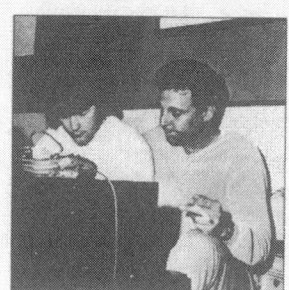

Brian with Hal Blaine.

BEACH BOYS JOURNALS PART 1

COMPUTER ENHANCED - DIGITALLY REMASTERED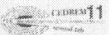

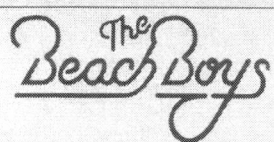

JOURNALS PART 1 VOL.3 (1965-1966)

CD - 11

VOL.3 OF OUR MUSIC HISTORY OF THE BEACH BOYS TAKES US INTO A MORE IMAGINATIVE PHASE IN BRIAN WILSON'S PRODUCTION STYLE. AS WE STEP FROM THE SUCCESS OF THE SURFING SOUND WITH 'CALIFORNIA GIRLS' SUDDENLY WE FIND OURSELVES LISTENING TO THE INCREDIBLE 'FANTASY WORLD' OF 'PET SOUNDS' WHICH UNDOUBTEDLY SPEARHEADED THE MOVE TO OPEN THE DOORS TO ALMOST AN 'ANYTHING GOES' ATTITUDE TO RECORDING ALBUMS IN '66 / '67. PAUL McCARTNEY HAS OPENLY ADMITTED THAT SGT. PEPPER WAS **ONLY** AS EXPERIMENTAL AND 'PSYCHEDELIC' AS IT WAS BECAUSE THE BEATLES HEARD 'PET SOUNDS' & DECIDED **THAT** WAS THE WAY TO RECORD IN 1967, UTILIZING HUGE HARMONICAS, FULL OBOES, CLARINETS......EVERYTHING !

#	SONGTITLE	TIME	SONGWRITERS	RECORDING DATE	COMMENTS
1.	CALIFORNIA GIRLS	2.49	MUSIC B.WILSON/LYRICS M.LOVE	April 6 '65	(INSTRUMENTAL) BACKING TRACK
2.	CALIFORNIA GIRLS	2.30	MUSIC B.WILSON/LYRICS M.LOVE	April 6 '65	(VOCALS ONLY)
3.	GRADUATION DAY	2.24	J.SHERMAN-N.SHERMAN	May 5 '65	(STUDIO VERSION)
4.	THE LITTLE GIRL I ONCE KNEW	1.33	BRIAN WILSON	Oct 13 '65	(INSTRUMENTAL) OVERDUB TRACK
5.	THE LITTLE GIRL I ONCE KNEW	3.27	BRIAN WILSON	Oct 13 '65	(FINAL MIX) 45 NON-ALBUM SINGLE
6.	TROMBONE DIXIE	2.52	BRIAN WILSON	Nov '65	(INSTRUMENTAL)
7.	WOULDN'T IT BE NICE	0.21	B.WILSON-T.ASHER	Jan 22 '66	(INSTR.) TAKE 18 (BACKING TRACK BREAKDOWN)
8.	WOULDN'T IT BE NICE	1.06	B.WILSON-T.ASHER	Jan 22 '66	(INSTR.) TAKE 19 (BACKING TRACK BREAKDOWN)
9.	WOULDN'T IT BE NICE	0.13	B.WILSON-T.ASHER	Jan 22 '66	(INSTR.) TAKE 20 (BACKING TRACK BREAKDOWN)
10.	WOULDN'T IT BE NICE	2.41	B.WILSON-T.ASHER	Jan 22 '66	FINAL W/'SEPARATED' MIX (TAKE 21) FINAL VOCALS WITH THE INSTRUMENTS & VOCALS TOTALLY SEPARATE IN THE MIX
11.	WOULDN'T IT BE NICE	2.30	B.WILSON-T.ASHER	Jan 22 '66	ALTERNATE VOCALS (TAKE 21) FEATURES DIFFERENT LEAD VOCALS TO THE RELEASED VERSION (FINAL BACKING TRACK)
12.	YOU STILL BELIEVE IN ME	17.36	B.WILSON-T.ASHER	Jan 24 '66	(SESSION) HIGHLIGHTS OF THE RECORDING SESSION (WITH **STEREO** BACKING TRACKS)
13.	YOU STILL BELIEVE IN ME	2.46	B.WILSON-T.ASHER	Jan 26 '66	(ALTERNATE VERSION) OUTTAKE FROM 'PET SOUNDS' SESSIONS
14.	HANG ON TO YOUR EGO	3.03	BRIAN WILSON	Feb 9 '66	(INSTR) TAKE #2 BACKING TRACK SESSIONS (I.D.'D AS 'LET GO OF YOUR EGO') BRIAN IS ASKED AT 6.10 IF THE UNION KNOWS HE'S RECORDING THESE SESSIONS (HMM....)
15.	HANG ON TO YOUR EGO	3.35	BRIAN WILSON	Feb 9 '66	(INSTR) TAKE #9 FINAL BACKING TRACK (I.D.'D AS 'LET GO OF YOUR LIBIDO')
16.	HANG ON TO YOUR EGO	3.18	BRIAN WILSON	Feb 9 '66	(INSTR) TAKE #2 EARLY MIX NO BACKING VOCALS, DOGS BARKING AT END (THE ORIGINAL LYRICS TO 'PET SOUNDS' TRACK 'I KNOW THERE'S AN ANSWER)
17.	HANG ON TO YOUR EGO	3.13	BRIAN WILSON	Feb 9 '66	TAKE #9 EARLY MIX 'LAID-BACK' VOCAL INTRO, WITH FULL BACKING VOCALS (THE ORIGINAL LYRICS TO 'PET SOUNDS' TRACK 'I KNOW THERE'S AN ANSWER)
18.	I JUST WASN'T MADE FOR THESE TIMES	15.53	B.WILSON-T.ASHER	Feb 14 '66	(INSTR) HIGHLIGHTS OF THE RECORDING SESSION (WITH STEREO BACKING TRACKS)

TOTAL CD TIME 71.00

Brother records

BEACH BOYS JOURNALS PART 1

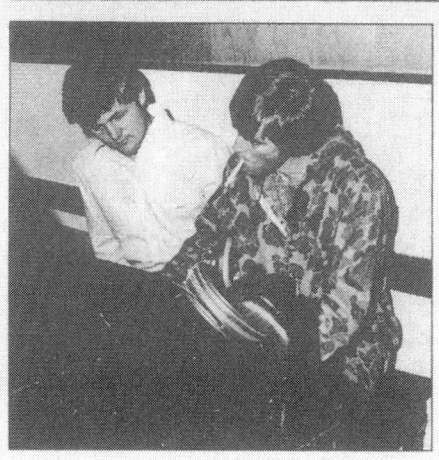

Brian Wilson – obviously a "valvie" – proudly demonstrates the discernible delights of his state-of-the-art four-track valve tape-recorder.

BEACH BOYS JOURNALS PART 1

COMPUTER ENHANCED - DIGITALLY REMASTERED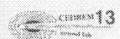

JOURNALS PART 1 VOL.4 (1966)

CD - 12

DEPENDING ON YOUR PERSONAL TASTE, THIS MAY BE YOUR FAVORITE CD IN THIS FIRST BOX. COMPRISING ABOUT HALF EACH OF OUTTAKES FROM 'PET SOUNDS' AND 'SMILE' WE FIND BRIAN WILSON AT HIS MOST INVENTIVE. 'GOOD VIBRATIONS' IS CERTAINLY A STAND-OUT & IF IT WERE NOT FOR TIME LIMITATIONS, WE WOULD HAVE PREFERRED TO HAVE PUT THE LATTER ONTO 'SMILE' ITSELF WHERE IT CLEARLY BELONGS. ALTHOUGH SOME OF THE MIXES HERE DIFFER ONLY **SLIGHTLY** FROM THE ISSUED VERSION (EG. TK #24) COUNTLESS HOURS HAVE BEEN SPENT COMPARING THE VERSIONS SO AS TO ENSURE THAT WE DON'T 'DOUBLE UP' ON ANY MIXES / VERSIONS & ACTUALLY INFORM YOU (VIA THE COMMENTS COLUMN) OF WHAT, WHERE & IN SOME CASES EXACTLY **WHEN** THE DIFFERENCES OCCUR.

#	SONGTITLE	TIME	SONGWRITERS	RECORDING DATE	COMMENTS
1.	I'M WAITING FOR THE DAY	3.08	B.WILSON-M.LOVE	Mar 6 '66	(INST) STEREO BACKING TRACK
2.	GOD ONLY KNOWS	2.50	B.WILSON-T.ASHER	Mar 9 '66	BACKING TRACK (OUTTAKE) SESSION
3.	GOD ONLY KNOWS	3.22	B.WILSON-T.ASHER	Mar 9 '66	(FINAL BACKING TRACK) COMPLETE VERSION
4.	GOD ONLY KNOWS	2.57	B.WILSON-T.ASHER	Mar 9 '66	(VOCAL OUTTAKE) FEATURES BRIAN WILSON'S 'GUIDE' VOCALS & AN EXTRA 'ACAPPELLA' (EXTENDED) VOCAL ENDING, NOT ON THE 'PET SOUNDS' VERSION.
5.	I'M WAITING FOR THE DAY	3.04	B.WILSON-M.LOVE	Mar10 '66	(ALTERNATIVE VERSION)
6.	I JUST WASN'T MADE FOR THESE TIMES	3.14	B.WILSON-T.ASHER	Mar10 '66	(ALTERNATE VERSION) OUTTAKE FROM 'PET SOUNDS' SESSIONS
7.	STUDIO CHAT	3.41		Mar10 '66	
8.	DON'T TALK (PUT YOUR HEAD ON MY SHOULDER)	1.27	B.WILSON-T.ASHER	April 3 '66	SESSION STUDIO TALK
9.	DON'T TALK (PUT YOUR HEAD ON MY SHOULDER)	3.00	B.WILSON-T.ASHER	April 3 '66	INSTR. TAKE #1 (BACKING TRACK)
10.	DON'T TALK (PUT YOUR HEAD ON MY SHOULDER)	0.50	B.WILSON-T.ASHER	April 3 '66	BACKING VOCAL RECORDINGS OF WHAT WAS PURPORTED TO BE A VOCAL INTRO TO 'DON'T TALK'.
11.	HEROES AND VILLAINS	0.50	B.WILSON-VAN DYKE PARKS	May 11 '66	(INSTR.) BACKING TRACK (EXCERPT)
12.	HEROES AND VILLAINS	2.11	B.WILSON-VAN DYKE PARKS	May 11 '66	EARLY BACKING TRACKS, PARTIAL MONO MIX THEN FULL MIX IN STEREO
13.	GOOD VIBRATIONS	1.17	B.WILSON-M.LOVE	Feb-Sep'66	(INSTR)TAKE 1 (BREAKDOWN)BACKING TRACK RECORDING SESSION
14.	GOOD VIBRATIONS	0.17	B.WILSON-M.LOVE	Feb-Sep'66	(INSTR)TAKE 2 (BREAKDOWN)BACKING TRACK RECORDING SESSION
15.	GOOD VIBRATIONS	0.34	B.WILSON-M.LOVE	Feb-Sep'66	(INSTR)TAKE 21 (BREAKDOWN)BACKING TRACK RECORDING SESSION
16.	GOOD VIBRATIONS	6.12	B.WILSON-M.LOVE	Feb-Sep'66	(INSTR)TAKE 28 EARLY FULL BACKING TRACK(W/ 2 BACKING VOCAL SEGMENTS)
17.	GOOD VIBRATIONS	1.00	B.WILSON-M.LOVE	Feb-Sep'66	(INSTR)TAKE 28 'INTERMEDIATE' (PART ONE)
18.	GOOD VIBRATIONS	0.50	B.WILSON-M.LOVE	Feb-Sep'66	(INSTR)TAKE 28 'INTERMEDIATE' (PART TWO)
19.	GOOD VIBRATIONS	3.52	B.WILSON-M.LOVE	Feb-Sep'66	(INSTR)TAKE UNKNOWN (EARLY FULL BACKING TRACK) EDITED RE-MIX (WITH 1 BACKING VOCAL SEGMENT)
20.	GOOD VIBRATIONS	3.52	B.WILSON-M.LOVE	Feb-Sep'66	(VOCALS / INSTR) # 1 REMIX #1 (MAINLY INSTR W/ SOME LEAD & BACKING VOCALS)
21.	GOOD VIBRATIONS	3.53	B.WILSON-M.LOVE	Feb-Sep'66	VOCALS / INSTR # 2 REMIX #2 (PIECES OF VERSES ONLY, FIRST APPEARANCE OF CHORUS / MIDDLE 8 VOCALS & THEREMIN ENDING)
22.	GOOD VIBRATIONS	3.02	B.WILSON-M.LOVE	Feb-Sep'66	(VOCALS / INSTR) # 3 EDITED REMIX #3 (MORE VOCALS, DIFF. LYRICS, MORE INSTR. OVERDUBS)
23.	DO YOU LIKE WORMS	3.54	B.WILSON-VAN DYKE PARKS	Oct 11 '66	(BACKING TRACK) SHORTER MIX. STOPS AT 1.10, AFRICAN CHANT IS MISSING OVER 'BICYCLE RIDER' PART
24.	DO YOU LIKE WORMS	3.55	B.WILSON-VAN DYKE PARKS	Oct 11 '66	(EARLY MIX) LONGER MIX, TALKING AT 38 SEC. AFRICAN CHANT OVERDUBBED ONTO SECOND HALF OF 'BICYCLE RIDER' SECTION & A COUGH AT 1.34 ! (HAWAIIAN BIT - 6 TIMES)

TOTAL CD TIME 63.13

Brother records

BEACH BOYS JOURNALS PART 1

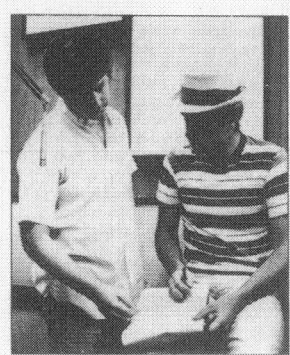
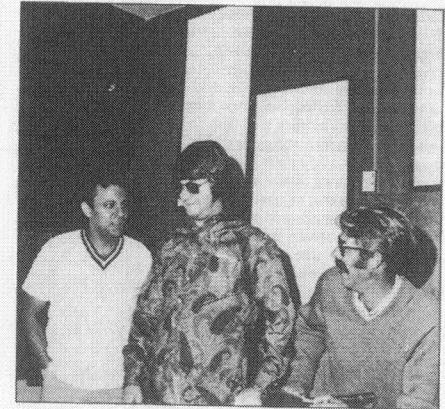

ABOVE - : DRUMMER HAL BLAINE (LEFT)

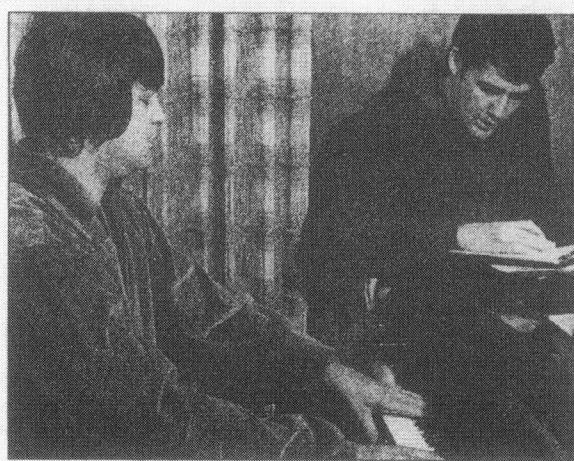

BOTTOM LEFT - : BRIAN WITH TONY ASHER ABOVE - : BRIAN WITH VAN DYKE PARKS

BEACH BOYS JOURNALS PART 1

COMPUTER ENHANCED - DIGITALLY REMASTERED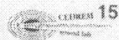

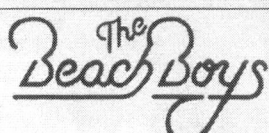

JOURNALS PART 1 VOL 5 (SMILE)

CD - 13

WHILE THERE MAY NEVER HAVE BEEN A FINISHED ALBUM CALLED 'SMILE', THIS REPRESENTS (AS CLOSE AS POSSIBLE) WHAT COULD-HAVE-BEEN. WE'VE ARRANGED THE TRACK ORDER IN SUCH A WAY THAT YOU CAN PICK WHICH VERSION OR MIX OF A PARTICULAR TRACK THAT YOU PREFER & PROGRAM YOUR CD PLAYER TO EXACTLY THE WAY YOU FEEL IT SOUNDS BEST. WE ACCEPT THAT OTHER ATTEMPTS HAVE BEEN MADE TO DO THIS BUT WE'RE CONFIDENT YOU'LL AGREE THIS IS THE BEST YET! PREVIOUSLY INFERIOR COPIES OF FINAL MIXES WERE USED (EG. WIND CHIMES, WONDERFUL, SURF'S UP & I'D LIKE TO SAY DADA) WHEREAS WE HAVE SUBSTITUTED THESE WITH THE MASTERS. THERE SEEMED NO POINT IN LISTENING TO 2 FINAL MIXES WHEN THERE WAS ABSOLUTELY NO DIFFERENCE BETWEEN THE TWO EXCEPT THAT THE OLDER TAPE HAS MASSIVE HISS, 'DROP-OUTS' ETC. LIKEWISE, WHEN 2 FINAL MIXES DID DIFFER ONLY SLIGHTLY, WE'VE PUT THESE (MINIMALLY DIFFERENT) MIXES ELSEWHERE ON THE BOX SET IN ORDER TO MAKE ROOM FOR OTHER MORE IMPORTANT MATERIAL (EG. 'DO YOU LIKE WORMS' HAD 4 MIXES IN TOTAL SO WE PUT 2 OF THEM ON VOL.4). COUNTLESS HOURS WERE SPENT CROSS-CHECKING MIXES TO ENSURE THAT YOU, THE FAN, 'GET IT ALL'. ONLY ONE VERSION OF 'GOOD VIBRATIONS' IS USED ON THIS CD SINCE THERE IS SO MUCH OF THAT AVAILABLE (WHICH WE'VE PLACED ON THE PREVIOUS CD IN THE SET). PERHAPS THE MOST EXCITING ADVANTAGE OF OUR FORMAT IS THAT YOU CAN (IF YOU WISH) PROGRAM 'HEROES AND VILLAINS' TO PLAY EXACTLY AS YOU'D LIKE IT TO (EG. THE ORIG. INTRO, FOLLOWED BY THE 'ALTERNATE' SUITE INTRO, MIDDLE 'MAIN' SECTION AND THE 'FINAL' SUITE END - HOWEVER YOU WANT IT !).

#	SONGTITLE	TIME	SONGWRITERS	RECORDING DATE	COMMENTS
1.	INTRO	0.11		Circa 66	THIS INTRIGUING BIT OF STUDIO CHAT MAKES IT CLEAR THAT BRIAN, IN FACT, HAD NOT INTENDED OUR PRAYER AS A SONG, BUT AS AN INTRO TO THE SMILE ALBUM.
2.	OUR PRAYER	1.09	B.WILSON	Circa 66	EARLY MIX W / LAUGHTER AT END (DIFFERENT VERSION TO THE '20 / 20' ALBUM)
3.	OUR PRAYER	1.07	B.WILSON	Circa 66	FINAL MIX NO LAUGHTER AT END (DIFFERENT VERSION TO THE '20 / 20' ALBUM)
4.	HEROES AND VILLAINS #1	0.37	B.WILSON-V.D.PARKS	Circa 66	(INTRO SEQU.) ABANDONED ORIG. INTRO. (PREVIOUSLY ACCREDITED TO MRS. LEARY'S COW 'FIRE' SEQUENCE.)
5.	HEROES AND VILLAINS #2	0.47	B.WILSON-V.D.PARKS	Circa 66	(SHORT INSTR.) BACKING TRACK WITH OVERDUBBED KEYBOARDS, HORNS & WHISTLE
6.	HEROES AND VILLAINS #3	0.53	B.WILSON-V.D.PARKS	Circa 66	('ALT.' SUITE INTRO) PRIOR TO 'BICYCLE RIDER' VOCALS.
7.	HEROES AND VILLAINS #4	0.58	B.WILSON-V.D.PARKS	Circa 66	('FINAL' SUITE INTR) WITH 'BICYCLE RIDER' VOCALS.
8.	HEROES AND VILLAINS #5	4.08	B.WILSON-V.D.PARKS	Circa 66	(MIDDLE SECTION) THIS SECTION IS CONSISTANT IN BOTH VERSIONS.
9.	HEROES AND VILLAINS #6	1.33	B.WILSON-V.D.PARKS	Circa 66	('FINAL' SUITE END) WITH BACKING VOCAL / HARMONICA ENDING
10.	HEROES AND VILLAINS #7	2.02	B.WILSON-V.D.PARKS	Circa 66	('ALT.' SUITE END) WITH FULL VOCAL ENDING
11.	HEROES AND VILLAINS #8	2.57	B.WILSON-V.D.PARKS	Circa 66	(FULL O/TAKE VERS.) DRASTICALLY DIFFERENT TO 45 VERSION
12.	DO YOU LIKE WORMS	3.57	B.WILSON-V.D.PARKS	Circa 66	(FINAL MIX)
13.	DO YOU LIKE WORMS	3.28	B.WILSON-V.D.PARKS	Circa 66	(ALT. VERSION) VOCALS OVER 'DRUM' START, MISSES 2ND. 'PLY MOUTH' VOCALS, DIFF. LEAD VOCALS, LONGER 'HAWAIIAN' BIT.
14	GOOD VIBRATIONS	3.35	B.WILSON-M.LOVE	Circa 66	(EARLY MIX) NUMEROUS VOCAL & MUSIC OVERDUBS (& EDITS) MISSING.
15.	WONDERFUL	2.09	B.WILSON-V.D.PARKS	Circa 66	BACKING TRACK WITH BACKING VOCALS ONLY ('COUNT !' AT 0.41) (COMPLETELY DIFFERENT TO THE 'SMILEY SMILE' ALBUM VERSION)
16.	WONDERFUL	2.04	B.WILSON-V.D.PARKS	Circa 66	(FINAL MIX) WITH LEAD VOCAL AND RE-MIXED BACKING VOCALS. (COMPLETELY DIFFERENT TO THE 'SMILEY SMILE' ALBUM VERSION)
17.	CHILD IS FATHER OF THE MAN	1.42	B.WILSON-V.D.PARKS	Circa 66	EARLIER SHORTER MIX (W/ COUNT-IN) ONLY 1 VOCAL SECTION (W/CELLO & TALKING AT END)
18.	CHILD IS FATHER OF THE MAN	1.54	B.WILSON-V.D.PARKS	Circa 66	FINAL MIX LONGER VERSION AND RE-MIXED VOCALS (W/EXTRA CHORUS AT 0.41)
19.	CABINESSENCE	3.59	B.WILSON-V.D.PARKS	Circa 66	(BACKING TRACK) FULL LENGTH VERSION (SAME BASIC TRACK WHICH WAS OVERDUBBED FOR INCLUSION ON 20/20 ALBUM)
20.	CABINESSENCE	4.04	B.WILSON-V.D.PARKS	Circa 66	(EARLY MIX) FULL LENGTH VERSION (W/BACKING VOCALS STARTING AT 0.43)
21.	CABINESSENCE	2.12	B.WILSON-V.D.PARKS	Circa 66	RE-MIX EDITED VERSION (W/MORE BACKING VOCALS)
	'THE ELEMENTS' (EARTH)				
22.	VEGA-TABLES / I'M IN GREAT SHAPE	3.32	B.WILSON-V.D.PARKS	Circa 66	EARLY MIX, COMPLETELY DIFFERENT TO 'SMILEY SMILE' VERSION. (WRAPPER LAUGHTER LYRIC REPEATED, FAR MORE 'GREAT SHAPE' PARTS)
23.	VEGA-TABLES / I'M IN GREAT SHAPE	3.30	B.WILSON-V.D.PARKS	Circa 66	FINAL MIX (ALTERED LYRICS AT 0.48. WITH EXTRA VOCAL PASSAGE AT END INSTEAD OF EXTENDED 'GREAT SHAPE') ('I'M IN GREAT SHAPE' LATER RE-RECORDED FOR 'WILD HONEY' AS 'MAMA SAYS')
	(WIND)				
24	WIND CHIMES	2.32	B.WILSON	Circa 66	(FINAL MIX) (COMPLETELY DIFFERENT TO THE VERSION ON 'SMILEY SMILE')
	(FIRE)				
25.	MRS. O'LEARY'S COW	1.37	B.WILSON	Circa 66	(FINAL MIX) (WHAT HAS BEEN OFFERED BEFORE HAS HAD AN EXTRA FIRST HALF WHICH CAN BE CORRECTLY SEPARATED AS TK#4 'HEROES AND VILLAINS' INTRO.)
	(WATER)				
26.	COOL COOL WATER	2.56	B.WILSON-M.LOVE	Circa 66	(FINAL MIX) (APPEARED LATER IN RADICALLY RE-MIXED FORM W/TK #27 &TK #17/18 AS FINALE FOR 'SUNFLOWER' ALBUM.) MIDDLE SECTION IS EDITED ON FROM 'GOOD VIBRATIONS' BOX SET & IS IN STEREO - REST IS MONO
27.	I'D LOVE TO SAY DADA	1.35	B.WILSON	Circa 66	(FINAL MIX) (USED FOR MIDDLE SECTION OF 'COOL COOL WATER' ON 'SUNFLOWER' ALBUM)
28.	SURF'S UP	1.36	B.WILSON-V.D.PARKS	Circa 66	INSTRUMENTAL INTRO) ORIGINAL INTRO TO WHAT BECAME THE TITLE TRACK TO THE SURF'S UP 1972 ALBUM, WITH CARL'S LEAD VOCAL (OVERDUBBED IN 1971)
29.	SURF'S UP	3.40	B.WILSON-V.D.PARKS	Circa 66	(FINAL MIX) (ORIGINAL VERSION, DIFFERENT TO 'SURF'S UP' ALBUM)
30.	THE OLD MASTER PAINTER / YOU ARE MY SUNSHINE	1.09	(TRAD.) / (H. GILLESPIE-B.SMITH-J.DAVIS)	Circa 66	(FINAL MIX) (1ST. PART IS AN OLD BLACK GOSPEL TUNE PLAYED ON CELLO. 2ND. PART IS POPULAR CLASSIC SUNG BY DENNIS WILSON)
	BONUS TRACKS ('SMILE' ERA INSTRUMENTAL OUTTAKES)				
31.	HOLIDAYS	2.36	B.WILSON	Circa 66	FROM 'SMILE' SESSIONS
32.	BARNYARD	0.58	B.WILSON	Circa 66	FROM 'SMILE' SESSIONS
33.	TONES	2.22	B.WILSON	Early 67	ALSO KNOWN AS 'PIXIES'
	TOTAL CD TIME 74.09				

Brother records

BEACH BOYS JOURNALS PART 1

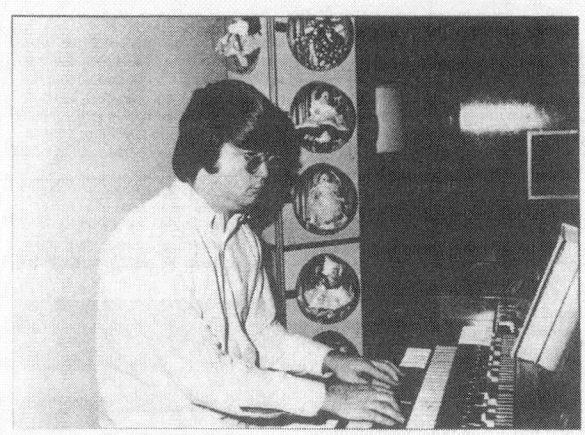

Brian instructs drummer Jim Gordon (in fire hat) while Larry Levine looks on (from the Fire sessions).

FOOTNOTE - : JIM GORDON WAS LATER TO PLAY ON NUMEROUS FAMOUS SESSIONS INCLUDING GEORGE HARRISON'S 'ALL THINGS MUST PASS', JOHN LENNON'S 'IMAGINE' ALBUM (AND LIVE WITH THE PLASTIC ONO BAND IN 1969) PLUS A STINT WITH JOE COCKER IN HIS 'MAD DOGS AND ENGLISHMEN' BAND (ALBUM & MOVIE). ALL OF THIS PALES IN COMPARISON TO HAVING CO-WRITTEN 'LAYLA' WITH ERIC CLAPTON (HE WAS ALSO A MEMBER OF ERIC'S 'DEREK & THE DOMINOES'.) NOW IN PRISON FOR MURDERING HIS OWN MOTHER WITH A HAMMER . (!)

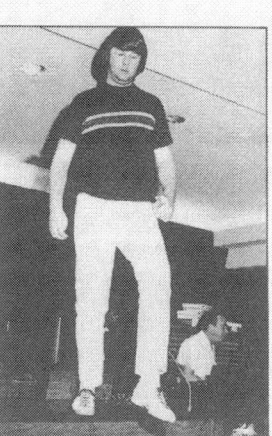

Above Frank Holmes created the front cover art for Smile as well as a series of drawings (seven in all) that were included in a twelve-page booklet that was to be part of the Smile package. The top sketch is for "Do You Like Worms"

Above, in Hawaii, August 25 and 26, 1967, the Beach Boys recorded a live album, Lei'd in Hawaii. For this LP, Brian made a rare live appearance (above middle).

BEACH BOYS JOURNALS PART 1

COMPUTER ENHANCED - DIGITALLY REMASTERED

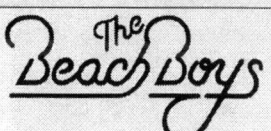

JOURNALS PART 1 VOL.6 (1966-1967)

CD - 14

THIS IS THE LAST OF 6 CD'S OF RARE STUDIO MATERIAL IN THIS BOX. THERE ARE SOME TRACKS HERE WHICH TRULY BELONG ON THE 'SMILE' CD BUT THERE JUST WASN'T ROOM, SO WE'VE PLACED THEM CHRONOLOGICALLY SO AS TO AT LEAST BE CONSISTENT WITH THE REST OF THE BOX SET. RECENTLY DISCOVERED GEMS SUCH AS THE REHEARSAL FOR THE 1967 HAWAII SHOW HAVE BEEN INCLUDED HERE ON OUR STUDIO CD, AS, IT'S NOT REALLY LIVE (I.E. IN FRONT OF AN AUDIENCE) EVEN TRACKS 20 - 22 WHICH APPEARED ON CAPITOL U.S.A.'S RARITIES LP IS **STILL** NOT ON CD TO THIS DAY.......UNTIL NOW !

#	SONGTITLE	TIME	SONGWRITERS	RECORDING DATE	COMMENTS
1.	SURF'S UP	2.14	B.WILSON-VAN DYKE PARKS	Nov 7 '66	(INSTR) TAKES 1 & 2 BACKING TRACK (W / PERCUSSION OVERDUB)
2.	SURF'S UP	2.10	B.WILSON-V.D.PARKS	Nov 7 '66	(INST) TAKE 3 BACKING TRACK (W / PERCUSSION OVERDUB)
3.	MEDLEY - : THE OLD MASTER PAINTER / YOU ARE MY SUNSHINE	1.07	TRADITIONAL / H. GILLESPIE-B.SMITH-J.DAVIS	Mid-late '66	INSTRUMENTAL BACKING TRACK (VOCAL VERSION CAN BE FOUND ON 'SMILE' CD)
4.	'SMILE' RADIO ADVERT	0.56		Late '66	CEDREM PROCESSED TO MAKE (AT LEAST) THE **MUSIC** MORE LISTENABLE
5.	TONES	1.02	BRIAN WILSON	Mar 13 '67	(INSTR) TAKE #1 BACKING TRACK (BREAKDOWN) UNRELEASED SONG
6.	TONES	0.12	BRIAN WILSON	Mar 13 '67	(INSTR) TAKE #2 BACKING TRACK (BREAKDOWN) UNRELEASED SONG
7.	TONES	1.46	BRIAN WILSON	Mar 13 '67	(INSTR) TAKE #3 BACKING TRACK (FULL VERSION) UNRELEASED SONG
8.	YOU'RE WELCOME	1.09	BRIAN WILSON	Mid '67	(45) RELEASED AS THE B-SIDE TO 'HEROES & VILLAINS' (JULY '67) NON-LP TRACK
9.	SHE'S GOIN' BALD	0.55	B.WILSON-M.LOVE-VAN DYKE PARKS	Mid '67	DEMO VERSION (SHORT SECTION ONLY)
10.	WITH ME TONIGHT	0.55	BRIAN WILSON	Mid '67	EARLY BACKING VOCALS (DIFF. TO BACKING VOCALS ON 'SMILEY SMILE')
11.	GOD ONLY KNOWS	2.50	B.WILSON-T.ASHER	Aug 25 '67	RECORDED LIVE DURING AFTERNOON REHEARSALS FOR THE CONCERT WHICH **WAS** TO BE THE 'LEI'D IN HAWAII' ALBUM, AT THE HONOLULU INTERNATIONAL CENTER, HAWAII, AUG 25 1967. RECORDED W/THE ORIGINAL LINE-UP OF BRIAN, CARL, DENNIS, MIKE & AL
12.	CALIFORNIA GIRLS	2.33	B.WILSON-M.LOVE	Aug 25 '67	"
13.	SURFER GIRL (#1)	2.55	BRIAN WILSON	Aug 25 '67	"
14.	SURFER GIRL (#2)	3.18	BRIAN WILSON	Aug 25 '67	"
15.	YOU'RE SO GOOD TO ME	2.41	BRIAN WILSON	Aug 25 '67	"
16.	THE LETTER	1.59	WAYNE CARSON	Aug 25 '67	"
17.	HELP ME RHONDA	2.35	BRIAN WILSON	Aug 25 '67	"
18.	HEROES AND VILLAINS	3.05	B.WILSON-VAN DYKE PARKS	Aug 25 '67	"
19.	THEIR HEARTS WERE FULL OF SPRING	2.33	BOBBY TROUP	Aug 25 '67	"
20.	WITH A LITTLE HELP FROM MY FRIENDS	2.23	LENNON-McCARTNEY	Late '67	RECORDED DURING WILD HONEY SESSIONS & ORIGINALLY SLATED FOR ISSUE ON ALBUM
21.	THE LETTER	1.47	WAYNE CARSON	Late '67	
22.	I WAS MADE TO LOVE HER	2.33	COSBY-HARDAWAY-MOY-WONDER	Late '67	ORIGINAL FRAGMENTS - PRIOR TO EDITING
23.	CAN'T WAIT TOO LONG	6.22	BRIAN WILSON	Late '67	(LONG VERSION)/FULL (EDITED) BACKING TRACK (W/OUT SPOKEN MIDDLE SECTION)
24.	CAN'T WAIT TOO LONG	5.35	BRIAN WILSON	Late '67	
25.	CAN'T WAIT TOO LONG	3.50	BRIAN WILSON	Late '67	(SHORT VERSION) EDITED. DIFF. MIX. **WITH** SPOKEN MIDDLE SECTION. 10 SEC EDITED OUT AT 1.42, 45 SEC. EDITED OUT AT 2.50, 32 SEC. EDITED OUT AT 3.01 (END ALSO EDITED & CUT)
	TOTAL CD TIME 58.34				

Brother records

BEACH BOYS JOURNALS PART 1

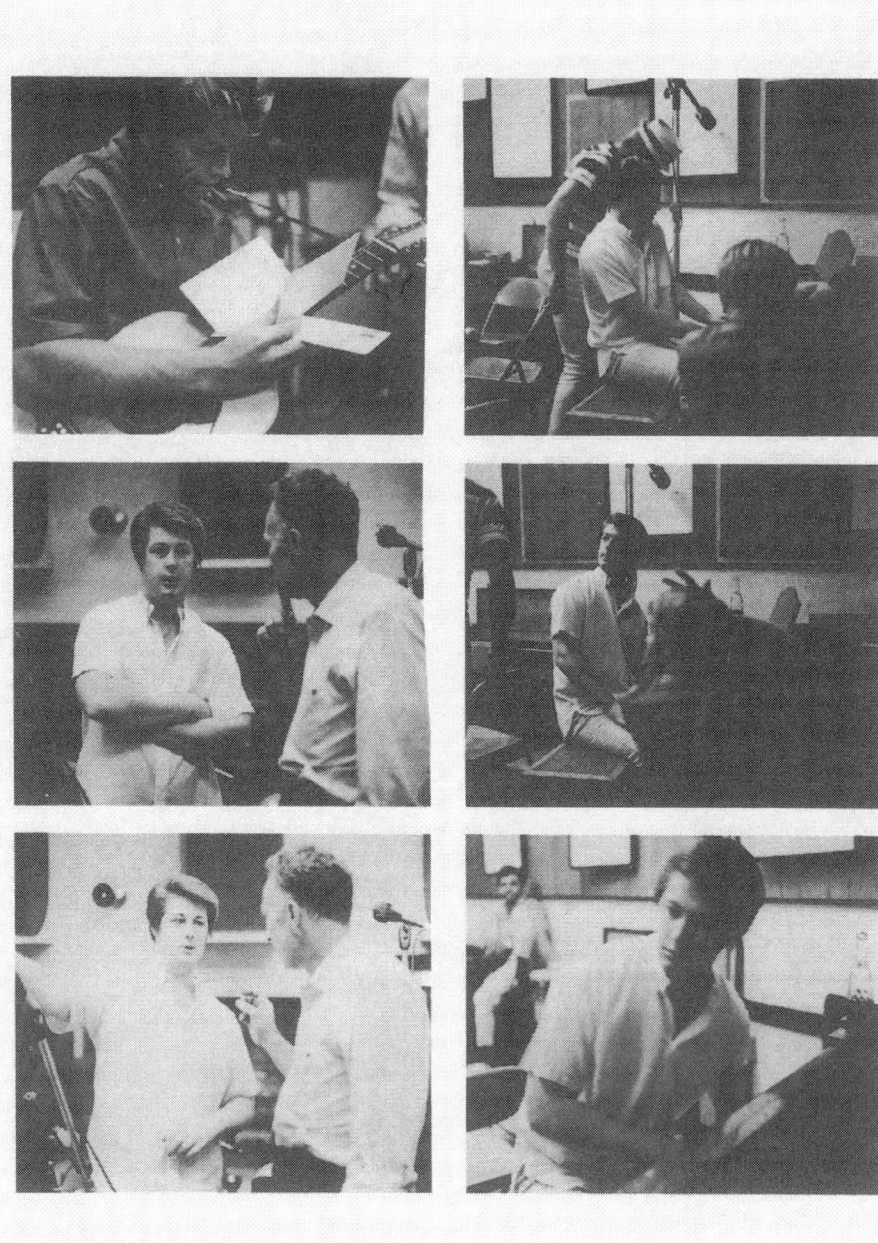

BEACH BOYS JOURNALS PART 1

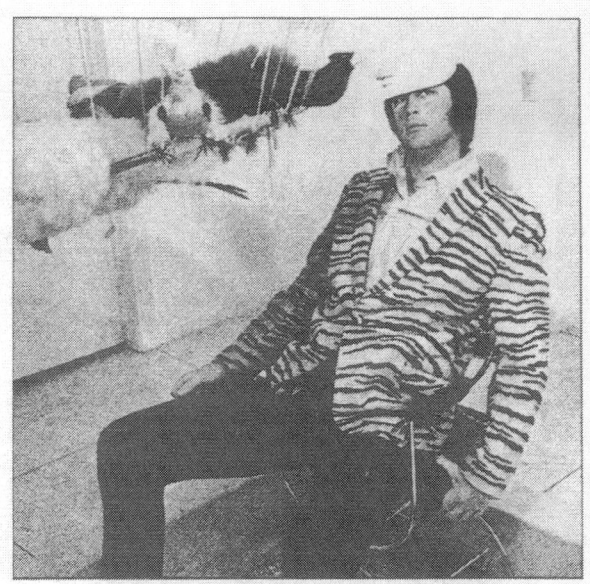

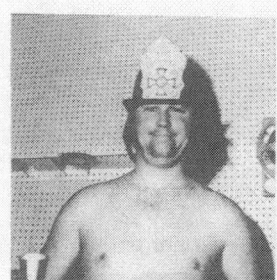
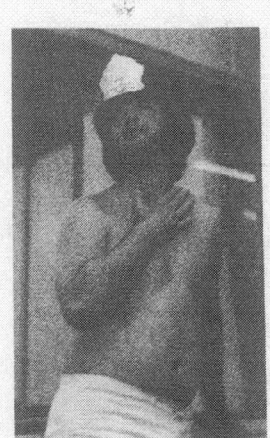

Above, Brian directs the action for a movie that was to complement the new music.

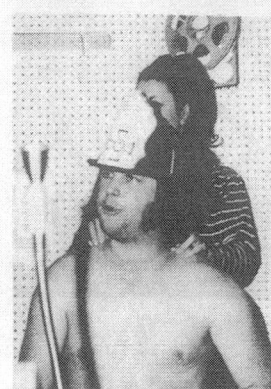

BEACH BOYS JOURNALS PART 1

Murry Wilson The 6th Beach Boy

Above........The Beach Boys at Hammersmith Odeon, 1968. Behind Bruce Johnston is bass player Ed Carter, who is still a member of the Beach Boys touring band.

BEACH BOYS JOURNALS PART 1

COMPUTER ENHANCED - DIGITALLY REMASTERED

JOURNALS PART 1 VOL.7 (LIVE 1964)

CD - 15

THE FIRST OF OUR 2 LIVE CD'S TO FINISH OFF THIS FIRST BOX SET COMPRISES ONE SONG FROM THE BEACH BOYS' HUGELY SUCCESSFUL 1964 AUSTRALIAN TOUR, FOLLOWED BY ALL THE VARIOUS OUTTAKES WHICH HAVE APPEARED OVER THE YEARS FROM THE 'CONCERT' ALBUM EDITED TOGETHER BY THE CEDREM LAB TO SOUND 'CONTINUOUS', WHICH MEANS YOU CAN NOW PLAY THESE TRACKS (#3 THRU #8) ALONGSIDE YOUR CONCERT & (MAYBE) HEAR THE ENTIRE CONCERT AT LAST ! A CONCERT FROM SWEDEN (W / INTERVIEW) AND A HOLLYWOOD BOWL CONCERT FROM LOS ANGELES COMPLETE A CD FULL OF 64 VINTAGE LIVE APPEARANCES.

#	SONGTITLE	TIME	SONGWRITERS	YEAR	COMMENTS
1.	CARL WILSON / INTRO	0.20		Circa '64	
2.	WHAT I'D SAY	4.36	RAY CHARLES	Jan.'64	SYDNEY, AUSTRALIA 1964
3.	INTRO - :	0.23		Aug.'64	CIVIC AUDITORIUM, SACRAMENTO, CALIFORNIA, USA '64 (THIS IS THE CONCERT WHICH RESULTED IN THE CAPITOL 'CONCERT' ALBUM IN '64)
4.	SURFIN' USA (#1)	2.04	C.BERRY-B. WILSON	Aug1'64	" " " "
5.	SURFER GIRL (#1)	2.33	BRIAN WILSON	Aug1'64	" " " "
6.	HUSHABYE	3.11	D.POMUS-M.SCHUMAN	Aug1'64	" " " "
7.	BE TRUE TO YOUR SCHOOL (#1)	1.54	BRIAN WILSON	Aug1'64	" " " "
8.	DON'T WORRY BABY (#1)	2.52	B.WILSON-R.CHRISTIAN	Aug1'64	" " " "
9.	INTERVIEW (ON SWEDISH TV)	4.09		Nov.'64	STOCKHOLM, SWEDEN NOV 1964
10.	FUN FUN FUN	1.59	B.WILSON-M.LOVE	Nov.'64	STOCKHOLM, SWEDEN NOV 1964
11.	LONG TALL TEXAN	2.19	H.STREZLECKI	Nov.'64	STOCKHOLM, SWEDEN NOV 1964
12.	IN MY ROOM (#1)	2.14	B.WILSON-G.USHER	Nov.'64	STOCKHOLM, SWEDEN NOV 1964
13.	GRADUATION DAY	2.29	J.SHERMAN-N.SHERMAN	Nov.'64	STOCKHOLM, SWEDEN NOV 1964
14.	PAPA-OOM-MOW-MOW	2.08	FRAZIER-WHITE-WILSON JR.-HARRIS	Nov.'64	STOCKHOLM, SWEDEN NOV 1964
15.	INTRODUCTION TO THE BAND	0.43		Nov.'64	STOCKHOLM, SWEDEN NOV 1964
16.	LITTLE DEUCE COUPE (#1)	1.41	B.WILSON-R.CHRISTIAN	Nov.'64	STOCKHOLM, SWEDEN NOV 1964
17.	SURFER GIRL (#2)	2.22	BRIAN WILSON	Nov.'64	STOCKHOLM, SWEDEN NOV 1964
18.	MONSTER MASH	2.42	B.PICKETT-L.CAPIZZI	Nov.'64	STOCKHOLM, SWEDEN NOV 1964
19.	LOUIE LOUIE	2.36	RICHARD BERRY	Nov.'64	STOCKHOLM, SWEDEN NOV 1964
20.	SURFIN' USA (#2)	2.24	C.BERRY-B. WILSON	Nov.'64	STOCKHOLM, SWEDEN NOV 1964
21.	DON'T WORRY BABY (#2)	2.48	B.WILSON-R.CHRISTIAN	Nov.'64	STOCKHOLM, SWEDEN NOV 1964
22.	I GET AROUND	2.36	BRIAN WILSON	Nov.'64	STOCKHOLM, SWEDEN NOV 1964
23.	JOHNNY B. GOODE	2.29	CHUCK BERRY	Nov.'64	STOCKHOLM, SWEDEN NOV 1964
24.	INTRODUCTION	1.07		1964	(BY ART LINKLETTER) HOLLYWOOD BOWL 1964 LOS ANGELES, CALIF. U.S.A. (JOINED ONSTAGE BY 'THE HONEYS' FOR TK #28)
25.	LITTLE DEUCE COUPE (#2)	2.26	B.WILSON-R.CHRISTIAN	1964	" " " "
26.	IN MY ROOM (#2)	2.25	B.WILSON-G.USHER	1964	" " " "
27.	BE TRUE TO YOUR SCHOOL (#2)	2.13	BRIAN WILSON	1964	" " " "
28.	SURFER GIRL (#3)	2.57	BRIAN WILSON	1964	" " " "
29.	KFWB THEME	0.27		1964	" " " "
30.	CLOSING CREDITS	1.16		1964	" " " "
	TOTAL CD TIME 66.19				

Brother records

BEACH BOYS JOURNALS PART 1

Glen Campbell, Carl, Dennis, Alan

ABOVE - : NOTE THE DATE ! HOW DO YOU PERFORM A SUCCESSFUL LIVE CONCERT ON THE EVENING OF JOHN F. KENNEDY'S ASSASSINATION ? A BRIEF MOMENT OF SILENCE AT THE START OF THEIR SET - AND IT'S 'ON WITH THE SHOW'. THE BEACH BOYS BROKE THE ALL-TIME ATTENDANCE RECORD AND HAD 3 ENCORES.....NOT BAD........

BEACH BOYS JOURNALS PART 1

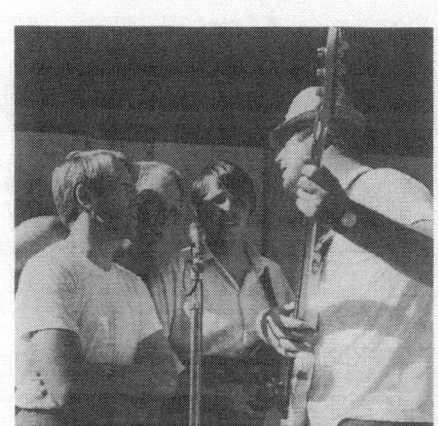
Alan, Mike, Carl, Brian at the Hollywood Bowl

BEACH BOYS JOURNALS PART 1

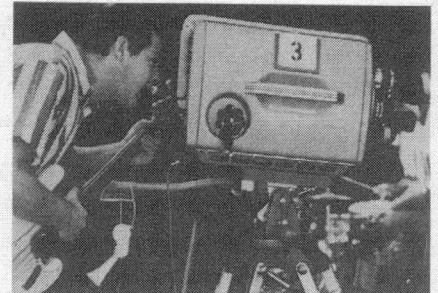

Dennis, Brian, Carl, Alan, Mike

Carl, Mike, Alan, Dennis, Glen Campbell

BEACH BOYS JOURNALS PART 1

COMPUTER ENHANCED - DIGITALLY REMASTERED

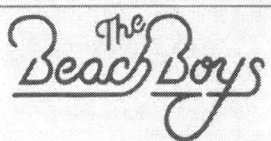

JOURNALS PART 1
VOL.8 (LIVE 1965-1968)

CD - 16

THE SECOND PART OF BOX #1'S LIVE DOUBLE DISC CONTAINS OUTTAKES FROM ONE OF THE MANY RECORDING SESSIONS WHICH BECAME THE 'PARTY' ALBUM, THE INCLUSION ON THIS TAPE ALONE OF 3 'COASTERS' SONGS IS A FAIR INDICATION OF HOW POPULAR THE COASTERS WERE WITH THE BEACH BOYS. FRICTION BETWEEN MIKE LOVE & DENNIS WILSON WAS APPARENTLY COMMON AND CAN BE HEARD ON TK #2 WHEN MIKE IS CRITICISING DENNIS FOR NOT SINGING THE **EXACT** LYRICS TO A BEATLES TUNE. FOLLOWING IS A CONCERT FROM 1966 OBVIOUSLY INTENDED FOR RADIO OR TV, GIVEN MIKE'S REFERENCE TO ADVERTS & THE RECORDING OF THE EVENING. THE SET FINISHES WITH THE ONLY TRACK ISSUED FROM THE PROPOSED 'LEI'D IN HAWAII' ALBUM AND A TRACK FROM THE US 'RARITIES' LP WHICH ACTUALLY GOES BEYOND THE BOXES' 1967 LIMIT BUT WE FELT THAT 'MUSICALLY' IT FITS BETTER HERE.

#	SONGTITLE	TIME	SONGWRITERS	RECORDING DATE	COMMENTS
	TRACKS 1-20 'PARTY' ALBUM OUTTAKES				
1.	RUBY BABY	2.06	LEIBER-STOLLER	Sep '65	BIG HIT SINGLE FOR 'DION' (DI MUCCI) CIRCA 61-62
2.	PREAMBLE	0.40		Sep '65	(PREAMBLE) BEATLES (JOHN LENNON) CLASSIC FROM THE 1964 'HELP !' ALBUM (& MOVIE SOUNDTRACK) ALTHOUGH **NOT** A SINGLE
3.	YOU'VE GOT TO HIDE YOUR LOVE AWAY	0.22	LENNON-McCARTNEY	Sep '65	(TAKE #1)
4.	YOU'VE GOT TO HIDE YOUR LOVE AWAY	2.14	LENNON-McCARTNEY	Sep '65	(TAKE #2)
5.	TICKET TO RIDE	1.30	LENNON-McCARTNEY	Sep '65	ANOTHER BEATLES SONG FROM HELP ! #1 HIT FOR THE BEATLES
6.	RIOT IN CELL BLOCK NO. 9	0.19		Sep '65	(PREAMBLE) ORIGINALLY A BIG HIT FOR THE COASTERS IN USA IN EARLY 60'S. MIKE LOVE RE-WROTE LYRICS (AS A REACTION TO THE KENT STATE UNIVERSITY INCIDENT) AS 'STUDENT DEMONSTRATION TIME' FOR 'SURF'S UP' ALBUM.
7.	RIOT IN CELL BLOCK NO. 9	2.30	LEIBER-STOLLER	Sep '65	(TAKE #1)
8.	RIOT IN CELL BLOCK NO. 9	0.56	LEIBER-STOLLER	Sep '65	(TAKE #2)
9.	LAUGH AT ME	2.13	SONNY BONO	Sep '65	SOLO SONNY BONO 45. TOP 10 IN USA & UK IN AUGUST 1965 FOR BONO
10.	ONE KISS LED TO ANOTHER	1.35	(PROBABLY) LEIBER-STOLLER	Sep '65	(TAKE #1) THIS OBSCURE SONG WAS THE COASTERS' FIRST SINGLE WHICH ONLY REACHED #79 IN USA ON SEP 9 1956 FOR **1 WEEK** ONLY
11.	ONE KISS LED TO ANOTHER	1.43	(PROBABLY) LEIBER-STOLLER	Sep '65	(TAKE #2)
12.	(PREAMBLE / JOKE)	0.39		Sep '65	WE CAN'T WORK OUT WHAT THE JOKE IS (BUT MAYBE YOU CAN)
13.	MOUNTAIN OF LOVE	1.43	HAROLD DORMAN	Sep '65	(TAKE #1) ORIGINALLY A #21 HIT FOR HAROLD DORMAN IN 60 AND A #9 HIT (AGAIN) THIS TIME BY JOHNNY RIVERS IN 1964
14.	MOUNTAIN OF LOVE	0.39	HAROLD DORMAN	Sep '65	(BREAKDOWN)
15.	MOUNTAIN OF LOVE	1.56	HAROLD DORMAN	Sep '65	(TAKE #2)
16.	MOUNTAIN OF LOVE	3.21	HAROLD DORMAN	Sep '65	(TAKE #3)
17.	CALIFORNIA GIRLS	1.29	BRIAN WILSON	Sep '65	US #20 HIT SINGLE IN JULY '65 ONLY 2 MONTHS BEFORE THIS WAS RECORDED (UK #26)
18.	I GET AROUND	0.55	BRIAN WILSON	Sep '65	(TAKE #1) #1 US SINGLE FROM MAY 64 (#7 IN UK)
19.	I GET AROUND	2.06	BRIAN WILSON	Sep '65	(TAKE #2) #1 US SINGLE FROM MAY 64 (#7 IN UK)
20.	POISON IVY / LITTLE DEUCE COUPE	2.34	LEIBER-STOLLER/B.WILSON-R.CHRISTIAN	Sep '65	'POISON IVY' WAS ORIGINALLY (AGAIN) A HIT FOR THE COASTERS THIS ONE A #7 US HIT IN OCT. 1959
21.	HELP ME RHONDA	2.20	BRIAN WILSON	Oct '66	LIVE AT THE MICHIGAN STATE UNIVERSITY (OCT 1966)
22.	I GET AROUND	2.27	BRIAN WILSON	Oct '66	LIVE AT THE MICHIGAN STATE UNIVERSITY (OCT 1966)
23.	MEDLEY - : SURFIN' SAFARI / FUN FUN FUN / SHUT DOWN / LITTLE DEUCE COUPE / SURFIN' USA	3.21	B.WILSON-M.LOVE / B.WILSON-M.LOVE / B.WILSON-R.CHRISTIAN/ C. BERRY / B.WILSON	Oct '66	"
24.	INTRO	1.21		Oct '66	"
25.	SURFER GIRL	2.26	BRIAN WILSON	Oct '66	"
26.	PAPA-OOM-MOW-MOW	2.15	FRAZIER-WHITE-HARRIS JNR	Oct '66	"
27.	INTRO	0.54		Oct '66	"
28.	YOU'RE SO GOOD TO ME	0.21	BRIAN WILSON	Oct '66	(BREAKDOWN)
29.	YOU'RE SO GOOD TO ME	2.17	BRIAN WILSON	Oct '66	"
30.	INTRO	0.26		Oct '66	"
31.	YOU'VE GOT TO HIDE YOUR LOVE AWAY	2.30	LENNON-McCARTNEY	Oct '66	"
32.	INTRO	1.11		Oct '66	"
33.	GOOD VIBRATIONS	3.52	B.WILSON-M.LOVE	Oct '66	"
34.	INTRO	0.21		Oct '66	"
35.	CALIFORNIA GIRLS	2.38	BRIAN WILSON	Oct '66	"
36.	INTRO	0.16		Oct '66	"
37.	SLOOP JOHN B	2.44	TRAD. ARR. BRIAN WILSON	Oct '66	"
38.	WOULDN'T IT BE NICE	2.00	B.WILSON-T.ASHER	Oct '66	"
39.	INTRO	0.41		Oct '66	"
40.	GOD ONLY KNOWS	2.46	B.WILSON-T.ASHER	Oct '66	"
41.	HEROES AND VILLAINS	3.33	B.WILSON-VAN DYKE PARKS	Aug 25 '67	HONOLULU INTERNATIONAL CENTER '67 (FROM THE NEVER RELEASED 'LEI'D IN HAWAII')
42.	ALL I WANNA DO	1.37	DENNIS WILSON	Nov 30 '68	LONDON PALLADIUM, ENGLAND '68 (REJECT FROM THE 'IN LONDON' ALBUM)
	TOTAL TRACK TIME 73.47				

Brother records

BEACH BOYS JOURNALS PART 1

Carl, Mike, Brian, Alan, Dennis

Brian, Mike, Alan and Carl two years later in Paris on tour

BEACH BOYS JOURNALS PART 1

BEACH BOYS JOURNALS PART 1

IT WAS THESE DRAFT PROBLEMS WHICH PROMPTED CARL TO GET INVOLVED WITH THE 'REGISTER TO VOTE' AND 'ANTI-HARD DRUG' MESSAGES.

BEACH BOYS JOURNALS PART 1

THE BEACH BOYS' LPs

MARK PAYTRESS LOOKS AT THE CLASSIC CAPITOL LPs FROM THE SIXTIES, WHEN BRIAN WILSON LED THE BAND FROM SURF AND SAND TO TRANSCENDENTAL MEDITATION AND PSYCHEDELIA

Everyone knows the Beach Boys' music; that harmony-led wash of sound which, perhaps more than anything else, seems to have been taken over by nostalgia radio as proof that life was better during the Sixties. And for much of the past 15 years, the group itself has survived on nostalgia, churning out the hits for sunshine soaked concert goers. All of this has unfairly obscured the fact that the Beach Boys — who were one of the most prolific recording groups of the Sixties — also produced an impressive run of albums, most of which repay close inspection, but have been unjustly ignored. In spite of the sheer volume of work they recorded for Capitol, the quality of much of the material stands as a testament to Brian Wilson's songwriting ability and incredible ear for production, and the group's master craftsmanship. In fact, the over-familiarity of the hits has, if anything, tended to dwarf the band's artistic worth; and the failure to recognise this has been one of the great injustices of rock history.

Capitol/EMI's magnificent job on the Beach Boys' CD reissue series last year prompted a sharp reappraisal of the band's back catalogue which, if you'd kept up with all the compilations issued over the past 25 years, consisted of a score of classic, fun-loving singles and little else. Not so: this, like the myth that paints the band as representative of American culture at its most sanitised, is a travesty of the truth. Anyone who has read Steve Gaines' warts'n'all biography, "Heroes And Villains", will know that the boys from Hawthorne High weren't exempt from the obvious distractions which litter the rock'n'roll byway; and of the three Wilson brothers, Dennis tragically succumbed to its lifestyle in December 1983. It almost claimed Brian too, but with a little help from his guru Dr. Eugene Landy, he made it back again. Cousin and enigmatic front-man Mike Love still adheres to that most esoteric of Sixties mysti philosophies, Transcendental Meditation, and only Carl, one-time draft-dodger, seems to have emerged with his all-American image anywhere near intact.

We shall be looking at the Beach Boys' post-Capitol recordings in a later issue: for the purposes of this feature, I shall stick closely to the original albums issued during the Sixties, a catalogue confused not only by Capitol's occasional rehashing of material in order to squeeze extra albums out of the band, but also by the haphazard fashion which they appeared in the U.K. To offer a more accurate account of the band's progression, I shall discuss each release in correct chronological order (U.S. release dates in brackets) which, when compared with the U.K. schedule given in the discography, gives you a rough idea just how stilted the Beach Boys' development must have seemed to unsuspecting British audiences.

Those wishing to read about the Beach Boys' pre-Capitol career should refer back to issue 40; while we covered the band's much-chronicled singles successes 40 issues later. Although Capitol have redeemed themselves with last year's handling of the CD reissues (all issued with detailed booklets giving session information, plenty of rare photographs and track-by-track accounts of the songs), the label must take some of the blame for the poor marketing of the Beach Boys career which, if the sleeves of the endless compilations and budget collections are anything to go by, consists of endless fun with surf, cars and girls, not necessarily in that order. Many British fans, to be fair, saw through the bland blanket marketing, so that when Capitol and the States resoundingly rejected "Pet Sounds" in 1966, this ground-breaking album achieved a No. 2 placing over here.

SURFIN' SAFARI (October 1962)

There's no mistaking which wave the Beach Boys sought to catch with their earliest recordings, although take away the title track and "Surfin' ", and you're left with a mixed fare of car and teen songs, plus a hilarious song about that ridiculous invention, the "Cuckoo Clock".

The bulk of this debut album was cut in one 13-hour session at Capitol's studios, and while primitive instrumentally, the boys' bedroom sessions (where they harmonised Four Freshman songs until the early hours) paid off with the distinctive harmonies that have remained the band's trademark. A mix of single cuts (though the version of "Surfin' " was not the same as the Candix hit single), cover versions, Brian Wilson-Gary Usher songs and the obligatory (at least until "Wild Honey") instrumental, this debut is full of period charm, and today suffices as a sentimental journey into U.S. pre-pop culture as much as for any real musical worth.

Although the album appeared in duophonic in the States, "Surfin' Safari" was intended to be heard in mono and remains that way on the CD reissue, where it is coupled with the group's second album. The CD also includes two bonus cuts dating from this time: "Cindy, Oh Cindy" and the amusing "Land Ahoy", previously aired on the "Rarities" album issued back in 1983.

SURFIN' U.S.A. (March 1963)

Though surfing was initially associated with instrumental music, pioneered by the likes of Dick Dale, the Beach Boys popularised the genre with a string of catchy vocal hits, which within months had transformed surfing into a worldwide phenomenon. They borrowed heavily from Chuck Berry's "Sweet Little Sixteen" for the title track, a move that was rewarded with their first U.K. chart entry; while in contrast to the mixed fare on their debut, the album was a surfers' delight, containing no less than five rousing instrumentals (including two popularised by Dick Dale, "Misirlou" and "Let's Go Trippin' ").

Nowhere near as commercial as "Surfin' USA", "Farmer's Daughter" or the car song "Shut Down" was "Lonely Sea", Brian Wilson's first introspective ballad (co-written with the late Gary Usher, as were many of his early efforts). It was the first in a long line of memorable compositions from the private world of the chief Beach Boy which would culminate in the confessional "Pet Sounds" album some three years later. Incredibly, "Lonely Sea" was taped back in June 1962, at the same session that produced "Surfin' Safari" and "409" for the previous album, but didn't really fit in on that record. If it hadn't made reference to the sea in the title, the song could well have escaped inclusion here too.

One out-take, "The Baker Man" (which took its cue from the Olympics' "Hully Gully"), was included on the CD reissue.

SURFER GIRL (September 1963)

As "Catch A Wave" amply illustrates, the Beach Boys' sound was developing quickly by this time, and a good deal more personality was injected into "Surfer Girl". With the assistance of top L.A. session musicians, the band were left to concentrate on their vocal work while Brian spent more time on achieving a bigger production (for which he received his first public credit).

Alongside hits like "Surfer Girl" (Brian Wilson's first song, dating from 1961),

Car and teen songs were the order of the day on "Surfin' Safari", the debut Beach Boys LP.

"Shut Down Vol. 2", the group's fifth album, was only the second to appear in the U.K.

"Catch A Wave" and "Little Deuce Coupe" was a second ballad from Brian, "In My Room". Long favoured by fans, "In My Room" was a step on from "Lonely Sea", though the incongruity of such introspection amidst a sea of tunes favouring the life-styles of the all-American teenager was lost on most casual listeners. If Capitol really feel they ought to squeeze another compilation out of the band, then there's certainly scope for a set of songs from "The Private Brian Wilson". A subsequent German-language version of "In My Room", taped in 1964, is included on the CD.

LITTLE DEUCE COUPE (October 1963)

Not content with getting three albums out of the band in less than a year, Capitol decided to cash in on the teenage obsession with cars on this collection comprising previously released material, plus several new songs cut in two days in September. Disc-jockey Roger Christian was Brian's co-composer on most of the car songs, and despite the inclusion of "Little Deuce Coupe" and "Our Car Club" from the third album, "409" from "Surfin' Safari" and "Shut Down" from "Surfin' USA", the album became one of the Beach Boys' most popular releases in the States.

The version of "Be True To Your School" (listen to Brian's effective use of horns — something that would be developed to perfection on the mid-Sixties recordings), differs from the single cut featured as a bonus on the CD, which includes the decidedly odd interjections from cheerleaders the Honeys. "Car Crazy Cutie" provided the basis of "Pamela Jean", a track taped by some of the band as the Survivors and issued as a single in January 1964.

It's worth mentioning that the CD reissue is (with the exception of "409") presented in stereo, although confirmed collectors will be aware that the original mono and stereo mixes done for the band's early albums differed markedly in some cases. It's also worth bearing in mind that the mono mixes were the ones worked on by Brian; while studio engineer Chuck Britz oversaw the stereo mixes right through to 1967's "Wild Honey". In the U.S., many of the early releases came in duophonic sound — a technique that, unlike electronically reprocessed stereo, which crudely pushed bass and treble frequencies into separate channels, employed a slight time-lag between channels, giving a 'wider' sound perspective — though today there is not a great deal of demand for these editions.

Despite the presence of David Marks on the rear sleeve photo, he'd been replaced during 1963 by the returning Al Jardine, who'd left the band in 1962 to continue with his High School studies.

SHUT DOWN VOLUME 2 (March 1964)

To avoid duplication of material, this album swaps places with "Little Deuce Coupe" in the CD reissue programme, and finds itself coupled with "Surfer Girl" (to which it is a more legitimate follow-up anyway). Although it has always been one of the more elusive albums (and was most welcome when See For Miles reissued it a couple of years back), "Shut Down Volume 2" finds the Beach Boys floundering somewhat, perhaps knocked back by the devastating (and extremely threatening) impression made by the Beatles in America earlier that year.

It was clear on this album (which was issued as a reply to Capitol's "Shut Down" various artists compilation, which many fans bought expecting it to be a Beach Boys album) that, despite coming up with masterful pop strokes like "Fun, Fun, Fun" and in particular the Spectoresque "Don't Worry Baby" (note big Brian's tear-wrenching falsetto, and all for a song about a car!), the band delighted in sending each other up, as on " 'Cassius' Love Vs. 'Sonny' Wilson", or letting Dennis have his 'Ringo' spot, singing on "This Car Of Mine" and pre-empting Ginger Baker's "Toad" on "Denny's Drums". And it wasn't only the gimmick songs that were filler: the version of "Louie Louie" too was barely passable. Only another lush Brian Wilson ballad, "The Warmth Of The Sun" (written in the aftermath of the Kennedy assassination), saved the day.

The CD reissue includes the single version of "Fun, Fun, Fun" and "I Do", which uses the same backing track as Brian's production for the Castells.

ALL SUMMER LONG (July 1964)

It would have made more sense had Brian Wilson packed in touring with the group after the release of "Shut Down Volume 2"; because there was little hint of his waning capabilities on this fine set, the last album to feature almost exclusively teenage obsessions.

Perhaps the comedy spot ("Our Favourite Recording Sessions") was wearing thin, the featured instrumental, "Carl's Big Chance" a wasted one, and "Do You Remember?" a pointless roll-call of the band's Fifties rock'n'roll favourites, but the rest of the disc far surpassed anything the band had done before. The opener, "I Get Around", was a vocal merry-go-round centred on the interplay between Brian and Mike Love and, not surprisingly, finally won the band a high placing in the U.K. chart. The title track was the U.S. single that never was, while "Girls On The Beach" showed Brian's dexterity in employing several key changes while avoiding the cliched and cumbersome traps which claim so many pop writers. "Don't Back Down" (mistitled "Don't Break Down" on early U.S. pressings), "Little Honda" (alternate versions of both contained on the CD) and "Wendy" kept the temperature high, for what was the Beach Boys' final 'beach' LP. Winter was around the corner, and so was Brian's collapse due to exhaustion (eight albums in two years by October 1964, remember); and then there was Xmas . . .

THE BEACH BOYS' CHRISTMAS ALBUM (October 1964)

This one's not yet out on CD in the U.K. (U.S. collectors have a baffling edition made available to them, which features half of the material in mono, the other half in stereo), although it's hoped that this set of standards and Brian Wilson originals will appear at some point. It was reissued in its original sleeve back in 1977, although next time round, Beach Boys collectors will be expecting several related bonus songs: "The Lord's Prayer" (already featured on "Rarities"), "Little Saint Nick (Single Mix)", "Auld Lang Syne" (without Dennis), "Jingle Bells" (backing track only) and "Little Saint Nick" (sung to the tune of "Drive-In"!). And then there's the matter of which version of "Merry Christmas, Baby" will be used: the stereo version was 30 seconds longer than its mono counterpart.

BEACH BOYS CONCERT (October 1964)

Incredible though it may now seem, it was this enthusiastic live set, recorded in Sacramento, California, which provided the Beach Boys with their first U.S. No. 1 album. True, it did feature several songs that had not appeared on disc before — a version of the Four Freshmen's "Graduation Day", Jan and Dean's "Little Old Lady From Pasadena", and Bobby Pickett's "Monster Mash", for example — but it hardly provides a benchmark in the band's creative development from today's perspective. Nevertheless, performed against the obligatory backdrop of pop's screaming audiences, the set stands up well, compared with other live documents of the day. The CD reissue sensibly coupled it with the 1968 "Live In London" set, and included a version of "Don't Worry Baby", although there was no room for three other songs taped at the time, "Don't Back Down", "Be True To Your School" (it would have been interesting to hear the audience response on that one!) and "Surfer Girl".

THE BEACH BOYS TODAY! (March 1965)

After the band completed their Xmas 1964 U.S. tour, with guitarist Glen Campbell standing in for the ailing Brian, old surf-hand Bruce Johnston was drafted in as a replacement, leaving Brian with time to concentrate on songwriting and producing. This move was instrumental in ushering in the Beach Boys' golden era, a time when the band had perfected their craft and when Brian began pushing the recording studio to new limits. "Today!" showed an increasing complexity in terms of both production and arrangement, a feat even more pronounced if you take into account that there's never been a true stereo edition of the album. With one notable exception, the inexplicable decision to destroy the album version of "Help Me Rhonda" with some ham-fisted fading, "Today!" remains a perfect introduction to the Beach Boys, full of glorious harmonies, exquisitely crafted two-minute mini-operas and infectious hooks and chorus lines.

Pick of the bunch had to be the sublime harmonies of "Please Let Me Wonder" and "I'm So Young" (an alternate take of the latter appears on the CD; "The Little Girl I Once Knew", plus an alternate "Dance, Dance, Dance" also appeared), plus the deceptively neat arrangement of the rather subdued hit "When I Grow Up (To Be A Man)". It's worth noting too that the arrangements of songs like "Kiss Me Baby", "In The Back Of My Mind" (featuring a fine vocal from soul brother Dennis) and "She Knows Me Too Well" pointed firmly in the direction which would climax a year (and three albums) later with "Pet Sounds".

SUMMER DAYS (AND SUMMER NIGHTS!!) (July 1965)

Some confusion surrounds this album, stemming from 1978 when Capitol re-released it as "California Girls" minus two tracks, "Amusement Parks U.S.A." and the (admittedly filler) "I'm Bugged At My Old Man". Now with its proper title and full running order reinstated, "Summer Days (And Summer Nights!!) can be seen as a solid follow-up to "Today!", although in some ways it did mark a step backwards. "California Girls" (and the album sleeve) reintroduced the obsession with girls and water, though the song's only crime was that it was too infectious a tune, rendering the backing music (and those marvellous opening bars) virtually redundant. This could be applied to much of the group's mid-Sixties work, when in fact a close listen to the backings reveal a sophistication hitherto unknown in the recording world.

The CD reissue includes an alternate take of "Let Him Run Wild", plus a fine studio recording of the Four Freshman hit, "Graduation Day", taped during the album sessions.

BEACH BOYS' PARTY! (November 1965)

Despite the far-reaching developments the Beach Boys were creating in the recording studios, it was this faked 'party' album which gave the band their biggest selling U.K. album to date. In fact, it was a compromise LP, enabling Brian could take a short breather after "Today!". So 12 songs were recorded, all acoustic bar some electric bass, and a few friends were invited into the studios (and to Mike Love's house, where a couple of tracks were taped) to add the all-important ambience. Out-takes are said to include the Stones' "(I Can't Get No) Satisfaction", "Smokey Joe's Cafe", "Long Tall Sally", "Heart And Soul" and "Ruby, Baby"; but sadly, none was added to the CD reissue.

Taken on its own, "Party!" was an inconsequential album of cover versions (bar the "I Get Around"/"Little Deuce Coupe" medley) tailor-made to add some zest to suburban garden parties. Spin it in 1991 and you'll find that it captures a pop era when pure pleasure was the most vital ingredient, an innocence that would be impossible today. And so for all its contrived joy, "Party!" remains an irreverent document, crucifying Dylan and Beatles songs in a way that pre-empted the current fascination for karaoke. Perhaps because pop music has only recently taken on 'art' proportions, irreverent recordings such as these hit a nerve that many critics find uncomfortable. But "Party!" is a welcome reminder that pop music is first and foremost a shared experience, and its best

BEACH BOYS JOURNALS PART 1

moments spontaneous explosions of sound and laughter. "Party!", in its premeditated attempt to capture those moments, is pure pop art: artifice masquerading as authenticity.

Collectors should note that the original U.S. edition of the album included a 12"x12" sheet of colour, wallet-sized photos, which alone are worth at least £10 today. Its best-known track, "Barbara Ann", actually featured lead vocals by band associate (Jan and) Dean Torrence.

PET SOUNDS (May 1966)

Given that Brian Wilson had almost ten months to work on this (time enough for many of today's established stars to cobble together enough material for a single release), rightly recognised masterpiece, one wonders what he could have done if he'd had more time in the years before this; and what he could have been capable of had the rest of the Beach Boys allowed him to pursue the direction he took on the abortive "Smile" project.

In common with most of the band's recordings during this time, "Pet Sounds" was written by Brian (much of it with lyricist Tony Asher) and played by a selection of top L.A. session musicians (including the likes of Leon Russell, Glen Campbell, Hal Blaine and Jim Gordon).

Although richly rewarded with a No. 2 chart position in the U.K., "Pet Sounds" disappointed the U.S. market which expected another selection of fun-loving tunes, instead of the introspective odes to teen angst which Brian had conjured up for them. By this time, competing with the likes of the Four Seasons (as explicitly stated on earlier recordings) was a thing of the past, and it was the Beatles' "Rubber Soul" which fired Wilson's imagination: "I'm gonna make the greatest album, the greatest rock album ever made," he enthused at the time. "Pet Sounds" didn't rock, exactly; but it was by far the most intricate pop album made at that time.

Reinstated in glorious mono for the CD reissue, "Pet Sounds" was, unlike the rest of the band's back catalogue, issued as a single disc, so as not to spoil its original identity, but complete with bonus tracks. Its best-known cuts, "Sloop John B", "God Only Knows" and "Wouldn't It Be Nice", are in no way adequate reflection of the breadth of material it contained, and if titles like "Don't Talk (Put Your Head On My Shoulder)", "You Still Believe In Me" and "I Just Wasn't Made For These Times" don't immediately spring to mind, it's because they failed to fit the mould of the obvious Beach Boys sound, and are too ethereal to ever warrant much radio play.

Collectors were surprised when, early in 1989, Toshiba/EMI in Japan issued a remastered "Pet Sounds" CD complete with two bonus cuts, "Unreleased Backgrounds" and "Hang On To Your Ego" ("I Know There's An Answer" with a different lyric). Copies quickly began to change hands for up to £100, although last summer's British CD reissue, complete with a third bonus track, "Trombone Dixie", has made that release somewhat redundant.

SMILEY SMILE (September 1967)

Brian Wilson's "Smile" project deserves a feature in itself, so for our purposes here, I will just sketch in its bare bones as background. Despite the commercial setbacks of "Pet Sounds", Wilson had been encouraged by the success of the "Good Vibrations" single that same year, and began work on what Beach Boy historian (and sleeve-note writer for the CD reissue series) David Leaf has called "a reflection of Brian's belief in the healing powers of laughter".

Recruiting lyricist Van Dyke Parks, Wilson spent the latter part of 1966 and the early months of 1967 in and out of recording studios working on what undoubtedly would have been a major musical achievement. Unfortunately, neither his fellow Beach Boys, nor Capitol Records for that matter, shared in his enthusiasm: certainly, much of the material was way off what had, up till that point, been regarded as suitable rock material, and the costs of recording were becoming prohibitive. By May 1967, it was clear that "Smile" would never come out as originally conceived, and while excerpts from the project have appeared here and there, it would be a great mistake to imagine that the eventual follow-up to "Pet Sounds", "Smiley Smile", was in any sense related to "Smile" other than in name and era. Those wishing to glimpse the nearest thing to the full "Smile" project needs to hear the most recent bootleg CD, which far exceeds any other out-take recordings, at least in terms of audio quality.

Ironically, it was "Smiley Smile", not "Smile", which was the antithesis of the recognised Beach Boys style. Produced by the band, it was sparse, under-produced and erratic, and lacked the sheer majesty of some of the big "Smile" productions. Both sides of "Smiley Smile" got off to the best possible start with "Heroes And Villains" and "Good Vibrations" respectively, but the rest of the material only gave a surface impression of the band's relationship with the burgeoning psychedelic movement. Surprisingly, though, it still works as acid-rock; while the likes of Jefferson Airplane and Pink Floyd seemed to focus on the intensity of the psychedelic experience, "Smiley Smile" conjures up those eerie moments of introspection and isolation, when the wonders of the world are reduced to sheer nonsense. Songs like "Little Pad", "Wind Chimes", and the potentially terrifying "Fall Breaks And Back To Winter" are fine examples; but the album's real saviours are "With Me Tonight" and "Wonderful", both of which grew out of the original "Smile" sessions.

Equally revealing, though, are the bonus tracks that turned up on the CD reissue. The alternate take of "Heroes And Villains" dates from "Smile" and includes an "In The Cantina" segment previously unheard by even the most avid collector; likewise, the various "Good Vibrations" out-takes offer a fascinating glimpse into the making of the song, while "Can't Wait Too Long" is Brian Wilson at his mesmerising best, proving that, even in this unfinished state, his music offered more than most contemporaries were able to in a lifetime. Two other bonus cuts were included: the meditative B-side, "You're Welcome", and a version of "Their Hearts Were Full Of Spring", recorded during rehearsals for their summer concerts in Hawaii.

During 1967, Brian also talked of other projects: LPs of water sounds, a fitness/exercise disc and an album of humour — it's a pity none were realised, for the head Beach Boy seemed to be divinely inspired during these few months.

Collectors should note that a U.S. Capitol record club edition of "Smiley Smile" was issued back in 1967, and now fetches £100.

WILD HONEY (December 1967)

Had the Beach Boys issued this 'back to the roots' release 12 months later, it probably would have caught the same wave as the Stones' "Beggars Banquet", the Beatles' "White Album", and the Band's first LP. But it took Bob Dylan's "John Wesley Harding",

Simple all-American boys off on a surfin' safari. The truth was that only Dennis was in any way proficient at the sport. The less well-known Beach Boy on the right is David Marks.

issued in February 1968, to break the mould and make a reacquaintance with simpler country, folk, soul and rock'n'roll styles fashionable once again.

Although, like its predecessor, "Wild Honey" was issued only in mono and electronically reprocessed stereo first time round, Capitol have sensibly stuck to the original mono mixes for the CD reissue series. It's never really had its champions, due mainly to the distinct lack of group vocals on the album (though this was in some way compensated for by the set's best known cut, "Darlin'"), but it proved a watershed recording for two reasons: Carl Wilson was beginning to assert himself within the band with no less than three lead vocals on "Wild Honey"; and for the first time since 1963, the instrumentation was recorded solely by the group members, rather than the experienced session musicians who were called in for Brian's earlier production extravaganzas.

Two out-takes from the sessions, covers of the Beatles' "With A Little Help From My Friends" and the Box Tops' "The Letter", turned up on 1983's "Rarities" collection, while an unreleased recording of "Cool Cool Water" remains in the vaults.

FRIENDS (June 1968)

It's just as well that EMI/Capitol decided to utilise a two-for-the-mid-price-of-one policy towards the CD reissues because the original albums weren't exactly generous on playing time: this one clocked in at around 24 minutes. Unfortunately, the initial batch of CD booklets contained a mix-up, and pages from the notes to "Stack-O-Tracks"/"Beach Boys' Party" seemed to have been swapped around with those for the "Friends"/"20/20" release.

The material on "Friends" was far superior to that on "Wild Honey", although the mood was, if anything, more mellow. Brian sang the autobiographical "Busy Doin' Nothin'", "Meant For You" and "Passing By" were lazy near-instrumentals, while "Transcendental Meditation" was the first of several songs the Beach Boys sang about the subject. This one, marked by discordant instrumentation and a fabulous swirling vocal, is often derided by fans of the group, but it certainly provided a memorable climax to one of the band's most under-rated albums. "Friends" is perhaps most notable for the emergence of drummer Dennis Wilson as a major musical force; of his two contributions, "Be Still" is one of the undiscovered gems from the Beach Boys' late-Sixties catalogue. Incidentally, the song did not stem from his relationship with Charles Manson as some believe: it was recorded in April 1968, weeks before the pair first met.

It's worth noting that while "Friends" was issued only in stereo in the States (mixed by Steve Desper, who also did the mixing on the subsequent Capitol albums), British collectors still had the choice of obtaining copies in glorious monophonic.

STACK-O-TRACKS (August 1968)

"You sing the words and play with the original instrumental backgrounds to 15 of their biggest hits" went the blurb on the back sleeve of this 'filler' album; 'filler' that is, if you'd already acquainted yourself with the complexity of instrumentation that went in to the making of those memorable Beach Boys hits. (Otherwise, it offers an indispensable insight into the band's lavish productions.)

First time round, this album came complete with chord sequences and a 16-page lyric booklet (although British fans had to

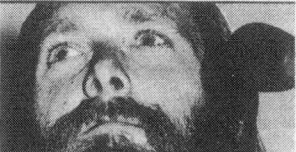

BEACH BOYS JOURNALS PART 1

wait a further eight years before it appeared over here; and then the lyrics simply appeared on the inner sleeve, with no chord shapes); and the album has long been one of the most sought-after releases in the band's back catalogue, not least because it was the first Capitol Beach Boys album not to chart. A U.S. Capitol Record Club edition (DKAO 8-2893) currently fetches £125, while original U.S. copies with the booklet can sell for up to £100.

Interestingly enough, several of the songs appear on the CD in true stereo — even though only mono/duophonic versions of the full songs have ever been made available. Among the aberrants are "Salt Lake City", "Sloop John B", "Wouldn't It Be Nice", "God Only Knows", "Little Honda", "Here Today", "You're So Good To Me", "Let Him Run Wild" and one of the featured bonus cuts, "California Girls". Instrumental versions of "Help Me Rhonda" and "Our Car Club" fleshed out the recent CD reissue. Collectors should note that the version of "Little Saint Nick" which appears is in fact the 45 version, complete with additional percussion.

20/20 (February 1969)

On the face of it a two-song album, with a slightly extended "Do It Again" and a remake of the Ronettes' "I Can Hear Music", "20/20" actually includes a couple of the band's finest late-Sixties recordings in "Never Learn Not To Love" and the wonderful "Smile" out-take "Cabinessence", where the group's exquisite harmonies take off in directions unheard of at the time it was recorded in December 1966. The legend of "Smile" may prove difficult to follow up with a posthumous release (hence the band's reluctance to sanction its issue), but on the strength of this track alone, it would have proved at least as groundbreaking as "Good Vibrations" (incredibly, another music paper recently omitted that 45 from their exhaustive list of influential records, despite the fact that it was the single most important release in recognising the recording studio as a vital part of the creative process — shameful!).

"Never Learn Not To Love" definitely sprang from the Wilson-Manson association, and the infamous "Lie" album contains Manson's original version (recorded as "Cease To Exist"). The Beach Boys took a good song, gave it a Spector-like production, had Dennis deliver another of his soulful vocals, and came up with one of the great B-sides of the decade (this album version features a slightly different mix). It certainly knocked spots off of the throwaway cover of "Bluebirds Over The Mountain" which the song backed. A unique version of "Bluebirds" appeared in Holland, while "Rarities" album offered a strange hybrid of the two.

"Brian Wilson Rarities" was an Australian-only package which was later withdrawn.

Perhaps hits collections like this mail-order only title will be the rarities of tomorrow.

LIVE IN LONDON (May 1970)

"20/20" was the Beach Boys' final Capitol studio album, but the story didn't end there. "Live In London" has been denigrated somewhat by a mid-price reissue on MfP, but the performances (taped in concert at Finsbury Park and the Palladium during the band's December 1968 U.K. tour) were far from throwaway.

If the track listing betrays the fact that the Beach Boys were always more concerned with crowd-pleasing rather than ground-breaking in the live situation, the arrangements stand as a testament to the group's musical integrity, proving them to be far more capable as musicians than they've ever been credited for.

"Wake The World" indicates just how well the late Sixties LP material stood up in concert, and it's a pity that more album tracks didn't receive the higher profile that they deserved. The group performance on "Their Hearts Were Full Of Spring" proved a perfect vehicle for the group's rich vocal sound, while versions of "Good Vibrations" and "God Only Knows" were more than passable renditions of studio-orientated songs.

"Live In London" is coupled with the 1964 live album, and ends up with a fascinating live bonus version of "Heroes And Villains", taped for the aborted "Lei'd In Hawaii" project in the summer of '67. A rare concert appearance with Brian on lead vocal (shared with Al Jardine), "Heroes And Villains" was an impressive performance, even by Beach Boys standards, leaving many fans hoping that perhaps the entire concert may find its way onto official release in the future.

The Beach Boys' memorable eight years with Capitol Records ended in 1970 when they decided to take their own Brother Records to Reprise. But, as every collector will know, for every album issued by Capitol during the Sixties, there's been at least a brace of releases during the following decades, with a seemingly endless barrage of mid-price reissues and ill-conceived compilations. Even the Sixties compilations weren't all they ought to have been, and collectors should look instead to last year's "Summer Dreams" as the ideal introduction to the band's most popular material.

But there have been several releases worth seeking out along the way. First off was World Records' "The Capitol Years" seven-album boxed set, issued in 1981. Taking a thematic approach to the group's material (discs were given titles like "Changes" and the inevitable "Sunshine Music"), the box was probably most sought-after because of the inclusion of a bonus disc of Brian Wilson productions, many of which had never been made available in Britain before. These included sides by the Honeys, Sharon Marie, Gary Usher, and Glen Campbell, plus two tracks by the Beach Boys masquerading as the Survivors, previously only available as a bonus single in EMI's boxed set of singles. And for those strictly concerned with bona fide Beach Boys rarities, the set also included the U.S. single mix of "Be True To Your School", now included on the "Little Deuce Coupe"/"All Summer Long" CD.

Two "Rarities" albums also appeared during the early 1980s, the first on Australian Capitol (ST 26463) which, due to an unauthorised live version of "What'd I Say" recorded live in Sydney in 1964, was withdrawn a few years later. In addition to several of the Brian Wilson productions which featured on the World Records box, the album also compiled both sides of Dennis's 1970 "Sound Of Free" single on LP for the first time.

A couple of years later, a British "Rarities" set was cobbled together (in a typically tasteless sleeve) which included several tracks that have since appeared as CD bonus tracks, plus a couple which haven't: alternate takes of "Good Vibrations" and "I Was Made To Love Her", plus a live version of "All I Want To Do".

THE BEACH BOYS
UK CAPITOL LP DISCOGRAPHY

LPs

Cat No.	Title	Current Mint Value
Capitol T 1808	SURFIN' SAFARI (4/63)	£25
Capitol T/ST 2027	SHUT DOWN VOLUME 2 (7/64)	£15/£18
Capitol T/ST 2164	THE BEACH BOYS' CHRISTMAS ALBUM (11/64)	£22/£25
Capitol T/ST 2198	BEACH BOYS CONCERT (2/65)	£14/£15
Capitol T/ST 2110	ALL SUMMER LONG (6/65)	£18/£20
Capitol T/ST 1980	SURFIN' USA (8/65, No. 17)	£15/£18
Capitol T/ST 1998	LITTLE DEUCE COUPE (10/65)	£15/£16
Capitol T/ST 2398	BEACH BOYS' PARTY! (2/66, No. 3)	£12/£10
Capitol T/ST 2269	THE BEACH BOYS TODAY! (4/66, No. 6)	£12
Capitol T/ST 2354	SUMMER DAYS (AND SUMMER NIGHTS!!) (6/66, No. 4)	£10
Capitol T/ST 2458	PET SOUNDS (5/66, No. 2)	£10
Capitol T/ST 20856	BEST OF THE BEACH BOYS (11/66, No. 2)	£10
Capitol T/ST 1981	SURFER GIRL (3/67, No. 13)	£10
Capitol T/ST 20956	BEST OF THE BEACH BOYS VOL. 2 (10/67, No. 3)	£10
Capitol T/ST 9001	SMILEY SMILE (11/67, No. 9)	£10
Capitol T/ST 2859	WILD HONEY (3/68, No. 7)	£10
Capitol T/ST 2895	FRIENDS (9/68, No. 13)	£12/£10
Capitol T/ST 21142	BEST OF THE BEACH BOYS VOL. 3 (11/68, No. 9)	£12/£10
Capitol ET/EST 133	20-20 (3/69, No. 3)	£12/£10
Regal Starline SRS 5014	BUG-IN (budget price, 3/70)	£5
MfP 1382	THE BEACH BOYS (budget price, 6/70)	£5
Capitol ST 21628	GREATEST HITS (9/70, No. 5)	£9
Regal Starline SRS 5074	THE BEACH BOYS (budget price, 6/71)	£5
MfP 5235	DO YOU WANNA DANCE (budget price reissue of "Beach Boys Today!", 1/72)	£6
Capitol ST 21715	LIVE IN LONDON (8/72)	£9
MfP 50065	ALL SUMMER LONG (budget reissue, 7/73)	£5
Capitol EAST 11307	ENDLESS SUMMER (11/74)	£9
Capitol ESTSP 14	WILD HONEY/FRIENDS (2-LP, reissue, 5/75)	£8.50
Capitol VMP 1007	SPIRIT OF AMERICA (9/75)	£9
MfP 50234	GOOD VIBRATIONS (budget price, 10/75)	£5
EMI EMTV 1	20 GOLDEN GREATS (6/76, No. 1)	£6
Capitol EST 24009	STACK O' TRACKS (12/76)	£8
MfP 50345	LIVE IN LONDON (budget price reissue, 9/77)	£4
Capitol CAPS 1014	THE BEACH BOYS' CHRISTMAS ALBUM (reissue, 12/77)	£8
Capitol CAPS 1023	SUMMER DAYS AND SUMMER NIGHTS!! (reissue, 6/78)	£8
EMI EMTV 1	20 GOLDEN GREATS (blue vinyl edition of 20,000, 1979)	£8
Capitol CAPS 1037	GIRLS ON THE BEACH (6/80)	£5
WRC SM 651/657	THE CAPITOL YEARS (7-LP box set, 1/81)	£30
Green Light GO 2002	PET SOUNDS (budget reissue, 6/81)	£4
Green Light GO 2005	BEACH BOYS CONCERT (budget reissue, 6/81)	£4
Green Light GO 2014	SURFIN' SAFARI (budget reissue, 6/81)	£4
Green Light GO 2025	LITTLE DEUCE COUPE (budget reissue, 6/81)	£4
MfP 50529	ENDLESS SUMMER (9/81)	£4
Fame FA 3018	PET SOUNDS (budget reissue, 5/82)	£4
Capitol BBTV 1867193	THE VERY BEST OF THE BEACH BOYS (2-LP, 1983)	£8
Capitol EMS 1174	LITTLE DEUCE COUPE (budget price reissue, 6/86)	£4
Capitol EMS 1175	SURFER GIRL (budget price reissue, 6/86)	£4
Capitol EMS 1176	ALL SUMMER LONG (budget reissue, 6/86)	£4
Capitol EMS 1177	BEACH BOYS' PARTY! (budget reissue, 6/86)	£4
Capitol EMS 1178	SUMMER DAYS AND SUMMER NIGHTS!! (budget reissue, 6/86)	£4
Capitol EMS 1179	PET SOUNDS (budget reissue, 6/86)	£4
EMI/Capitol EN 5005	MADE IN THE U.S.A. (2-LP, 8/86)	£9
EMI/Capitol EMTVD 51	SUMMER DREAMS (2-LP, 6/90, No. 1)	£8

All prices refer to original issues of albums. Where albums were released in mono and stereo, the mono price is given first, unless there is no difference in the two values, in which case a single value is given.

CDs

Cat No.	Title	
Capitol CDEN 5005	MADE IN THE USA (11/86)	£10
EMI CDP 746 467 2	ENDLESS SUMMER (2/87)	£10
Capitol CDP 746 618 2	SPIRIT OF AMERICA (6/87)	£10
EMI CDEMTV 1	20 GOLDEN GREATS (11/87)	£10
Capitol CDP 748 421 2	PET SOUNDS (budget price, 6/90)	£7.50
Capitol CDP 7 93691 2	SURFIN' SAFARI/SURFIN' USA (budget price, 6/90)	£7.50
Capitol CDP 7 93692 2	SURFER GIRL/SHUT DOWN VOLUME 2 (budget price, 6/90)	£7.50
Capitol CDP 7 94620 2	SUMMER DREAMS (6/90)	£10
Capitol CDP 7 93693 2	LITTLE DEUCE COUPE/ALL SUMMER LONG (budget price, 7/90)	£7.50
Capitol CDP 7 93694 2	TODAY/SUMMER DAYS AND SUMMER NIGHTS!! (budget price, 7/90)	£7.50
Capitol CDP 7 93695 2	BEACH BOYS' CONCERT/LIVE IN LONDON (budget price, 8/90)	£7.50
Capitol CDP 7 93696 2	SMILEY SMILE/WILD HONEY (budget price, 8/90)	£7.50
Capitol CDP 7 93598 2	BEACH BOYS' PARTY!/STACK-O-TRACKS (budget price, 9/90)	£7.50
Capitol CDP 7 93697 2	FRIENDS/20/20 (budget price, 9/90)	£7.50

BEACH BOYS JOURNALS PART 1

MUSICAL EXPRESS

21, 1975   12p

10cc. a Man mewn cyngerdd yng Nghaerydd
— SEE PAGE 3

BEGINS THIS WEEK:

THE LAST BEACH MOVIE
A Story of Brian Wilson

By NICK KENT

THE LAST BEACH MOVIE

BRIAN WILSON 1942-

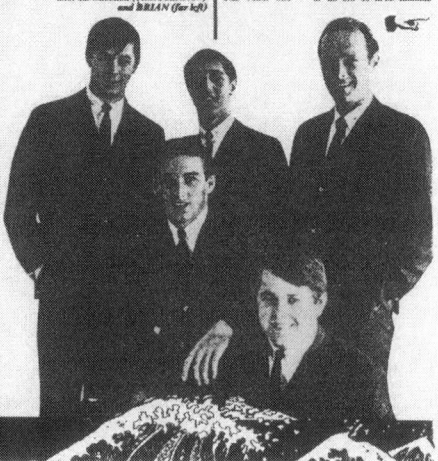

THE INCIDENT MUST HAVE occured a little over a year ago.

Paul McCartney, complete with the inevitable Linda, had just flown into Los Angeles — for business talks and the like — and already he was trying to get in touch with Brian Wilson.

McCartney and Wilson were no strangers. Derek Taylor, back in 1966 when he was The Beach Boys' publicist, had convened an encounter between the two composers — an encounter, moreover, that had proven totally successful as regards compatability.

Conversation had been easy and verbal bouquets had constantly changed hands throughout an evening that had reached its peak when Wilson had played back the final mix of a new composition of his, mooted to be the next Beach Boys single — a song called "Good Vibrations". McCartney of course had been mightily impressed.

But that was all some eight years ago, and times and personalities change.

Now there was no Beatles to contend with. Instead, McCartney was married, domesticated, a father and the composer of music that, if it

suffered in comparison to the giddier heights of yore, was still cast in a meticulous workmanlike idiom.

Brian Wilson, however, hadn't seemed to have stood the rigours of the period as buoyantly as McCartney. His personality, always as fitful as it was fanatical in any given direction, was supposedly weighed down by brooding hermetic traits, and he was often erratic, paranoid, crazed — cursed by a weight problem that had ultimately got out of all proportion and which consequently seemed to be reinforcing his numerous complexes.

Moreover, his creative output had lessened dramatically, giving rise to contentions that his muse was practically inert.

Wilson soon enough got the message that McCartney was trying to contact him, and he just froze up, became terrified. Apparently he'd been informed of a quote attributed to McCartney to the effect that the latter considered "God Only Knows" to be the highest achievement in composition. Something like that.

Anyway Brian couldn't handle it. What was originally meant as just another verbal bouquet from one of his peers became twisted in the Wilson psyche. If he'd created the greatest song ever . . . I mean, now . . . what was there left to achieve? He just couldn't . . .

Paul McCartney never got to see Brian Wilson face-to-face. The latter reportedly locked himself away in the "cabanya" of his Bel Air swimming pool.

Paul and Linda stood for maybe an hour (who knows?) that night knocking on the door, trying to lure him out: "Brian . . . Brian, it's alright. Really!"

An eye witness states that they could hear him crying quietly to himself.

PART 1:

20,000 Leagues Under The Surf

by

NICK KENT

IT WAS TWO WEEKS into last December when Brian Wilson phoned Warner Bros' Dave Bursyn with the news of a new single. He'd written and recorded a brand new track and was wild with enthusiasm.

"Dave . . . Dave we've got to put it out right now . . . right now"

There was one slight problem though: the song was a novelty Christmas ditty complete with quirky lyrics about babes in arms with stockings at the foot of their beds and Santa Claus careering over the snowy tundras beladen with gifts.

The music itself was dumb as hell, right down to the two-chord coda and the trashy organ sound underpinning a morass of sleigh bells jangling through the mix. Wilson thought it tremendous though — he'd even added a wiggy spoken bit performed in his best near-retarded "Wizard of Oz" voice — and just couldn't understand Bursyn's hesitancy about the whole project.

It wasn't as though Bursyn even disliked the song, it was *just* . . . A song specifically about Christmas conceived at least two months too late? There just wasn't any point . . .

Wilson, though, was adamant. He started manipulating Bursyn's better nature the only way he knew how. He started cracking up . . . pleading . . . "Dave won't you do it . . . for me?" Bursyn ultimately was left with no real choice.

"A Child for Winter", The Beach Boys' Christmas single for 1974, was released December 27 of that year — a limited pressing with an old Al Jardine song "Suzi Cincinatti" (dating back to the "Sunflower" era circa 1970) as the B-side.

The pressing, in fact, was so limited that, in five months, the single has already become, for better or worse, a bonafide collector's item on par with obscurities like the Dennis Wilson solo track "Sound of Free" or the vintage Beach Boys/Annette Funicello collaboration "The Monkey's Uncle."

To call Dave Bursyn's position as Warner Bros' mediator for The Beach Boys a "thankless" one is to commit something of the grand understatement.

It's not merely that the rest of the band both hate and resent his very presence — it was Bursyn, for example, who rejected the original finished tapes of both "Holland" and the "Beach Boys In Concert" set, holding out on the former until Van Dyke Parks had literally forced Brian Wilson onto the piano to finish off what at first were just vague fragments of a song eventually to take shape as "Sail On Sailor" (thus nixing the inclusion of Mike Love's dreadful "We Got Love" on that album) — it's more that Bursyn is just one more figure directly involved in the whole heartbreaking task of attempting to forcibly extract 'product' out of 'confused' genius Brian Wilson.

LOS ANGELES is seemingly full of characters who've at one time or another been involved in trying to extricate Wilson from his brooding complexes, if only long enough for him to spread out and create.

Tony Asher, for example, who collaborated with Brian as lyricist on the "Pet Sounds" album of 1966, is employed by the Wes Farrell Organisation. (Farrell, arguably America's very own Mickie Most, was responsible for both the Partridge Family and David Cassidy until the latter recently left his supervision to be produced, interestingly enough by ex-Beach Boy Bruce Johnston for R.C.A.).

David Anderle — once upon a time the unofficial "mayor of hipness" in L.A., later the head of "Brother", Wilson's dream record label, and consequently a key figure in the period that saw the giddy rise and disintegration of The Beach Boys' now legenderay "Smile" album debacle — is now working at A & M records. His latest triumph being the impressive success of The Ozark Mountain Daredevils.

And then there is the Burbank Warner's contingent. The unfortunate Bursyn, the infamous Andy "Wipeout" Wickham, to whom the topic of The Beach Boys is a very tender issue indeed and one he refuses to discuss with journalists, and, finally, of course, there is the ever incorrigible Van Dyke Parks, lyricist of "Surf's Up", once upon a time the House of Warner's 'mad professor' archetype, who will still walk into a room, make a scatterbrained statement like "Do you know — I was in South Carolina last week and a guy came up to me and said 'It's O.K. to be a fraud' " and promptly disappear again.

It's like Derek Taylor says: Van Dyke Parks is mad, but it's a constant thing and on that level, anyone with the appropriate quotient of sensitivity can relate.

"Brian, though — one day he's coherent . . . bright, and then the next he can be just so damn illogical . . . strange . . . scarey".

Maybe Phil Spector is the nearest living equivalent to the Brian Wilson condition. Spector's another one who's now working for the Warners catalogue and it's maybe just a little too convenient to wax enigmatic about the ironies inherent in it all.

Phil Spector and Brian Wilson: two living legends from the 60's, visually the total antithesis of the other (Spector small, unhealthy looking, rodent-like; Wilson large, almost bovine in aspect), both obsessed by "Sound" so gargantuan it was more akin at times to a tonal approximation of the Niagara Falls.

And now? Both time-warp casualties, supposed Bel Air hermits locked way in small darkened rooms where they reportedly play their old records for hours on end. The image is as madly appealing, as potentially tragic as it may well be stupidly misguided.

Whatever, in 1967 one of Brian Wilson's main paranoias, created via his almost hysterical sense of competition, was that Spector was infuriated by the former's manipulation of "his sound" and was out to "get" him.

Even today they may still be in competition — as the current highest contenders for the dubious "Orson Welles of rock" soubriquet.

If one actually desires to hold credence by such hypothetical comparisons then Spector must at the very least have the advantage simply in regard to the particular nature of his art. But then again, Brian Wilson has the weight problem! And so it goes.

"WE FIRST GOT . . . no, well . . . ah . . . my brother Dennis came home from school one day and he said . . . um . . . 'Listen you guys, it looks like surfin's gonna be the next big craze and . . . uh . . . you guys oughta write a song about it.' 'Cos at that time we were writing songs for friends and . . . um . . . school assemblies.

"So it happened we wrote a song just due to Dennis' suggestion and from there we just got on the surf wagon 'cos we figured . . . y'know . . . it'd be a hot craze. It's all because of my brother though.

"And he didn't know . . . he didn't . . .

"It just happened
by chance."

THE BASIC FACTS are pretty straightforward: Brian Douglas Wilson was born on June 20, 1942, the first of three sons to be brought into the world by parents Murray and Audrey Wilson.

The three brothers were brought up in the post-war stucco community of Hawthorne, one of the utterly characterless Californian suburbs positioned some thirty miles from the Pacific Ocean.

At Christmas-time, for example, the shops would be stocked up with postcards of the community, artificial snow on the roofs, reindeer

Illustrations by EDWARD

gambolling across the lawns (similarly layered in said artificial snow). That sort of thing.

Anyway, the Wilson family was an acutely tight-knit unit, due mostly to Murray, a domineering father who adhered stolidly to all the arch-American maxims.

In his younger days, Murray Wilson would have been referred to as a "pistol", an extrovert boisterous sort who never got out of the habit of cracking terrible jokes and anticipating the response by slapping listeners on the back.

The whole family lived comfortably due to his moderately successful self invested business dealing in heavy machinery, but Murray's hankering was towards making inroads into the music biz.

If his prowess as composer was pretty dismal, his lack of success as a father is rather more significant. Strict to the point of being a bully at times, his rapport with his sons was fairly one-dimensional.

Derek Taylor: "Murray was always out of his depth. There was no malice in him whatsoever, mind. He was just a hot-shot from the suburbs . . . rather like someone who I heard being referred to as 'being heavier the nearer he gets to Manchester'.

"He knocked them about emotionally to the point where they became the image he'd set up for them. Carl had to take so much weight, be so calm. Dennis had to be such a crack shot son.

"A daft man, really. He really scared the hell out of his boys. Mike (Love) had some great stories about him. I was always trying to get them out of him. 'Tell me more about Murray, Mike'." (Laughs).

Stories like the one about Murray's two glass eyes — one for normal use and a special blood-shot model for when he was hung over. Dennis once stole the bloodshot model, after Murray had spent the evening drinking somewhat to excess, and took it to school. He was soundly beaten.

Or the now legendary tale, printed in *Rolling Stone* some three years ago, about the time Brian took his father's plate just before Murray had seated himself at the dinner table, went to the bathroom and excreted two large turds onto it. He returned to the table, replaced the bestooled plate, and waited. He too was soundly beaten.

But that was Brian. Wiggy, sure. But not mad.

Not at that point anyway.

He was conscientious, hard-working, though a none-too brilliant scholar — as his report-books from both El Camino Junior High and El Camino College (Fall 1960-Winter '62) willingly testified.

Music was his thing. Most of all he loved The Four Freshmen, a clean-cut close harmony team who specialised in 'respectable' pop, and would sit for hours by the record player singing along . . . testing his vocal range until he could reach an effortless, impressive falsetto pitch.

And he wrote songs.

IT ALL PICKS UP from here. The high-school bands. First there was Carl And The Passions, then they became Kenny And The Cadets. Brian was Kenny.

Finally there was The Beach Boys and a record called "Surfin' " on Candix records. It hit.

From Candix to mighty Capitol and producer Nik Venet who — in an era of tired chinless

"Listen, guys — why don't we put on a show?" Early B.B. publicity shot with DAVID MARKS (centre back row) and BRIAN (far left)

£3

The Great Outdoors: a Hollywood rehearsal for Big Bri — Dennis in the foreground

"The only time I actually enjoyed myself with Brian was when I was standing by the piano working with him. Otherwise, I felt hideous!

"Brian Wilson has to be the single most irresponsible person I've ever met . . ."

—TONY ASHER

(Lyricist: "Pet Sounds")

record executives — was sharp, into hip slogans and camel hair coats. He and Murray didn't see eye to eye though.

The Beach Boys, see — this high-school band which featured the three Wilson brothers, a slightly older cousin called Mike Love and a weedy-looking local boy soprano named David Marks — had struck oil and Murray Wilson, their father, was determined to make up for lost time.

Photos of the band at the very outset of their career — before the weedy Marks was ousted over him not being strictly "kin" and the equally weedy Al Jardine, rescued from a tentative future as a dentist, was brought in — are still pretty hilarious. They all smiled like rabbits, had big ears and over-sized lumberjacker shirts.

Carl the archetypal fat boy, Mike Love, even then with a receding forehead, and Dennis, his features not developed enough for him to be described as in any way good-looking.

Only Brian showed any visual promise: tall and at that time almost lean, he instinctively showed himself to be the leader.

Which he was, even though father Murray called the shots in most respects. As their manager, he stood for heavy discipline. Work, work, work. The guys just seemed to comply willingly.

Especially Brian whose songwriting was really the key to it all. Wilson was not merely a bonafide teen visionary as far as a multiplicity of trends were concerned — he could almost calculate the longevity of each so that, by the time any given fad had burned itself out, The Beach Boys were inevitably long long gone — his instinct for pure rock expression was as impressive as it was seemingly effortless.

Indeed, Wilson's talents were such that from the sparsest of influences he created a whole California sound — a tonal feel complemented by lyrics that exploded Chuck Berry's more incisive observations in "The Promised Land" into a full-blown utterly irresistible myth.

As Nik Cohn observed in his "Awopbopaloobop" book:

"He (Wilson) worked a loose-limbed group sound and added his own falsetto. Then he stuck in some lazy twang guitar and rounded it all out with jumped-up Four Freshmen harmonies. No sweat, he'd created a bonafide surf music out of nothing. More, he had invented California."

BRIAN HAD the whole surfing-beach craze cased all by himself.

In 1962, he took Chuck Berry's "Sweet Little Sixteen" and transformed it into "Surfin' U.S.A.," again in Cohn's words — "the great surf anthem, the clincher: a hymn of unlimited praise."

In 1963 he even eclipsed his own fantasies for The Beach Boys when, with Jan Berry of Jan & Dean fame, he created "Surf City" — a virile all-American sun-kissed Valhalla where the ratio was strictly "two girls for every boy".

And who really cared if such fantasies were basically as dumb as hell — their very naivety only compounded the appeal. When the Beach Boys sang "The girls on the beach/Are all within reach/And one waits there for you" they were automatically giving hope to every clumsy adolescent dreamer struggling through his awkward years. And that's all that really mattered. Plus the fact that they were inevitably damn fine rock 'n' roll music.

Almost simultaneous to the surf hiatus, Wilson quickly expanded his range of topics to embrace the motor sports fad of the early '60s.

For this masterful transition, he started investing in other lyric-writers — principally one Roger Christian who "was really . . . really a guiding light for me. I'd go over there, see . . . he'd get off at midnight, OK, he'd do a night-time radio show from 9 to 12 every night and we'd go over to Otto's, order a hot fudge sundae and just . . . whew! talk and talk.

"We'd be writing lyrics . . . hussling, y'know and all of a sudden we'd realise we'd just written fifteen songs."

Christian's lyrics were the acorn all-American gospel — stout-hearted salutations to the competitive spirit littered with patriotic references to "daring young men playing dangerous games" and in depth motor mechanic descriptions of stripped-down cherry coupes.

The most famous Wilson-Christian collaboration has to be the classic "Don't Worry Baby" wherein Brian utilised a perfect Spector-Ronettes-styled melody to underpin what at first seems a straightforward teen passion declaration. It's only on closer inspection that you realise the young lover's angst is focused on Christian's hero having bragged his way into a "chicken-run". Romance in Roger Christian's lyrics was always a strict second runner to heavy machinery.

Cohn again:

"There was by now no subject too soap-opera for him (Wilson/Christian) to take on. He churned out 'A Young Man is Gone', an ode to the departed James Dean, and 'Spirit of America' and 'Be True to Your School'. At the same time, he did some fine rejoicings, full of energy and imagination — 'Shut Down', '40s', 'Little Deuce Coupe'. Fine rock 'n' roll music but brought up to date, kept moving and not left to atrophy. Best of all was 'I Get Around'.

"What Brian Wilson was doing now was making genuine pop art. Not camp word plays on pop, but the real thing. He was taking the potential heroics that surrounded him and, not being arty, not being coy in the least, turning them into live music. Simply, he'd taken high-school and raised it to completely new levels. He'd turned it into myth. As far as I'm concerned, this was his best period."

Cohn's contentions do make for an impressive dogma but, by failing to connect with the vital post-faddism of Brian Wilson's emergent "New" music he chooses to first ignore and then to belittle an incomparable creative bent that begins with "In My Room" and reaches its full blown swan-song hiatus with "Caroline No" the final track on "Pet Sounds".

Having perhaps conveniently failed to connect with this streak, Cohn is left with this rather too-pat disclaimer:

"Musically, meanwhile, he travelled a long way, most of it backwards. As he became more and more of a recluse, so he got increasingly hooked on the concept of Wilson as creative artist. No more surf-boards and hot rods, no more amateur myth-making. Instead, he emerged as a full blown solemn romantic, turning out successions of near tone poems, fragile pools of sound, very limpid. Small choirs running through mock fugues and rambling boy sopranos. Sad songs about loneliness and heartache. Sad songs even about happiness. Sometimes it works and then it's exquisite — 'Caroline No', 'Here Today', 'Don't Talk (Put Your Head On My Shoulder)'. More often, it's just sloppy."

IT'S NIGH impossible to affix a date or, perhaps more appropriate, a direct *incident* to explain this transformation from Brian Wilson, Cohn's faceless Californian fad-visionary, to Brian Wilson the self-conscious 'creative artist' of "Pet Sounds."

Nonetheless, December 23rd, 1964, remains symbolically an important date for The Beach Boys and Wilson in particular.

It was the day that Brian Wilson finally cracked up on a plane winging from L.A. to Houston where The Beach Boys were set to play a Christmas show.

The "wig-out" was a fairly obvious precursor to a complete nervous breakdown brought about by the hefty build-up of innumerable pressures and by sheer overwork. In fact, Brian's "condition" was so ragged at this point he went on to suffer two more similar breakdowns in quick succession.

The traumas, though, were providential in that they extricated Wilson from all his touring commitments with The Beach Boys and set him aside to concentrate almost solely on composing and recording.

Seen strategically, the move was perfectly timed. Brian could now concentrate on what he did best and moreover be allowed the creative elbow-room to experiment a little more, develop new formulae to combat the likes of The Beatles (who, it had to be admitted, had swiped The Beach Boys' teen titan throne that very year).

Brian Wilson, left to his own devices, could settle that score easily enough. The other guys knew that. At that time, they trusted Brian implicitly.

Off the road and away from all those pressures that must have undermined his personality and basically flattened his whole character, Brian Wilson started getting wise to a few things.

Ego, for one — the unfettered dynamic pitting of one's talents against all the other bands. This new band for example — The Rolling Stones. They weren't so damn hot!

The Beatles — now The Beatles were different. Brian dug the hell out of those albums. And that Paul? Boy what a talented guy!

And Bob Dylan . . . Well actually Dylan scared Brian a little, made him uneasy. Brian was frightened in this almost child-like way — scared of something you can't quite fully comprehend, yet fascinated all the same.

And then again, Brian was getting this . . . uh thing from Dylan's whole sound . . . his feel, y'know. He confided with friends that he honestly believed Bob Dylan was out to destroy music with his genius.

Very quickly Brian Wilson was becoming besotted with 'Art'.

People would tell him the most common-place facts about such-and-such a composer or painter and Brian would just flip right out.

You mean to say Beethoven wrote some of these works when he was completely deaf? Boy, I bet . . . I bet this whole painting thing has been going on for thousands of years, right?

A visitor would read a fragment from a volume of Omar Khayyam and Brian Wilson would get up right there and then, his head positively swimming with all this magical dumb inspiration and just *know* that this guy had *all* the answers.

ALL THESE quasi-revelations were to start making tentative infringements on Wilson's music itself —but not for a while yet. The first post-touring album for example, was "The Beach Boys — Today" and it found Wilson both taking care of "business" with teen beat retreads like "Dance, Dance, Dance" and high school romance rock ("Good To My Baby") while exploring more adventurous aspects of both production and composition.

What Wilson was now aiming for, in terms of production at least, was to pick up on all that had made Phil Spector's records great — that majestic *presence* — and modify the very essentials to accomodate an almost self-effacingly 'clean' all-American white harmony combo sound. Less of that marvellously over-bearing Wagnerian pomp and circumstance stuff: more clarity, more fragility.

On "Today" there is one criminally overlooked track, "She Knows Me Too Well" which both lyrically and melodically anticipates the maturity of expression to be found in "Pet Sounds". Both "She Knows Me Too Well" and "In The Back Of My Mind" — another little known "Today" gem — used breathtakingly gorgeous melodies and arrangements as a foil for more 'adult' lyrics.

Wilson's dream lovers were suddenly no longer simple happy souls harmonising their sunkissed innocence and undying devotion over a muted halcyon backdrop of surf and sand. They were vulnerable, insecure, at times almost neurotic.

Brian's whole approach to romance was becoming more and more personalised, more honest in a distinctly autobiographical way.

The innocence was still there, for sure — God, it had to be . . . it was the absolute deciding factor, the master-plan that dictated to almost every aspect of his creativity — but it was becoming more worldly now. The rigours of experience were impinging themselves upon the very nature of his muse and Brian Wilson could no longer comfortably dream on like before.

For starters, he was married now.

His wife's name was Marilyn and she was the elder daughter of the Rovelles, a good Jewish family, comfortable enough to allow their younger off spring Diane the benefits of a good nose-job.

Visually Marilyn was no beauty and at times she and Brian's relationship seemed, to say the least, a trifle strained. Also it seemed even to the casual on-looker that Wilson held the younger Rovelle in higher esteem. Maybe he was just a little infatuated with her. She was certainly prettier.

And younger . . . more 'innocent'.

Brian Wilson's penchant for "the great all-American teen *anthem*" hadn't deserted him yet awhile. In 1965, he composed arguably his greatest work in that field.

"California Girls" at once took all that was best in Wilson's heroic myth-weaving patriotism stand and combined it with his new melodic and arranging sophistication. The results created an even more irresistible myth than the ones that had gone before:

"Well, East Coast girls are hip — I really dig the style they wear
And the Southern girls with the way they talk, they knock me out when I'm down there.
The Midwest farmers' daughters really make you feel alright
And the Northern girls with the way they kiss — they keep their boyfriends warm at night."

Diplomatic, sure, but Brian and the guys were adamant:

"I wish they all could be California/I wish they all could be California/I WISH THEY ALL COULD BE CALIFORNIA GURLS"

That was the thing, see, with The Beach Boys. They were always "gurls".

So anyway it was 1965 and the Beach Boys were still on the beach. Only this time there was a new West Coast "sound" coming up — a "sound" which had nothing to do with sun and surfing and though it concentrated on harmonies in part, used the little jangling of a 12-string Richenbacker guitar for a musical back-drop as opposed to the fat twang of the surf guitar.

The Byrds hailed from Los Angeles too but they were almost the complete antithesis of the Beach Boys.

For a start, they were more into a very defined "bohemian" thing — very cerebral in contrast to the Beach Boys more "physical" predilections. Their harmonies, though they lacked a clearly defined falsetto and anchored bass voice, were "effete" by comparison and their trip was seemingly to make uneven ratios of folk/rock music. Ostensibly they were around to electrically 'interpret' Dylan — spread the word on the new Messiah. Whatever, it was new and it caught on. Fast.

No one actually bothered to verbally gauge the reaction of Brian as regards these Californian upstarts who in all honesty, sounded more anglophiliac than true blue American.

Possibly, he was worried by their appearance. More probably, he didn't give it a second thought.

There were two more Beach Boys albums before the advent of "Pet Sounds" and both were, in their own way, cop-outs or, more to the point, "manufactured" product put out to satisfy Capitol. Both "Summer Days (and Summer Nights)" and "Beach Boys Party" were easy-formula halcyon-days fare, no real surprises. The latter seems almost symbolic in retrospect: a supposedly informal 'live' recording of a Beach Boys Beach Party (it was of course done in the studio) it featured lotsa accapella singing, acoustic guitars strumming over the crackling of weenies, bongoes, the girls joining in on the chorus, everybody making merry.

Al Jardine sang an impromptu "Times They Are A-changing", Mike Love goofed out on "I Get Around" and Brian did a very reverent ver

BEACH BOYS JOURNALS PART 1

BEACH BOYS JOURNALS PART 1

BEACH BOYS JOURNALS PART 1

Beach Boys Latest To Earn Goldie

The Beach Boys were greeted with some nice news when they made their triumphant return from England this weekend. Their latest single, "Good Vibrations," has surpassed the 925,000 mark in sales and has thus become the biggest-selling single in Beach Boy history.

"Good Vibrations" has now outsold such big Beach Boy hits as "Help Me, Rhonda," "I Get Around" and "Sloop John B.," all of which were in the 900,000 category. If "Vibrations" continues its sales pace it will become the first million selling single for the group.

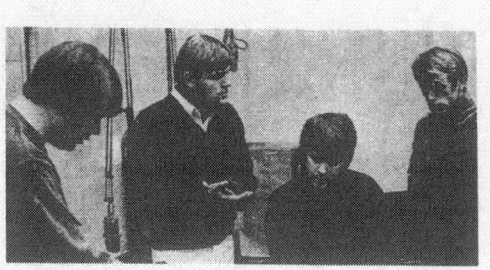

VARIETY

BEACH BOYS' GOLDISK VIA 'VIBRATIONS' SINGLE

The Beach Boys, who have been hot album artists for Capitol Records with six gold LPs, finally entered the golden circle for singles with their current "Good Vibrations" hit. Disk was released late in October and soared over the 1,000,000 marker last week, cueing Capitol to ask for RIAA gold record certification.

The Beach Boys are also approaching the 1,000,000 mark on two previous singles, "Help Me Rhonda" and "I Get Around."

Capitol Sales Splurge Paced By Beach Boys

HOLLYWOOD — "Good Vibrations," the latest single by the Beach Boys, has taken off faster than any previous Beach Boys single in their recording history, according to Capitol Records.

The Brian Wilson-penned tune racked up sales of 293,000 in four days of sales with an additional 100,000 copies back-ordered from customers, reports the company. Disk is number 10 on the Top 100 this week.

Also setting a solid sales pace are a trio of new albums... Al Martino's "This Is Love," which topped the 67,000 mark in sales after one week; "For Christmas This Year" by the Lettermen, with sales of 88,000 after one week; and Jackie Gleason's "How Sweet It Is," sales of 42,000 in two weeks—the largest two-week sale of any previous Gleason album. The LP is also part of a nationwide "How Sweet It Is" promotion.

Beach Boys Set Up Label

LOS ANGELES — Brothers Records has been formed by the Beach Boys with domestic and foreign distribution being sought. The vocalists will not cut for their own company which falls under the umbrella of Beach Boys Enterprises. They remain tied to Capitol. Brian Wilson will be executive producer for the teen-oriented company.

Over at Capitol, the group has just earned gold disks for the single "Good Vibrations" and for the LP's "Little Deuce Coupe" and "Shut Down," vol. II.

BEACH BOYS JOURNALS PART 1

THE GREAT LOST ALBUMS

"SMILE"

PETER DOGGETT LAUNCHES A NEW SERIES BY EXPLORING THE MYSTERY AND MYSTIQUE BEHIND THE BEACH BOYS' LOST MASTERPIECE

Whether your obsession is love or rock'n'roll, "what might have been" is always more romantic than "what was". Across the forty-year history of rock music, legends have grown, or in some cases deliberately been constructed, around the records that never were — the great lost albums that were doomed by a combination of fate, loss of artistic nerve, or physical or psychological collapse.

This series will single out the most momentous and tragic of rock's lost albums, examining not only what went wrong, but also whether the music can ever stand up to the myth. What almost all these projects share is the sense that they form a missing link in a major artist's career. If they'd been released, then the course of rock history might have been ... well, better, perhaps, or maybe worse, but undoubtedly different. For some artists, the sacrifice of an almost complete record liberated them from a musical straitjacket; for others, like Brian Wilson and the Beach Boys in the case of "Smile", the loss is measurable in personal as well as artistic terms.

To understand exactly what "Smile" might have been, you have to think yourself back into the mind-set of 1966, when the Beach Boys were not a rather embarrassing oldies act touring on fading glory, but in the eyes of many musicians and fans the most innovative and ambitious rock group in the world. Or, at least, their creative leader, Brian Wilson was: while he laboured over grandiose projects in the studio, the rest of the band were doing what they've always done, performing their hits in public. And that, as we'll see shortly, was part of the problem.

1966 was the year when the Beach Boys toppled the Beatles as the most popular group in the world — a judgement cemented into fact that December, when they triumphed in the 'New Musical Express' readers' poll, a result that sent shockwaves around the world.

A year or two earlier, the Beach Boys had been one of the few American acts to survive the onset of Beatlemania. Emerging as spokesmen for the male hedonists of California, with nothing more than surf, speed and sex on their minds, they'd gradually widened their palette, with Brian Wilson — devotee in equal doses of Phil Spector, George Gershwin and the Four Freshmen — established as one of the most inventive melodists and arrangers in pop.

Their label, Capitol, had treated them as fan fodder from the start, whipping Brian Wilson into completing three or four albums a year, and driving him into a nervous breakdown in the process. By the end of 1964, Wilson was ensconced in the studio, leaving the rest of the group to tour as his representatives on earth. Freed from the need to complete his records in hours rather than days, Wilson began to give his creative talent free rein. At first, he was content to give the accepted boundaries of teen pop a gentle tug, introducing the anthem "California Girls" with a mournful, touching instrumental progression that undercut the message of the song, or scoring album tracks like "In The Back Of My Mind" as if they were a mini-symphony.

CLASSICAL

By late 1965, however, Brian was thinking beyond the 'Billboard' charts. His next album, "Pet Sounds", brought the tone-poems of 20th century classical music into the pop field for the first time, and tied them to lyrics — mostly written by advertising man Tony Asher — which explored the emotional roller-coaster of adult romance. In Britain, "Pet Sounds" was greeted as a masterpiece; musicians as diverse as Paul McCartney and John Cale have described it as pop's finest moment. But in America, where the Beach Boys' pleasure-seeking image was set in stone, it failed to match the sales of their earlier releases.

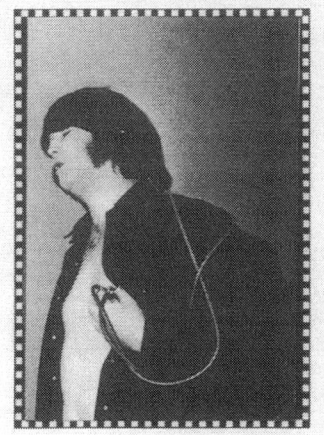

From then on, Wilson was back under the heat — Capitol wanted more teen-oriented hits, and various members of the band, notably Brian's cousin, lead singer Mike Love, were suspicious of Wilson's increasingly obsessive work habits.

Meanwhile, Brian was blowing his mind — partly on drugs ("I totally fried my brain", he admitted in one of his pathetically revealing interviews a decade later), partly on the possibilities of music, and partly on the artistic and intellectual stimulus of new friends like Van Dyke Parks and David Anderle. They persuaded Brian that being ambitious didn't mean that he was crazy, and encouraged him to follow his whims wherever they took him.

That place turned out to be, after months of studio work, "Good Vibrations". Wilson had been toying with the concept, and the title, since the "Pet Sounds" sessions; in February 1966, he began to work on the basic track. Over the next five months, through 90 hours of sessions at four Los Angeles studios, Wilson perfected the single which became a worldwide hit in November, greeted universally as the most breathtaking and adventurous piece of pop music ever released.

"Good Vibrations" set the style for what was to follow, linking together several apparently unrelated musical fragments with stunning self-confidence — and leaving the Beach Boys the puzzle of how to reproduce the complex changes of key and tempo on stage. Around 30 minutes of out-takes from the "Good Vibrations" sessions have emerged on official and bootleg releases; they show Brian Wilson in absolute control of the sessions, experimenting endlessly with different combinations of instruments, months before the rest of the group were pulled in to add the vocals. Brian himself sang lead on some of these out-takes, unveiling lyrics that didn't make the final record; his brother Carl contributed the final lead vocal to the single.

With lyricist Van Dyke Parks as his collaborator, Brian now embarked on what Parks called "an American Gothic trip". Van Dyke dragged Brian away from the familiar territory of romantic love towards a new style of writing, full of elliptical images and verbal free-association. "I tried to contribute to the idea that perhaps all music did not have to be for dancing", Parks explained later, though "Good Vibrations" had already drawn complaints from a minority of pop fans who found its sudden switches of tempo unsettling on the discotheque floor.

Another vital ingredient was humour, or at least Brian Wilson's version of it. The Beach Boys had already indulged themselves on album with rather weak verbal battles like "'Cassius' Love Vs. 'Sonny' Wilson"; now Brian wanted to make music that would encompass the Universal Smile he'd found from mind-expanding drugs. And so the album-in-the-making, originally titled "Dumb Angel" in an astute piece of self-analysis, became "Smile". As 'Rolling Stone' writer Tom Nolan noted in 1971, "Humour was salvation, the Holy Grail, for Brian"; and Wilson's associates remember his ambitious, unrealisable plans around this

BEACH BOYS JOURNALS PART 1

The distinctive cartoon sleeve for "Smile".

The rear artwork, with proposed line-up.

One of several "Smile" bootlegs, this picture CD has an impressive hour-long running time.

time for records of water noises, comedy and even a health food album, based around one of the "Smile" tracks, "Vega-Tables".

That was still a long way off in May 1966, when Wilson and Parks began to assemble the pieces of "Smile". Remarkably, that was when work commenced on the centre-piece of "Smile", "a three-minute musical comedy" in Brian's words called "Heroes And Villains". That was still being recorded eight months later, long after its proposed release date.

The saga of that single is in many ways a microcosm of the entire "Smile" tragicomedy. On previous albums, Brian Wilson had conceived each song as a separate entity. With "Smile", all boundaries were knocked aside, and he crafted two dozen or so fragmentary pieces of music, some conventional, others totally off-the-wall, which he then tried to shape into some kind of coherent whole.

The problem was, Brian never quite decided which combination of fragments should make up a particular song. That's why it's never been possible for anyone to reconstitute the complete "Smile", even though there is around two hours of material circulating among collectors. Around the end of 1966, Capitol were demanding finished cover artwork, which Brian duly provided; for the back of the sleeve, he wrote out by hand a list of a dozen song titles, which were printed up with the note, "see labels for correct playing order".

We have the song titles, then, and a large proportion of the tapes; but how do the two fit together? "Heroes And Villains", for instance, was originally planned to run for seven minutes, across both sides of a single. That complete version, which Beach Boys stalwart Bruce Johnston insists is still in existence, has never surfaced. The "Smiley Smile" CD issued last year did, however, unveil for the first time several additional melodic sections of the song, while various bootleg releases contain variations on the existing themes.

Also available on bootleg is a 23-second fragment called "Bicycle Rider" — a theme which was incorporated into "Heroes And Villains" when the group performed the song live in the 1970s. Equally fragmentary is a piece called "Barnyard", though most sources again suggest that this was meant to form part of the finished "Heroes And Villains". The shifts and breaks on the CD out-take of the song are so dramatic that virtually anything could have been considered part of the song; in Brian Wilson's mind, virtually anything was.

"Heroes And Villains" was eventually issued in July 1967 — almost two months after the Beatles' "Sgt. Pepper" had sent rock spinning in an entirely new direction. It's no secret that the Beatles intended parts of "Revolver" as a direct response to "Pet Sounds"; the friendly competition between the two groups was so intense that the release of anything like a full-bore "Smile" would surely have set the Beatles back for months while they considered a suitable reply.

Beautiful and intriguing, "Heroes And Villains" was nowhere near as commercial as "Good Vibrations"; and just as they had done with "Pet Sounds", Capitol did their best to overshadow its release by rushing a greatest hits set onto the market. (In Britain, of course, Capitol had grown so weary waiting for the Beach Boys to capitalise on their 'NME' poll victory that they had issued the 1965 track "Then I Kissed Her" as a single, against the wishes of the group. It reached No. 4; "Heroes And Villains" stalled at No. 8.)

In September 1967, the Beach Boys finally released their new album — only it wasn't "Smile", but "Smiley Smile", which wasn't exactly the same thing. "Good Vibrations" and "Heroes And Villains" were on board, together with new versions of songs originally intended for "Smile", like "Vega-Tables", "Wind Chimes" and "Wonderful"; but the overall effect was trivial and unfocused, like a stoned hippie's playpen set to music. Compared to the lavish orchestrations of "Pepper", it didn't stand a chance. Another comparison: "Smiley Smile" spent two months in the U.K. chart and reached No. 9; "Pepper" was on the lists for upwards of two years, and stayed at No. 1 for six months.

The anti-climax of "Smiley Smile" convinced most onlookers that "Smile" was more hype than reality. Even the smattering of pro-Wilson press coverage, from insiders like Jules Siegel, cast more doubt on Brian's sanity than anything else. But the myth of this impossibly perfect album grew — particularly as tales spread of a track called

BEACH BOYS JOURNALS PART 1

"Fire", which Brian had destroyed after a series of conflagrations had affected the area of L.A. around his studio; and when the public heard Brian's solo rendition of another "Smile" extract, "Surf's Up", on the U.S. TV show "Inside Pop: The Rock Revolution", complete with appreciative commentary by composer/conductor Leonard Bernstein.

Beach Boys historian Brad Elliott has revealed that internal Capitol memos suggest the company were still expecting "Smile" to be released as a follow-up to "Smiley Smile". A photo booklet had already been prepared for "Smile" early in 1967; Capitol staff were advised not to include it as a bonus with "Smiley Smile", but to save it for the group's next LP. In the event, "Smile" was completely abandoned, and most of the booklets were destroyed.

The subsequent trickling-down release of "Smile" material — "Cabinessence" and "Our Prayer" on the "20/20" album in 1969, "Surf's Up" as the title track of a 1971 album — helped restore the legend. Then in 1972, Carl Wilson announced that "Smile" would be issued later that year, as part of a double set with the group's latest album. "Carl & The Passions" duly appeared, but with "Pet Sounds", not "Smile", as its companion.

Almost a decade later, Bruce Johnston told the American magazine 'Goldmine' that he was intending to assemble a "Smile" suite for the Beach Boys' upcoming retrospective. "Ten Years Of Harmony" followed a few months later, without a hint of "Smile".

Most recently, Brian Wilson delighted his supporters by announcing that he was in the process of piecing together the complete "Smile" album, along with his "Brian Wilson" solo set. That record came out, but "Smile" was consigned to the vaults once again; word emerged that Brian had never actually tackled the archive tapes at all.

Over the last decade, however, an increasing amount of "Smile" material has leaked onto the collector's market, forming the basis for several LPs and CDs, plus — within the last few months — a comprehensive, though not exactly hi-fi quality, three-album set. None of this is adequate compensation for a finished "Smile", but the tapes that have escaped give us a clear indication of what was going on at Brian Wilson's sessions between February 1966 and May 1967. What follows is an A-Z listing of "Smile" songs, together with a guide to their eventual resting place, on official or unofficial releases.

BARNYARD: This title is given to two entirely different fragments of music. The first is a vocal refrain which was later reworked for the opening of "With Me Tonight" on "Smiley Smile"; the second emerged alongside "Do You Like Worms" on a bootleg album, and may form part of that track, or "Heroes And Villains". Confusingly, there's a set of lyrics for "Barnyard" which doesn't fit either fragment; again, these may belong to the extended "Heroes And Villains".

BEEN WAY TOO LONG: This is an alternate title for "Can't Wait Too Long".

BICYCLE RIDER: Less than 25 seconds long, this keyboard refrain matches the chorus melody of "Heroes And Villains"; as noted elsewhere, some "Bicycle Rider" lyrics were added to live renditions of that song in the 1970s.

CABIN ESSENCE: As the final track on "20/20", "Cabinessence" (one word!) is one of the highlights of the Beach Boys' catalogue. That recording was obtained by overdubbing existing "Smile" versions of "Cabin Essence" (two words), "Who Ran The Iron Horse" and "Home On The Range", and editing them into one track — which may or may not have been Brian Wilson's original intention.

The original two-word title supports the 'Americana' theme of the album, with the song trying (among many other things) to evoke the essence of life in the cabins for the American pioneers.

A bootleg tape of "Cabin Essence" exists in its original form — i.e. without Carl's lead vocal, but edited into "Who Ran The Iron Horse", a typically opaque vocal chorus.

CAN'T WAIT TOO LONG: One of the most beautiful Beach Boys' tracks of all, this is grouped among the "Smile" recordings purely because it sounds as if it should be. It was actually recorded after the "Smile" sessions, in October/November 1967 and July 1968, and was finally released in unfinished form on the "Smiley Smile"/"Wild Honey" CD set.

CHILD IS FATHER TO THE MAN: William Wordsworth's poem inspired not only Blood, Sweat & Tears' first album but also this two-minute fragment — which opens with a gentle keyboard pattern and a distant French horn, and then merges into a circular vocal refrain. The instrumental track was used as the basis for the "Child Is Father To The Man" section added to "Surf's Up" for official release in 1971, and then overdubbed with fresh vocals.

DO YOU LIKE WORMS: One of the highlights of the "Smile" tapes is this track, which begins with a ponderous instrumental section, moves into a vocal harmony piece known to fans as "Plymouth Rock", segues into the familiar "Bicycle Rider" tune with additional vocals that sound like an Indian chant, and then returns to "Plymouth Rock" — repeating the same structure but adding a separate 'Hawaiian' vocal piece. The reappearance of the 'Bicycle Rider' theme merely helps to heighten the symphony feel of the album. Sadly, this track remains unreleased.

THE ELEMENTS: There is no single track called "The Elements" or even "The Elements Suite", though Brian Wilson intended there would be. There are four basic elements — earth, air, fire and water. 'Fire' would have been represented by "Mrs O'Leary's Cow"; 'water' by "Love To Say Da-Da"; but 'air' and 'earth' are more mysterious, although both seem to have been instrumental themes.

FIRE: The common title given to the track officially known as "Mrs O'Leary's Cow".

FRIDAY NIGHT: A variant title for the mysterious "I'm In Great Shape".

GEORGE FELL INTO HIS FRENCH

Quite apart from the breathtaking music, one of the highlights of the unreleased "Smile" LP would have been the lavish booklet illustrations.

BEACH BOYS JOURNALS PART 1

The Beach Boys caught in a happier moment, away from the arguments, drug habits and internal pressures that resulted from being America's most creative outfit of the mid-Sixties.

HORN: The title given by bootleggers to the session logged at Capitol as "Talking Horns".
GOOD VIBRATIONS: Besides the hit single, also included on "Smiley Smile", additional out-takes from the lengthy sessions for this song have been included on "Beach Boys Rarities" and the "Smiley Smile"/"Wild Honey" double CD set. An extended, 15-minute medley of session out-takes was included on one of the numerous "Smile" CD bootlegs. Without exception, these working fragments document the taping of the backing track, plus Brian's guide vocals, rather than the layering of the Beach Boys' final harmony parts.
HEROES AND VILLAINS: As explained above, the single/"Smiley Smile" version of this song was merely part of the original blueprint; additional fragments were included on an alternate take on "Smiley Smile"/"Wild Honey", while further rehearsal takes appear on the best "Smile" bootleg, alongside the 15 minutes of "Good Vibrations".
HOLIDAYS: A muted tenor saxophone cries over a piano figure as this instrumental track begins, followed by an uptempo theme which breaks into a fairground motif and hints at the melodies of several other "Smile" tracks, notably "Child Is Father To The Man". A pocket symphony in less than three minutes. "Holidays" remains officially unreleased. Incidentally, the instrumental piece included on the first "Smile" bootleg under the name "Holidays" was actually an extract from Miles Davis's "Porgy And Bess" album.
HOME ON THE RANGE: One of the themes which were incorporated into the "20/20" version of "Cabinessence".
INSPIRATION: Taped on June 2nd 1966, this otherwise unidentified track remains buried in the vaults.
I DON'T KNOW: Me neither; the identity of this track remains unconfirmed, though Dennis Wilson did record a song of this title a decade later — itself still unreleased.
I RAN: Another track yet to surface, unofficially or officially.
LOVE TO SAY DA-DA: "Cool Cool Water" on "Sunflower" is a fully developed version of the original "Smile" concept, although only the chaotic 'flowing river' vocals in the middle of that track actually date from the "Smile" sessions. Available on bootleg is a much sparser "Cool Cool Water", which is presumably the "Love To Say Da-Da" recorded at the end of the "Smile" sessions in May 1967.
MRS O'LEARY'S COW: Like the orchestral session for the Beatles' "A Day In The Life", the recording of this purely instrumental track has become part of rock legend. The intention was to create a track that conjured up the sound of fire: the musicians were presented with firemen's helmets and rubber axes to create the mood, and then began to perform a terrifying, sliding piece of music which evoked the ebb and flow of flames burning out of control, while percussion instruments imitated the crackling of the flames.
The session was filmed, and combined with madcap footage of the Beach Boys riding a fire engine; the results can be seen in the video, "The Beach Boys: An American Band". A couple of versions of the 'fire' music remain intact — Brian didn't, as he claimed at the time, destroy the master tapes — but they are only available on bootleg.
THE OLD MASTER PAINTER/YOU ARE MY SUNSHINE: This one-minute track combined a Brian Wilson instrumental theme for cello and percussion with a mournful arrangement of the familiar country hit by Tex Davis which ended with the string section sliding to a stop as if their powerpacks had just run down. Dennis Wilson overdubbed a lead vocal for "You Are My Sunshine" in late November 1966.
PRAYER: A soaring vocal harmony piece — a spiritual tribute to the power of the human voice — this "Smile" track was overdubbed and extended by editing the tape to make up "Our Prayer" on the "20/20" album.
SURF'S UP: The pinnacle of the "Smile" writing sessions was this remarkable Wilson/Parks composition, which in turn provided the Beach Boys' finest recorded moment on the 1971 album to which it gave its name. Though it was difficult to tell, that recording was salvaged from a mess of fragments — adding a new Carl Wilson vocal to a 1966 backing track of the initial verses, then switching to the recording that Brian Wilson made, solo at the piano, in December 1966, at the same time as the "Inside Pop" TV clip was filmed. The 1971 cut ended with the addition of a revamped "Child Is Father To The Man". The "Smile" cut was worked on intermittently between November 1966 and January 1967, but never completed. A session out-take demonstrates the musicians using shakers to evoke the sound of the opening lyric: "a diamond necklace plays the pawn". What we *don't* have, as yet, is a complete 1966 vocal performance over the finished backing track.
TALKIN' HORNS: Take a room full of top hornmen; tell them to communicate to each other through their instruments; and the result is a glorious three-minute extravaganza that is part Ornette Coleman avant-garde, part Disney fantasy, part pure stupidity. This piece, which surely can't have been intended for "Smile", is otherwise known as "George Fell Into His French Horn", after a line of the saxophone 'dialogue' heard during the track.
TONES: The bootleg tape of this track opens with Brian Wilson exalting his instrumentalists to go "all out". The track that follows epitomises the humour of "Smile", with a xylophone playing a ridiculous solo theme, before a bank of drums, percussive pianos and brass venture into a catchy, irrepressible march tune. Another shorter take exists, with additional woodwind instrumentation taking us closer to the sound of a fairground — before the tape abruptly switches into a few seconds of "Heroes And Villains" vocal riffs, and then fades away.
TUNE X: An alternate title for "Tones".
VEGA-TABLES: After "Mrs O'Leary's Cow", the sessions for "Vega-Tables" attracted most media attention at the time — simply because Paul McCartney dropped in midway through the fortnight of sessions spent on the track to chew some carrots and drop some radishes in the mix. A snippet of the "Smile" cut surfaced at the end of the re-recording of the song on "Smiley Smile", while an entire backing track was used for Laughing Gravy's cover of the track — Gravy being a pseudonym for Beach Boys buddies Jan & Dean. Note also that the original "Vege-Tables" incorporated the vocal chant issued as "Mama Says" on the "Wild Honey" album.
WHO RAN THE IRON HORSE: Another of the themes that constituted "Cabinessence".
WIND CHIMES: Recut for "Smiley Smile", this tribute to the ethereal music of the air around us was originally recorded in August and October 1966. The original version, which remains unissued, featured a Brian Wilson solo vocal, and none of the bubbly, stoned atmosphere of the July 1967 cut on "Smiley Smile".
WONDERFUL: On "Smiley Smile", "Wonderful" — a mysteriously lovely Van Dyke Parks love song — had a lead vocal by Carl Wilson. The "Smile" original, taped in August, October and December 1966, was something else entirely, with Brian's vocal adding another layer of emotion to the piece. A complete backing track for the song is also in circulation.
THE WOODSHOP: One night at Goldstar Studios, Brian Wilson persuaded a team of experienced session musicians to down their violins and attack other pieces of wood — with hammers, nails and saws. The results appeared as a coda to the 1968 recording "Do It Again", but only on the "20/20" LP version.
YOU ARE MY SUNSHINE: See "The Old Master Painter".
YOU'RE WELCOME: An eerie, heavily echoed vocal chant, which had the air of a mantra, "You're Welcome" was a genuine "Smile" out-take, taped on 15th December 1966. Not included in the original handwritten track listing for the LP, it emerged finally as the flipside of "Heroes And Villains".

Those were the ingredients; but someone left the cake out in the rain, and (to complete a ridiculous metaphor) Brian Wilson could never find that recipe again.
What went wrong? Back in 1971, Brian himself tried to explain: "That was because Van Dyke Parks had written lyrics that were all Van Dyke Parks and none of the Beach Boys. The lyrics were so poetic and symbolic they were abstract, we couldn't . . . Oh no, wait, it was, no, really, I remember, this is it, this is why, it didn't come out because, I'd bought a lot of hashish . . ." and off he rambled into a convoluted and ultimately meaningless

BEACH BOYS JOURNALS PART 1

anecdote about being stoned.

In all his confusion, however, Brian had fingered the two main reasons for the non-appearance of "Smile". First, the album was indeed a Brian Wilson/Van Dyke Parks project, not a Beach Boys album, and when certain members of the Beach Boys confronted the pair with what they saw as the meaninglessness of the new songs, Brian didn't have the strength to stand his ground. Then, as on many occasions thereafter, Brian reacted to a threat by adopting the ostrich position and leaving the rest of the Beach Boys to deal with the crisis. They concocted the semi-brilliant "Smiley Smile", and then saw themselves through two dark years of collapsing sales figures by draping the mirage of "Smile" over their next few albums.

Sadly, the drugs played an equally vital role in snuffing out Wilson's creative flame. Brian's massive ingestion of LSD induced first euphoria ("I'm writing a teenage symphony to God", he announced in 1966), then rampant paranoia, followed by some kind of personality collapse — documented in style, if not entirely accurately, in Wilson's 'autobiography'. "Wouldn't It Be Nice". After the enormous emotional and physical stress of the "Smile" episode, Wilson was unable to give his all to any recording project for the next two decades. Almost every Beach Boys album had some contribution from Brian, but he remained unable to focus his energies in one coherent direction until he completed his epic solo album, "Brian Wilson", in 1988.

There was a third, less dramatic reason for the shelving of "Smile". During late 1966 and early 1967, the Beach Boys were in dispute with Capitol Records over royalty payments and the renewal of their contract. The group eventually decided to form their own Brother Records label, to give themselves total artistic control over their product, and distribute their releases through Capitol. Capitol objected, and slapped in an injunction on the release of the original two-part "Heroes And Villains". By the time the dispute was settled, four months had passed, and Brian Wilson's will to complete and issue the project had dissipated.

So "Smile" remains a fantasy in the minds of Beach Boys fanatics, and a room full of tape in the Capitol Records archive. Imagine an alternative scenario, however: it's March 1967, the seven-minute "Heroes And Villains" has just reached the American Top 10, and "Smile" is just about to reach the stores. Pre-publicity has been enormous; the world is ready for a masterpiece from the group who toppled the Beatles.

Here's the rare picture sleeve for the U.S. Brother edition of "Heroes And Villains".

Fantasy No. 1 comes from the unofficial Brian Wilson fan club: in their version of the fairy-tale, "Smile" astounds the world, alters the course of rock, forces the Beatles to scrap "Sgt. Pepper", establishes Brian Wilson as a modern-day Gershwin, and redirects the sound of California from acid-rock to the "American Gothic trip" of the Beach Boys' shifting melodic structures and painstakingly layered harmonies. Brian escapes his drug paranoia, and is presumably awarded the Nobel Prize for Music — a category invented just for him — around 1975. The world lives happily ever after.

I'd love to believe that story too, but somehow I think the world is fiercer than that. On the evidence of what we have, "Smile" would have been a remarkable record, stunningly original, full of daredevil melodies and abstract lyricism that transcended the bounds of the popular song. But it wouldn't have been commercial, in the way that the Doors, or Love, or Jefferson Airplane were. Unless your fantasy insists that the entire Summer Of Love — the extension of the Haight-Ashbury across the Western world — is abandoned, then it's unlikely that "Smile" would have beaten back the advent of psychedelia from San Francisco, or London.

So Fantasy No. 2 goes like this. "Smile" is greeted with an initial intake of breath, and immediate cult adulation. Devotion to the album is compulsory among hip persons on both sides of the Atlantic. But like "Pet Sounds" in the States, the album fails to find a mass audience. You can't dance to it; you can't even sing along to most of it without taking a course in harmony; and letters in the pop papers complain that the Beach Boys should go back to what they do best, and cut another surfing album. Brian Wilson is crushed with disappointment, and the remaining Beach Boys don't even have the salvation of unused "Smile" tracks with which to bolster their subsequent albums. Otherwise, life carries on much as before. It's less romantic that way, but then life is rarely as romantic as fantasy.

Thanks to Mike Grant and 'Beach Boys Stomp' magazine. Dominic Priore produced a massive 260-page paperback edition of his fanzine 'The Dumb Angel Gazette' entirely devoted to "Smile"; write for more details to P.O. Box 4131, Carlsbad, CA 92008, U.S.A.

DISCOGRAPHY OF "SMILE"-RELATED RELEASES

BEACH BOYS U.S. SINGLES

Cat. No.	Title	Current Mint Value
Capitol 5676	GOOD VIBRATIONS/LET'S GO AWAY FOR A WHILE (10/66, p/s)	£20
Brother 1001	HEROES AND VILLAINS/YOU'RE WELCOME (7/67, p/s)	£30
Brother-Reprise 1058	SURF'S UP/DON'T GO NEAR THE WATER (11/71)	£20

Pic. sleeves also exist for the cancelled Capitol 5826 release of "Heroes And Villains Pts 1 & 2"; these sell for £300+.

BEACH BOYS U.S. LPs

Cat. No.	Title	Current Mint Value
Brother T/ST 9001	SMILEY SMILE (9/67, mono/stereo)	£10
Capitol ST8 2891	SMILEY SMILE (5/68, Capitol Record Club release)	£100
Capitol SKAO 133	20/20 (2/69, includes "Cabinessence" and "Our Prayer", plus "The Woodshop" fragment after "Do It Again")	£10
Brother-Reprise RS 6382	SUNFLOWER (8/70; includes "Cool, Cool Water")	£10
Brother-Reprise RS 6453	SURF'S UP (8/71; includes "Surf's Up")	£10

LAUGHING GRAVY U.S. SINGLE

Cat. No.	Title	Current Mint Value
White Whale WW 261	VEGETABLES/SNOW FLAKES ON LAUGHING GRAVY'S WHISKERS (10/67; A-side uses "Smile" backing track)	£75

JAN AND DEAN U.S. SINGLE

Cat. No.	Title	Current Mint Value
United Artists UP 50859	JENNIE LEE/VEGETABLES (1/72, p/s; B-side uses "Smile" backing track)	£20

BEACH BOYS U.K. SINGLES

Cat. No.	Title	Current Mint Value
Capitol CL 15475	GOOD VIBRATIONS/WENDY (10/66, No. 1)	£4
Capitol CL 15510	HEROES AND VILLAINS/YOU'RE WELCOME (8/67, No. 8)	£4

BEACH BOYS U.K. LPs

Cat. No.	Title	Current Mint Value
Capitol T/ST 9001	SMILEY SMILE (11/67, No. 9; mono/stereo)	£10
Capitol E-T/E-ST 133	20/20 (3/69, No. 3; mono/stereo)	£12/£10
Stateside SSL 8251	SUNFLOWER (11/70, No. 29)	£10
Stateside SSL 10313	SURF'S UP (11/71, No. 15)	£10

BEACH BOYS U.K. CDs

Cat. No.	Title	Current Mint Value
Capitol CZ 326	SMILEY SMILE/WILD HONEY (7/90)	£8
Capitol CZ 341	FRIENDS/20/20 (9/90)	£8
CBS	SUNFLOWER (1991)	£8
CBS	SURF'S UP (1991)	£8

BEACH BOYS JOURNALS PART 1

Disc and Music Echo—February 18, 1967

your award is . . . . .

AMPLY APPRECIATED AND
BENIGNLY ACCEPTED. IT WAS
CAUTIOUSLY ANTICIPATED BUT NOT
DELIBERATELY SOUGHT YET, SUBCONSCIOUSLY, IT WAS
EARNESTLY COVETED AND IT IS, IN ANY CASE,
FRIGHTFULLY NICE OF YOU TO VOTE
GOOD VIBRATIONS SINGLE OF THE YEAR.

We are the Beach Boys and we will see you in May and thank you

BEACH BOYS JOURNALS PART 1

Page 12—MELODY MAKER, March 10, 1973

RICHARD WILLIAMS is granted a rare audience with the elusive genius behind the Beach Boys

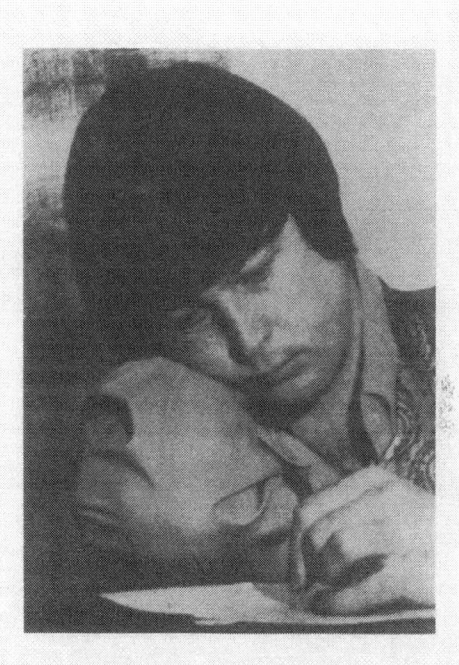

LOS ANGELES — Wheeling down Beverly Glen Boulevard from Coldwater Canyon in a yellow Checker cab, the desirability of the residences increases almost every quarter-mile.

The stilt-houses jutting out of the Canyon's sides give way to expensive ranch-style bungalows and mock-Georgian mini-mansions, their hedges trimmed down to just 18 inches, so that passers-by can stare in envy at the Lincoln Continental, the Mercedes coupe, and the kids' twin Stingrays. Gardeners fuss over the flower-beds, surrounded by lawns which look like they're trimmed by nail-clippers, daily.

Make a right turn at the bottom of Beverly Glen, onto Sunset Boulevard, past the baroque pink elegance of the Beverly Hills Hotel (where workmen are, at this moment, retouching the equatorial-forest murals in miles of corridor — by hand, with little brushes and pots of paint), and in a couple of minutes you enter Bel Air.

"Well," says the cab-driver in his native bar, "I've been working in L.A. for eight years, and I've been inside here maybe twenty times." Cab-drivers, especially Americans, don't impress easily. Right now, this one is impressed.

Bel Air is a residential estate, the quintessence of gracious living, Hollywood style. Whereas the board members of Beverly Drive are anxious to show you how far they've come, status-wise, the chairmen up in Bel Air will go to considerable lengths to keep the peekers away.

Just inside the East Gate of the estate, a clean white prowl car barks behind some bushes. The foliage, a dazzling early-spring green, thickens along Bellagio Road until all that's visible of the houses is a rash of brick chimneys, or the glint from a leaded window.

Bellagio is the main artery of Bel Air, running from east to west and numbering into the thousands. It's where Brian Wilson lives.

The tension started when I got to the gate, and looked beyond it to the low greenish house, built in the Thirties for Tarzan's creator, Edgar Rice Burroughs. It was quiet — nothin' shakin' but the leaves on the trees, and the ligaments in my knees.

On the gatepost, a sign said that the house was protected by some patrol or other. I remembered the cabbie's instruction: "You better watch out, all them Bel Air people got German Shepherds." And beside it was an intercom grille, with a buzzer-button and the legend: STAND BACK! SPEAK NORMAL.

It seemed like a good motto for the occasion.

I pressed the buzzer, stood back and waited until Brian's wife Marilyn activated the electric gate-opener. Actually, the gate turned out to be busted and open anyway.

The drive. The front door. Hello Marilyn. The dark hall. Hello Dog. Hello second dog. The living room. Hello third dog. Hello Cat. Hello Diane (Marilyn's sister) Hello.

Brian was lying on his front, almost under a big pool table. Diane bent over him, wielding a small electric massage appliance around the back of his neck and the tops of his shoulders. He was wearing an old red and white shirt outside tatty blue jeans, and battered brown indoor moccasins.

"Brian, this is Richard," said Marilyn.

"Uhh," he said Brian, trying to screw his head round and back to see me. He failed, because his long hair fell across his eyes as he gave up and faced the carpet again. "I'm sorry, but I woke up this morning, and I had this ...uhh... headache. I can't get rid of it ... real bad."

Okay, I told myself. Perch on the pool table and talk with Marilyn. Stand back, speak normal.

I WANTED to hear the new (American) Spring material Diane and Marilyn had just finished cutting, with Brian's help, in Iowa. Why Iowa? Seems they had a friend there, and the friend had a friend with a studio, and more friends, who're musicians, and one thing led to another.

It was snowing in Iowa (it's in the 70s in L.A.) but Brian looked round again to say that it's the best studio he's ever used. They had a great time, using unknown musicians and working hard.

Marilyn got on the copy tape of the sessions, and played me four completed tracks over the new set of JBL studio monitor speakers suspended from each corner of the room.

First there was the one they hope will be the single, "Shyin' Away," written by David Sandler. David co-produced the first Spring album, and has worked on Beach Boys material.

It's a great Top 40 song — the Ronell sisters retain the innocence they purveyed when they were the Honeys, back in the Sixties, and Sandler's melody caters perfectly to their best qualities. I didn't think they wrote songs like that any more.

Then there's David's "Snowflakes," a pretty Christmas song with whispered vocals, and Brian's "Had To Phone You," which he wrote when Marilyn was in Europe and he was still in California. Lastly there's a ballad by Dennis Wilson, one of the prettiest love songs he's written, beautifully sung by Diane.

They all sound like smashes to me, and Brian's production work — reminiscent in many places of his "Pet Sounds" touches, with perfectly-placed oddities like a clarinet solo and a bass line provided by the bottom end of the piano keyboard — is tremendous.

Marilyn explained that they were no longer with United Artists.

"Now how can they drop somebody after only one album? But I'm glad I mean they worked hard for us in Europe but over here..."

Columbia Records are interested in them at the moment, and amazingly they're all like young, kids on the brink of their first contract — excited, a bit breathless, wishin' and hopin' like mad. They really want Columbia to like their stuff.

"They were crazy about the first album," said Diane, still stroking Brian's neck with the vibro-massager. "But we're wondering whether they're going to like the new stuff ... it's so different. Don't worry, girls — the only difference is that it's better.

Brian was still lying on the floor, groaning, and while we discussed Spring I was cajoled by a small beggish dog called Banana into playing catch with a tennis ball.

It was fun for awhile, but I couldn't help feeling that we were stalling. Time for a prod.

"Oh," I said, feigning nonchalance. "I'm really happy — I've just got hold of a copy of the Students' "I'm So Young'."

THAT did the trick. Brian leapt to his feet, brushed the massager aside, forgot his headache and spoke.

"You did? Oh that's fantastic, I'm So Young' by the Students ... that record took me through senior year in high school. Oh, it's great."

This sudden burst of activity almost overbalanced his Stand back, speak normal, stand back, speak normal, stand back ... I only had time to nod in knowing assent before he spoke again.

"Listen here, I think I have that record somewhere. I'll go find it."

Finally, Brian reappeared. He hadn't found the record, but he started flipping through a pile of 45s lying on a chair, next to the upright piano.

Then he started putting them on the record-player. First there was "Da Doo Ron Ron," which he played twice. Then "Fool For You" by the Impressions — "That's Curtis Mayfield," he said. I know, I said. He sang and mimed along with the chorus.

"Does Phil live near here," I queried innocently.

"Oh ... umm ... I'm not sure. In Los Angeles or does he live in New York? Maybe he lives with Paul McCartney?" He laughed mischievously, like a little boy. "Where does Paul McCartney live?"

In London, I told him. I think he knew, and it looked like I was getting a put-on, so I asked him about this song called "This Could Be The Night," that he'd told me about before Spector had apparently recorded it with the Modern Folk Quartet around 1965, and Brian had heard it during the recording, but Phil never released it. Brian walked to the piano and demonstrated how, if went. He remembered it very clearly, except for a couple of verses. He told me that he was trying to get the lyrics from Phil so that he could record it with Spring, but every time he called Spector seemed strangely reluctant to part with them.

It's a great song, and Brian obviously got a buzz from singing it with differently-harmonised bass lines and new riffs, and it was fascinating to hear how, even though he was only mucking about, the harmonies and rhythms were pure Brian Wilson. No-one else could've been playing that piano.

He also sang the Platter's old "Twilight Time," then sprang up and led me through into a big room which used to be his home recording studio, where many of the finest Beach Boys cuts since 1966 were made. Now it's bare: wooden floor, a grand piano, a few chairs, and many pictures of Marilyn and the kids.

He took me through the room and up some stairs into a smaller chamber which used to be the studio's control room, pointing out where the monitor speakers had been. New-to-look bricks filled the hole which had been the window between booth and studio.

"Marilyn wanted some more room," he said. "She was tired of having musicians coming in and out of the house ... but it was a great studio. We got a nice sound here."

He sat down at the piano. It was the very same instrument. Marilyn told me, that had been placed in a sandbox back in the days of "Smile," when Brian had wanted to try and get a certain feeling into his music — the same kind of trip that he went through on the "Fire" section of "Elements," when he got the reversion musicians to dress up in firemen's uniforms.

WAS there still, I asked him, any truth in the recurring rumour that the "Smile" tracks would be released one day? No, he said emphatically. There just wasn't enough left to get together — only fragments, like the snatch of "Surf's Up" around where they recorded the song last year. That, then, seems to be it, the final confirmation that the original "Smile," with all its mystical reputation, will never be heard.

But we continued to talk about it for a while, and suddenly Brian hammered out the beginning of "Heroes and Villains." I've been in this town so long and back in in the city I've been taken.

After one verse, he switched into an unfamiliar lyric and tune, and when it was over explained that this was the full original version, as written by himself and Van Dyke Parks. Like several other songs, "Vegetables," for instance, they were hacked around and edited before being released on "Smiley Smile" and 45s. Had "Smile" come to fruition, we'd have heard them in all their glory.

(Later, when Diane told Marilyn what Brian had been singing, she said: "No. NOT REALLY? He hasn't done that in years. That's fantastic!"

Back at the piano, Brian told me about this other song he was working on for Spring. He made me promise not to divulge its identity, but I can say that it's in the Cottonfields mould — a Stephen Foster-type song, this time with an arrangement inspired by the Spencer Davis Group's "Gimme Some Lovin."

"I gotta get David," he said. "David," he hollered up the stairs. The slight, pale figure of David Sandler appeared, and they sang it together, trying out harmonies and tags — and if it ever comes out, it'll be a classic record.

No wonder Brian didn't want the secret giving away, because anyone who had the formula could do it — and probably botch it up.

Before supper, Diane told Brian to show me round the house. He took me out as far as the gates of the pool, which were locked, and back onto the patio, where kids' toys cluttered the concrete.

He took me upstairs, where the guest rooms were piled with bric-a-brac, and the "master bedroom," where his own bed lurches drunkenly. One snapped off. One thing's for sure — the place looks lived-in and comfortable.

By this time, I'd given up standing back and speaking normal. Brian, too, had lost most of his jitteriness.

Next time, I thought, we'll get down to the interview. But meanwhile, it was nice to know that Brian Wilson is not the madman that legend suggests.

He's just shy, and very nice.

Shyin' Away

BEACH BOYS JOURNALS PART 1

THE BEACH BOYS DOWN - UNDER

An Australian History from Surfside '64

by Stephen McParland

Australia and America have very similar climates and cultures and it was as a result of these similarities that the Beach Boys became quite popular in Australia during the early to mid sixties. The "beach culture" existed in Australia as it did in Southern California and it was only a matter of time before The Beach Boys' music also gained a foothold here.

The groups' first releases in Australia, "**Surfin' Safari**" and "**Ten Little Indians**", received only mild success, but paved the way for their Top Ten smash, "**Surfin' USA**"

The increasing popularity of The Beach Boys' music prompted Harry M. Miller, one of Australia's pioneer entrepreneurs, to bring them to Australia in a tour package billed as SURFSIDE '64. Accompanying the Beach Boys were The Surfaris, Paul & Paula and Roy Orbison. Chosen as support group was The Joy Boys, who at the time were riding high with their hit record, "Murphy The Surfie" (Later recorded by The Surfaris). It is interesting to note that Roy Orbison was the tour headliner, The Beach Boys were second bill!

SURFSIDE '64 was a whirlwind tour and covered five Australian States in nine days. Misinformed as usual, the media had David Marks listed as one of The Beach Boys, but it was Alan Jardine who stepped off the plane at Brisbane, the site of the group's first concert. It was also here that The Beach Boys' Official Australian Fan Club was formed.

The beginning of the Fan Club was instigated by a competition put together by the national television guide magazine, TV WEEK, in which prospective Fan Club presidents were given the chance to elaborate their ideas of how they would operate such a club, John Kubler, then a resident of Sandgate (a Brisbane suburb) won. He did tell me however, that there had been some 'behind the scenes' manipulation. Nonetheless, he did possess the best and most creative ideas and that is what counted.

At its' peak, The Beach Boys Official (Australian) Fan Club boasted a membership of some three thousand members and issued a monthly newsletter. Members were also issued with photos of the group, a membership card and cloth badges (to be sewn onto whatever). All these items were designed by John at his own expense. As usual, the record company aided very little even though they were making quite a tidy sum out of The Beach Boys product.

The Beach Boys arrive at Brisbane for their 1964 tour

The Fan Club (under John's leadership) lasted for three years, ending in 1967. This was not a reflection on the fans disinterest but rather the economic situation John found himself in. Fan clubs cannot operate successfully without the help and support of the respective record company: There is only so much one individual can contribute out of his or her own pocket!

The Fan Club also catered for New Zealand, having a National President there as well as State Presidents throughout Australia. It was great while it lasted.

Following the success of the SURFSIDE '64 tour, Capitol in Australia issued the single **Hawaii** b/w **The Rocking Surfer** (CP 1551). Hawaii (featuring a lead vocal by Brian and Dennis) had been one of the most popular songs at their Australian concerts. The single quickly climed the charts and peaked Nationally at in the Top Five. Towards the end of the tour, The Beach Boys promised they would return the following year, but this never happened.

A SURFSIDE '65 show was planned (featuring The Hondells) but shelved before 1964 had come to a close. A new tide in music had hit Australia, spearheaded by The

BEACH BOYS JOURNALS PART 1

Beatles. Surf and Hot Rod music was quickly inundated as teenagers everywhere traded in their surfboards for a pair of Beatle boots !

The Beach Boys, however, in a wise move to more all-encompassing Californian subjects, continued their popularity with a further three hit records during 1964. The times were a changin' but so were The Beach Boys and their music! Record release-wise, Australia closely followed America during this period. Apart from the "Hawaii" single , the only other odd release was **Then I Kissed Her** b/w **Mountain Of Love** (CP1689) in 1967, prompted by the success of the same single in England (where it peaked at # 4). Australia was ans still is influenced by both the US and UK markets. One American release that did not reach Australia was the 1964 Christmas single **The Man With All The Toys** b/w **Blue Christmas** (US Capitol 5312). This was primarily due to the failure of their previous seasonal release, **Little Saint Nick** (CP 1585).

Album releases were also similar in nature to the US product, although Australia often missed out on the nmore elaborate packaging of the US originals. All The Beach Boys' original Capitol Records' albums were released in Australia, with one exception. **Shut Down (Vol.1)** failed to appear. It was not really a Beach Boys albumbecause it only contained two Beach Boys' tunes; the title song and the Wilson-Usher automobile ode **409**. The remainder of the package comprised material from such diverse groups and individuals as Robert Mitchum, The Cheers, The Piltdown Men, The Eligibles,, Jimmy Dolan and the Gary Usher lead Super Stocks. In mid-1964 The Beach Boys issued their own **Shut Down Volume 2** album, but because the first volume had not been released downunder Capitol (EMI Australia) altered the album title and graphics accordingly to read simply **Shut Down** (Capitol T/ST 2027).

In all the sixties was quite a successful period for The Beach Boys in Australia. The group acheived seventeen Top Forty records (sixteen in the Top 30) despite little major media coverage. Radio stations were somewhat more receptive. One in particular, Sydney station 2SM 9together with affiliated stations in other States), organised a competition during the 1964 tour whereby lucky girls were given the opportunity of winning a luau breakfast with The Beach Boys or supper with The Surfaris. 2SM disk jockeys, Bob Rogers and Tony "Murph The Surf" Murphy, were the chaperons.

When The Beach Boys finally returned to Australia it was again a Sydney radio station that paved the way. This time it was 2UW and affiliates that promoted the tour. The actual promoters were John Keefe and David Trew, together with Paul Dainty and Des Cox. This partnership was called Creative Artists Management, London and Australia. This second tour kicked off in New Zealand on Friday, April 17th, 1970 and after a lightening tour of that country, the4 group (without Brian, but including Bruce Johnston as his replacement) landed on Australian soil at Essenden Airport, Melbourne, on wednesday evening the 22nd. Then followed concerts in Perth, Adelaide, Canberra, Sydney, Wollongong, Newcastle and Brisbane. All in the space of one week !

While in Sydney, the group performed at The Sydney Stadium (as in 1964) hosted by 2UW personalities and also appeared in caberet at the Chevron Hilton with Billy Burton's Orchestra. Both shows were well received but lacked the intense crowds of their previous visit. The Stadium concert was unfortunately marred by the absence of the groups' "elaborate electronic equipment" which had been mislaid by the airline !! Likewise, the Chevron appearances were hampered by poor acoustics and sound board mixing.

The Australian television network SEVEN (and affiliates) was also involved in the tour and as a result the group appeared on ATN 7 in Sydney. On the same program was local recording artist Ted Mulry, then enjoying success with the song "Julia". Al Jardine was so impressed with the tune that he approached Albert Productions for the recording rights. His idea was to take the song back to america and release it on the groups' own Brother Records label. This never happened - nor did a one hour colour film the group were to make whilst in Australia. It is not known exactly how much of the film was completed. I have personally seen only one clip from it. The story line of the show was tied in with Australias' Bi-Centenary (of Captain Cooks' landing in 1770) and accordinmg to John Bonney, the films' co-producer, it featured a Mac Sennett type chase scene with The Beach Boys (playing Captain Cooks' crew) being chased through Sydneys' streets after they had jumped ship to have a good time in town. Captain Cook was played by Dave Allenby, an English comedian who accompanied The Beach Boys on the tour. Basically the film was a satire on the overseas idea of Australia. Artistic relief was to be provided by some colour sequences filmed during the groups' concert at the famous TIKI VILLAGE in Surfers' Paradise, Queensland. The one and only film clip I saw featured The Beach Boys in an old car being chased by Dave allenby on a bicycle. The accompanying soundtrack was a non-released live version of the group singing **I Get Around.**

The press conference during the 1970 tour was quite gruelling for the group. Most of the questions revolved around rumours that they had run out of money and that they were heavily involved in drugs. There were also discussions of why their record sales had been slowly dwindling since the mid-sixties.

Compared to the 1964 tour, the 1970 tour proved quite dissapointing with half-filled concert arenas. Dennis hinted that he would like to buy a small beachside home near Perth and spend a good deal of his free time there but this was just another unsupported statement, one of many the group made whilst savouring what Australia had to offer.

BEACH BOYS JOURNALS PART 1

AUSTRALIAN SINGLES (1962 - 1988)

Discographical notes on the singles:

All **CP** prefixes are CAPITOL releases through EMI (Australia)
Label colour for CP 1484 to CP 1709 inclusive - Purple with Silver writing
Label colour for CP 1715 to CP 8809 inclusive - Yellow and Orange swirl
Label colour for CP 9122 - Red and Orange circular
Label colour for CP 10617 and CP 11280 - Orange
Label colour for CP 556 - Purple with Silver writing
Label colour for CP 1852, CP 1843, CP 2156, CP 2195, CP 2285 and CP 2339
- Black with Silver writing and Rainbow band around edge
OSS prefix denotes STATESIDE singles distributed through EMI (Australia)
Label colour - Black with Silver writing
Prefixes R, RPS and REP denote Brother / Reprise singles distributed through WEA (Australia). All feature the Brother Records and Reprise Records logos.
Label colour - Yellow with Orange edging
DS prefix denotes Caribou singles distributed through CBS (Australia)
Label design - picture label of Caribou
Note that DS 005, DS 008 and DS 009 also feature the Brother Records logo.
ES prefix denotes Caribou single distributed through CBS (Australia)
Label design is identical to DS prefixes.
BA prefix denotes CBS single distributed through CBS (Australia)
Label colour - Yellow/Orange/Red fade
885-9607 denotes a Polydor single distributed through Polygram Records Pty. Ltd.
Label colour - Red with black lettering
7-99392 denotes an Atlantic single distributed through WEA Records
Label colour - Red and Black with Black lettering
7-69385 denotes an Elektra single distributed through WEA Records
Label colour - Red and Black with Silver lettering

Cat #	Title	Year
CP 1484	Surfin' Safari / 409	1962
CP 1503	Ten Little Indians / County Fair	1962
CP 1517	Surfin' U.S.A. / Shut Down	1963
	(features the sole songwriting credit Brian Wilson, later altered to read Chuck Berry due to copyright action. Surfin' U.S.A. is based on "Sweet Little Sixteen". Brian simply used Chucks' music and wrote new lyrics	
CP 1533	Surfer Girl / Little Deuce Coupe	1963
CP 1545	Be True To Your School / In My Room	1963
CP 1551	Hawaii / The Rocking Surfer	1964
	(Released due to the success of the "live" version performed during the 1964 tour)	
CP 1557	Fun, Fun, Fun / Why Do Fools Fall In Love?	1964
CP 1569	I Get Around / Don't Worry Baby	1964
CP 1581	When I Grow Up / She Knows Me Too Well	1964
CP 1585	Little Saint Nick / The Lord's Prayer	1964
CP 1588	Dance, Dance, Dance / The Warmth Of The Sun	1964
CP 1598	Do You Wanna Dance? / Please Let Me Wonder	1965
CP 1602	Help Me, Rhonda / Kiss Me, Baby	1965
CP 1614	California Girls / Let Him Run Wild	1965
CP 1628	The Little Girl I Once Knew / There's No Other (Like My Baby)	1965
CP 1632	Barbara Ann / Girl Don't Tell Me	1966
CP 1642	Caroline, No / Summer Means New Love	1966
	(released under the name of Brian Wilson)	
CP 1643	Sloop John B / You're So Good To Me	1966
CP 1663	Wouldn't It Be Nice / God Only Knows	1966
CP 1673	Good Vibrations / Let's Go Away For Awhile	1966
CP 1689	Then I Kissed Her / Mountain Of Love	1967
	(released due to the success of the same single in England)	
CP 1699	Heroes And Villains / You're Welcome	1967
CP 1704	Gettin' Hungry / Devoted To You	1967
	(released under the name of Brian Wilson and Mike Love)	
CP 1709	Wild Honey / Wind Chimes	1967
CP 1715	Darlin' / Here Today	1968
CP 8358	Friends / Little Bird	1968
CP 8429	Do It Again / Wake The World	1968
CP 8619	Bluebirds Over The Mountain / Never Learn Not To Love	1969
CP 8709	I Can Hear Music / All I Want To Do	1969
CP 8809	Break Away / Celebrate The News	1969
CP 9122	Cottonfields / The Nearest Faraway Place (Steel guitar version)	1970
OSS 9319	Tears In The Morning / It's About Time	1971
OSS 9772	Don't Go Near The Water / Student Demonstration Time	1971
R 1091	You Need A Mess Of Help To Stand Alone / Cuddle Up	1972
R 1101	Marcella / Hold On Dear Brother	1972
RPS 1325	Sail On Sailor / Only With You	1973
R 3583	California Saga, California / Sail On Sailor	1973
CP 10617	Surfin' U.S.A. / The Warmth Of The Sun	1974
R 3621	Surfer Girl / Wouldn't It Be Nice?	1975
	(Live versions of songs as featured on the "In Concert" double LP)	
RPS 1354	Rock & Roll Music / The TM Song	1976
RPS 1368	It's O.K. / Had To Phone Ya	1976
CP 11280	Be True To Your School / Graduation	1977
RPS 1394	Peggy Sue / Hey Little Tomboy	1978
REP 3882	Come Go With Me / Diane	1978
DS 003	Here Comes The Night / Baby Blue	1979
	(released in both 7" and 12" formats 12" Cat # DS 12000)	
DS 004	Good Timin' / Love Surrounds Me	1979
DS 005	Lady Lynda / Full Sail	1980
DS 007	School Day / Keepin' The Summer Alive	1980
	(not issued - no copies pressed)	
DS 008	Oh Darlin' / Endless Harmony	1980
DS 009	School Day (Ring, Ring Goes The Bell) / Sunshine	1980
	(A side slightly speeded up from LP version)	
CP 556	"Beach Boys Medley" / God Only Knows	Sept. 1981
	(actual A side title is not Beach Boys Medley but : Good Vibrations/ Help Me Rhonda/I Get Around/Shut Down/Surfin' Safari/Barbara Ann/Surfin' U.S.A./Fun, Fun, Fun)	
ES 711	Come Go With Me / Don't Go Near The Water	Feb. 1982
	(both sides are re-issues. Don't Go Near The Water was originally released in Australia on the Stateside label. Come Go With Me was originally issued in Australia on the W.E.A.(Australia) label. Songs are taken from the compilation LP Ten Years Of Harmony.)	
BA 3317	Getcha Back / Male Ego	June 1985
	(first Beach Boys single issued in Australia with a picture sleeve. Design is basically identical to that of LP from which single is taken. Male Ego is <u>not</u> on LP)	
BA 3341	California Calling / It's OK	Oct. 1985
	(It's OK is a re-issue originally released in Australia on the W.E.A. (Australia) label)	
CP 1852	Rock 'N' Roll To The Rescue / Good Vibrations	Nov. 1986
	(live in London)(released in 7" and 12" versions with identical picture sleeves 12" Cat # is ED 217)	
CP 1843	California Dreamin' / Lady Liberty	Dec. 1986
885 9607	Wipe Out / Crushin' (Fat Boys with Beach Boys)	July 1987
	(released in both 7" and 12" formats. 12" Cat # is 885 960-1)	
7-99392	Happy Endings / California Girls (Beach Boys & Little Richard)	Dec. 1987
	(issued with picture sleeve featuring photo of the Beach Boys and Little Richard with notation "Happy Endings" from the motion picture "The Telephone")	
7-69385	Kokomo / Tutti Frutti (by Little Richard)	Sep. 1988
	(Kokomo by the Beach Boys.Tutti Frutti by Little Richard <u>without</u> Beach Boys. Sleeve note "From the Elektra Original Motion Picture Soundtrack 'Cocktail' ")	
CP 2156	Do It Again / Wouldn't It Be Nice	Oct. 1988
	(issued with a mid-sixties photo of The Beach Boys on the front and a picture of Hamilton Island holiday resort on the back. Do It Again is an edit with The Beach Boys singing and was used in TV commercials for Hamilton Island. Rear sleeve note " As featured in the six album box set THE CAPITOL YEARS on album, cassette and CD.")	

BEACH BOYS JOURNALS PART 1

AUSTRALIAN CARIBOU SINGLES

DS 001	O.C. SMITH Together / Just Couldn't Help Myself	1978
DS 002	DENNIS WILSON River Song / Farewell My Friend	1978
DS 003	THE BEACH BOYS Here Comes The Night / Baby Blue	1979
DS 004	THE BEACH BOYS Good Timin' / Love Surrounds Me	1980
DS 005	THE BEACH BOYS Lady Lynda / Full Sail	1980
DS 006	THE BEACH BOYS It's A Beautiful Day / Sumahama (released in New Zealand only. Reported to have been only approx. 200 pressed. CBS (Australia) allot catalogue numbers for New Zealand as well as for Australia.	1980
DS 007	THE BEACH BOYS School Day / Keepin' The Summer Alive (not released and no copies pressed)	1980
DS 008	THE BEACH BOYS Oh Darlin' / Endless Harmony	1980
DS 009	THE BEACH BOYS School Day (Ring, Ring Goes The Bell) / Sunshine (A side is slightly speeded up version of LP cut)	1980
DS 010	CARL WILSON What You Do To Me / Time (taken from Carl's first solo album "Youngblood" LP - which was not released in Australia)	1983

THE BEACH BOYS DOWN - UNDER (PART 2)
An Australian History from Surfside '64

by Stephen McParland

One of the most amusing and entertaining situations that occurred whilst the Beach Boys were in Australia happened during their 1964 tour. While performing at the Sydney stadium, Mike Love noticed a pretty young blonde in the audience named Sandra Rice. After the show he sought her out and spent the rest of the evening with her in Sydney's Kings Cross. Assumedly a romance blossomed. Following the groups tour of New Zealand, Mike flew back to Australia to find her again and after a radio appeal by 25M disc jockey, Mad Mel, he was reunited with his "lost love". After a few days Mike was convinced that he had found his perfect match (yes, another one!) and promised he would be back to ask her parents' permission to marry her after he had completed engagements in Los Angeles. He never did come back and I'm sure I remember hearing an interview with Brian and an Australian disc jockey, in which Brian admitted that the inspiration for "help Me Rhonda" came from Mike's ill-fated romance with Sandra!

After the 1970 tour the group's fortunes in Australia waned. They were no longer a commercial success. Their last chart record for years was to be the 45 version of "Cottonfields" (CP 9122) which reached the top ten in early 1970 (obviously aided by the group's visit). Even an in-depth interview with the group by radio station 25M, talking about drugs, Creedence Clearwater Revival, themselves, their hang-ups and their music, did little to bring about a more general acceptance of the group by the then "with-it" generation. 25M had gone to the trouble of sending three interviewers to New Zealand to spend two days with the Beach Boys at a farm on a NZ island, all for nothing! The majority of the listening public had lost interest in both the group and their music.

BEACH BOYS JOURNALS PART 1

THE SEVENTIES

The years from 1971 to 1976 saw little chart activity for the group in Australia. Record sales were down and their singles, particularly the two on Stateside and those on the Warner/Reprise/Brother label, became instant collector's items. This period was not only a bad one for the group in Australia, but also worldwide; However the situation began to change with Capitol Records repackaging some of the group's earlier material under the album titles ENDLESS SUMMER and SPIRIT OF AMERICA. Surprisingly, two singles culled from these compilations (CP 10617 and CP 11280) failed to make any impact on the Australian charts - or worldwide for that matter.

The mid to late seventies saw a resurgence of interest chart-wise in the group. Their updated version of Chuck Berry's *Rock and Roll Music* (1976) peaked in the National Top Thirty and two other singles *Peggy Sue* (1978) and *Lady Lynda* (1980) achieved a modicum of success. In 1981 Capitol Records issued a medley of the group's most remembered songs (in line with the then fascination with the "medley" concept) and by late spring/early summer, the release was riding at the top of many regional charts. Unfortunately this was not new material and the "juke box" concept of the Beach Boys "band" became more fully entrenched.

In 1978, The Beach Boys made their last (to date) tour of Australia, this time accompanied by Brian Wilson. Absent was Murray Wilson, who had died a few years earlier and who had been with the group on their two preceding tours as their "manager". Together with sell-out concerts around Australia and New Zealand (predominantly populated by the under twenties), the group was presented with Gold and Platinum records, attained from sales in Australia alone. These awards were for:

GOLD ALBUMS:
*BEST OF THE BEACH BOYS VOLUME 1
*BEST OF THE BEACH BOYS VOLUME 2
 *BEST OF THE BEACH BOYS VOLUME 3
 *SPIRIT OF AMERICA
 *BEACH BOYS CONCERT (1964)

PLATINUM ALBUMS
*ENDLESS SUMMER - awarded a single platinum
*20 GOLDEN GREATS - awarded a double platinum

Apart from leaving Australia loaded with over thirty five gold and platinum discs, the 1978 tour proved to be the most successful of all the tours. However it must also rank as the worst musical sounding tour of all. The newspapers were particularly critical of the group's performances, but the fans loved them nonetheless. Not many groups can boast of fans willing to sit for hours in the rain and mud just to get a glimpse of their idols. These were not just the "oldies" who remember them, but young kids who think it is all new. It is just a pity this younger audience was not buying the group's "new" material.

THE EIGHTIES

The early eighties were full of rumours of a Beach Boys return visit, but sadly nothing happened. A planned live concert tie-in with Sydney television station TEN's entry into the stereo broadcast medium was an incentive for the group to once again appear down-under, but this fizzled out. So too did the planned February 1986 tour. Tickets went on sale and the hype began, but poor sales eventually caused the scheduled shows to be, at first, postponed (until the following year) and then finally cancelled. Everyone was wondering what happened to the forty odd thousand people who packed the group's 1978 performances. Had their concerts been that bad?

The group's 1985 self titled album fared reasonably well down-under and the single *Getcha Back* peaked high on a number of regional charts, but nothing Nationally. The same situation applied to the group's follow-up releases. *Rock & Roll To The Rescue* (1986) and *California Dreamin'* (1986), yet their teaming with THE FAT BOYS for a 1987 rap version of The Surfaris' *Wipe Out* proved more successful. Unfortunately, little was made of the Beach Boys' involvement with the record.

In 1988 Brian Wilson shocked and pleased the music world with the release of his long awaited solo album. A solo single, *Let's Go To Heaven In My Car*, preceded the album's appearance, but did not find its' way down-under although the song was included on the *Police Academy 4* soundtrack (and at the end credits of the film) which was issued (through WEA) in Australia; However Brian's self titled album did make an antipodean appearance, together with two more singles *Love And Mercy* and *Night Time*. It is interesting to add that Night Time was NOT ISSUED as a single in the U.S. Brian's debut received excellent reviews from much of the Australian media and even though neither the album nor the singles achieved any major chart success, focus was once again placed on The Beach Boys, albeit in an indirect manner.

At the same time that Brian was pursuing his own direction, The Beach Boys (under the production of old cohort, Terry Melcher) completed a new waxing, *Kokomo*. Attached to the Bryan Brown-Tom Cruise film *Cocktail* the song soon began a slow climb up the charts, achieving chart topping status towards the end of 1988 in both America and Australia and once again the sun was shining for the boys from Hawthorne!

Australian Extended Plays

Discographical Notes: All EAP prefix EPs were released on the Capitol label, distributed by EMI (Australia). Label colour was GREEN with SILVER writing. All EPs were issued with cardboard picture sleeves. AUSEP prefix EP was issued by DISCONTINUED RECORDS under license from EMI, pressed by EMI (New Zealand) and issued in 1986. The label colour was BLACK with SILVER writing with RAINBOW band around the edge (same label as CP prefix singles).

EAP-1 20529 SURFIN' SAFARI
Surfin' Safari; Ten Little Indians; Shut Down; Surfin' U.S.A.
Front cover picture is the same as the LP. The back cover lists the tracks plus it features an advertisement for two other albums by the Beach Boys. The interesting thing about the advertisement is that the two albums mentioned (T 1886 Surfer's Choice and T1930 King Of The Surf Guitar) are NOT by the Beach Boys but by DICK DALE & HIS DEL-TONES!

EAP-1 20548 SURFER GIRL
409; Little Deuce Coupe; Summertime Blues; Surfer Girl

EAP-1 20618 FUN FUN FUN WITH THE BEACH BOYS
Be True To Your School; Fun Fun Fun; Hawaii; Why Do Fools Fall In Love
"Be True To Your School" is the single version (featuring the Honeys). The back cover features a photo of the Beach Boys holding Australia's "surfer girl" Little PATTIE.

EAP-5267 LITTLE HONDA
Wendy; Don't Back Down; Little Honda; Hushabye
Track listing and cover correspond to the American release - 4 BY THE BEACH BOYS, issued in September 1964 (CAPITOL R 5267) - reached #44 on US BILLBOARD.

EAP-4 2198 BEACH BOYS' CONCERT
The Little Old Lady From Pasadena; Papa-Oom-Mow-Mow; Let's Go Trippin'; Johnny B. Goode

EAP-1 20708 DANCE DANCE DANCE WITH THE BEACH BOYS
Dance Dance Dance; Do You Wanna Dance; Help Me Rhonda; California Girls

EAP-1 20709 I GET AROUND
In My Room; I Get Around; Don't Worry Baby; When I Grow Up (To Be A Man)

EAP-1 20794 BARBARA ANN
Sloop John B; The Little Girl I Once Knew; There's No Other (Like My Baby); Barbara Ann

EAP-1 20866 GOOD VIBRATIONS
God Only Knows'; Wouldn't It Be Nice; Let's Go Away For Awhile; Good Vibrations

EAP-21048 WILD HONEY
Then I Kissed Her; Heroes & Villains; Darlin'; Wild Honey

EAP 21325 I CAN HEAR MUSIC
I Can Hear Music; Do It Again; Bluebirds Over The Mountain; Friends

AUSEP 138 4 THE BEACH BOYS
Good Vibrations; Hawaii; Surfin' U.S.A.; I Get Around
Issued with a cardboard picture cover with an early photo of the Beach Boys (with David Marks) on the front cover. BEACH BOYS AUSTRALIA address included on rear cover.

BEACH BOYS JOURNALS PART 1

Australian LP's (Period covered is 1963 to end 1988).
General Information:
T/ST denotes CAPITOL releases through EMI (Australia). T is MONO; ST is STEREO. CAPITOL releases T-1808 to ST-133 inclusive were issued on the black/rainbow label. ST-21715 was issued on the light green Capitol label with black and purple logo. ST-26463 was issued on the purple Capitol label with silver writing and logo and ST-12293 was issued on the purple Capitol label with silver writing and logo. SOSL denotes STATESIDE releases through EMI (Australia). STATESIDE LPs were issued on an orange label with black lettering and logo. MS, 2RS and MSK denotes Reprise/Brother releases through WEA (Australia). WEA LPs were issued on the yellow/light brown label with Brother and Reprise Records logos (as were the W.E.A. singles). DL, GOLDE and SBP denotes CBS (Australia) releases. The DL prefix signifies a Caribou Records release. CARIBOU/CBS LPs all feature caribou logo label as per the singles. GOLDE release was on the Caribou label, compiled by CBS executive Andy Yavasis. SBP release was on the CBS label - yellow/orange/red bleed label with white logo.

Surfin' Safari	T-1808	1963
Surfin' USA	T-1890	1963
Surfer Girl	T/ST-1981	1963
Little Deuce Coupe	T-1998	1964
Shut Down Volume 2	T/ST-2027	1964
All Summer Long	T/ST-2110	1964

Features the mis-spelled track "Don't BREAK Down" on the front cover

Beach Boys Christmas Album	T-2164	1964
Beach Boys' Concert	T/ST-2198	1964
Beach Boys Today	T-2269	1965
Summer Days (And Summer Nights!!)	T/ST-2324	1965
Beach Boys' Party	T/ST-2398	1965
Pet Sounds	T-2458	1966
Best Of The Beach Boys Volume 1	T/ST-20796	1966

Different track listing than the American release of the same name

Best Of The Beach Boys Volume 2	T/ST-20797	1966

Different track listing than the American release of the same name

Smiley Smile	T/ST-9001	1967
Wild Honey	T/ST-2858	1968
Friends	ST-2895	1968
Best Of The Beach Boys Volume 3	ST-21487	1968

Different track listing than the American release of the same name

20/20	ST-133	1969
Live In London	ST-21715	1970

Original release features a red/grey/black and purple art cover with a picture of the Beach Boys, less Brian but including Bruce

Sunflower	SOSL 8251	1970

No foldout cover but 45 version of "Cottonfields" included as bonus track

Surf's Up	SOSL 10313	1971
Carl & The Passions - So Tough	MS 2090	1972
Holland	MS 2118	1973

NO booklet or "Mt. Vernon & Fairway" 7" disc as in America

Beach Boys In Concert	2RS 6484	1974
15 Big Ones	MS 2251	1976
The Beach Boys Love You	MSK 2258	1977
M.I.U.	MSK 2268	1978
L.A. (Light Album)	DL 3008	1979
Keepin' The Summer Alive	DL 3009	1980
Sunflower	DL 3010	1980

Foldout cover as per American original but issued on the Caribou/CBS label and no "Cottonfields" included.

Surf's Up	Dl 3011	1980
Beach Boys/Brian Wilson Rarities	ST 26463	9/81

Gatefold (fold-out) cover. Album compiled and conceived by Stephen J. McParland with help from Glenn A. Baker. Subsequently withdrawn after protests from Dave Nowlen (a member of the Survivors). The dispute was over the liner notes which infer that the Survivors were the Beach Boys under alias (long believed to be the case)

Ten Years Of Harmony	2ELPS 0039	2/82
In Harmony	GOLDE 102	11/83

A shorter version of the double LP set "Ten Years Of Harmony" compiled by CBS (Australia) executive Andy Yavasis. This release was a budget line issue. Track listing: Side A: Rock and Roll Music; Cool, Cool Water; The Trader; Disney Girls; San Miguel; Surf's Up; Wontcha Come Out Tonight; School Day (Ring Ring Goes The Bell); Good Timin'; Sail On Sailor. Side B:Darlin' (Live); Lady Lynda; Sea Cruise; Roller Skating Child; River Song (Dennis Wilson); Long Promised Road; Marcella; Don't Go Near The Water; California Saga/California; 'Till I Die.

Beach Boys Rarities	ST 12293	11/83
The Beach Boys	SBP 8090	6/85

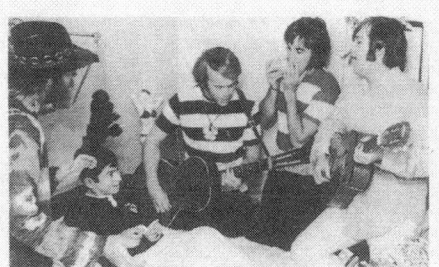

Mike, Alan, Dennis, Carl

Alan, Carl, Bruce, Mike, Brian, Dennis (seated)

BEACH BOYS JOURNALS PART 1

Brian Wilson in his Los Angeles health-food store, The Radiant Radish.

Left, Chuck Britz with Brian at Western Studios. Brian: "We went to at least ten of the studios around town, but I preferred Western.... It seemed to have the best echo chamber for what we were doing vocally." Above, Brian.

THE BEACH BOYS

The Beach Boys are hard to put in words. You might more easily associate them with pictures of the surf or T-Birds—or what it was like when you were younger and heard "Surfin' Safari" for the very first time. (Art is a kind of scrapbook.)
The Beach Boys do not offer a clear conception of the nature of man like, say, the Stones, nor like the Beatles, true images of themselves, but rather a fuzzy composite image that turns out to be written in clear musical concepts.
Something may be learned from this.
Mostly, the Beach Boys belong to rock 'n roll (our own special art) and not to literature or sociology.
And so it's hard to write about them.
Their music invented its own special genre, based, of course, on the foundations of others. It exists in a pure state, lyric and poetic, exhilarating, essentially non-verbal and funfunfun, with voices and instruments weaving in and out to form a convincing and kaleidoscopic musical tapestry.
Yes, but the Beach Boys?
It takes a strong swallow to accept how far the Beach Boys (three brothers, a cousin and a friend) have come since 1961 when they stepped out of Hawthorne, California obscurity with "Surfin'." The group rode the crest of the surfing and custom car crazes with Four Freshmen harmonies, candy-striped shirts and hit-after-hit: "I Get Around," "Surfer Girl," "Little Deuce Coupe," "California Girls," "Help Me Rhonda," "Shut Down"...
The music was (and remains) basically easy, accessible, lilting often with tricky, completely integral mood and rhythmic changes, as unmistakably white middle-class American as the Kinks and the Beatles are undeniably white middle-class British, and had a vitality far more provocative than the standard brand of pre-acne pap prevalent in the early and middle 60s.
And then came Pet Sounds (one of best albums ever) and "Good Vibrations" (ditto for singles) and John Lennon called Brian Wilson a genius and Wilson believed

BEACH BOYS JOURNALS PART 1

it and then came the strange marriage with Van Dyke Parks and the non-appearance of Smile.

The Beach Boys vanished into commercial semi-obscurity, although their subsequent LPs (Smiley Smile, Wild Honey, Friends, 20/20) became more personal, more imaginative, more (and then less) ethereal notations on the state of their collective musical heads.

Within each song—soft hymns to life, complex tapestries of nature, evocative instrumentals, tender songs to innocence of all sorts—the Beach Boys have created an impressionistic half-dream, half-spiritual world, which turns its head and runs back into the womb of Brian Wilson romanticism. Their records hint at the tranquil beauty lying just beneath the surface of each man's consciousness than can be reached if, like the Beatles, he can only "relax and float downstream."

The Beach Boys have made a series of positive statements about experiencing life to its fullest. You might call the Beach Boys' music religious.

It's good.

Do you wanna dance?

"As I sit and close my eyes,
There's peace in my heart
And I'm hoping that you'll find it too
And these feelings in my heart
Are meant for you . . ."

BEACH BOYS JOURNALS PART 1

"Heroes and Villains" was one of the most highly publicized single records in rock history. Because it was the follow-up to "Good Vibrations," expectations were high. Restless anticipation increased to such a peak that the record's actual release could only seem anticlimactic.

The Beach Boys never submitted Smile to Warner Brothers nor does it appear to exist in one complete tape that could be released.

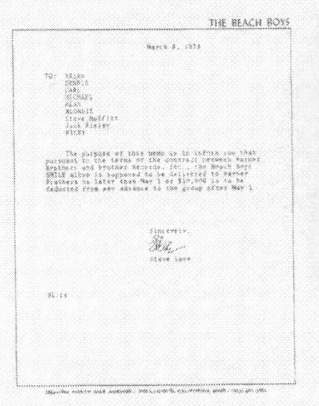

THE BEACH BOYS — SMiLE!
SMiLE is the name of the new Beach Boys album which will be released in January 1967 and with a happy album cover, the really happy sounds inside, and a happy in-store display piece, you can't miss! We're sure to sell a million units....
in January.

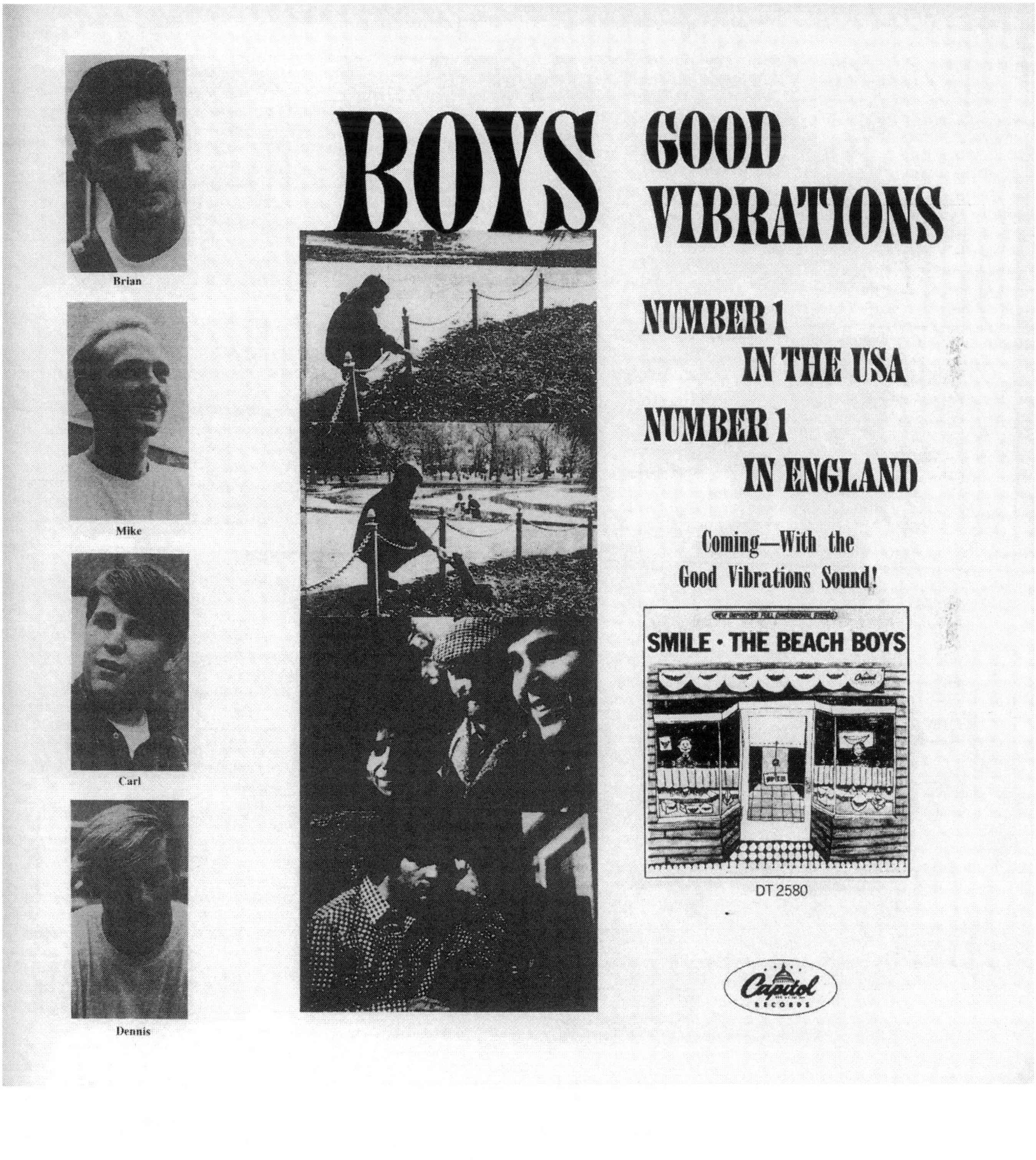

BEACH BOYS JOURNALS PART 1

BOYS GOOD VIBRATIONS

NUMBER 1 IN THE USA

NUMBER 1 IN ENGLAND

Coming—With the Good Vibrations Sound!

SMILE · THE BEACH BOYS

DT 2580

Capitol RECORDS

Brian

Mike

Carl

Dennis

BEACH BOYS JOURNALS PART 1

The Beach Boys Smile

- Do You Like Worms
- Wind Chimes
- Heros and Villains
- Surf's Up
- Good Vibrations
- Cabin Essence
- Wonderful
- I'm in Great Shape
- Child Is Father of the Man
- The Elements
- Vega-tables
- The Old Master Painter

BEACH BOYS JOURNALS PART 1

BEACH BOYS JOURNALS PART 1

BEACH BOYS JOURNALS PART 1

BEACH BOYS JOURNALS PART 1

BRIAN WITH
EX-WIFE
MARILYN
ROVELL

BEACH BOYS JOURNALS PART 1

BEACH BOYS JOURNALS PART 1

BEACH BOYS JOURNALS PART 1

BEACH BOYS JOURNALS PART 1

BEACH BOYS JOURNALS PART 2

The Beach Boys

JOURNALS PART 2 (1968-88)

BEACH BOYS JOURNALS PART 2

BEACH BOYS JOURNALS PART 2

COMPUTER ENHANCED - DIGITALLY REMASTERED

The Beach Boys

JOURNALS PART 2 (1968 - 88)

DISC ONE
1. LOOP DE LOOP
2. SUSIE CINCINNATI
3. SAN MIGUEL
4. H.E.L.P. IS ON THE WAY
5. TAKE A LOAD OFF YOUR FEET
6. OVER THE WAVES (A.K.A. CARNIVAL)
7. I JUST GOT MY PAY
8. 'TIL I DIE
9. GOOD TIME
10. BIG SUR
11. LADY
12. WHEN GIRLS GET TOGETHER
13. LOOKIN' AT TOMORROW (A WELFARE SONG)
14. 'TIL I DIE (REPRISE) (BONUS TRACKS)
15. WE'RE TOGETHER AGAIN
16. CELEBRATE THE NEWS
17. GAMES TWO CAN PLAY
18. SOUND OF FREE
19. TEARS IN THE MORNING
20. OUR TEAM
21. 4TH OF JULY
22. FAIRY TALE MUSIC
23. FAIRY TALE MUSIC
24. FAIRY TALE MUSIC
25. FAIRY TALE MUSIC
26. FAIRY TALE MUSIC
27. BRIAN'S BACK
28. SANTA ANA WINDS
29. LOOKING DOWN THE COAST
30. H.E.L.P. IS ON THE WAY
31. SANTA ANA WINDS
TOTAL CD TIME 74.39

DISC TWO
1. CHRISTMAS TIME IS HERE AGAIN
2. CHILD OF WINTER
3. WINTER SYMPHONY
4. MICHAEL ROW THE BOAT ASHORE
5. SEASONS IN THE SUN
6. HOLY EVENING
7. ALONE ON CHRISTMAS DAY
8. GO & GET THAT GIRL
9. SANTA'S GOT AN AIRPLANE
10. I SAW MOMMY KISSING SANTA CLAUS - OUTTAKES -
11. I SAW MOMMY KISSING SANTA CLAUS
12. I SAW MOMMY KISSING SANTA CLAUS
13. XMAS MEDLEY
14. KONA CHRISTMAS (MELE KALIKI MAKO)
15. BELLS OF CHRISTMAS (BONUS TRACKS)
16. JINGLE BELL ROCK
17. HAVE YOURSELF A MERRY LITTLE CHRISTMAS
18. DO YOU HEAR WHAT I HEAR ?
19. LITTLE SAINT NICK
20. LITTLE SAINT NICK
21. AULD LANG SYNE
22. THINGS WE DID LAST SUMMER
23. THE LORD'S PRAYER
24. LITTLE SAINT NICK
25. HOLY EVENING
26. BRIAN WILSON XMAS MESSAGE
TOTAL CD TIME 65.55

DISC THREE
1. WALK ON BY
2. OLD FOLKS AT HOME / OL' MAN RIVER
3. WE'RE TOGETHER AGAIN
4. WE'RE TOGETHER AGAIN
5. WE'RE TOGETHER AGAIN
6. BLUEBIRDS OVER THE MOUNTAIN
7. BREAKAWAY
8. WE GOTTA GROOVE
9. MY SOLUTION
10. (INTRO-:)
11. VEGETABLES
12. (INTRO-:)
13. FALLIN' IN LOVE (A.K.A.'LADY')
14. (INTRO-:)
15. SEARCHIN'
16. RIOT IN CELL BLOCK #9
17. HELP ME RHONDA
18. OKIE FROM MUSKOGEE
19. JOHNNY B. GOODE
20. 'CARL AND THE PASSIONS/ RADIO AD
21. 'CARL AND THE PASSIONS/ RADIO AD
22. YOU NEED A MESS OF HELP TO STAND ALONE (REG. TO VOTE ADS)
23. DENNIS WILSON
24. CARL WILSON
25. RICKY FATAAR
26. MIKE LOVE
27. AL JARDINE
28. WE GOT LOVE
29. 'HOLLAND' (RADIO AD)
30. CALIFORNIA FEELING
31. CARL WILSON (ANTI-DRUGS AD.)
TOTAL CD TIME 64.11

DISC FOUR
1. HONKIN' DOWN THE HIGHWAY
2. BRIAN'S BACK
3. SEA CRUISE
4. ON BROADWAY
5. MONY MONY
6. HEY LITTLE TOMBOY
7. SHORTENIN' BREAD
8. BE MY BABY
9. IT'S TRYING TO SAY (A.K.A. 'BASEBALL')
10. LINES
11. IT'S OVER NOW
12. EVERYBODY WANTS TO LIVE
13. DIANE
14. HOW'S ABOUT A LITTLE BIT OF YOUR SWEET LOVIN'
15. LADY LYNDA
16. RIVER SONG
17. RIVER SONG
18. FAREWELL MY FRIEND
19. CARRY ME HOME
20. GETTING HUNGRY
21. HOW'S ABOUT A LITTLE BIT
22. SHE'S JUST OUT TO GET YOU
23. BABY BLUE
24. IT'S NOT TOO LATE
25. WILD SITUATION
TOTAL CD TIME 70.15

DISC FIVE
1. SCHOOLGIRL
2. MOONLIGHT
3. COMPANION
4. HE'S A BUM
5. CALENDER GIRL
6. CALENDER GIRL
7. CALIFORNIA BEACH
8. LET'S VISIT HEAVEN TONIGHT
9. ALMOST SUMMER
10. ALMOST SUMMER
11. TODAY I STARTED LOVIN' YOU AGAIN
12. TODAY I STARTED LOVIN' YOU AGAIN
13. HEY GOOD LOOKIN'
14. SKATETOWN U.S.A.
15. IT'S A BEAUTIFUL DAY
16. ANGEL COME HOME
17. GOOD TIMIN'
18. OH! THOSE GIRLS
19. LOOKING BACK WITH LOVE
20. HOT SUMMER LOVERS
21. ALLEY OOP / PAPA OOM-MOW-MOW
22. SUN CITY
23. HAWAII
24. SUMMERTIME MUSIC
25. HYATT REGENCY
26. HYATT REGENCY
27. BE TRUE TO YOUR BUD
28. BERMUDA SHORTS
29. DA DOO RON RON
TOTAL CD TIME 74.06

DISC SIX
1. LET'S PARTY
2. HER BOYFRIEND'S BACK
3. LIGHTNIN' STRIKES
4. SUGAR SHACK
5. THE LETTER
6. THE LOCOMOTION
7. WHAT YOU DO TO ME
8. CALIFORNIA DREAMIN'
9. PROBLEM CHILD
10. PROBLEM CHILD
11. EAST MEETS WEST
12. CHASIN' THE SKY
13. BACK IN THE U.S.S.R.
14. COME GO WITH ME
15. SURFER GIRL
16. BARBARA ANN
17. HAPPY BIRTHDAY AMERICA
18. HAPPY ENDINGS
19. KOKOMO
TOTAL CD TIME 74.00

DISC SEVEN
1. WOULDN'T IT BE NICE
2. INTRO
3. VEGETABLES
4. 'SURF CITY' REQUEST
5. COOL COOL WATER
6. IT'S ABOUT TIME
7. INTRO
8. SURF'S UP
9. INTRO
10. STUDENT DEMONSTRATION TIME
11. SHORTENIN' BREAD
12. PEGGY SUE
13. ROLLER SKATING CHILD
14. IT'S OK
15. 409 (EXCERPT)
16. SUMAHAMA
17. ANGEL COME HOME
18. YOU ARE SO BEAUTIFUL
19. GOOD TIMIN'
20. SOME OF YOUR LOVE
21. GOIN' ON
22. LIVING WITH A HEARTACHE
23. DISNEY GIRLS
24. KEEPIN' THE SUMMER ALIVE
25. SCHOOLDAY (RING! RING! GOES THE BELL)
26. LADY LYNDA
27. I WRITE THE SONGS
28. RUNAWAY
TOTAL CD TIME 73.43

DISC EIGHT
1. COTTONFIELDS
2. CAROLINE NO
3. INTRO
4. AREN'T YOU GLAD
5. YOU STILL BELIEVE IN ME
6. CATCH A WAVE
7. SURFER GIRL
8. HEROES & VILLAINS
9. BARBARA ANN
10. IN MY ROOM
11. BE TRUE TO YOUR SCHOOL
12. HELP ME RHONDA
13. FUN FUN FUN
14. CALIFORNIA GIRLS
15. SLOOP JOHN B
16. DARLIN'
17. GOD ONLY KNOWS
18. DO IT AGAIN
19. LITTLE DEUCE COUPE
20. ROCK AND ROLL MUSIC
21. I GET AROUND
22. WOULDN'T IT BE NICE
23. GOOD VIBRATIONS
24. SURFIN' USA
25. SUMMER IN PARADISE
TOTAL CD TIME 72.33

Brother records

THIS IS THE SECOND (8 CD) BOX SET IN OUR HISTORY OF THE BEACH BOYS WHICH OFFERS (IN CHRONOLOGICAL ORDER) THE PICK OF THE RARITIES IN **BEST EVER** SOUND QUALITY. OUR CEDREM SOUND LAB HAS BEEN UTILIZED ON **ALL** THE CD'S IN BOTH SETS, GUARANTEEING UNSURPASSED QUALITY THROUGHOUT. LANDLOCKED, FOR EXAMPLE, IS PRESENTED HERE IN BEST EVER SOUND QUALITY, PLUS, ABOUT 80 TRACKS HAVE NEVER BEFORE APPEARED ON CD & SOME TRACKS HAVE NEVER BEFORE APPEARED IN ANY FORM (NOT EVEN VINYL LP). FROM THE WEALTH OF LIVE MATERIAL AVAILABLE WE'VE ELECTED TO ONLY USE THE VERY **BEST** SOUND QUALITY RECORDINGS, ALTHOUGH MANY 'AUDIENCE' TAPES WERE AVAILABLE TO US, WE CHOSE TO ONLY USE 'IN-LINE' OR 'SOUNDBOARD' TAPES TO MAINTAIN THE QUALITY OF THE JOURNALS SETS. ON THE 2 CD'S OF LIVE MATERIAL WE'VE ALSO SEPARATED THE HITS & ALBUM TRACKS SO AS TO ENABLE THE FANS TO LISTEN TO **EITHER** JUST THE 'HITS' (DISC 8) OR (DISC 7) A CD WITH 23 MORE OBSCURE SONGS NONE OF WHICH APPEAR ON ANY OF THE BEACH BOYS' OFFICIAL LIVE ALBUMS (EG. 'VEGETABLES', 'SURF'S UP', 'YOU ARE SO BEAUTIFUL', 'I WRITE THE SONGS' OR 'RUNAWAY'). THIS SET (LIKE JOURNALS PART 1) WAS PREPARED BY A **FAN**, WHO KNOWS HOW IMPORTANT IT IS TO 'GET IT RIGHT' & WE'VE SUBSEQUENTLY GIVEN YOU A FEAST OF RARITIES INCLUDING ALL OF DENNIS WILSON'S 'BAMBOO' ALBUM. ALL 'BONUS TRACKS' WHICH APPEARED ON THE VARIOUS CD ISSUES IN RECENT YEARS HAVE BEEN PLACED WITHIN OUR BOX SET IN CHRONOLOGICAL ORDER.
A DELUXE 68 PAGE COLOR BOOK FILLED WITH AN INCREDIBLY DETAILED TRACK BY TRACK ANALYSIS OF EVERY SONG, PLUS HEAPS OF RARE PHOTOS, ARTICLES, INTERVIEWS & A FULL DISCOGRAPHY IS ALSO INCLUDED.

NUMBER ____ OF LIMITED EDITION OF 1,000 COPIES

BEACH BOYS JOURNALS PART 2

BEACH BOYS JOURNALS PART 2

COMPUTER ENHANCED - DIGITALLY REMASTERED

The Beach Boys
JOURNALS PART 2
VOL.1 LANDLOCKED

CD - 17

THE 'LANDLOCKED' ALBUM WAS RECORDED AROUND 1970 BUT WAS NEVER ISSUED AS SUCH. MANY SONGS WERE EVENTUALLY ISSUED IN MOSTLY REMIXED OR RE-RECORDED FORM & SOME WERE LEFT INTACT BUT THIS IS HOW THE ALBUM **SHOULD** HAVE SOUNDED. IN ORDER TO GIVE YOU THE BEST POSSIBLE VALUE FOR MONEY, WE'VE FILLED THE REST OF THE DISC WITH SONGS WHICH FALL ROUGHLY INTO THE MUSICAL STYLE RESERVATIVE OF 'LANDLOCKED' WHICH (WE FEEL AT LEAST) MAKES THIS CD PARTICULARLY STRONG. THE CEDREM SOUND LAB HAS BEEN UTILIZED TO PROVIDE THE BEST EVER SOUND QUALITY. TRACK 13 WAS REPRISED AS 'LAZY LIZZIE' IN 1970'S BY BRIAN & APPEARS ON THE 'OUTTAKES' CD IN BRIAN WILSON'S OWN CEDREM BOX SET.

#	SONGTITLE	TIME	SONGWRITERS	RECORDING DATE	COMMENTS
1.	LOOP DE LOOP	2.58	B WILSON-AL JARDINE	1970	STILL UNRELEASED IN ANY FORM, A MUCH LONGER VERSION IS RUMOURED TO EXIST
2.	SUSIE CINCINNATI	2.56	AL JARDINE	1970	1ST APPEARED AS THE B-SIDE TO 'ADD SOME MUSIC TO YOUR DAY' IN MARCH 1970, THEN AGAIN AS A B-SIDE FOR 'CHILD OF WINTER' (DEC '74) AND FINALLY '15 BIG ONES' ALBUM IN JULY '76.
3.	SAN MIGUEL	2.25	D WILSON-G JACOBSON	1970	EVENTUALLY ISSUED ON THE '10 YEARS OF HARMONY' ALBUM IN REMIXED FORM
4.	H.E.L.P. IS ON THE WAY	2.18	BRIAN WILSON	1970	(ORIGINAL 1970 MIX) BRIAN'S ODE TO A HEALTH FOOD STORE HE ONCE OWNED IN WEST HOLLYWOOD 'THE RADIANT RADISH' (BACKING VOCALS START AT 0.21)
5.	TAKE A LOAD OFF YOUR FEET	2.33	BRIAN WILSON-A JARDINE-G WINFREY	1970	ALTERNATE MIX TO 'SURF'S UP' ALBUM
6.	OVER THE WAVES (A.K.A. CARNIVAL)	1.01	TRADITIONAL	1970	STILL UNRELEASED IN ANY FORM. A TUNE WHICH WILL BE FAMILIAR TO ALL, HOWEVER, FROM 'FAIRGROUNDS AND CAROUSELS'.
7.	I JUST GOT MY PAY	2.22	BRIAN WILSON	1970	THIS TUNE FIRST APPEARED AS THE VERSES IN 'ALL DRESSED UP FOR SCHOOL' (WHICH WAS LEFT UNISSUED) THEN USED ON THIS (UNISSUED AT THE TIME) THEN RELEASED AS THE VERSE FOR 'MARCELLA' FROM THE 'CARL & THE PASSIONS' ALBUM
8.	'TIL I DIE	5.01	BRIAN WILSON	1970	REMIXED VERSION APPEARED LATER ON 'SURF'S UP' ALBUM
9.	GOOD TIME	3.07	BRIAN WILSON-AL JARDINE	1970	REMIXED VERSION APPEARED LATER ON 'THE BEACH BOYS LOVE YOU' ALBUM
10.	BIG SUR	2.40	MIKE LOVE	1970	TOTALLY RE-WORKED VERSION APPEARED LATER ON 'HOLLAND' (WITH CALIFORNIA)
11.	LADY	2.22	DENNIS WILSON	1969	AS ISSUED AUG 1969. ACTUALLY ISSUED AS A SINGLE BY DENNIS AS DENNIS WILSON & RUMBO, WHICH FEATURED DARYL DRAGON (1/2 OF THE CAPTAIN & TENNILE)
12.	WHEN GIRLS GET TOGETHER	3.20	B WILSON-M LOVE	1970	REMIX APPEARED ON THE 'KEEPIN' THE SUMMER ALIVE' ALBUM IN 1980
13.	LOOKIN' AT TOMORROW (A WELFARE SONG)	2.05	A JARDINE-G WINFREY	1970	REMIXED VERSION APPEARED LATER ON 'SURF'S UP' ALBUM WITH HORRID PHASING ETC. THIS IS HOW IT SHOULD SOUND
14.	'TIL I DIE (REPRISE)	2.38	BRIAN WILSON	1970	EARLY MIX WITH NO VERSES (EG 'I LOST MY WAY' AT 0.23 AND 'IT KILLS MY SOUL' AT 0.57)
	- BONUS TRACKS -				
15.	WE'RE TOGETHER AGAIN	1.50	B WILSON-R WILSON	Sep11'68	(FINAL MIX) VOCALS BY BRIAN AND CARL
16.	CELEBRATE THE NEWS	3.04	D WILSON-G JACOBSON	Feb25'69	B-SIDE OF 'BREAKAWAY' SINGLE
17.	GAMES TWO CAN PLAY	2.02	BRIAN WILSON	Early '69	(FINAL MIX) LEAD VOCAL BY BRIAN (FROM REJECTED 'ADULT CHILD' LP)
18.	SOUND OF FREE	2.21	D WILSON-M LOVE	Mid '69	B-SIDE TO LADY SINGLE BY DENNIS WILSON AND RUMBO. REMASTERED FROM 2 SOURCES TO GIVE US A COMPLETE START (FOR THE 1ST TIME ON CD THERE'S NO SKIP AT THE START)
19.	TEARS IN THE MORNING	4.12	BRUCE JOHNSTON	Circa '70	ORIGINAL MIX OF A CLASSIC SONG FOR THE 'SUNFLOWER' ALBUM. LEAD VOCAL IS COMPLETELY DIFFERENT & ALL THE BACKING VOCALS ARE MISSING
20.	OUR TEAM	2.33	B WILSON-C WILSON-D WILSON-A JARDINE-M LOVE	Circa '70	FINAL MIX
21.	4TH OF JULY	2.45	DENNIS WILSON	Circa '71	FINAL MIX
22.	FAIRY TALE MUSIC (PART 1)	1.29	B WILSON	Circa '73	('MT VERNON & FAIRWAY') PART 1. (MUSIC ONLY)
23.	FAIRY TALE MUSIC (PART 2)	0.42	B WILSON	Circa '73	('BETTER GET BACK IN BED') PART 2.(MUSIC ONLY)
24.	FAIRY TALE MUSIC (PART 3)	0.34	B WILSON	Circa '73	('MAGIC TRANSISTOR RADIO') PART 3. 'BONUS' 7" DISC (EP)(MUSIC ONLY)
25.	FAIRY TALE MUSIC (PART 4)	0.43	B WILSON-C WILSON	Circa '73	('I'M THE PIED PIPER') PART 4 (MUSIC ONLY)
26.	FAIRY TALE MUSIC (PART 5)	0.41	B WILSON-J RIELEY	Circa '73	('RADIO KINGDOM') PART 5 (MUSIC ONLY)
27.	BRIAN'S BACK	2.42	M LOVE	Circa '76	TOTALLY UNRELEASED SONG FEATURING MIKE & CARL. SUPPOSED TO BE PART OF MIKE'S NEVER ISSUED 1ST SOLO LP, BUT ORIGINALLY EARMARKED FOR INCLUSION ON '15 BIG ONES' WHEN IT WAS GOING TO BE A DOUBLE ALBUM TO BE CALLED 'PICK YA UP AT 8'
28.	SANTA ANA WINDS	2.50	B WILSON-A JARDINE	Circa '78	ORIGINAL TAKE. COMPLETELY DIFFERENT VERSION ON THE 'KEEPIN' THE SUMMER ALIVE' ALBUM (WHICH WE FEEL IS VASTLY INFERIOR TO THIS).
29.	LOOKING DOWN THE COAST	3.13	AL JARDINE	Circa '78	TOTALLY UNRELEASED SONG, BRIAN SINGS INTRO W/ AL JARDINE HANDLING LEAD VOCALS.
	- ALTERNATE MIXES -				
30.	H.E.L.P. IS ON THE WAY	2.29	BRIAN WILSON	1970	(REMIX) LONGER AND DIFFERENT MIX TO THE ORIGINAL (TK #4), BACKING VOCALS DON'T APPEAR UNTIL 0.25 AND THE ENDING IS LONGER AND ALLOWS US TO HEAR BRIAN'S PLUG FOR 'THE RADIANT RADISH' AS THE FINAL WORDS ON THIS DISC.
31.	SANTA ANA WINDS	2.55	B WILSON-A JARDINE	Circa '78	(REMIX) SIMILAR TO TK #28 BUT DOUBLE TRACKED LEAD VOCALS

TOTAL CD TIME 74.39

Brother records

BEACH BOYS JOURNALS PART 2

BRIAN DRESSED UP AS SANTA CLAUS (A.K.A. ST. NICHOLAS, LITTLE SAINT NICK)

OUTTAKE PHOTO FROM 'THE BEACH BOYS CHRISTMAS ALBUM' 1964

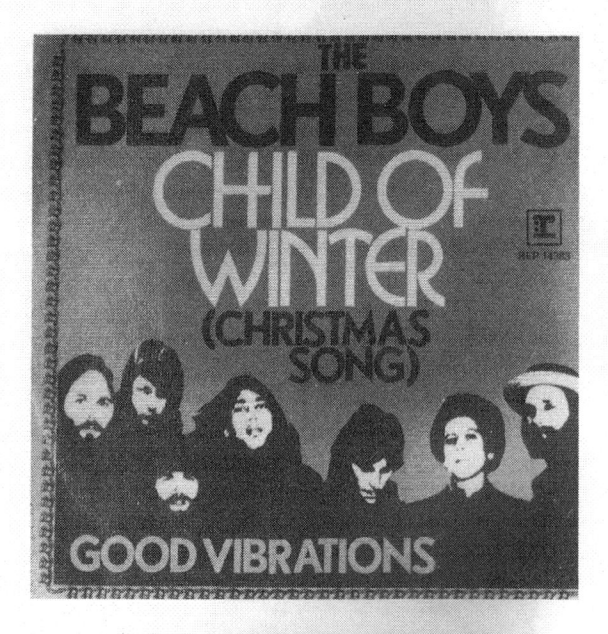

POSTER PROMOTING CONCERT WHICH WAS RECORDED FOR TH 'CONCERT' ALBUM. **EXTRA** TRACKS FROM THIS CONCERT AVAILABLE IN JOURNALS (VOL.1

BEACH BOYS JOURNALS PART 2

COMPUTER ENHANCED - DIGITALLY REMASTERED

The Beach Boys
JOURNALS PART 2
VOL.2 1977 XMAS ALBUM

CD-18

DURING 1976/77 THE BEACH BOYS RECORDED SOME TRACKS FOR INCLUSION ON A FOLLOW UP TO THEIR 1964 XMAS ALBUM TO BE TITLED 'MERRY CHRISTMAS FROM THE BEACH BOYS'. ORIGINAL SONGS WERE WRITTEN AND RECORDED PLUS A COUPLE WERE RECYCLED FOR POSSIBLE INCLUSION. WARNER BROS. REFUSED TO RELEASE THE ALBUM, SO IT HAS REMAINED FIRMLY ENTRENCHED IN THE VAULTS UNTIL NOW. WE'VE WORKED ON THE ORIGINAL TAPES TO PROVIDE NEAR PERFECT SOUND QUALITY THROUGHOUT, SO THE END RESULT IS SOMETHING WE ARE VERY PROUD OF & UNLESS THE BEACH BOYS RELEASE THIS THEMSELVES, **THIS** IS THE VERSION TO BUY. WE'VE ADDED TO THIS OUTTAKES FROM THAT ALBUM, SOME MIKE LOVE XMAS SONGS, 'BONUS' TRACKS WITH A YULETIDE FEEL & A BRIAN WILSON CHRISTMAS / NEW YEAR MESSAGE WHICH MAKES THIS IDEAL TO PLAY ON 'REPEAT' DURING YOUR NEXT XMAS DAY AT HOME.

#	SONGTITLE	TIME	SONGWRITERS	RECORDING DATE	COMMENTS
1.	CHRISTMAS TIME IS HERE AGAIN	3.00	BRIAN WILSON	Circa76/77	GREAT OPENING TRACK TO THE WHOLE ALBUM WHICH APART FROM 'CHILD OF WINTER' REMAINS TOTALLY UNRELEASED TO THIS DAY
2.	CHILD OF WINTER	2.42	B.WILSON-S.KALINICH-OAKLEY-HALDEMANN-AUTREY	Circa 74	ACTUALLY ISSUED AS A BROTHER/REPRISE SINGLE, DEC 1974 WITH 'LANDLOCKED'S' 'SUSIE CINCINNATI' AS THE B-SIDE
3.	WINTER SYMPHONY	2.56	BRIAN WILSON	Early 70's	ORIGINALLY WRITTEN SEVERAL YEARS BEFORE THIS PROJECT
4.	MICHAEL ROW THE BOAT ASHORE	3.32	TRAD.	Early 70's	RECORDED DURING THE 'BIG 15 ONES' SESSIONS
5.	SEASONS IN THE SUN	3.20	BREL-MCKUEN	1968	ACTUALLY RECORDED CIRCA LATE '68, PRODUCED BY TERRY JACKS WHO LATER RECORDED HIS OWN VERSION & HAD A MASSIVE HIT WITH IT.
6.	HOLY EVENING	3.20	DENNIS WILSON	Circa76/77	ESSENTIALLY A DENNIS WILSON SOLO EFFORT
7.	ALONE ON CHRISTMAS DAY	2.53	B WILSON-M LOVE	Circa76/77	COMPLETELY DIFFERENT SONG TO 'CHRISTMAS DAY' WHICH APPEARED ON THEIR 1964 XMAS ALBUM
8.	GO AND GET THAT GIRL	2.59	C.TULEJA-R.ALTBACH	Circa76/77	THIS ONE ONLY SCRAPES IN AS HAVING ANY RELEVANCE TO XMAS AT ALL
9.	SANTA'S GOT AN AIRPLANE	3.26	B.WILSON-M.LOVE	Circa76/77	THIS IS BASICALLY 'H.E.L.P. IS ON THE WAY' WITH XMAS LYRICS
10.	I SAW MOMMY KISSING SANTA CLAUS	2.17	BRIAN WILSON	Circa76/77	NOT THE FAMOUS SONG, BUT A 'NEW SONG WITH THE ONLY SIMILARITY BEING THE LYRICS
	- OUTTAKES -				
11.	I SAW MOMMY KISSING SANTA CLAUS (A.K.A. 'WALKIN')	2.12	BRIAN WILSON	Circa76/77	INSTRUMENTAL & BACKING VOCALS ONLY
12.	I SAW MOMMY KISSING SANTA CLAUS	1.11	CONNOR	Circa76/77	THE ORIGINAL SONG WITH THE BEACH BOYS OWN CHILDRENS' CHORUS
13.	XMAS MEDLEY : GOD REST YE MERRY GENTLEMEN, COME ALL YE FAITHFUL, HARK THE HERALD ANGELS SING, WE WISH YOU A MERRY CHRISTMAS	2.19	TRADITIONAL	Circa76/77	FEAT. THE BEACH BOYS, FAMILIES AND CHILDRENS' CHORUS
14.	KONA CHRISTMAS (MELE KALIKI MAKO)	2.27	A.JARDINE-M.LOVE	Circa76/77	'M.I.U.' ALBUM SONG, 'KONA COAST' W / CHRISTMAS LYRICS
15.	BELLS OF CHRISTMAS	2.20	B.WILSON-M.LOVE-R.ALTBACH	Circa76/77	REJECTED FROM THE ALBUM'S FINAL LINE-UP, LATER APPEARED ON 'M.I.U.' LP AS 'BELLES OF PARIS' WITH NEW NON-XMAS LYRICS
	- BONUS TRACKS -				
16.	JINGLE BELL ROCK	2.26	JOE BEAL-JIM BOOTH	1983	RARE 45 ISSUED BY MIKE LOVE & DEAN TORRENCE AS A DUO
17.	HAVE YOURSELF A MERRY LITTLE CHRISTMAS	3.01	MARTIN-BLANE	1983	FROM THE U.S. ONLY, (CASSETTE ONLY) RELEASE ON 'HITBOUND' CALLED 'CHRISTMAS PARTY' (MIKE SOLO)
18.	DO YOU HEAR WHAT I HEAR ?	3.30	MANNING-RAGNEY-SHAYNE	1983	THIS SONG FORMED THE BASIS FOR MICHAEL JACKSON'S 'WE ARE THE WORLD' - A TRULY LOVELY MELODY
19.	LITTLE SAINT NICK	1.56	BRIAN WILSON	1964	(ALTERNATE VERSION) SUCH A RADICAL RE-WORKING MOST CONSIDER IT AS A DIFFERENT SONG ALL TOGETHER
20.	LITTLE SAINT NICK	2.01	BRIAN WILSON	1964	(SINGLE VERSION) DIFFERENT TO LP VERSION
21.	AULD LANG SYNE	1.21	TRADITIONAL	1964	(ALTERNATE VERSION) DIFFERENT TO LP VERSION
22.	THINGS WE DID LAST SUMMER	2.29	J.STYNE-S.CAHN	Circa '63	ESSENTIALLY A CHRISTMAS SONG, THE ORCHESTRA WAS ARRANGED BY DICK REYNOLDS WHO ALSO DID THE '64 XMAS ALBUM
23.	THE LORD'S PRAYER	2.33	ALBERT HAY MALOTTE	1964	ORIGINAL B-SIDE OF THE 'LITTLE SAINT NICK' SINGLE
24.	LITTLE SAINT NICK	1.50	BRIAN WILSON	1964	BACKING TRACK ONLY FROM THE 'STACKS OF TRACKS' ALBUM
25.	HOLY EVENING	3.22	DENNIS WILSON	Circa76/77	FINAL MIX
26.	BRIAN WILSON XMAS MESSAGE	0.15	BRIAN WILSON	1987	WARNER BROS PROMO LP TRACK FOR XMAS 1987

TOTAL CD TIME 65.55

Brother records

BEACH BOYS JOURNALS PART 2

Above, the man in the mask is Billy Hinsche. Dennis missed this Halloween 1971 session at Brian's house. Carl and Brian have make-up on. The costumes got the group in the mood to record a special Halloween message that was to be mailed to radio stations but apparently never was.

BEACH BOYS JOURNALS PART 2

COMPUTER ENHANCED - DIGITALLY REMASTERED

The Beach Boys

JOURNALS PART 2 VOL.3 (1968-75)

CD - 19

AFTER MUCH DELIBERATION WE DECIDED TO PLACE ALL THE **BEST** RARITIES INTO CHRONOLOGICAL ORDER TO CREATE A 'LISTENING HISTORY' OF THE BAND THROUGH '18 YEARS OF HARMONY'. WE WOULD NORMALLY KEEP SPOKEN MESSAGES & LIVE TRACKS SEPARATE, BUT IN THE CHRONOLOGICAL SENSE, WE FELT IT NECESSARY TO INTEGRATE THEM WITH STUDIO MATERIAL SO AS TO CREATE A BETTER 'FEEL' FOR THE MUSICAL CIRCUMSTANCES THAT THESE TRACKS WERE RECORDED IN (& THE AUDIENCE'S PERCEPTION OF THE GROUP). **ONLY** 4 OF THESE TRACKS HAVE EVER BEEN OFFICIALLY RELEASED WORLD WIDE (TKS 1, 2, 6 &7) AMONG THE TRACKS MAKING THEIR DEBUT APPEARANCE ON CD ARE VEGETABLES' & 'LADY' WHICH HAD DAYS SPENT ON THEM IN OUR CEDREM SOUND LAB 'DE-CLICKING' AN ACETATE TO MAKE IT LISTENABLE - THE END RESULT IS SENSATIONAL !

#	SONGTITLE	TIME	SONGWRITERS	RECORDING DATE	COMMENTS
1.	WALK ON BY	0.56	BACHARACH-DAVID	May 26 '68	SHORT (BUT EXCELLENT) TRIBUTE TO 1 OF BRIAN'S FAVORITE SONGWRITING TEAMS.
2.	OLD FOLKS AT HOME / OL' MAN RIVER	2.34	STEPHEN FOSTER / KERN-HAMMERSTEIN II	May 26 '68	BRIAN'S ON-GOING LOVE AFFAIR WITH TRADITIONAL SONGS CONTINUES
3.	WE'RE TOGETHER AGAIN	2.32	B.WILSON-R.WILSON	Sep 11 '68	(INSTR) BACKING TRACK
4.	WE'RE TOGETHER AGAIN	2.08	B.WILSON-R.WILSON	Sep 11 '68	(INSTR) 'SLIDE' GUITAR (ETC) OVERDUBS ONTO BACKING TRACK
5.	WE'RE TOGETHER AGAIN	2.14	B.WILSON-R.WILSON	Sep 11 '68	(EARLY MIX) DIFF. TO 'FINAL MIX' (ON 'LANDLOCKED') & SLIGHTLY LONGER
6.	BLUEBIRDS OVER THE MOUNTAIN	2.50	ERSEL HICKEY	Nov '68	SINGLE A-SIDE. 'DRASTICALLY' STEREO MIX WITH ALMOST NO BRASS (COMPLETELY DIFFERENT MIX TO THE '20 / 20' LP)
7.	BREAKAWAY	2.53	BRIAN WILSON-R.DUNBAR (AKA MURRY WILSON)	Mar/Apr '69	SINGLE A-SIDE (NON LP TRACK) & SELDOM FOUND ON 'HITS' COMPILATIONS AS IT WAS A 'FLOP' IN MOST COUNTRIES
8.	WE GOTTA GROOVE	2.09	UNKNOWN	Circa '70	LITTLE IS KNOWN OF THIS EXCEPT THAT IT COOKS
9.	MY SOLUTION	3.37	BRIAN WILSON	Oct '70	NO DOUBT 'SUBSTANCE ASSISTED' LEAD VOCAL IS BILLY HINSCHE WITH BRIAN, CARL, AL, MIKE AND BRUCE (RECORDED DURING EVENING OF HALLOWEEN).
10.	(INTRO-:)	0.42		Feb '71	LIVE ON U.K. TV'S 'DAVID FROST SHOW' IN FEB 1971 WITH CARL, AL MIKE AND DENNIS (BRIAN NOT PRESENT)
11.	VEGETABLES	2.15	B.WILSON-VAN DYKE PARKS	Feb '71	" " "
12.	(INTRO-:)	1.30		Feb '71	" " "
13.	FALLIN' IN LOVE (A.K.A. 'LADY')	2.33	D.WILSON-G.JACOBSON	Feb '71	" " "
14.	(INTRO-:)	0.28		Feb '71	WITH THE GRATEFUL DEAD APRIL 27 1971 AT NEW YORK'S FILLMORE EAST. AFTER 'SEARCHIN' THEY PLAYED 2 SONGS BY THEMSELVES - (GOOD VIBRATIONS & I GET AROUND) - THEN WERE JOINED AGAIN BY 'THE DEAD' (FOR TRACKS #17 - 19)
15.	SEARCHIN'	4.47	LEIBER-STOLLER	Feb '71	
16.	RIOT IN CELL BLOCK #9	4.18	LEIBER-STOLLER	April 27 '71	" " "
17.	HELP ME RHONDA	3.08	B.WILSON	April 27 '71	" " "
18.	OKIE FROM MUSKOGEE	3.08	MERLE HAGGARD	April 27 '71	" " "
19.	JOHNNY B. GOODE	3.10	CHUCK BERRY	April 27 '71	" " "
20.	'CARL AND THE PASSIONS/ PET SOUNDS'	1.00		Early '72	(60 SEC RADIO AD) CARL & THE PASSIONS 'SO TOUGH' WAS ONLY RELEASED SEPARATELY IN A FEW COUNTRIES, NOT IN USA WHERE IT WAS AVAILABLE AS A DOUBLE LP WITH 'PET SOUNDS'
21.	'CARL AND THE PASSIONS/ PET SOUNDS'	0.30		May '72	(30 SEC RADIO AD)
22.	YOU NEED A MESS OF HELP TO STAND ALONE	3.28	B.WILSON-J.RIELEY	Early '72	ALTERNATE MIX TO THE CARL & THE PASSIONS' ALBUM
23.	DENNIS WILSON	0.18		Mid '72	(REGISTER TO VOTE RADIO SPOT) THE BEACH BOYS WERE STILL FIGHTING THEIR 'UN-COOL' IMAGE, SO THESE RADIO SPOTS WERE PART OF AN OVERALL EFFORT TO IMPROVE THEIR PUBLIC PROFILE. CARL WAS ALSO FIGHTING A BATTLE AGAINST BEING CONSCRIPTED INTO THE ARMY.
24.	CARL WILSON	0.21		Mid '72	" " "
25.	RICKY FATAAR	0.26		Mid '72	" " "
26.	MIKE LOVE	0.26		Mid '72	" " "
27.	AL JARDINE	0.17		Mid '72	" " "
28.	WE GOT LOVE	4.45	R.FATAAR-B.CHAPLIN-M.LOVE	Late '72	RECORDED FOR 'HOLLAND' AND ACTUALLY MADE THE FIRST (ONLY) GERMAN PRESSING, WAS THEN CULLED AND REPLACED BY 'SAIL ON SAILOR'
29.	'HOLLAND'	1.00		Jan '73	(60 SEC RADIO AD) 'SAIL ON SAILOR' WAS THOUGHT TO BE 'HOLLAND'S' SAVING GRACE, HENCE THE PREDOMINANCE DURING THE OPENING OF THIS PROMO SPOT.
30.	CALIFORNIA FEELING	2.46	B.WILSON-S. KALINICH	Late '74	REPORTED BY U.K. MAG. N.M.E. AS BEING A TRACK RECORDED FOR AN UP-AND-COMING ALBUM RELEASE (WHICH DIDN'T EVENTUATE)
31.	CARL WILSON 'GETT OFF'	0.30		1975	(ANTI HARD DRUG MESSAGE) WHO BETTER TO ADVISE YOUTH ON THE DANGERS OF DRUGS THAN A MEMBER OF THE BEACH BOYS ?
	TOTAL CD TIME 64.11				

Brother records

BEACH BOYS JOURNALS PART 2

BEACH BOYS JOURNALS PART 2

COMPUTER ENHANCED - DIGITALLY REMASTERED

The Beach Boys
JOURNALS PART 2 VOL.4 (1976-78)

CD - 20

ON THIS CD WE'VE BEEN ABLE TO OFFER 3 OUTTAKES FROM DENNIS WILSON'S ABANDONED 'BAMBOO' ALBUM. WE ALSO HAVE 3 REJECTS FROM '15 BIG ONES' 8 TRACKS ORIGINALLY SLATED FOR RELEASE ON THE 'ADULT CHILD' LP, PLUS A LOT OF SOLO OFFERINGS THROUGH THE LATE '70'S UNTIL THE EARLY '80'S. MANY OF THESE TRACKS, IN FACT, HAVE NEVER BEEN ON CD **OR** VINYL BEFORE AND COME FROM PERSONAL TAPE COLLECTIONS FROM AROUND THE WORLD. 'BRIAN'S BACK' HERE IN DEMO FORM, A COMPLETED VERSION BEING AVAILABLE ON THE 'LANDLOCKED' CD IN THIS SET.

#	SONGTITLE	TIME	SONGWRITERS	RECORDING DATE	COMMENTS
1.	HONKIN' DOWN THE HIGHWAY	2.48	BRIAN WILSON	Early '76	ORIGINAL SESSION FOR 'LOVE YOU' ALBUM
2.	BRIAN'S BACK	2.54	MIKE LOVE	Early '76	ORIGINAL DEMO
3.	SEA CRUISE	3.26	HUEY P. SMITH	Early '76	OUTTAKES FROM '15 BIG ONES' SESSIONS. AS THE ALBUM'S RECORDING SESSIONS CONTINUED, A DOUBLE ALBUM WAS ENVISAGED WITH A WORKING TITLE OF 'PICK YA UP AT 5'. THESE THREE WERE CULLED WHEN THE SINGLE LP '15 BIG ONES' WAS DECIDED ON. (SEA CRUISE WAS EVENTUALLY ISSUED ON '10 YEARS OF HARMONY')
4.	ON BROADWAY	3.10	MANN-WEILL-SPECTOR	Early '76	"
5.	MONY MONY	2.50	JAMES-CORDELL-BLOOM-GENTRY	Early '76	"
6.	HEY LITTLE TOMBOY	2.22	BRIAN WILSON	Early '76	TRACKS FROM THE UNREALIZED 'ADULT CHILD' ALBUM, WHICH DESPITE BEING HERALDED AS A BRIAN WILSON SOLO PROJECT, CONTAINED MANY BEACH BOY TRACKS INCLUDING THESE
7.	SHORTENIN' BREAD	2.50	TRAD. ADAPTED BRIAN WILSON	Early '76	"
8.	BE MY BABY	2.57	SPECTOR-GREENWICH-BARRY	Early '76	"
9.	IT'S TRYING TO SAY (A.K.A. 'BASEBALL')	2.09	BRIAN WILSON	Circa 76/77	(DENNIS SINGS) "
10.	LINES	1.46	BRIAN WILSON	Circa 76/77	(BRIAN SINGS) "
11.	IT'S OVER NOW	2.52	BRIAN WILSON	Circa 76/77	(CARL SINGS) "
12.	EVERYBODY WANTS TO LIVE	3.08	BRIAN WILSON	Circa 76/77	"
13.	MY DIANE	2.15	BRIAN WILSON	Circa 76/77	(DENNIS SINGS) "
14.	HOW'S ABOUT A LITTLE BIT OF YOUR SWEET LOVIN'	1.31	B WILSON-D ROVELL-M LOVE-R ALTBACH	Mid '77	REJECT FROM THE M.I.U. ALBUM
15.	LADY LYNDA	3.23	A.JARDINE-R.ALTBACH	Mid '77	ORIGINAL VERSION (CAN BE HEARD PLAYING ON A RADIO IN THE '78 FILM 'ALMOST SUMMER')
16.	RIVER SONG	4.08	D.WILSON-C.WILSON	Mid '77	ORIGINAL VERSION (TOUGHER MIX WITHOUT CHOIR)
17.	RIVER SONG	3.47	D.WILSON-C.WILSON	Mid '77	A-SIDE SINGLE
18.	FAREWELL MY FRIEND	2.27	DENNIS WILSON	Mid '77	B-SIDE TO ABOVE (THIS SONG WAS PLAYED AT DENNIS'S FUNERAL)
19.	CARRY ME HOME	3.38	D.WILSON-G.JACOBSON	Mid '77	WRITTEN FOR 'HOLLAND' BUT WAS UNRECORDED AT THE TIME AS IT WAS CONSIDERED A BIT HEAVY FOR THE BEACH BOYS. SUBJECT MATTER (AS DENNIS HIMSELF SAID) WAS A SOLDIER DYING IN VIETNAM (DENNIS IMAGINED IT WAS HIMSELF FOR INSPIRATION)
20.	GETTING HUNGRY	3.56	B.WILSON-M.LOVE	1978	RELEASED FEB '79 ON 'CELEBRATION' ALBUM FEATURING MIKE LOVE & RON ALTBACH (TK #20 ALSO SINGLE B-SIDE) TK #21 SAME SONG AS TRACK #14
21.	HOW'S ABOUT A LITTLE BIT	2.32	B.WILSON-D.ROVELL-M.LOVE-R.ALTBACH	1978	
22.	SHE'S JUST OUT TO GET YOU	3.12	M.LOVE	1978	
23.	BABY BLUE	3.19	D.WILSON-G.JACOBSON-K.LAMM	1978	SONG INTENDED FOR DENNIS WILSON'S FOLLOW-UP TO 'PACIFIC OCEAN BLUE' TENTATIVELY TITLED 'BAMBOO'. DENNIS ABANDONED THESE SESSIONS PREFERRING TO CONCENTRATE ON HIS 2 SONGS TO BE INCLUDED ON THE L.A. ALBUM 'BABY BLUE' (WHICH APPEARS HERE WITH AN EARLY MIX. NO VOCALS OVER INTRO AND NO VOCALS DURING MIDDLE SECTION) & 'LOVE SURROUND ME'.
24.	IT'S NOT TOO LATE	4.21	DENNIS WILSON	1978	"
25.	WILD SITUATION	2.16	DENNIS WILSON	1978	"

TOTAL CD TIME 70.15

Brother records

BEACH BOYS JOURNALS PART 2

BEACH BOYS JOURNALS PART 2

COMPUTER ENHANCED - DIGITALLY REMASTERED

The Beach Boys

JOURNALS PART 2 VOL.5 (1978-82)

CD - 21

OUR CHRONOLOGY CONTINUES WITH A FINE SELECTION OF BEACH BOYS' RARITIES MIXED IN WITH SOME MIKE LOVE ADVERTS AND SOME EXCELLENT SOLO MATERIAL. CERTAINLY NO ONE IN THE BEACH BOYS HAS MILKED THEIR 'SURFING' DYNASTY MORE THAN MIKE LOVE AND ON THIS DISC YOU'LL HEAR (NOT ONLY) MIKE RE-RECORDING OLD BEACH BOYS CLASSICS BUT (EGAD!) CHANGING THE LYRICS ON ONE TO MAKE 'BE TRUE TO YOUR SCHOOL' INTO A BEER AD. WE'VE ALSO BEEN ABLE TO INCLUDE ANOTHER 4 TRACKS FROM DENNIS WILSON'S ABANDONED FOLLOW-UP TO 'PACIFIC OCEAN BLUE' TITLED 'BAMBOO' & THE BEACH BOYS' EXCELLENT REVIVAL OF NEIL SEDAKA'S 'CALENDAR GIRL'. FOR THE FANS OF DENNIS WE HAVE HIM SINGING 'GOOD TIMIN'' WHICH SEEMS AS THOUGH IT WAS THE ONE & **ONLY** TIME HE EVER DID SO!

#	SONGTITLE	TIME	SONGWRITERS	RECORDING DATE	COMMENTS
1.	SCHOOLGIRL	2.04	D.WILSON	1978	SONGS INTENDED FOR DENNIS WILSON'S FOLLOW-UP TO 'PACIFIC OCEAN BLUE' TENTATIVELY TITLED 'BAMBOO'. DENNIS ABANDONED THESE SESSIONS PREFERRING TO CONCENTRATE ON HIS 2 SONGS TO BE INCLUDED ON THE L.A. ALBUM.
2.	MOONLIGHT	3.26	D.WILSON	1978	"
3.	COMPANION	3.26	D.WILSON-C.MUNOZ	1978	"
4.	HE'S A BUM	2.10	D.WILSON	1978	"
5.	CALENDER GIRL	3.36	NEIL SEDAKA-H.GREENFIELD	1978	OUTTAKE FROM THE 'L.A.' ALBUM
6.	CALENDER GIRL	3.02	NEIL SEDAKA-H.GREENFIELD	1978	ALTERNATE MIX
7.	CALIFORNIA BEACH	2.41	A.JARDINE-M.LOVE	1978	ORIGINAL VERSION (LATER BECAME 'SKATETOWN U.S.A.')
8.	LET'S VISIT HEAVEN TONIGHT	3.18	B.JOHNSTON	1978	BRUCE JOHNSTON (SOLO)
9.	ALMOST SUMMER	2.20	B.WILSON-M.LOVE-A.JARDINE	1978	ORIGINAL DEMO
10.	ALMOST SUMMER	3.24	B.WILSON-M.LOVE-A.JARDINE	1978	STUDIO PLAYBACK WITH EARLY OVERDUBS
11.	TODAY I STARTED LOVIN' YOU AGAIN	0.51	UNKNOWN	End '78	(SLOW) MIKE (SOLO), FROM AN UNRELEASED ALBUM 'COUNTRY LOVE'
12.	TODAY I STARTED LOVIN' YOU AGAIN	2.00	UNKNOWN	End '78	(FAST) "
13.	HEY GOOD LOOKIN'	2.12	HANK WILLIAMS	End '78	"
14.	SKATETOWN U.S.A.	2.12	A.JARDINE-M.LOVE	Early '79	CALIFORNIA BEACH' (W/NEW LYRICS) REJECTED BY COLUMBIA PICTURES AS THE TITLE SONG FOR A SKATING MOVIE (LOST OUT TO DAVE MASON - EX 'TRAFFIC')
15.	IT'S A BEAUTIFUL DAY	3.16	A.JARDINE-M.LOVE	Early '79	BEACH BOYS SINGLE ISSUED AUG '79. ALSO ON 'AMERICATHON' SOUNDTRACK AND '10 YEARS OF HARMONY' ALBUM
16.	ANGEL COME HOME	3.55	C.WILSON-G.CUSHING-MURRAY	Apr 28 '79	LIVE IN FRONT OF AUDREY WILSON & INVITED GUESTS ON US 'MIDNIGHT SPECIAL' TV SHOW. AMAZINGLY, **DENNIS** SINGS 'GOOD TIMIN'!
17.	GOOD TIMIN'	2.46	B.WILSON-C.WILSON	Apr 28 '79	"
18.	OH! THOSE GIRLS	3.00	UNKNOWN	Circa '80	UNRELEASED MIKE (SOLO) TRACK
19.	LOOKING BACK WITH LOVE	3.28	UNKNOWN	Circa '81	OUTTAKE VERSION (OF RELEASED SINGLE) BY MIKE LOVE (SOLO)
20.	HOT SUMMER LOVERS	2.40	UNKNOWN	Circa '81/82	UNRELEASED MIKE (SOLO) TRACK
21.	ALLEY OOP / PAPA OOM-MOW-MOW	3.03	DALLAS FRAZIER / FRAZIER-WHITE-WILSON JNR-HARRIS	Circa '82	MIKE & DEAN (NO KNOWN RELEASE, BUT WAS PLAYED ON U.S. RADIO)
22.	SUN CITY	2.45	UNKNOWN	Circa '82	MIKE (SOLO) FROM A PERIOD WHEN MIKE WAS BUSY PROMOTING HAWAII AS A HOLIDAY DESTINATION.
23.	HAWAII	2.05	B.WILSON	Circa '82	MIKE'S RE-RECORDING "
24.	SUMMERTIME MUSIC	2.51	UNKNOWN	Circa '82	MIKE (SOLO) "
25.	HYATT REGENCY (WAIKIKI)	1.00	UNKNOWN	Circa '82	60 SEC ADVERTISMENT "
26.	HYATT REGENCY (MAUI)	1.00	UNKNOWN	Circa '82	60 SEC ADVERTISEMENT "
27.	BE TRUE TO YOUR BUD	2.00	BRIAN WILSON (W / NEW LYRICS)	Circa '82	2 MINUTE ADVERT FOR 'BUDWEISER' BEER (NEIL YOUNG LAMPOONED THIS SORT OF 'ROCK-STAR SELL-OUT' IN HIS SONG 'THIS NOTE'S FOR YOU')
28.	BERMUDA SHORTS	0.56	UNKNOWN	Circa '82	RECORDED DURING SOUNDCHECK
29.	DA DOO RON RON	2.56	BARRY-SPECTOR-GREENWICH	1982	MIKE LOVE & DEAN TORRENCE. FROM THE (HITBOUND / RADIO SHACK) CASSETTE ONLY RELEASE 'ROCK N' ROLL CITY' WHICH ALSO FEATURED DEAN TORRENCE (SOLO) & THE BEACH BOYS

TOTAL CD TIME 74.06

Brother records

BEACH BOYS JOURNALS PART 2

BEACH BOYS JOURNALS PART 2

COMPUTER ENHANCED - DIGITALLY REMASTERED

The Beach Boys — JOURNALS PART 2 VOL.6 (1982-88)

CD - 22

CHRONOLOGICALLY, THIS CD FINALISES THE HISTORY OF THE BEACH BOYS WITH 1988'S HIT KOKOMO (USING THE RARE SPANISH VERSION) & PROVIDES SOME OF THE RELEASED (BUT RARE) TRACKS FROM 82 THRU' 87. THIS VOLUME HAS MANY SPECIAL GUESTS INCLUDING BEATLE RINGO STARR WHO DRUMS **AND** SINGS LEAD VOCALS ON TRACK #13, 'BACK IN THE USSR' (A BEATLES SONG OBVIOUSLY INFLUENCED BY THE BEACH BOYS) THE SAME YEAR RINGO HAD PLAYED DRUMS ON A TRACK ON 'THE BEACH BOYS' ALBUM ('CALIFORNIA CALLING'). WE ALSO HAVE JULIO IGLESIAS, JIMMY PAGE & THE OAKRIDGE BOYS GUESTING AT THE ANNUAL 4TH. OF JULY CONCERT. WE'VE ALSO TAKEN THE OPPORTUNITY TO PRESENT SOME SOLO EFFORTS DURING THE 80'S, BRIAN'S EFFORTS HAVE BEEN KEPT ASIDE FOR THE CEDREM 'BRIAN WILSON' BOX SET. FOR THOSE OF YOU WHO ASSUMED THAT THE 'ROCK N' ROLL CITY' VERSION OF 'CALIFORNIA DREAMIN'' WAS THE TRACK USED FOR THE 'MADE IN U.S.A.' HITS COMPILATION WILL NO DOUBT SURPRISED TO LEARN THAT THEY ARE COMPLETELY DIFFERENT RECORDINGS & SUBSEQUENTLY THE EARLIER (CASSETTE ONLY) ROCK N' ROLL CITY VERSION APPEARS HERE.

#	SONGTITLE	TIME	SONGWRITERS	RECORDING DATE	COMMENTS
1.	LET'S PARTY	3.19	ADRIAN BAKER-MIKE LOVE	1982	MIKE LOVE & DEAN TORRENCE. FROM THE (HITBOUND / RADIO SHACK) CASSETTE ONLY RELEASE 'ROCK N' ROLL CITY' WHICH ALSO FEATURED DEAN TORRENCE (SOLO) & THE BEACH BOYS (TK #9)
2.	HER BOYFRIEND'S BACK	2.13	FELDMAN-GOLDSTEIN-GOTTEHRER	1983	MIKE LOVE & DEAN TORRENCE. " " "
3.	LIGHTNIN' STRIKES	3.05	LOU CHRISTIE-T.HERBERT	1983	MIKE LOVE & DEAN TORRENCE. " " "
4.	SUGAR SHACK	3.01	McCORMACK-VOSS	1983	MIKE LOVE (SOLO) " " "
5.	THE LETTER	2.25	W.THOMPSON	1983	MIKE LOVE (SOLO) " " "
6.	THE LOCOMOTION	3.00	GOFFIN-KING	1983	MIKE LOVE (SOLO)
7.	WHAT YOU DO TO ME	3.50	C.WILSON	1983	CARL WILSON (SOLO) SINGLE RELEASED WORLD-WIDE. A HIT IN SOME COUNTRIES
8.	CALIFORNIA DREAMIN'	2.55	J.PHILLIPS-M.GILLIAM	1983	THE BEACH BOYS ORIGINAL VERSION (FROM 'ROCK 'N' ROLL CITY') A COMPLETELY DIFFERENT RECORDING TO THE 'MADE IN THE U.S.A.' VERSION.
9.	PROBLEM CHILD	4.28	TERRY MELCHER	1984	FROM THE MOVIE SOUND TRACK 'PROBLEM CHILD' (THE FIRST BEACH BOY RECORDING AFTER DENNIS DIED.
10.	PROBLEM CHILD	3.40	TERRY MELCHER	1984	INSTRUMENTAL BACKING TRACK
11.	EAST MEETS WEST	4.14	UNKNOWN	1984	(WITH FRANKIE VALLI) FLOP 45 COLLABORATION
12.	CHASIN' THE SKY	4.10	UNKNOWN	1985	FROM THE RARE SOUNDTRACK TO THE MOVIE 'UP THE CREEK'
13.	BACK IN THE U.S.S.R.	3.01	LENNON-McCARTNEY	1985	(FEAT. RINGO STARR) WASHINGTON DC, USA (LIVE)
14.	COME GO WITH ME	2.35	C.E.QUICK	1985	(WITH THE OAKRIDGE BOYS) WASHINGTON DC, USA (LIVE)
15.	SURFER GIRL	2.12	BRIAN WILSON	1985	(WITH JULIO IGLESIAS) WASHINGTON DC, USA (LIVE)
16.	BARBARA ANN	2.57	FRED FASSERT	1985	(WITH JIMMY PAGE & FRIENDS) WASHINGTON DC, USA (LIVE)
17.	HAPPY BIRTHDAY AMERICA	4.30	UNKNOWN	1986	MIKE LOVE'S '4TH OF JULY' ALBUM TRACK, UNCREDITED ON ALBUM'S SLEEVE OR LABEL, ONLY A 'POST PRESSING' STICKER ON THE SHRINK WRAP INDICATED ITS EXISTANCE (STUDIO **NOT** LIVE)
18.	HAPPY ENDINGS	4.24	B.JOHNSTON-T.MELCHER	1987	(WITH LITTLE RICHARD) 45 FROM SOUND TRACK FOR 'THE TELEPHONE' STARRING WHOOPI GOLDBERG.
19.	KOKOMO	3.27	PHILLIPS-MELCHER-LOVE-McKENZIE	1988	(SPANISH VERSION) ISSUED IN SOME COUNTRIES AS A BONUS TRACK ON THE VINYL (ONLY) RELEASE OF THE 'STILL CRUISIN'' ALBUM (& AS A 45 IN SPANISH SPEAKING COUNTRIES)

TOTAL CD TIME 74.00

Brother records

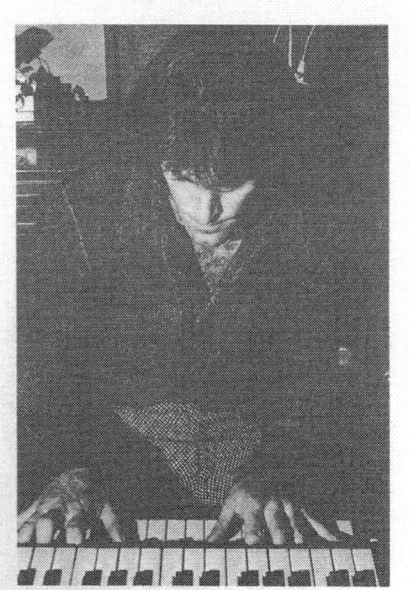

BEACH BOYS JOURNALS PART 2

Above, The Beach Boys in 1977. Opposite bottom, From behind the stage of the Oakland Stadium, July 2, 1976.

BEACH BOYS JOURNALS PART 2

COMPUTER ENHANCED - DIGITALLY REMASTERED
CEDREM 17

The Beach Boys

JOURNALS PART 2 VOL.7 LIVE RARITIES (71-86)
CD - 23

RATHER THAN PROVIDING JUST ANOTHER CD OF MOSTLY 'HITS', WE THOUGHT THE TRUE FANS WOULD MUCH PREFER A COLLECTION OF SONGS RARELY HEARD LIVE IN CONCERT. COUPLED WITH A RARE LIVE RELEASE FROM 1986'S (USA & VINYL) 'SUNKIST' COMPILATION '25 YEARS OF GOOD VIBRATIONS'. THE ONLY COVER VERSION ON THIS DISC WHICH IS NOT 'TRADITIONAL' OR AN OLDIE FROM THE 50'S OR 60'S IS ONE OF DENNIS WILSON'S LEAD VOCAL EFFORTS 'YOU ARE SO BEAUTIFUL' CO-WRITTEN BY **BILLY PRESTON**, THE ONLY ARTIST TO HAVE (SHARED BILLING WITH AND) PLAYED **LIVE** WITH THE BEATLES (**AND THE ROLLING STONES!**). ONLY THE FIRST & LAST SONGS HAVE EVER BEEN OFFICIALLY RELEASED IN LIVE FORM & EVEN 'RUNAWAYS' LP RELEASE IS VERY RARE WORLDWIDE. SANDWICHED BETWEEN THOSE TWO IS A FEAST OF RARITIES PERFORMED LIVE WHICH ARE NOT ON **ANY** OF THE BEACH BOYS 4 OFFICIAL LIVE ALBUMS - : 'CONCERT', 'LIVE IN LONDON' & THE DOUBLE LP 'IN CONCERT'. IF YOU OMIT 6 TRACKS FROM 'IN CONCERT' & SKIP TRACK #1 HERE, THIS CD IS PERFECT TO PLAY WITH ALL 4 RELEASED LIVE ALBUMS TO CREATE (IF YOU WISH) YOUR OWN 'CONCERT HISTORY' FROM 1964 TO 1986.

#	SONGTITLE	TIME	SONGWRITERS	YEAR	COMMENTS
1.	WOULDN'T IT BE NICE	1.54	B.WILSON-T.ASHER	1971	SINGLE ISSUED IN MAY '71, PERFORMED OCT '70 'BIG SUR', CALIFORNIA, USA ALSO APPEARED ON 'CELEBRATION AT BIG SUR' ALBUM.
2.	INTRO	0.44			
3.	VEGETABLES	2.04	B.WILSON-VAN DYKE PARKS	1971	SYRACUSE UNIVERSITY, NEW YORK, USA MAY 1 1971. (ONLY CARL, MIKE, AL & BRUCE - DENNIS & BRIAN NOT PRESENT)
4.	'SURF CITY' REQUEST	0.14		1971	" " "
5.	COOL COOL WATER	3.27	BRIAN WILSON	1971	" " "
6.	IT'S ABOUT TIME	3.24	D.WILSON-B.BURCHMAN-A.JARDINE-C.WILSON	1971	" " "
7.	INTRO	0.25		Feb 24 '72	LIVE IN HOLLAND 1972, DUTCH TV SHOW 'GRAN GALA DU DISQUE'
8.	SURF'S UP	5.06	B.WILSON-VAN DYKE PARKS	Feb 24 '72	" " "
9.	INTRO	0.25		Feb 24 '72	" " "
10.	STUDENT DEMONSTRATION TIME	5.19	LEIBER-STOLLER (W / NEW LYRICS MIKE LOVE)	Feb 24 '72	" " "
11.	SHORTENIN' BREAD	2.44	TRAD. ADAPTED BY B WILSON	1979	NASSAU COLISEUM LONG ISLAND, NEW YORK U.S.A. MAY 14, 1979 (WITH DENNIS)
12.	PEGGY SUE	2.03	HOLLY-ALLISON-PETTY	1979	" " "
13.	ROLLER SKATING CHILD	1.55	BRIAN WILSON	1979	" " "
14.	IT'S OK	1.54	B.WILSON-M.LOVE	1979	" " "
15.	409 (EXCERPT)	0.36	B.WILSON-G.USHER	1979	" " "
16.	SUMAHAMA	2.44	M.LOVE	1979	" " "
17.	ANGEL COME HOME	3.31	C.WILSON-G.CUSHING-MURRAY	1979	" " "
18.	YOU ARE SO BEAUTIFUL	1.39	BILLY PRESTON-BRUCE FISHER	1979	" " "
19.	GOOD TIMIN'	2.11	B.WILSON-C.WILSON	1980	PHILADELPHIA, PENNSYLVANIA, U.S.A. MAY 18 1980
20.	SOME OF YOUR LOVE	2.17	B.WILSON-M.LOVE	1980	" " "
21.	GOIN' ON	2.38	B.WILSON-M.LOVE	1980	" " "
22.	LIVING WITH A HEARTACHE	4.02	C.WILSON-R.BACHMAN	1980	" " "
23.	DISNEY GIRLS	4.25	B.JOHNSTON	1980	" " "
24.	KEEPIN' THE SUMMER ALIVE	3.37	C.WILSON-R.BACHMAN	1980	KNEBWORTH, LONDON, ENGLAND JUNE 21, 1980
25.	SCHOOLDAY (RING! RING! GOES THE BELL)	3.16	CHUCK BERRY	1980	" " "
26.	LADY LYNDA	4.37	A.JARDINE-R.ALTBACH	1980	" " "
27.	I WRITE THE SONGS	3.55	B.JOHNSTON	1980	" " "
28.	RUNAWAY	2.30	M.CROOK-DEL SHANNON	1986	U.S.A; 1986
	TOTAL CD TIME 73.43				

Brother records

BEACH BOYS JOURNALS PART 2

Above, Dennis streaks

Above, Onstage Oakland Coliseum, December, 1976.

BEACH BOYS JOURNALS PART 2

COMPUTER ENHANCED - DIGITALLY REMASTERED

The Beach Boys

JOURNALS PART 2 VOL.8 LIVE HITS (71-93)

CD - 24

THE LAST OF THE CD'S IN THIS SET & THE FINAL IN OUR 16CD 'HISTORY' IS A SELECTION OF MOSTLY HIT SINGLES PERFORMED LIVE OVER A 22YEAR PERIOD. WE FINISH IT WITH THE MOST RECENT LIVE APPEARANCE AVAILABLE (1993) PLUS A RARE 3 SONG SELECTION AIRED DURING THE 'LIVE AID' CONCERT IN 1985. ALTHOUGH 'COOL COOL WATER' & 'IT'S ABOUT TIME' WERE NOT HITS, THEY WERE A-SIDE SINGLES, SO WE'VE INCLUDED THEM HERE. FOR MORE OBSCURE TRACKS LIKE 'ANGEL COME HOME' CHECK OUT 'LIVE RARITIES'. AS WITH 'LIVE RARITIES' YOU CAN USE THIS TO MAKE UP YOUR OWN 'LIVE HISTORY' (BY UTILIZING SONGS #1, 6, 11, 19, 20, 24 & 25 ALTHOUGH #11 & 24 CAN BE ALSO FOUND ON 'JOURNALS' VOL.1.) INTERESTING TO NOTE THAT CARL SINGS THE 'BICYCLE RIDER' LYRICS DURING 'HEROES & VILLAINS' WHICH IS MISSING FROM THE RELEASED VERSION. SOME OTHER HITS WHICH ARE MISSING HERE CAN BE FOUND ELSEWHERE IN THIS SERIES IN LIVE FORM, FOR EXAMPLE, YOU CAN FIND 'COME GO WITH ME' ON DISC 6 IN THIS BOX SET & 'DON'T WORRY BABY' IS IN 'JOURNALS' VOL.1.

#	SONGTITLE	TIME	SONGWRITERS	RECORDING DATE	COMMENTS
1.	COTTONFIELDS	3.04	HUDDIE LEDBETTER	May 1 '71	SYRACUSE UNI, NEW YORK, USA (FEAT. CARL, MIKE, AL & BRUCE ONLY, DENNIS & BRIAN NOT PRESENT) 1971
2.	CAROLINE NO	3.07	B.WILSON-T.ASHER	May 1 '71	" " "
3.	INTRO	0.34		May 1 '71	" " "
4.	AREN'T YOU GLAD	3.06	B.WILSON-M.LOVE	May 1 '71	" " "
5.	YOU STILL BELIEVE IN ME	2.35	B.WILSON-T.ASHER	May 1 '71	" " "
6.	CATCH A WAVE	2.48	BRIAN WILSON	May14'79	NASSAU COLISEUM, LONG IS., NEW YORK, USA (W / DENNIS)
7.	SURFER GIRL	2.33	BRIAN WILSON	May14'79	" " "
8.	HEROES AND VILLAINS	3.47	B.WILSON-VAN DYKE PARKS	May14'79	" " "
9.	BARBARA ANN	2.32	FRED FASSERT	May14'79	" " "
10.	IN MY ROOM	2.20	B.WILSON-G.USHER	May18'80	PHILADELPHIA, PENNSYLVANIA, USA 1980
11.	BE TRUE TO YOUR SCHOOL	2.28	BRIAN WILSON	May18'80	" " "
12.	HELP ME RHONDA	3.49	BRIAN WILSON	May18'80	" " "
13.	FUN FUN FUN	3.50	B.WILSON-M.LOVE	May18'80	" " "
14.	CALIFORNIA GIRLS	3.13	BRIAN WILSON	June21'80	KNEBWORTH, LONDON, ENGLAND 1980
15.	SLOOP JOHN B	3.08	TRAD. ARR. BRIAN WILSON	June21'80	" " "
16.	DARLIN'	2.32	B.WILSON-M.LOVE	June21'80	" " "
17.	GOD ONLY KNOWS	2.28	B.WILSON-T.ASHER	June21'80	" " "
18.	DO IT AGAIN	3.11	B.WILSON-M.LOVE	June21'80	" " "
19.	LITTLE DEUCE COUPE	1.46	BRIAN WILSON	June21'80	" " "
20.	ROCK AND ROLL MUSIC	2.34	CHUCK BERRY	June21'80	" " "
21.	I GET AROUND	2.07	BRIAN WILSON	June21'80	" " "
22.	WOULDN'T IT BE NICE	2.55	B.WILSON-T.ASHER	July '85	'LIVE AID', PHILADELPHIA, PENNSYLVANIA, USA 1985
23.	GOOD VIBRATIONS	4.34	B.WILSON-M.LOVE	July '85	" " "
24.	SURFIN' USA	3.04	CHUCK BERRY (W/ LYRICS BY B.WILSON)	July '85	" " "
25.	SUMMER IN PARADISE	4.26	M.LOVE-T.MELCHER-C.FALL	July '93	WEMBLY, LONDON, ENGLAND, UK 1993

TOTAL CD TIME 72.33

Brother records

BEACH BOYS JOURNALS PART 2

Below, Sunflower originally had a different song alignment and a different title.

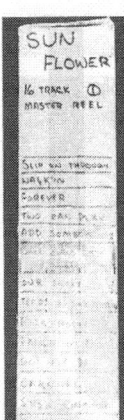

Bruce, Dennis, Mike, Brian, Alan, and Carl

BEACH BOYS JOURNALS PART 2

Gone are the white Levis, tennies and striped shirts. Gone too are the odes to affluent hedonism, replaced by a host of ecologic, mystic and poetic preoccupations. Yet despite the beards, beads and plugs for TM, the Beach Boys, after 15 years in the business, remain identifiably the Beach Boys. Alone among white American rock groups, their ingenuity has sustained them over a decade, at times shaping, at times ignoring the whims of passing fancy.

The elements of their style are by now legend: the vocals, densely clustered or moving in counterpoint, simultaneously frail and precise; the compositions, some complex, others elementary, some anthemlike, others confessional, some a catalog of clichés, others a revision of rock orthodoxy.

In the Sixties, when they were at the height of their original popularity, the Beach Boys propagated their own variant on the American dream, painting a dazzling picture of beaches, parties and endless summers, a paradise of escape into private as often as shared pleasures. Yet by the late Sixties, the band was articulating, with less success, a disenchantment with that suburban ethos, and a search for transcendence. It has been a curious trek from hot rods and high times to religion and conservation; yet through it all, the Beach Boys have remained wed to the California that Chuck Berry once called the "promised land"—and their resurgent popularity says as much about the potency of that chimera as it does about the Beach Boys.

They were winners from the start: "Surfin'," their first release on a local L.A. label, made the city's charts in 1961. At a time when rock had become a game for Tin Pan Alley pros, the Beach Boys were very much a family affair: Brian Wilson, 19, his brother Dennis, 17, and Carl, at 15 the youngest Wilson, formed the original group, together with cousin Mike Love and their Hawthorne neighbor, Alan Jardine.

In surfing, the Beach Boys had hit upon a potent image. Leisure, mobility and privacy—it was the suburban myth transported to the Pacific Ocean, but rendered heroic. There had been "surf bands" (such as Dick Dale's) in California before the Beach Boys, but these bands played a homogeneous brand of instrumental rock, crossed with rhythm and blues; the Beach Boys, with their neatly trimmed harmonies, were projecting a world view.

"Surfin' Safari," the group's first national hit on Capitol, launched surf music as a fad; by "Surfin' U.S.A.," the Beach Boys' followup in early 1963, the group had perfected a style. Working off a cop from Chuck Berry's "Sweet Little Sixteen," Brian and Mike contrived a set of lyrics that revealed no small flair for constructing teen utopias ("If everybody had an ocean . . ."); and the music itself was no less striking. While the blanched vocals harked back to the Four Preps, the guitars had the crude drive of a high school band; coming in the midst of teen idols, Brill Building pop and seductive "girl groups," the first Beach Boys hits managed to sound raunchy and vital, yet clean, somehow safe—for here was a rock and roll band aspiring to the instrumental sleekness of the Ventures, the lyric sophistication of Chuck Berry, and the vocal expertise of some weird cross between the Lettermen and Frankie Lymon and the Teenagers.

Surfin' U.S.A., the group's second album, sold extraordinarily well at a time when singles were still the barometer of pop success. When the Beach Boys returned to the studio, it was under the tutelage of Brian Wilson, who became the band's producer. The Beach Boys thus were one of the first rock groups with studio control; and to a large extent, their history is the story of the records Brian made.

He was not your average rock and roll star. Moody and withdrawn, Brian never quite fit the carefree stereotype the early Beach Boys so carefully cultivated. Onstage, he smiled a lot, but looked awkward; the show focused on the mugging of Mike and Carl, and the athletic sex appeal of Dennis. In the safety of the studio, on the other hand, he was the group's dominant voice, always plotting fresh departures and refining old ideas, rarely content to recycle a tried and true formula. Like his idol Phil Spector, he came to be considered something of an oddball genius.

The first LP he produced for the Beach Boys, *Surfer Girl*, hinted at things to come. For the first time, Brian used his falsetto extensively, sharing lead vocals with Mike Love, whose nasal drone propelled all of the group's early uptempo hits. The group's harmonies veered toward the modern voicings of the Four Freshmen, and the success of "Surfer Girl," a cool ballad, enabled Brian to fill the album with similarly romantic fare, tied to surfing in name only. More importantly, Brian let a little of himself be expressed; on "In My Room," his pure falsetto, soaring over violins (another innovation), carried a message of suburban-bred agoraphobia at variance with (although not unrelated to) the Beach Boys' official posture of nonstop kicks: "There's a world where I can go/And tell my secrets to/In my room. . . ."

Throughout this early period, the Beach Boys refined their sound. On straight rockers, they sang tight harmonies behind Love's lead, with Carl contributing crisp, if rudimentary, guitar lines; on the ballads, Brian played his falsetto off against lush, jazz-tinged voicings, often using (for rock) unorthodox harmonic structures. At the same time, the group's pursuit of Fun, whether on a surfboard or in a car, set them apart and assured them of an audience, no matter how restrictive the specific motifs—although surfing, cars and the California locale all became emblematic, of course.

California—in 1963, it was the one place west of the Mississippi where everyone wanted to be. Rich and fast, cars, women, one suburban plot for everyone: a sea of happy humanity sandwiched between frosty mountains and toasty beaches, all an

The Beach Boys

BEACH BOYS JOURNALS PART 2

easy drive down the freeway. But was it that simple and bright? Behind the pursuit of fun, you might hear a hint of tedium, or a realization that each day blemished the pristine Youth this culture coveted. Brian Wilson understood this perfectly, and, characteristically, made it attractive and not a little heroic, as in "I Get Around," in which he expresses sheer frustration: "I'm gettin' bugged drivin' up and down the same old strip...." His business was the revitalization of myths he wished were true and knew were false. The hollowness, properly dressed up as adolescent yearning, could itself be marketed in "teen feel" pop songs.

Brian Wilson in any case was after something more than simple celebrations of suburbia. Throughout 1963, Phil Spector's Crystals and Ronettes recordings poured epic crescendos of sound into three-minute singles. The resonance and self-conscious imagery of Spector's records caught Brian's ear. From 1964 to *Pet Sounds* (May 1966), he dedicated himself to duplicating that oceanic sound. He would wed the Beach Boys' own harmonic expertise to Spector's use of layered percussion and orchestration. But Brian was not after mere imitation; the same impacted density would amplify his own lyrical themes. Suburban values wouldn't be abandoned—they'd be rendered profound, their ambiguities expressed.

"Fun, Fun, Fun" and "Don't Worry Baby" marked the break. "Don't Worry," ostensibly about a drag race, represented an earnest confession of insecurity: "Well, it's been buildin' up inside of me for, oh, I don't know how long/I don't know why, but I keep thinkin' something's bound to go wrong." The vocal arrangement underlined this vulnerability at every turn, casting the lyric's anxiety against a soothing expanse of overdubbed harmony parts. The Beach Boys were beginning to push pop conventions to their limits.

Meanwhile, hit followed hit, each marking some small advance over its predecessor. After "I Get Around," a brilliant teen anthem mounted with unorthodox chord changes, the singles toyed with an ever broader palette of colors. "Dance, Dance, Dance" was the most successful musically, an unabashed rocker driven by Spectoresque percussion (sleigh bells, castanets, tambourine). But "When I Grow Up (to Be a Man)" stands as Brian's most touching work of the period. Its sad queries ("Will I dig the same things that turned me on as a kid?") formed an admission of the ephemerality of youth, the passage of time underlined by the tolling of years on the refrain ("16, 17").

By 1965, "California Girls" and *Summer Days (and Summer Nights)*, Brian's style had fully developed. The group's last unadulterated fling at summer in the suburbs, *Summer Days* included such highlights as "Let Him Run Wild," a cyclical construct that recalled Holland-Dozier-Holland at Motown as much as it evoked Phil Spector. Brian had tamed the studio, just as the group had mastered his daunting arrangements.

Yet Brian increasingly played the recluse, dropping all concert dates with the band to concentrate on composing and producing. Commercially, the Beach Boys stayed on top, churning out virtually flawless singles, which, after "Surfin' U.S.A.," almost always reached the Top 30 nationally. Brian Wilson, however, wasn't looking back.

Not without regret, the Beach Boys, presumably at Brian's behest, abandoned their search for the perpetual followup. Perhaps, as some have claimed, Brian Wilson was consumed by a desire to better the Beatles; or perhaps, more simply, he was intent on working out the music already in his mind. Whatever the reasons, Wilson now focused all of his energy on creating an album that would fully reflect the Beach Boys' capabilities, by elaborating a new intricacy and a new seriousness of intent.

Their next album, *Pet Sounds*, ushered in a turbulent period for the group. While "Wouldn't It Be Nice," the opening cut, presented Brian's fantasy of marital bliss, the rest of the record vented Wilson's obsession with isolation, cataloging a forlorn quest for security. The whole enterprise, which smacked slightly of song cycle pretensions, was streaked with regret and romantic languor: "I had to prove that I could make it alone now/But that's not me." But it worked; sweetening each cut with everything from chamber strings to a lonesome koto, Wilson distilled a potent brew, both confessional and maudlin, in the melodramatic fashion of Paul Anka. The Beach Boys have never quite recaptured the sustained brilliance of Brian's settings for these songs; and it was his music that carried the lyrics and made them evocative rather than trite.

The record's conclusion was pessimistic, charting the inevitability of change. By closing the cycle on a note of resignation ("Where did your long hair go?/Where is the little girl I used to know?"), "Caroline, No" revealed the emptiness of Brian's daydream on "Wouldn't It Be Nice." Unfortunately, such expressions of adolescent angst were not everybody's cup of tea: compared to previous Beach Boy albums, *Pet Sounds* sold poorly.

As if to prove the Beach Boys could still cut a happy-go-lucky Top 40 single, Brian countered with "Good Vibrations," a foray into full-fledged psychedelia. Through dozens of overdubs and six months of painstaking work, the group created their biggest hit to date.

It was Brian Wilson's finest hour as a producer. Opening over muted bass, organ triplets and a brace of flutes, Carl's lead vocal lent the song a hushed intimacy; and the voicings on the refrain were scored over a rapidly bowed bass and theremin, the song's "psychedelic" ingredient. In midstream, harpsichord, jew's-harp, tambourine, sleigh bells and thickly carpeted vocals swirled into a retard—and suddenly "Good Vibrations" became a meditation for organ, breathy vocals and possibly wind chimes (Brian's penchant for weird per-

BEACH BOYS JOURNALS PART 2

cussion reached new heights here).

Not satisfied with this symphonic million-seller, Wilson pressed on. In 1967 he and lyricist Van Dyke Parks were hard at work on a new, more humorous song cycle. The work was to be called *Smile*, and would include a four-part suite on the elements, as well as "Heroes and Villains," "Vegetables," "Cabinessence" and "Surf's Up." Designed as Brian's crowning achievement, *Smile* would supposedly place the Beach Boys right next to the Beatles in the pantheon of arty rock.

But personality problems had begun to take their toll. As legend has it, Brian, suddenly paranoid, destroyed most of the album's laboriously assembled vocal tracks. The group began objecting to Brian's increasing eccentricity, and Brian himself was reportedly depressed by the appearance of *Sgt. Pepper*. *Smile* finally collapsed under the accumulated pressures.

In its wake, the Beach Boys issued an abridged version of "Heroes and Villians," and *Smiley Smile*, a substitute for *Smile*. Long on parched humor and short on ambitious new music, the album was anticlimactic, to put it mildly. It was also the first album produced by the Beach Boys collectively.

Smiley and its successor, *Wild Honey*, marked a turning point for the Beach Boys. In its heyday, the band had dominated the charts thanks to Brian's skill at cutting hit singles; since the early songs were composed by a performing member of a performing group, they could be successfully re-created onstage. But starting with *Pet Sounds*, the music's complexity virtually precluded live performance; even worse, many of the new lyrics hardly hinted at the sunny fare Beach Boy fans expected. Perhaps sensing defeat in his effort to broaden the group's scope, Brian retreated; after *Wild Honey*, his contributions diminished, often taking the shape of writing three or four tunes for an album.

A few scattered tracks like "Darlin' " and "Do It Again" dented the Top 20 in 1967 and 1968; and in Europe, the Beach Boys' popularity continued unabated. But the days of coasting on the charts were over.

Unhappy with their Capitol contract, the band played out their last two years with the label. On albums like *Friends*, it almost seemed as if they were attempting, defiantly, to be uncommercial. A return to *Smiley's* dryness, minus the weirdness, *Friends* cast the Beach Boys as auteurs: coming from anybody else, the album would have been embarrassing; coming from them, it had the ring of autobiographical truth.

Brian, in the songs he contributed to the venture, returned to the suburban themes that have always preoccupied him; only now, the good life appeared as an exercise in ennui: "I get a lot of thoughts in the mornin'," sang Brian in "Busy Doin' Nothin'." "I write 'em all down/If it wasn't for that, I'd forget 'em in a while." At their best, the Beach Boys have never flinched before their own banality. "Busy Doin' Nothin'," for example, featured an entire verse devoted to dialing a telephone and not getting an answer. It is one of Brian's most subtle lyrical conquests.

Friends, when set against the success of "Do It Again," a summer-fun rehash, illustrated the band's dilemma. On the one hand, by milking familiar formulas, they could still command an audience; on the other hand, whenever they released a personal statement, or experimental material, the group found themselves performing in a vacuum.

With the expiration of their Capitol contract in 1969, the Beach Boys thus faced several questions. Should they disband in the face of sporadic sales and indifferent response? Should they change their name, a liability in "hip" circles, and aim exclusively at the burgeoning market for "progressive rock"? Or should they continue as before, retain their original name and identity, and record whatever material they felt appropriate?

The answers came in 1970. The Beach Boys signed with Reprise Records, reactivated their own Brother Records logo (which had appeared on *Smiley Smile's* label), played the Big Sur Folk Festival, and issued *Sunflower*, their strongest album since *Pet Sounds*. In name, style and sound, they remained the Beach Boys.

In the five years since, the group has reestablished a loyal following among a new generation, and emerged as one of the biggest live acts in the U.S. In addition, they have continued to record new original material, with fitful public response.

Surf's Up, released in 1971, epitomized the post-*Pet Sounds* Beach Boys. On such tracks as "Long Promised Road," Carl Wilson emerged as Brian's heir apparent, a composer with an intuitive grasp of the Beach Boys' style. But *Surf's Up* also contained large doses of puffery, pretentiousness and ecological nonsense. Truth to tell, the Beach Boys had evolved into an accomplished, idiosyncratic but sometimes sterile ensemble, at least in the studio.

On the road it was a different story. Although the band had been a concert draw in the mid-Sixties, its skid on the charts had brought a virtual halt to touring. The group's pact with Reprise, however, dictated a new strategy: since most of America hadn't heard them since the Sixties, or had never heard them, the Beach Boys decided to return to the road and perfect their live performance. Initially, they labored over contemporary material, finally mastering such difficult songs as "Wouldn't It Be Nice."

But it was the surfing and car songs that brought audiences to their feet. At first the group persisted in largely performing recent material, but as the crowds grew, the pressure to concentrate on the oldies became irresistible. Eventually, in 1974, they found themselves blessed with a million-selling Number One album. They were back on top. There was only one small problem: *Endless Summer*, their first gold record since "Good Vibrations," consisted entirely of tracks cut before 1965.

Left: (1) The Beach Boys circa 1966 (with Brian in the car next to Mike Love); (2) The first album; (3) The Boys in 1967; (4) and (5) Two group shots, sans Brian, from 1966. (1, 3 & 4, Capitol Records)

BEACH BOYS JOURNALS PART 2

To Brian, the problem must have seemed particularly acute. On the one hand, he now composed moody, introspective miniature operas, like " 'Til I Die" on *Surf's Up*—although he was reportedly reluctant to release the song, because it wasn't "fun." On the other hand, he was still capable of writing happy-go-lucky songs like those behind the Beach Boys' initial popularity, as "Marcella" on *Carl and the Passions* showed. Unfortunately, almost all of his writing had become baroque, condensed, difficult to execute forcefully, and, apparently, difficult for an audience to hear. They wanted the cheerful values of the early Sixties reaffirmed, resoundingly, in the compelling and straightforward fashion of the early hits. What Brian for his part wanted was considerably less clear: perhaps just to trundle around the house and run the Radiant Radish, his organic-foods shop in Hollywood.

Buried by a tidal wave of nostalgia, and more or less abandoned by Brian, their greatest creative asset, the Beach Boys had little choice but to embrace their past. Hooking up with Jim Guercio, managing and marketing mastermind for Chicago, they triumphantly toured to sellout crowds. But in the meantime, little new material emerged from the studios.

Ironically, Brian Wilson remains the group's guiding light. It is Brian's old songs that the band plays night after night; and it is Brian's new songs that stand out on the later Beach Boy albums. Indeed, the Beach Boys remain beholden to a style bequeathed them by Brian. From the nasal raunch of "Surfin' Safari" to the convoluted elegance of "Surf's Up," that style has become a nearly autonomous fund of favored themes, production tricks and chord progressions. In tacit acknowledgment of his continued preeminence, even in absentia, 1973's *Holland* opened and closed with a new song by Brian Wilson.

But the future remains uncertain. For one thing, Brian by the end of 1975 had yet to resume an active role within the group despite persistent rumors to the contrary; for another, the group is almost exclusively identified in the public's mind with its hits from the early Sixties. Like Chuck Berry, the Beach Boys lyrically and musically reflect an era; yet like the Beatles, the band has matured and progressed within the confines of a unique style. In many respects, they are the most innovative white rock and roll band the United States has ever seen. But whether they will ever be able to lead their audience beyond the uncomplicated suburban utopia their early hits so brilliantly depicted is another question entirely.

Discography

Singles
"Surfin' " (Candix 331; ☆75, 1962). "Surfin' Safari" (Capitol 4777; ☆14, 1962). "Ten Little Indians" (Capitol 4880; ☆49, 1962). "Surfin' U.S.A." b/w "Shut Down" (Capitol 4932; ☆3, 1963). "Surfer Girl" b/w "Little Deuce Coupe" (Capitol 5009; ☆7, 1963). "Be True to Your School" b/w "In My Room" (Capitol 5069; ☆6, 1963). "Fun, Fun, Fun" (Capitol 5118; ☆5, 1964). "I Get Around" b/w "Don't Worry Baby" (Capitol 5174; ☆1, 1964). "When I Grow Up (to Be a Man)" (Capitol 5245; ☆9, 1964). "Wendy" (Capitol E.P. 5267; ☆44, 1964). "Dance, Dance, Dance" (Capitol 5306; ☆8, 1964). "Do You Wanna Dance?" (Capitol 5372; ☆12, 1965). "Help Me, Rhonda" (Capitol 5395; ☆1, 1965). "California Girls" (Capitol 5464; ☆3, 1965). "The Little Girl I Once Knew" (Capitol 5540; ☆20, 1965). "Barbara Ann" (Capitol 5561; ☆2, 1966). "Sloop John B" (Capitol 5602; ☆3, 1966). "Wouldn't It Be Nice" b/w "God Only Knows" (Capitol 5706; ☆8, 1966). "Good Vibrations" (Capitol 5676; ☆1, 1966). "Heroes and Villains" (Brother 1001; ☆12, 1967). "Wild Honey" (Capitol 2028; ☆31, 1967). "Darlin' " (Capitol 2068; ☆19, 1967). "Friends" (Capitol 2160; ☆47, 1968). "Do It Again" (Capitol 2239; ☆20, 1968). "I Can Hear Music" (Capitol 2432; ☆24, 1969). "Break Away" (Capitol 2530; ☆63, 1969). "Add Some Music to Your Day" (Reprise 0894; ☆64, 1970). "Long Promised Road" (Brother/Reprise 1047; ☆89, 1971). "Sail On Sailor" (Brother 1138; ☆79, 1973). "Surfin' U.S.A." (Capitol 3924; ☆36, 1974).

Albums
Surfin' Safari (Capitol 1808; ☆32, 1962). *Surfin' U.S.A.* (Capitol 1890; ☆2, 1963). *Surfer Girl* (Capitol 1981; ☆7, 1963). *Little Deuce Coupe* (Capitol 1998; ☆4, 1963). *Shut Down—Vol. 2* (Capitol 2027; ☆13, 1964). *All Summer Long* (Capitol 2110; ☆4, 1964). *The Beach Boys' Concert* (Capitol 2198; ☆1, 1964). *The Beach Boys Today* (Capitol 2269; ☆4, 1965). *Summer Days (and Summer Nights)* (Capitol 2354; ☆2, 1965). *The Beach Boys' Party* (Capitol 2398; ☆6, 1965). *Pet Sounds* (Capitol 2458; ☆10, 1966). *Best of the Beach Boys—Vol. 1* (Capitol 2545; ☆8, 1966). *Best of the Beach Boys—Vol. 2* (Capitol 2706; ☆50, 1967). *Smiley Smile* (Brother 9001; ☆41, 1967). *Wild Honey* (Capitol 2859; ☆24, 1967). *Friends* (Capitol 2895; ☆126, 1968). *Best of the Beach Boys—Vol. 3* (Capitol 2945; ☆153, 1968). *20/20* (Capitol 133; ☆68, 1969). *Close Up* (Capitol 253; ☆136, 1969). *Sunflower* (Reprise 6382; ☆151, 1970). *Surf's Up* (Reprise 6453; ☆29, 1971). *Pet Sounds/Carl and the Passions "So Tough"* (Reprise 2083; ☆50, 1972). *Holland* (Reprise 2118; ☆36, 1973). *The Beach Boys in Concert* (Reprise 6484; ☆25, 1973). *Endless Summer* (Capitol 11307; ☆1, 1974). *Spirit of America* (Capitol 11384; ☆8, 1975). *Good Vibrations: Best of the Beach Boys* (Reprise 6484/Brother 2223; ☆25, 1975). *20/20 and Wild Honey* (Reprise 2166; ☆50, 1974). *Friends and Smiley Smile* (Reprise 2167; ☆125, 1974).
(Chart positions taken from Joel Whitburn's *Record Research*, compiled from *Billboard* Pop and LPs charts.)

The Beach Boys in 1971 (clockwise from top left: Brian, Mike Love, Al Jardine, Bruce Johnston, Dennis Wilson, and, in the center, Carl Wilson). (Annie Leibovitz)

BEACH BOYS JOURNALS PART 2

BEACH BOYS JOURNALS PART 2

Surf's Up In Central Park

The Beach Boys pulled their woodie into Central Park's Great Lawn and celebrated over fifteen years of California high-life while a capacity New York City crowd danced and cheered along with them. Photographer Lynn Goldsmith donned her wet suit and dived right into the swim of things for *ROCK SCENE*.

Mike Love urges everyone to sing together ... and they do!

Carl and Mike had better not be messed with ... or are they meditating?

The eternal Beach Boys gather together for a group photo by their backstage trailer. That's Carl, Al, Dennis, Brian (looking quite sprightly!) and Mike.

BEACH BOYS JOURNALS PART 2

BEACH BOYS PARTY!

Photos: Lynn Goldsmith

This is how it looked for the 100,000 plus Beach Boys fans who were treated to a free concert by this legendary group.

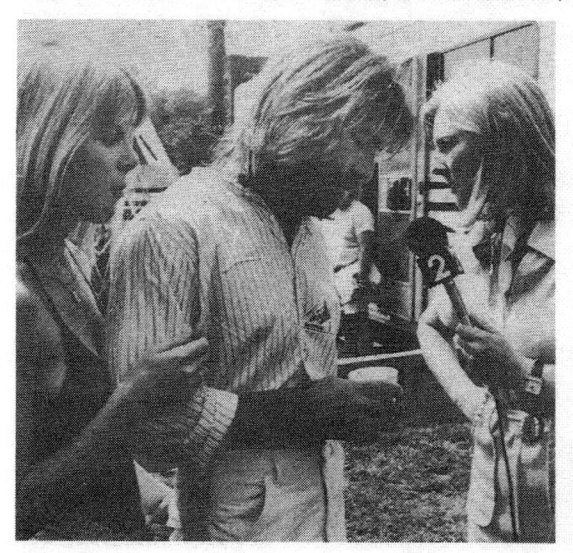

Dennis and the new Mrs. Wilson have a chat with a local television news reporter. And while you're at it, check out Dennis' new solo debut album as well, "Pacific Ocean Blue."

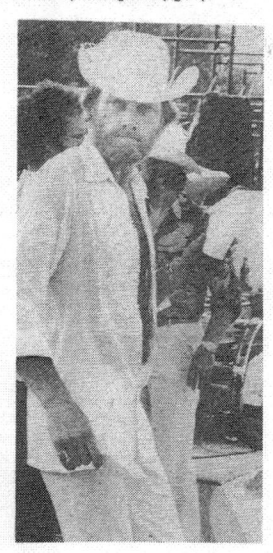

The pause that refreshes. Now what did you say the next song was...?

BEACH BOYS JOURNALS PART 2

Brian's wife, Marilyn, oversees the backstage area in ante-bellum splendor... five tiers, count 'em!

"Well, east coast girls are hip/I really dig those styles they wear...."

Here's a fan who believes in putting an unmistakable message across.

And another....!

The concert was a joyous success for all concerned. Here's hoping the Beach Boys come back for a visit soon, and keep carrying those world-wide Good Vibrations... at least until Daddy takes their T-Bird away. Bust your buns! □

BEACH BOYS JOURNALS PART 2

THE BEACH BOYS (AND BRIAN WILSON) LOVE YOU

Richard Cromelin probes the Wilson mind in Los Angeles

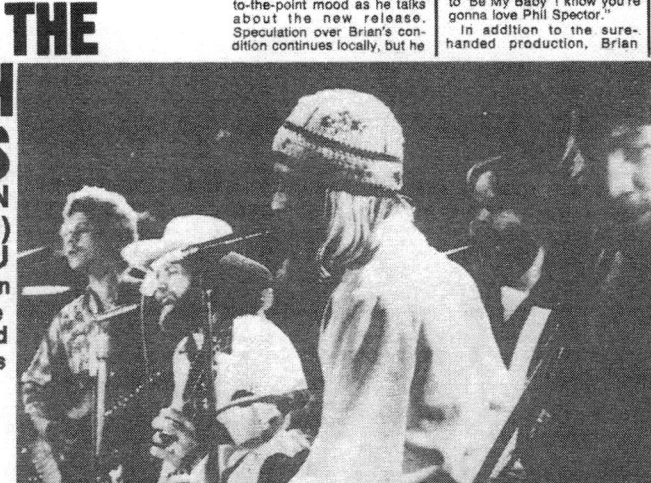

LAST YEAR'S '15 Big Ones,' in which Brian became reacquainted with the Beach Boys, must be considered something of an interim album, what with its several antique rock'n'roll numbers, one backdated Beach Boys song and its aura of a band working to find its feet. The follow-up, it figured, would be the one to watch for a broader, accurate reading on the Beach Boys condition.

The album, 'The Beach Boys Love You', is done, and here's what Brian Wilson thinks: "This is really the first time since 'Pet Sounds' that I've felt this thoroughly satisfied with an album. I think it gives a little bit — it *gives*, it has a little extra. There's more to it than just throwing the stuff in there and getting it over with and getting it out to make money."

Brian, framed against a bay window in his Bel Air living room on a rainy, decidedly un-Beach Boys day, is in a terse, to-the-point mood as he talks about the new release. Speculation over Brian's condition continues locally, but he appears to be functioning just fine, he's parted company with his psychiatrist, he played a bundle of live sets with the Beach Boys last year, and now 'The Beach Boys Love You' testifies that his participation in the group is more than tokenism.

People may persist in finding lost marbles all over the Wilson estate, but his knack for producing records is undiminished. Brian's mention of 'Pet Sounds' is appropriate, not because 'Love You' matches the classic stride for stride, but because the sound — emphasizing a very versatile and musical synthesizer over conventional rock-band structure — regains the dense, spacious volumes and the delectably textured wall-of-sound carryover that marked 'Pet Sounds'.

In one lyric, Brian tips his hat to the boss: "Come on, listen to 'Da Doo Ron Ron' now/Listen to 'Be My Baby'! I know you're gonna love Phil Spector."

In addition to the sure-handed production, Brian wrote everything on the album, collaborating only on "Good Time" (with Mike Love) and "Ding Dang" (Roger McGuinn). Brian explains his recent compositional outburst:

"Well, my (then) psychiatrist took me to the studio and put me on a program of songwriting. He just said, 'I want you to write songs. That's your job in life, you're supposed to write songs, and you might as well just sit down and start writing songs.' I said, 'Alright, I'll give it a try.' So I sat down and I wrote a song a day for 14 or 15 days."

The songs he came up with stick close to the Beach Boys basics, dealing in a disarmingly direct fashion with teenage recreation and romance. There's also a bit of Wilson whimsy, a touch of the offbeat, and, especially on side two, some personal, poignant verses that are substantial without being weighty. The primary thrust of the album, though — particularly cuts like "Good Time", "Roller Skating Child" and "Honkin' Down the Highway" — is that old-fashioned, "Fun, Fun, Fun" exhilaration.

Brian's comparison of the 'Love You' sessions with last year's studio stint points up the contrast: "15 Big Ones" was harder. We had a difficult time amongst us. We quibbled a lot and there were strange weird feelings that kind of fouled me up. I got through it.

"These last sessions were much more productive. The guys were a lot happier, they seemed really with it. Of course, Mike and Al being meditators, they're always with it. Carl was a little more receptive to everything, and Dennis of course. The Beach Boys were much more receptive this time around, and I was in a much better frame of mind than I'd been in for a long time, so we were able to work on the album *together*."

Brian also sings six leads, and while the charitable listener might point out the raw urgency and the new R&B flavor his vocals provide, the fact remains that his erratic pitch and intonation are more distracting than satisfying. Brian won't admit to such shortcomings, but he does have his regrets:

"I wish I hadn't done that many leads. We should really mix it up so we all get a chance at it. I did a little more than my share this time, and next time we'll divide it up so it's not quite like that."

Brian's summation of the current Beach Boys temper and his own role in the band support the encouraging tone of "The Beach Boys Love You":

"I do feel more like a member now again. It's a little easier to cope now. I played about 35 shows last year. It was a little scary to be out there, but it was very productive, and the group worked hard together, and I was just thrilled to be part of it.

"The group's very positive about it. They act a lot more positive than they ever have before, especially about doing tours and everything like that. The boys believe in themselves, they believe they have something good to offer people and they're doing their job."

Lest you think Brian Wilson has gone completely normal and neutral, though, he leaves us with a little preview of his latest creative process:

"There's a song called 'Everybody Wants to Live.' It's about how you throw a cigarette butt in the toilet and it goes, 'Pft.' I think it's a cute song. It could be a smash. It's a moody thing. It starts out, 'A cigarette butt when you throw it in the water goes "Pft,"' but the trick is you shouldn't laugh.' It's a funny song. It starts off funny and gets serious."

Not *too* serious, we hope.

The Beach Boys — It's not all happiness and love inside The Sand Box

While we've all joyously reported the return of Brian Wilson to the Beach Boys flock, it seems the band themselves are not too ecstatic about the whole deal.

Apparently, it was Brian's wife Marilyn who insisted on her hubby's return, a decision which has divided the group sharply down the middle. Dennis and Carl Wilson were very annoyed and, though Al Jardine and Mike Love were all for letting Brian take over the controls, it is Love who seems to resent his intrusion most vehemently. "I'm not going on the road like some broken-down rock star," said Love.

Diplomatic Carl, who has really outclassed Brian's recent Beach Boys contributions with his own and not gained sufficient credit, was "depressed" after the release of the current 15 Big Ones album, while Dennis Wilson put it more strongly: "We were heartbroken. People have waited a long time, anticipating a new album — I hated to give them this. It was a great mistake to put Brian in full control. He was always the absolute producer, but little did he know that in his absence people grew up; we became as sensitive as the next guy. Why should I relinquish my rights as an artist? The whole process was a little bruising".

In fact the group used to sneak into the studio after Brian left to add extra backing vocals and instrumentation. As one critic said of Brian: "There is no logical definition of art that says past genius justifies present sterility."

C. Side

BEACH BOYS JOURNALS PART 2

'BACKSTABBING BEACH BOYS

A special Movin' on report from Los Angeles

Why the band nearly broke up

AFTER 16 years together, and after the triumphant comeback of leader Brian Wilson, the Beach Boys recently came perilously close to disbanding completely.

Shortly after they signed a multi-million-dollar contract with CBS-distributed Caribou Records, an argument over their management nearly split the group at the seams.

The immediate problem, according to a source close to the Beach Boys, centred on Dennis and Carl Wilson's dissatisfaction with manager Steve Love (brother of Beach Boy, Mike Love, and Brian's bodyguard Stan Love).

On September 2, the last day of their whirlwind East Coast tour and the day after a large free concert in Central Park, the simmering disagreement erupted into a bitter shouting match between Dennis Wilson and Mike, Steve and Stan Love.

DENNIS WILSON... alone and (left) with the Beach Boys he nearly left.

BEACH BOYS JOURNALS PART 2

The first indication that something was amiss came during an interview at the hotel where Dennis stayed while the band was in New York. Dennis had been talking about the free concert the day before and about his recently released solo album, "Pacific Ocean Blue", when he suddenly announced: "This could be the last Beach Boys concert tonight (in Providence, Rhode Island). I see the Beach Boys coming to a close, and there's a lot of backstabbing and maliciousness going on.

The band and its entourage of more than 30 people was due to fly from Providence to Los Angeles in two private planes. The flight was broken by a brief stop at Newark airport.

Dennis was planning to avoid the seven-hour flight back to L.A. by staying overnight in New York and catching a commercial flight the following day. In the process of saying goodbye to everyone, Dennis and Karen mentioned their plans, and Brian decided it would be a good idea to stay, too. But the Love contingent overruled him.

Dennis had been working on a short fuse and this ignited him. He said something to Al Jardine, the white-cowboy-suited Beach Boy who was still wearing his ten-gallon hat.

Jardine turned on Dennis with controlled fury: "We don't need you," he said. "We can make it without you."

Dennis played his hand, indicating that the group was through. Brian sat with his head bowed, unable to react. Mike Love walked out, followed closely by Dennis and Mike's two brothers.

The three Loves, Dennis and Dennis's bodyguard ended up standing in a tight circle about a metre from where I was sitting in the limousine. It was a scene right out of "Casablanca".

Both planes had their motors running, ready for takeoff, as the group of men stood and yelled at each other.

"You got into this band on Brian Wilson's coattails!" Stan Love screamed, as he towered over the others, gesticulating wildly, the veins in his neck bulging.

"You've been riding on his coattails! I'm the one that's brought him around. I'm the one that keeps him from walking out in front of buses. And, you're gonna quit on us after all that?"

Love was yelling very loudly and his was the only clearly intelligible part of the argument. I stepped out of the car to get a bead on Dennis's actual words.

The band's road manager charged at me and said: "John, why don't you get back in the car until this blows over."

His teeth were bared and he was clenching his fists. "Now I'm tellin' you nice if you know what's good for you get back in that car. This is a family argument that's been going on for 16 years and *you're not supposed to see this*."

Back in the car I could still hear Stan Love screaming at Dennis that he was riding on Brian's coattails.

It was after midnight as the limousine headed toward Manhattan. Dennis sighed heavily: "What's today's date?" he asked. "September 3? I'll remember it. The Beach Boys broke up on Al Jardine's birthday."

"They keep telling me I had my own solo album now, like I should go off in a corner and leave the Beach Boys to them. The album really bothers them. They don't like to admit it's doing so well; they never even acknowledge it in interviews.

"Mike Love never wanted me in the band. For that matter, apparently Brian didn't either, or at least not at first. My mother took my part and told Brian I had to be in the group. I never even knew about this myself until about two years ago."

A week later the situation apparently resolved itself. "The group got back together." Dennis explained at the band's Brother Studio.

Dennis Wilson insisted however, that the reconciliation may only be temporary. "What you witnessed is what you witnessed," he said.

Beach Boy: I was dead drunk

CARL Wilson of the Beach Boys quietly slipped into Sydney today freely admitting he had been "dead drunk" before he performed in Perth on Tuesday night when he fell over twice

"I had taken a valium tablet earlier in the day and then drank a couple of Polynesian maitais, so, by the time I was to go on stage, I was right out of it," he said.

Wilson, the 30-year-old youngest member of the five man group said he could remember nothing leading up to the concert.

"All I can say is I'm really sorry"

More than 300 disgusted Beach Boy fans walked out of the concert and demanded their money back after Wilson forgot words, missed high notes and fell

Beach Boy Carl Wilson . . . missed notes, words and fell over

Beach Boys face dumper

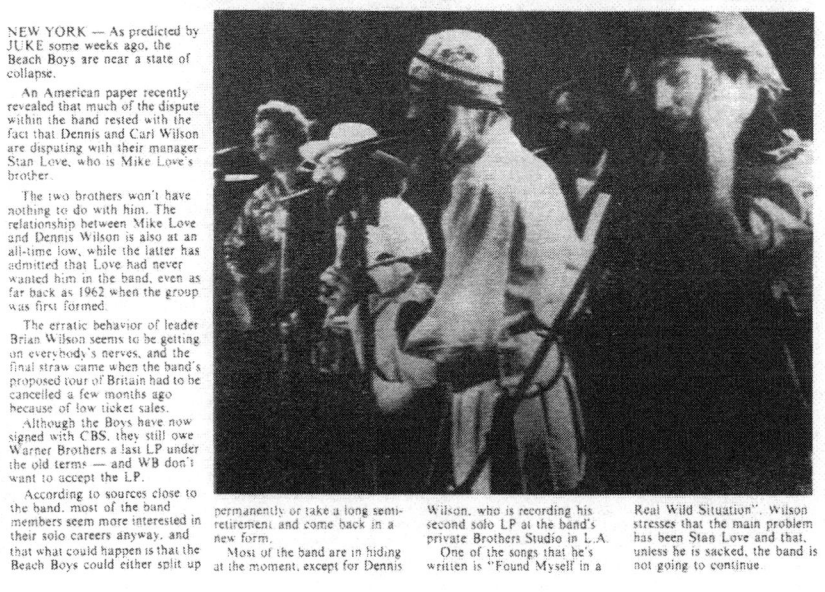

NEW YORK — As predicted by JUKE some weeks ago, the Beach Boys are near a state of collapse.

An American paper recently revealed that much of the dispute within the band rested with the fact that Dennis and Carl Wilson are disputing with their manager Stan Love, who is Mike Love's brother.

The two brothers won't have nothing to do with him. The relationship between Mike Love and Dennis Wilson is also at an all-time low, while the latter has admitted that Love had never wanted him in the band, even as far back as 1962 when the group was first formed.

The erratic behavior of leader Brian Wilson seems to be getting on everybody's nerves, and the final straw came when the band's proposed tour of Britain had to be cancelled a few months ago because of low ticket sales.

Although the Boys have now signed with CBS, they still owe Warner Brothers a last LP under the old terms — and WB don't want to accept the LP.

According to sources close to the band, most of the band members seem more interested in their solo careers anyway, and that what could happen is that the Beach Boys could either split up permanently or take a long semi-retirement and come back in a new form.

Most of the band are in hiding at the moment, except for Dennis Wilson, who is recording his second solo LP at the band's private Brothers Studio in L.A.

One of the songs that he's written is "Found Myself in a Real Wild Situation". Wilson stresses that the main problem has been Stan Love and that, unless he is sacked, the band is not going to continue.

BEACH BOYS JOURNALS PART 2

The BEACH BOYS

Nobody seems to know exactly what is happening between The Beach Boys and their record *companies*. Yes *companies*. Currently they seem to be swaying between two of 'em.

Last year I sat down with Brian Wilson and engineer Earl Mankey and heard the album that was supposed to follow *The Beach Boys Love You*. This new album, tentatively titled *Adult Child*, was supposed to come out last September. We all know that didn't happen.

What *did* happen was the Beach Boys had a flare-up with the Warner Bros Record Co. in America and announced they'd be giving their next album to CBS. They even flew to London to perform at a CBS convention; not surprisingly that performance was slagged to the outhouse and back by the English music papers – The Beach Boys had after all just cancelled a mammoth *public* London show.

And now, according to tales from the Corridors of Power, the Boys have re-opened negotiations with Warners in America.

All this has left the Australian record companies in something of a quandry. CBS and WEA don't quite know whether to bung on the limos, champagne and caviar, or ignore their arrival.

In the meantime, you can soothe your surfin' soul by running through the track listing for the mysteriously 'lost' *Adult Child* album:

Life Is For Living, (not the Sherbet song) *Hey There Little Tom Boy, Help Is On The Way* (not the Little River Band track) *It's Over Now, Everyone's Got To Live, Shortnin' Bread, Lines, On Broadway, Games, Base Ball,* and *Still I Dream Of It.*

Some of the tracks are now nearly three years old. They were originally recorded for *15 Big Ones*, the album featuring Brian's return to recording with the Beach Boys.

So there I was last year, in the studio with Earl Mankey and B. Wilson, listening to *Adult Child* and finding it very, very good.

Also in the can is a frantic reworking of the old Spencer Davis hit, **Gimme Some Lovin'**. "*Brian wants to work,*" says Earl. "*He's looking for a goal. Some of the new songs reflect his everyday situation, like* Help Is On The Way."

"It's getting easier to write songs," explains Brian.

Wilson has lost 50 pounds since the last time I saw him, and looks healthy. He spits his words out quickly. We talk about his songwriting.

"I don't carry a notebook or use a tape player," he begins. "I like to tell a story in the songs with as few words as possible. I sort of tend to write what I've been through and look inside myself. Some of the songs are messages."

Yet Brian's lyrics have never been cosmic wordplays. "I've always been insecure about my lyrics. I always felt that what I wanted to say was never really imparted in my lyrics – that the message just wasn't there.

"I'm extremely confident that the group will always get across in some way. With *The Beach Boys Love You*, there are a lot of simple you-me type songs, like the Beatles did in their early songs – things that occur between two people. I've kept it on a very simple level."

Rodney Bingenheimer arrives on the scene. Brian hugs the lad. "Rodney is as cool as honey," he grins. Bingenheimer now has a top-rated radio programme on KROQ AM, and recently did a two-hour salute to Brian on his 35th birthday.

Through glitter or this latest punk period, Bingenheimer has always played Beach Boys records. "I first met Brian and the Beach Boys at a concert in San Jose in 1963," he says.

"One time I went to a Phil Spector recording session when he was doing *River Deep, Mountain High*. Brian, Mick Jagger and myself were all in the room next to Phil. When Phil records, it's a performance, an act. When Brian records it's a very serious thing.

"Every week on my programme kids call from all over L.A. and ask if I can play some Beach Boys records. After I play *Surfer Girl* or *Mona* from the last album, more people will ring and ask where they can buy the record or who was that playing. The Beach Boys have outlasted all the fads."

Rod eventually says goodbye and proclaims, "the Beach Boys have always had the best-looking girls at their concerts." And winking, he adds, "*the Beach Boys are permanent wave!*"

Earl, Brian and myself then reminisce about Phil Spector. "The man is my hero," Brian enthuses. "He gave rock 'n' roll just what it needed at the time and obviously influenced us a lot. His productions . . . they're so large and emotional. Powerful . . . the Christmas album is still one of my favourites."

I remember checking out Brian's record collection. McCartney, Stevie Wonder and Fleetwood Mac were current tops, but his old Ronettes and Crystals 45s were so worn-out from constant play that the grooves had become mirror-like.

"It's kinda funny," says Brian. "The Bay City Rollers did one of our songs, and now B. J. Thomas had a hit with *Don't Worry Baby*. Shaun Cassidy had a number one record with Phil's *Da Doo Ron Ron*, and this group Kiss has just done *Then She Kissed Me*. And Leif Garrett's Top 5 with our *Surfin' USA*.

"We've done a lot of Phil's songs: *I Can Hear Music, Just Once In My Life, There's No Other, Chapel Of Love* . . . I used to go to his sessions and watch him record. I learned a lot . . ."

"I've always been flattered that Brian continues to say nice things about me and keeps recording my songs," says Phil Spector. "Brian is a very sweet guy and a nice human being, I'm glad he's coming out of his shell. I think he got caught in a trap with *Good Vibrations*. I think he got condemned more than condoned.

"He became a prisoner instead of a poet. He had the plaudits, the accolades and touched the masses. I know music is a very important thing to him, besides a vocation. It became cluttered the last few years. Your attitude is in the grooves, and it's a very personal thing. But Brian thrived on competition.

"I remember when *Fun Fun Fun* came out. He wasn't interested in the money, but a top ten record. He wanted to know how the song would do against the Beatles and if KFWB would play it. But I never saw Brian as a competitor."

The next day I travel to American Productions, where the Beach Boys minus Mike Love are rehearsing at noon.

Their live show is approximately two hours and 45 minutes long, the songs the group has been performing the last five years.

"A lot of the kids coming to see us now weren't even born when the first surfing hits were recorded in 1961. For a long time we refused to sing stuff like *Surfin' USA*," Carl once mentioned in an interview. "But finally we realised that we were resisting our own history. Now we've learned to embrace our past."

Later in the afternoon Brian and myself retire to a small office away from the music and noise.

"I look forward to touring. Artists like Paul McCartney, Elton John have always said nice things about the Beach Boys and myself. We've influenced a lot of groups, especially our harmonies: Electric Light Orchestra, 10cc, Queen."

What about the Beach Boys' longevity? Especially in the light of the swathe of rumours (all denied) the group is "tired" and "disintegrating".

"We're still happening. New people are picking up on us all the time. I don't really analyse why we're successful. I'm sure the Beach Boys are viewed as an institution, but the main reason for our popularity has to be the songs.

"I didn't ever think I would be back touring with the Beach Boys again. They asked me to do it and I said OK. It's like racketball (*Brian's favourite sport along with basketball*). You make a commitment once you get on the court. The other guy serves and you have to play."

Wilson's official return to the stage was July 1976 at Oakland Stadium, California. Early shows were full of chaos, bodyguards, and general hoopla.

"I feel more into it now. Rehearsals went real good. I got some of the old fire back, and I feel more positive. I feel good about myself, and once you feel good about yourself, you can touch other people. I lost weight and acquired self-discipline.

"I got really constructive. I wanted to be a full band member again. And it was the right time to tour. At first there was some pressure and high expectations from a lot of friends. I was told not to take it so seriously. But the period of adjustment wasn't as traumatic as some people think.

"I was prepared, emotionally and physically, for the task. In the early days I would also play bass, but now I'm sticking exclusively to piano. I'm a little fearful of the organ," he adds.

"It's a very haunting instrument. I like the simplicity of the piano. But the greatest addition to the Beach Boys sound is the ARP string synthesizer. I prefer it to real string sections.

"I think a lot of the songs I've written and sung reflect my life. *I Just Wasn't Made For These Times* is very deep. *Surfer Girl, Caroline No, Till I Die, California Girls* . . . These songs have a lot of strength to them; they are very pretty and have deep meanings."

On a recent Mike Douglas show he spent his whole segment talking about his drug problem and regards his retreat as *"like the Maharishi being in bed. I took anything to get me high. Insecurity set in. I took my dose of LSD and it shattered my mind, but thank God I came back.

"Cocaine at first was a beautiful high, but the comedown was awful. Heaven and hell. I lived in my room for a few years and became very paranoid. But that period is over. I feel very inspired now, and I'm even cutting down on cigarettes."*

Contrary to popular belief, he is a very accessible person. He never was guarded during his seclusion, and a number of times I'd seen him at the market or the library. He's also become used to interviews.

"Self-examination is good. My life at one time depended on the success of the Beach Boys. I kick back a bit now. I like the fact we get publicity. I think just being written about is the main thing. Public retention."

The Beach Boys' music has always gone well with films. *Shampoo* and *American Graffiti* both employed Beach Boys songs in their soundtracks. Kim Fowley, who compiled the *American Graffiti* double album soundtrack, picked *All Summer Long* for its pathos.

"This was in late '71, way before the Beach Boys became popular again to the mass audience. I grew up with them and see great film possibilities for their songs," says Fowley.

"Yes, we're thinking about movies very much. We're going to get into movies very soon," predicts Brian.

BEACH BOYS JOURNALS PART 2

March 4, 1978

The Beach Boys
IN THE PIPELINE

THE Beachboys, the longest surviving major rock band in the world, return to Australia for their first tour since the band's re-emergence with Brian Wilson at the helm.

Wilson, the band's chief songwriter who is responsible for all the band's major songs, "retired" from the group after the release of "Pet Sounds".

The album is still held by many (myself included) to be the band's greatest achievement and one of the all-time greatest rock albums.

Although he continued to contribute to the band's recorded sound, as both producer and principal songwriter, after "Pet Sounds" he ceased playing with the Beachboys in concert, and only reappeared on stage with the band following the release of "16 Big Ones", the second last album.

In the intervening years, Wilson became something of a legend in America, as the reclusive genius who never left his home and sporadically wrote songs on his piano, which was situated in a huge sandpit in the middle of his living room.

His paranoia of meeting and talking to strangers was legendary.

At one time Paul McCartney stood outside the Wilson front door one night calling out to Brian Wilson to come down and talk to him.

Wilson sat in bed listening to McCartney trying to entice him downstairs, with tears rolling down his cheeks because he couldn't bring himself to meet McCartney.

It was also well-known in rock circles, and Wilson has since openly discussed it in interviews he has done in the last 15 months as part of his "cure", that he had a drug problem.

Around the time of recording "Pet Sounds" in 1967, and the ill-fated "Smile" album, Wilson was, like The Beatles and many others, experimenting with LSD.

It was while recording the "Smile" album, part of which was eventually released as "Smiley Smile", that Wilson "flipped out".

Wilson's music was becoming breathtakingly adventurous and it was no secret that during the recording of "Pet Sounds", the other Beachboys were not at all pleased with Wilson's new musical direction, although years later when history rated "Pet Sounds" a masterpiece, they naturally maintained they could see what Brian Wilson had been trying to do.

But back then Wilson had only his own artistic instinct to tell him what to do, because he got precious little moral support from the others.

And when drugs started playing around with his judgement, Wilson began losing grip on reality, and more importantly, his music. While drugs had helped him create such masterpieces as "Good Vibrations" and "Heroes and Villians" it was also responsible for the effective demise of the Beachboys as a performing and recording band for several years.

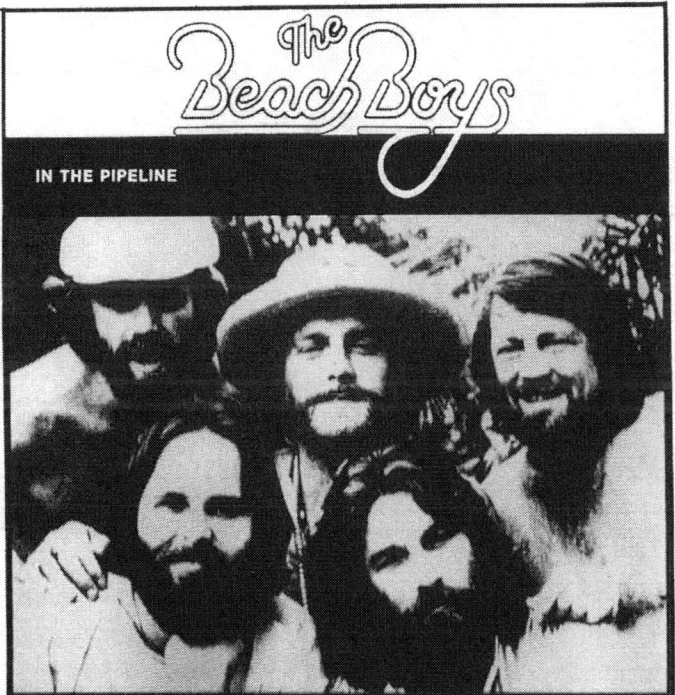

With Brian Wilson off the road and needing every encouragement to step into a recording studio or write new songs, the Beachboys began to slow slide downhill. They could still cut it as a singles band with songs like "Wild Honey", "Darling", "I Can Hear Music" and "Do It Again", but the albums of this period were patchy, to say the least.

The turning point came with the release of "Surf's Up". The title song had originally been a victim of Wilson's decision to destroy the "Smile" album tapes.

After several years of languishing in no-man's land, living off the reputation of their golden oldie classics such as "Surfing U.S.A.", "California Girls", "Fun, Fun, Fun", "Help Me Rhonda" etc., suddenly the Beachboys materialized with the goods.

It was not only notable for some of Wilson's best songs in years, but "Surf's Up" also showed that the other Beachboys had matured as songwriters.

The critical success of "Surf's Up" was encouragement to Wilson to withdraw more from his own problems, and begin to concentrate more on the world around him. But it was the release of "Holland" that was responsible for introducing a whole new generation of rock fans to the Beachboys magic.

It was now apparent that the group was functioning more as a collective, with Brian's brothers Dennis and Carl, and Mike Love, realising they could no longer rely on the brilliant but erratic Brian to always deliver the goods.

So while they continued to try and help Brian overcome his seemingly insurmountable personal problems, which now included acute paranoia about his obesity, and drugs continued to make him even more irrational and unforgotten, the others increasingly took charge of their own artistic destinies by decreasing their reliance on Brian Wilson.

That they were successful in doing this can be seen on "Surf's Up", but more importantly on "Holland", particularly on the "California Suite," the record's highpoint.

With two recent major artistic successes behind them, fans and critics alike who had become disinterested in the Beachboys late '60s early '70s output, began to sit up and take notice once more of a band which had previously seemed destined to become musically redundant.

It was only the Beachboys monumental contribution to the sounds of the early '60s that kept the band functioning as a viable musical force, during their years in the wilderness prior to "Surf's Up".

The fans who continued to make them one of America's top live attractions did so out of reverence to the early Beachboys, and the band realising the essence of its continued appeal as a live band, wisely built their act around their repertoire of golden oldies.

The strength of the newer material though, at last allowed the Beachboys the opportunity to extend themselves musically on stage, and helped rid them of the feeling of seeming to be more akin to a jukebox, than a '70s rock band.

Their stage sound was fleshed out with the addition of extra musicians, including Ricky Fataar and Blondie Chaplin for a time as permanent members of the band.

"Holland" provided the Beachboys with the opportunity to really consolidate their standing as one of the front rank rock bands, but for one reason or another it took them more than three years to record a follow-up to "16 Big Ones".

This album heralded the return as a fully functioning member, of Brian Wilson. Wilson's rejuvenation was due to the intervention of a psychiatrist who, with the assistance of personal "helpers", kept an around the clock watch on Wilson, who was suddenly put on a drug-free diet. Wilson gradually began to achieve some degree of normality as his rocketing weight was first checked, then reduced. The transformation from stumblebum drug freak to a more coherent and industrious person, inevitably led to his reunion artistically and musically with the Beachboys.

Despite worrying deafness which was another contributing factor to his original withdrawal from live performing, he once more took to the road with the band.

After a cautious start, he gradually got back into stride, to the point where sitting at the keyboards up on stage with the Beachboys seemed the most natural thing in the world for the man who before could not bring himself to meet the Beatle who wanted to tell him how much he admired the songwriter in him.

If "16 Big Ones" and its successor "Beach boys Love You", are not the gems we might have expected from a rejuvenated Brian Wilson, then perhaps we are expecting too much too soon.

Where before the group had agonized for years over the recorded of "Holland" as a follow-up album after "Carl And The Passions", they recorded two albums in the space of six months. It illustrated the band's newfound enthusiasm for recording upon Brian's return, but in retrospect it was undoubtedly a mistake.

The new album which is due any day has been much longer coming and hopefully the wait will be worthwhile.

Important as it is that the new album should confirm the Beachboys claim to today's rock 'n roll hall of fame, it won't be the end of the road if it doesn't. For already the Beachboys long career has guaranteed their immortality.

musically with the Beachboys.

Despite worrying deafness which was another contributing factor to his original withdrawal from live performing, he once more took to the road with the band.

Anyone who seeks confirmation of that fact needs only to catch one of their Australian concerts to realise the immense contribution the Beachboys have made to rock music.

It will also give many of us the first chance to glimpse Brian Wilson back on stage where he belongs.

After years of listening to "Pet Sounds" and believing in the sheer genius of Wilson, it's a bit like finally coming face to face with Elvis after all these years. Well Elvis is gone but Brian Wilson remains, and anyone who aspires to pay homage to one of the half dozen greatest contributors to the evolution of rock 'n roll, will beg, borrow or steal a ticket to see the Beachboys while they are here.

And if you want to catch up on one of the other half dozen greats, Mr. Zimmerman will be following close behind.

BEACH BOYS JOURNALS PART 2

Beach-Combin' '76

SUNTAN LOTION, shades, surfboard, deckchair, towel, paperbacks, transistor radio... there's still something missing to make Summertime complete.

The sun is hot, the mood is right, turn on the radio and there it is 'Good, good, good vibrations... instant Summer.

There seems to be a big connection between Beach Boys records and the British Summer. As soon as the sun shines, out come one of those bouncy, sunkissed numbers — or is it the other way round?

No Summer would be complete without a Beach Boys revival, and 1976 is no exception.

'Good Vibrations' was first released in late 1966 and represented the Beach Boys at their peak. Ever since it has been a popular revived 45 and popped up every now and then so as not to be forgotten — as if we could.

Now it's featuring again in the charts as a single, and as a part of Capitol Record's 'Beach Boys 20 Golden Greats' compilation.

At the same time there is The Tonics 1976 version of their 'All Summer Long' happening here, and Todd Rundgren's version of 'Good Vibrations' is strangely enough climbing the American charts.

The Beach Boys formed 15 years ago when teenager Dennis Wilson suggested to his relation Mike Love that a song about the craze of the day, surfing, would be a good idea.

A group was formed consisting of the Wilson brothers Dennis, Brian and Carl, plus Mike and a friend Al Jardine.

Fortunately for the band their first record, unsurprisingly titled 'Surfin'', was heard by a Capitol Records executive who signed them up.

Their debut for Capitol was a Brian Wilson / Mike Love composition 'Surfin' Safari' which hit the US Top 20 in 1962.

This first song set the scene for several to come. Their sound was established, and within 12 months they followed through with 'Surfin' USA', 'Surfer Girl', 'Little Deuce Coupe' and 'Be True To Your School'. Brian Wilson also worked on Jan and Dean's classic of the same period 'Surf City'.

From those early days they came up with a fantastic collection of unforgettable hits such as 'I Get Around', 'Fun, Fun, Fun', 'When I Grow Up To Be A Man', 'Help Me Rhonda', 'California Girls', 'Barbara Ann', 'Sloop John B'... the list goes on and on.

Gradually they became more sophisticated with their music, though those amazing vocal harmonies that had been evident even at the beginning were still very much part of their sound. But the songs, production and arrangements became more complex.

In Britain they first made an impact on the Top Ten with 'I Get Around' in 1964, and have been firm favourites here ever since.

'Good Vibrations' showed their new direction, and was followed by more masterpieces such as 'Heroes And Villains', 'Darlin'' and 'Break Away'.

By 1972 the band had moved to Warner Brothers and their direction and intention seemed rather muddled. The albums 'Carl And The Passions — So Tough' and 'Holland' serve to confirm this, though the track 'Sail On Sailor' from 'Holland' is a recognised classic.

Now they seem to have returned to square one, with a line up of the five original members producing '15 Big Ones' reflecting a Sixties - type feel, but comparing poorly with all those golden oldies on '20 Golden Greats'.

BEACH BOYS: sunny connection

NEW MUSICAL EXPRESS — April 16th, 1977

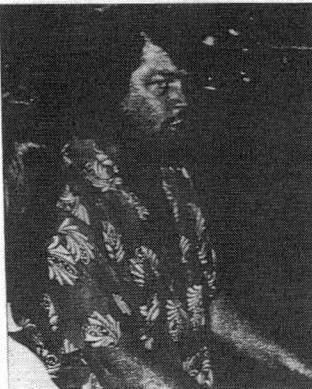

Waitin' for The Man

Waitin' for Brian Wilson, to be precise. Next to surfin' that's been THE BEACH BOYS' fave leisure pursuit. But now Brian is back and Dennis is making a solo album and... ROY CARR reports

SOME THINGS just stick in your mind. Like the very first time I ever met Dennis Wilson, during The Beach Boys' first expedition to Britain. I was a musician at the time, and by sheer coincidence we were both appearing on a Radio Luxembourg EMI-sponsored plug show with the highly imaginative title *Friday Spectacular*.

Perhaps the only lip-sync radio show in history, *Friday Spectacular* was taped each week in EMI House before an audience of around 300 precocious little horrors who knew it was all a con and acted accordingly.

After being plied with free samples courtesy of the Milk Marketing Board, these kids were more interested in seeing who could belch the loudest during transmission than in who was up on stage trying to impress the EMI warlords. Gary Glitter, or Paul Raven as he was then called, was also on the bill.

Brian Wilson was still an active member of the candy-striped shirted Californians, who were on a whistle-stop Eurotour to promote "Help Me Rhonda".

It was all a bit of a lark. Backstage, Mike Love made no secret that he was infatuated by programme-presenter Muriel Young's cleavage; Dennis Wilson was scoring the phone numbers of anything in skirts and over the age of consent; Carl Wilson and Al Jardine were on their best behaviour; while every few minutes someone had to be despatched to drag Bro' Brian out of the loo.

Meanwhile, a music publishing company rep was trying to persuade every act on the show to cover a Beach Boys song. I was offered "Little Deuce Coupe". Lambrettas I could relate to — but what the hell was a Little Deuce Coupe? Anyway, I wasn't buying.

My attention was distracted by the sound of the Brothers Wilson trying to sort out the chords of some Beatles songs.

My guitarist and I ended up teaching them both chords and lyrics to The Fabs' "I Should Have Known Better" and "Tell Me Why". And a few months later both songs appeared on The Beach Boys' best-selling "Party" album.

WE'VE ALL grown beards since then. On a recent visit to The Beach Boys' Brothers Studio at Santa Monica I hadn't been inside more than half-an-hour when Dennis suddenly leapt up from behind the control desk, wrapped a pair of cans around my ears and, joined by his extrovert friend Baron Stewart, began laying down backing vocal tracks for Dennis' first solo album, "Pacific Ocean Blues".

By the way Dennis, my bill's in the mail...

BRO' BRIAN may be projected as the creative, eccentric brains of the organisation, but it has always been left up to Dennis Wilson to live out The Beach Boys fantasy of the All-American Red Blooded Male. While - the others count the calories and meditate on mountains, Dennis is the only one who avidly follows the outdoor pursuits The Beach Boys songs have celebrated.

Dennis is an extremely physical person. When the pressures of recording become too intense he doesn't lock himself away in a closet. He lets off steam the only way he knows how.

This afternoon a thrash on a Captain Fantastic Pinball table isn't enough, and so he straps on a pair of speed-racing rollerskates and tears up 10 miles of Santa Monica's sidewalks. And later on he enters a powerboat race along the seaboard.

Come to think of it, drummers are a bit like bass players. Dark horses.

Perhaps it has something to do with being stuck either right at the back of the stage or to one side. For the most part, the rhythm section isn't called upon to do anything but lay down a backbeat, and that kinda job gives a man plenty of time to think and build up frustrations.

The result is that bass players and drummers are frequently the first sidemen to cut loose and make solo albums.

So Dennis has been recording his own album.

After just one more week of overdubbing, re-mixing and programming the set he has co-produced with Gregg Jakobson will be ready for delivery to James Guercio's CBS-distributed Caribou label.

During a break in the session, Dean Torrence (the Dean in Jan And...) arrives in the control room with a selection of visually attractive album sleeve mock-ups. Dennis agrees with Dean's choice and guarantees the artwork will be completed around the same time as the mastertape.

Dennis has recorded 14 songs (tentatively titled): "Rainbow", "Thoughts Of You", "Taking Off", "Time", "You And I", "Tug Of Love", "Pacific Ocean Blues", "River Song", "Dreamer", "Schoolgirl", "What's Wrong", "Moonshine", "Friday Night", "Farewell My Friend", "I Don't Know", "Holy Man" as well as re-recording "Only With You" from off "Holland". From these tracks he'll make a final selection.

This isn't the first time he has flown solo. In 1965 he and Gary Usher cut some singles as The Four Speeds, and, as late as 1969, cut an obscure British single "Sound Of Free" as Rumbo.

But "Pacific Ocean Blues" (originally entitled "Freckles") is his first serious commitment. Instead of hauling a bunch of El Lay's finest into the studio and completing the project in a few weeks, Wilson has chosen to play almost every instrument himself. It's taken him nine months. The sound is impressionistic in texture, and from what I've heard of it the music appears to be an ethereal reflection of the album's title.

He tells me that "Pacific Ocean Blues" is totally entrenched from any official Beach-Boys project. It's his brainchild and his alone. The only stipulation placed on it by Warner Brothers/ President Mo Ostin was that Bro' Brian should not contribute material, and that the rest of the gang should not sign on as deckhands.

IT'S COMMON knowledge that since signing The Beach Boys and Brothers in 1970, Warner-Reprise have been less than ecstatic about the group's recording schedule and their selling power. According to one Warner Executive, up until the release of "15 Big Ones" The Beach Boys had only scored one gold album for the office wall.

Hi, I'm Brian.

BEACH BOYS JOURNALS PART 2

The hey-day of The Candy-Striped Surfers.

Originally, "15 Big Ones" — one of three albums The Beach Boys were working on simultaneously to fulfil their contractual obligations to Warner-Reprise — was intended as The Beach Boys "Pin-ups". But as it transpired, only about half of the album was given over to re-running other artists' oldies: songs like "On Broadway" and "You've Lost That Loving Feelin'" being shelved, "The Beach Boys Love You" roots album is just out as I write, and a third set is in preparation.

Actually, The Beach Boys' problem started showing as far back as 1966. After the controversy that greeted "Pet Sounds", the subsequent emergence of The Beatles' "Sgt. Pepper" motivated Bro' Brian to abort his meisterwerk "Smile" and withdraw even further into his paranoid shell. Nine of the 15 "Smile" tracks were dispersed over subsequent albums, but consecutive collections like "Smiley Smile", "Wild Honey", "Friends", and "20/20" did little to transform The Beach Boys from a successful singles band into a hotshot album act.

And the move to Warner-Reprise did little either. "Sunflower" — their first offering under the new agreement — was the last album on which Bro' Brian participated.

Warner-Reprise went into shock. The Beach Boys without Brian Wilson in the driving seat just wasn't on.

Under pressure, "Surf's Up" — a collection of old unreleased masters plus some new material — temporarily pulled the band out of a skid, partly due to much emphasis being made of The Boy Wonder's involvement.

But "Carl & The Passions — So Tough" / "Pet Sounds" bombed. And the costly, highly publicised "Holland" junket was rejected and refurbished before being given a release date.

Allegedly, "Holland" didn't recoup its production costs, while "Concert" — originally a single album — had to be re-submitted before being unleashed.

Taking into consideration that The Beach Boys have been far from prolific, it's a wonder that Dennis Wilson should feel able to devote so much time and energy to producing the first of what he insists will be half-a-dozen solo albums.

"My material," he states, running his hands through his shag of hair, "doesn't necessarily concur with what The Beach Boys are doing. When there's a quorum there's a vote, and that's it. I also happen to respect Brian's judgement on such matters".

Dennis Wilson has been quoted as saying: "Brian *is* The Beach Boys. He *is* the band. We're *his* messengers. *He* is all of it. Period. We're nothing. *He's* everything".

He's still adamant. This time he tells me: "Everything I do is a stepping stone from Brian — he's taught me so much".

Whether he and the rest of the band are just playing up The Living Legend syndrome of The Troubled Genius, no one will ever admit. That's the party line and everyone toes it.

When tackled about their sporadic releases, the reply has always been that The Beach Boys are awaiting Bro' Brian's availability.

Now, it's not that Al, Carl, Dennis and Mike (or Bruce Johnston) are without talent, but it certainly does often appear that, as a collective unit, The Beach Boys are reluctant to take a major step without Brian's involvement — even though Brian's Wilson's greatest achievements have often been misunderstood. (It's a fact, that both the band and Capitol had second thoughts about "Pet Sounds" when they first heard it.)

Dennis Wilson can't offer what he feels to be an adequate explanation for depleted record sales and other similar traumas.

"I guess," he begins, "maybe the people who normally buy records just didn't want to buy ours . . . it's hard to try and understand why . . . truthfully, I dunno.

"As an artist," he continues, "and I'm speaking for myself, I have always been a little intimidated by Brian's immense talent."

He pauses. "It's like if you're in a team and the person who plays in the position you prefer also happens to be a far superior player. You tend to stand back and help his game. And like I've already stated, Brian is The Beach Boys."

Waiting on Brian Wilson's recovery has been a long, drawn-out process. In the meantime, Capitol Records re-packaging programme has kept the band hot poop by proxy, with compilations like "Endless Summer" and "Spirit Of America" topping the American best-sellers.

Dennis says he doesn't feel haunted by an illustrious past and the problems in living up to their reputation as *The All-American Rock Band*. But one doesn't have to resort to force to get him to admit that towards the close of the 60's, the Boys were beached by their American fans even though abroad their stature remained intact.

"Yeah," he sighs "The Beach Boys went through a big slump. This is what happened. At the end of the 60s there was a transition from surfin', and the record companies were so used to promoting us as surfers that they didn't realise things were changing.

"With people like Jimi Hendrix coming up, it was an image than was extremely difficult for us to try and outlive. It was a time of great change and we found it almost impossible to shake off our old identity."

Ironically, during the Beatles Boom, The Beach Boys didn't have to contend with such problems. In terms of popularity, they were at their zenith. But with Second Assault, American suddenly grew apathetic.

"I'd put it much stronger than that, they ignored us," he insists. "There's no use denying it, we suddenly went from being a very large group into being a very small group again."

He's not exaggerating — The Beach Boys actually went back to playing small clubs like the Whiskey A Go Go on Sunset Strip.

"Maybe," he reflects, "at the time, we were in the right frame of mind. Look, I could offer all kinds of theories . . . but the plain fact is that The Beach Boys went through a big dip in popularity."

How did you react?

"It broke my heart. It hurt. It's no use me saying it didn't. Believe me, it really does hurt to suddenly realise that you're *not* what you used to be. And that people don't want to know."

Hi, I'm Dennis.

AFTER 15 years in business, The Beach Boys fortunes have now turned full circle. Despite their sparse vinyl output, they're one of Planet Earth's major concert attractions.

Dennis Wilson still does a mental double-take on that count.

The final stage of their comeback began last summer. Bro' Brian had finally gotten out of bed and returned to active public life.

"Fifteen Big Ones" — the album around which his artistic re-entry was enacted and according to reliable sources, The Beach Boys first all-new album in 42 months — took a supporting role in the carnival, however, because most people seemed more intrigued by Brian's presence than the actual purpose of his resurrection.

While some treated the album as The Second Coming, the more cynical viewed it as a Mad Hatter's Tea Party. The music took a backseat as in interview after interview Brian Wilson acted . . . er, a little weird and fuelled his own Madcap Mystique.

Dennis doesn't really give a shit about what people think.

"We were more concerned with Brian's return to the group. Everyday he just gets better and better — more so when he's in the studio. And that's all that really matters."

"He's lost weight, he's healthy again and working well. I suppose a sign of any artist's true greatness is when, against all odds, they make a successful comeback."

So the Beach Boys have been let off the hook, but Dennis doesn't disguise the years of anxiety.

"I'll be truthful with you. There were many times when I'd look at my brother and think to myself, maybe he won't ever pull it together again. He went through a lot of bad times. Drugs didn't help.

"If we had lost Brian, I guess we'd have had to go on without him but we always felt in our hearts that things would turn out the way they have and we were prepared to wait and wait.

"But there were other things as well. Michael and his meditation . . . there were our divorces . . . Carl fighting the draft board . . . so many things can come down at the same time, and they did. Also, when it came to the matter of business affairs, I have to admit The Beach Boys weren't the smartest guys around."

THINGS HAVE changed quite drastically. They've tidied up their affairs both marital and business, taken stock of where the money is coming from, and more important, where it's going to. The album that led them back into the big time however, fared much better in America than it did in Europe.

And it's an album with which Dennis is dis-satisfied. He insists it should have been all-original, and that an oldies album should have been shelved for later. But he was out-voted on that score.

Dennis puts the lack of success abroad down to marketing — bearing in mind EMI's TV blitzkreig here for their "20 Golden Greats".

As a matter of interest, at the peak of its sales EMI's "20 Golden Greats" sold more copies than the combined sales of Britain's next four best-selling albums.)

However, Dennis isn't perturbed that the old still continues to outsell the new. He's philosophical on the subject. "It's all part of the same thing," he muses. "Our roots go right back to 'Surfin' and we don't try to dis-associate ourselves from our past. I'm honoured by our achievements and proud to still be around, so ultimately it doesn't really matter if the public bought more copies of '20 Golden Greats' than '15 Big Ones'. The one thing that they all had in common was that they were buying The Beach Boys."

BEACH BOYS JOURNALS PART 2

BEACH BOYS JOURNALS PART 2

THE BEACH BOYS/ A CHRONOLOGICAL DISCOGRAPHY
Compiled by Jeff Deutch

KEY:
- Album (A)
- Single (S)
- Multiple album packages (A)S
- Reissue (R)
- (B) Produced and/or written by Brian Wilson
- (C) Produced by Carl Wilson
- (D) Written and/or performed by Dennis Wilson
- (BB) Performed by the Beach Boys under another name
- (A) Produced by Ron Alibach
- (J) Produced by Bruce Johnston
- (G) Produced by James William Guercio
- (X) Produced by Jeff Baxter
- (E) Compiled by Brad Elliot

BEACH BOYS/BEACH BOYS LEAD VOCALS/BEACH BOYS PRODUCED AMERICAN LP AND SINGLE RECORDS

Date	Artist	Title	Label	(S) or (A)
12/61	BEACH BOYS	Surfin'/Luau	X 301	(S)
2/62	BEACH BOYS	Surfin'/Laua	Candix 301	(S)
3/62	KENNY & THE CADETS	Barbie/What a Young Girl Is Made Of	Randy 422	(S)
5/62	BEACH BOYS	409/Surfin' Safari	Capital 4777	(S)
6/62	RACHEL & THE REVOLVERS (B)	The Revolution/Number One	Dot 16392	(S)
11/62	BEACH BOYS	Ten Little Indians/County Fair	Capitol 4880	(S)
12/62	BEACH BOYS	Surfin' Safari	Capitol 1808	(A)
/63	BOB & SHERRY (B)	The Surfer Moon/Do the Humpty Dumpty	Safari 101	(S)
3/63	BEACH BOYS	Surfin' U.S.A./Shut Down	Capitol 4932	(S)
4/63	BEACH BOYS	Surfin' U.S.A.	Capitol 1890	(A)
5/63	FOUR SPEEDS (D)	RPM/My Sting Ray	Challenge 9187	(S)
5/63	HONEYS (B)	Surfin' Down the Swanee River/Shoot the Curl	Capitol 4952	(S)
7/63	BEACH BOYS (B)	Surfer Girl/Little Deuce Coupe	Capitol	(S)
7/63	BEACH BOYS (B)	Surfer Girl	Capitol 1981	(A)
8/63	HONEYS (B)	Pray for Surf/Hide Go Seek	Capitol 5034	(S)
9/63	FOUR SPEEDS (D)	Cheater Slicks/Four on the Floor	Challenge 9202	(S)
10/63	BEACH BOYS (B)	Little Deuce Coupe	Capital 1998	(A)
10/63	BEACH BOYS (B)	Be True to Your School/In My Room	Capitol 5069	(S)
11/63	SHARON MARIE (B)	Runaround Lover/Summertime	Capitol 5064	(S)
12/63	HONEYS (B)	The One You Can't Have/From Jimmy with Tears	Capitol 5093	(S)
12/63	BEACH BOYS (B)	Little Saint Nick/Lord's Prayer	Capitol 5096	(S)
1/64	SURVIVORS (B)	Pamela Jean/After the Game	Capitol 5102	(S)
2/64	BEACH BOYS (B)	Fun, Fun, Fun/Why Do Fools Fall in Love	Capitol 5118	(S)
3/64	PAUL PETERSON (B)	She Rides with Me/Poorest Boy in Town	Colpix 720	(S)
3/64	CASTELLS (B)	I Do/Teardrops	Warner Bros. 5421	(S)
3/64	BEACH BOYS (B)	Shut Down Vol. 2	Capitol 2027	(A)
4/64	HONEYS (B)	He's a Doll/Love of a Boy and Girl	Warner Bros. 5430	(S)
5/64	BEACH BOYS (B)	I Get Around/Don't Worry Baby	Capitol 5174	(S)
6/64	GARY USHER (B)	Sacramento/Just the Way I Feel	Capitol 5193	(S)
6/64	SHARON MARIE (B)	Thinkin' 'Bout You Baby/Story of My Life	Capitol 5195	(S)
7/64	BEACH BOYS (B)	All Summer Long	Capitol 2110	(A)
8/64	BEACH BOYS (B)	When I Grow Up/She Knows Me Too Well	Capitol 5245	(S)
10/64	BEACH BOYS (B)	Wendy/Little Honda/Hushabye/Don't Back Down	Capitol 5267	(ELP)
10/64	BEACH BOYS (B)	Beach Boys' Concert Live	Capitol 2198	(A)
10/64	BEACH BOYS (B)	Beach Boys' Christmas Album	Capitol 2164	(A)
11/64	BEACH BOYS (B)	Dance Dance Dance/Warmth of the Sun	Capitol 5306	(S)
12/64	BEACH BOYS (B)	The Man With All The Toys/Blue Christmas	Capitol 5312	(S)
2/65	BEACH BOYS (B)	Do You Wanna Dance/Please Let Me Wonder	Capitol 5372	(S)
3/65	BEACH BOYS (B)	The Beach Boys Today	Capitol 2269	(S)
5/65	GLEN CAMPBELL (B)	Guess I'm Dumb/That's All Right	Capitol 5441	(S)
5/65	BEACH BOYS (B)	Help Me Rhonda/Kiss Me Baby	Capitol 5395	(S)
7/65	BEACH BOYS (B)	Summer Days (and Summer Nights)	Capitol 2354	(A)
8/65	BEACH BOYS (B)	California Girls/Let Him Run Wild	Capitol 5464	(S)
10/65	BEACH BOYS (B)	Beach Boys' Party	Capitol 2398	(A)
11/65	BEACH BOYS (B)	The Little Girl I Once Knew/There's No Other	Capitol 5540	(S)
1/66	BEACH BOYS (B)	Barbara Ann/Girl Don't Tell Me	Capitol 5561	(S)
3/66	BEACH BOYS (B)	Sloop John B./You're So Good to Me	Capitol 5602	(S)
4/66	ANNETTE (B)	The Monkey's Uncle/How Will I Know My Love	Vista 440	(S)
4/66	BRIAN WILSON (B)	Caroline, No/Summer Means New Love	Capitol	(S)
5/66	BEACH BOYS (B)	Pet Sounds	Capitol 2458	(A)
7/66	BEACH BOYS	Best of the Beach Boys	Capitol 2445	(A)

BEACH BOYS JOURNALS PART 2

Date	Artist	Title	Label	Type
7/66	BEACH BOYS (B)	Wouldn't It Be Nice/God Only Knows	Capitol 5706	(S)
10/66	BEACH BOYS (B)	Good Vibrations/Let's Go Away for a While	Capitol 5676	(S)
	BEACH BOYS	Smile	Capitol 2580	UNR
7/67	BEACH BOYS (B)	Heroes and Villians/You're Welcome	Brother 1001	(S)
8/67	BEACH BOYS	Best of the Beach Boys Vol. 2	Capitol 2706	(A)
9/67	BEACH BOYS (BB)	Smiley Smile	Brother 1002	(A)
9/67	BRIAN WILSON & MIKE LOVE (B)	Gettin' Hungry/Devoted to You	Brother (Capitol)	(S)
10/67	BEACH BOYS	Deluxe Set	Capitol 2818	(A)S(R)
10/67	BEACH BOYS	Wild Honey/Wind Chimes	Capitol 2028	(S)
12/67	BEACH BOYS	Wild Honey	Capitol 2068	(A)
12/67	BEACH BOYS	Darlin'/Here Today	Capitol 2160	(S)
4/68	BEACH BOYS	Friends/Little Bird	Capitol	(S)
5/68	BEACH BOYS	Friends	Capitol	(A)
6/68	BEACH BOYS	Stack-O-Tracks	Capitol 2893	(A)
7/68	BEACH BOYS (B)	Do It Again/Wake the World	Capitol 2239	(S)
8/68	BEACH BOYS	Best of the Beach Boys Vol. 3	Capitol 2945	(A)
11/68	BEACH BOYS	Bluebirds Over the Mountain/Never Learn Not to Love	Capitol 2432	(S)
1/69	BEACH BOYS	20/20	Capitol 133	(A)
2/69	HONEYS (B)	Tonight I'll Be Loving You/Goodnight My Love	Capitol 2454	(S)
2/69	BEACH BOYS	I Can Hear Music/All I Want to Do	Capitol	(S)
5/69	BEACH BOYS	Close-Up	Capitol 253	(A)
6/69	BEACH BOYS (B)	Breakaway/Celebrate The News	Capitol 2530	(S)
8/69	DENNIS WILSON & RUMBO (D)	Sound of Free/Lady	Stateside	UK(S)
2/70	BEACH BOYS	Good Vibrations	Capitol 442	(A)
3/70	BEACH BOYS	Add Some Music to Your Day/Susie Cincinnati	Brother-Reprise 0894	(S)
4/70	BEACH BOYS	Cottonfields/The Nearest Faraway Place	Capitol 2765	(S)
7/70	BEACH BOYS	The Whole World/Slip on Through	Brother-Reprise 0929	(S)
8/70	BEACH BOYS	Sunflower	Brother-Reprise 6382	(A)
8/70	BEACH BOYS (B)	All Summer Long/California Girls	Capitol 500	(A)S(R)
10/70	BEACH BOYS (B)	Dance, Dance, Dance/Fun, Fun, Fun	Capitol 701	(A)S(R)
10/70	FLAME (C)	See the Light/Get Your Mind Made Up	Brother 3500	(S)
11/70	BEACH BOYS	It's About Time/Tears in the Morning	Brother-Reprise 0957	(S)
1/71	FLAME (C)	The Flame	Brother 2500	(A)
1/71	FLAME (C)	Another Day Like Heaven/I'm So Happy	Brother 3501	(S)
3/71	BEACH BOYS	Cool, Cool Water/Forever	Brother-Reprise 0998	(S)
5/71	BEACH BOYS	Wouldn't It Be Nice (Live)	Ode 70 66016	(S)
5/71	BEACH BOYS	Long Promised Road/Deirdre	Brother-Reprise 1015	(S)
8/71	BEACH BOYS	Surf's Up	Brother-Reprise 6454	(A)
9/71	BEACH BOYS	Till I Die/Long Promised Road	Brother Reprise 1047	(S)
11/71	BEACH BOYS	Surf's Up/Don't Go Near the Water	Brother-Reprise 1055	(S)
11/71	SPRING (B)	Now That Everything's Been Said/Awake	United Artists 50848	(S)
3/72	BEACH BOYS	You Need A Mess of Help to Stand Alone/Cuddle Up	Brother-Reprise 1091	(S)
5/72	BEACH BOYS	Carl and the Passions—Pet Sounds	Brother-Reprise 2083	(A)S
5/72	SPRING (B)	Spring	United Artists 5571	(A)
5/72	SPRING (B)	Good Time/Sweet Mountain	United Artists 50907	(S)
7/72	BEACH BOYS	Marcella/Hold on Dear Brother	Brother-Reprise 1101	(S)
1/73	BEACH BOYS	Sail On Sailor/Only With You	Brother-Reprise 1138	(S)
1/73	BEACH BOYS	Holland/Mt. Vernon & Fairway	Brother-Reprise	(A)EP
4/73	BEACH BOYS	California Saga/Funky Pretty	Columbia 45834	(S)
6/73	AMERICAN SPRING (B)	Shyin' Away/Fallin' in Love	Brother-Reprise 6484	(A)S
11/73	BEACH BOYS	Beach Boys in Concert	Brother-Reprise 2197	(A)(R)
5/74	BEACH BOYS (B)	Pet Sounds	Capitol 11307	(A)
6/74	BEACH BOYS	Endless Summer	Capitol 3924	(S)(R)
7/74	BEACH BOYS (B)	Surfin' U.S.A./The Warmth of the Sun	Brother-Reprise 2166	(A)(R)
7/74	BEACH BOYS	Wild Honey/20/20	Brother-Reprise 1310	(S)
8/74	BEACH BOYS	I Can Hear Music	Brother-Reprise 2167	(A)S(R)
10/74	BEACH BOYS (B)	Friends/Smiley Smile	Brother-Reprise 1321	(S)
12/74	BEACH BOYS	Child of Winter/Susie Cincinnati	Brother-Reprise	(S)(R)
3/75	BEACH BOYS	Sail On Sailor/Only With You	Capitol 11384	(A)
4/75	BEACH BOYS	Spirit of America	Capitol	(S)(R)
6/75	BEACH BOYS (B)	Little Honda/Hawaii	Capitol	(S)(R)
7/75	BEACH BOYS (B)	Barbara Ann/Little Honda	Brother-Reprise 2223	(A)
7/75	BEACH BOYS	Good Vibrations/Best of the Beach Boys	Brother-Reprise	(S)(R)
8/75	BEACH BOYS (B)	Wouldn't It Be Nice/Caroline, No	Capitol 4164	(S)
1/76	RICCA MARTIN (C)	Stop Look Around/I Had A Dream	Brother-Reprise 1354	(S)
6/76	BEACH BOYS (B)	Rock and Roll Music/TM Song	Brother-Reprise 2251	(A)
7/76	BEACH BOYS (B)	Fifteen Big Ones	Brother-Reprise 1368	(A)
9/76	BEACH BOYS (B)	It's OK/Had to Phone Ya	Brother-Reprise 1375	(S)
11/76	BEACH BOYS (B)	Everyone's in Love/Susie Cincinnati	Capitol 11584	(A)(R)
11/76	BEACH BOYS	'69/Live in London	Brother-Reprise 2258	(A)
4/77	BEACH BOYS (B)	The Beach Boys Love You	Brother-Reprise 2258	(A)
6/77	BEACH BOYS (B)	Honkin' Down The Highway/Solar System	Caribou 34354	(A)
8/77	DENNIS WILSON (D)	Pacific Ocean Blue	Caribou 34354	(A)

BEACH BOYS JOURNALS PART 2

10/77	RICCA MARTIN (C)	Beached	Epic 34834	(A)
10/77	DENNIS WILSON (D)	You and I	Caribou	(S)
4/78	CELEBRATION FEATURING MIKE LOVE (A)	Almost Summer/Lookin' Good	MCA 40891	(S)
5/78	ORIGINAL SOUNDTRACK (A)	Almost Summer	MCA 3037	(S)
8/78	BEACH BOYS (BB)	Peggy Sue	Brother-Reprise RPS 1394	(S)
9/78	BEACH BOYS	M.I.U. Album	Brother-Reprise MSK 2268	(A)
2/79	BEACH BOYS	Here Comes the Night/Baby Blue	Caribou ZS9026	(S)
2/79	BEACH BOYS	Here Comes the Night/Here Comes the Night (instrumental)	Caribou 2ZS9028 12" disco	(S)
2/79	CELEBRATION (A)	Celebration	Pacific Arts pAC7122	(A)
3/79	BEACH BOYS	L.A. Light Album	Caribou JZ35752	(A)
4/79	BEACH BOYS	Good Timin'/Love Surrounds Me	Caribou ZS9029	(S)
5/79	CELEBRATION	Star Baby/Gettin' Hungry	Pacific Arts PAC45105	(S)
8/79	VARIOUS ARTISTS	Americathon	Lorimar JS 36174	(A)
8/79	BEACH BOYS	Lady Lynda/Full Sail	Caribou ZS9030	(S)
10/79	BEACH BOYS	It's a Beautiful Day/Sumahama	Caribou/Lorimar ZS9031	(S)
3/80	BEACH BOYS (J)	Goin' On/Endless Harmony	Caribou ZS9032	(S)
3/80	BEACH BOYS (J)	Keepin' the Summer Alive	Caribou JZ36293	(A)
5/80	BEACH BOYS (J)	Livin' with a Heartache/Santa Ana Winds	Caribou ZS9033	(S)
3/81	CARL WILSON (G)	Hold Me/Hurry Love	Caribou ZS601049	(S)
3/81	CARL WILSON (G)	Carl Wilson	Caribou NJZ37010	(A)
6/81	CARL WILSON (G)	Heaven/Hurry Love	Caribou ZS602136	(S)
7/81	BEACH BOYS (B)	Beach Boys Medley/God Only Knows	Capitol A 5030	(S)
9/81	MIKE LOVE	Lookin' Back with Love/One Good Reason	Boardwalk NB7-11-128	(S)
10/81	MIKE LOVE	Lookin' Back with Love	Boardwalk NB1-33242	(A)
11/81	BEACH BOYS	Come Go With Me/Don't Go Near the Water	Caribou ZS50263	(S)
11/81	BEACH BOYS (BB)	Ten Years of Harmony	Caribou Z2X37445	(A)
6/82	BEACH BOYS (BB)	Sunshine Dream	Capitol SVBB12220	(A)
6/82	BEACH BOYS	Be True to Your School	Capitol N-16273	(A)
4/83	VARIOUS ARTISTS	Rock 'N' Roll City	Hitbound/Realistic 51-3009	(C)
4/83	CARL WILSON (X)	What You Do to Me/Time	Caribou	(S)
5/83	CARL WILSON (X)	Youngblood	Caribou BFZ37970	(A)
8/83	BEACH BOYS (E)	Rarities	Capitol ST-12293	(A)
8/83	CARL WILSON (X)	Givin' You Up	Caribou ZS404020	(S)

BEACH BOYS ORIGINAL AMERICAN ALBUMS

12/62 SURFIN' SAFARI — Capitol DT/T 1808 — Producer: Nick Venet
Surfin' Safari; County Fair; Ten Little Indians; Chug-A-Lug; Little Miss America; 409/Surfin'; Heads You Win-Tails I Lose; Summertime Blues; Cuckoo Clock; Moon Dawg; The Shift

4/63 SURFIN' U.S.A. — Capitol ST/T 1890 — Producer: Nick Venet
Surfin' U.S.A.; Farmer's Daughter; Misirlou; Stoked; Lonely Sea; Shut Down/Noble Surfer; Honky Tonk; Lana; Surf Jam; Let's Go Trippin'; Finders Keepers

7/63 SURFER GIRL — Capitol ST/T 1981 — Producer: Brian Wilson
Surfer Girl; Catch a Wave; The Surfer Moon; South Bay Surfer; The Rocking Surfer; Little Deuce Coupe/In My Room; Hawaii; Surfer's Rule; Our Car Club; Your Summer Dream; Boogie Woogie

10/63 LITTLE DEUCE COUPE — Capitol ST/T 1998 — Producer: Brian Wilson
Little Deuce Coupe; Ballad of Ole Betsy; Be True to Your School; Car Crazy Cutie; Cherry, Cherry Coupe; 409/Shut Down; Spirit of America; Our Car Club; No-Go Showboat; A Young Man Is Gone; Custom Machine

3/64 SHUT DOWN VOL. 2 — Capitol ST/T 2027 — Producer: Brian Wilson
Fun, Fun, Fun; Don't Worry Baby; In the Parkin' Lot; "Cassius" Love vs. "Sonny" Wilson; The Warmth of the Sun; This Car of Mine/Why Do Fools Fall in Love; Pom Pom Play Girl; Keep an Eye on Summer; Shut Down Part II; Louie, Louie; Denny's Drums

7/64 ALL SUMMER LONG — Capitol ST/T 2110 — Producer: Brian Wilson
I Get Around; All Summer Long; Hushabye; Little Honda; We'll Run Away; Carl's Big Chance/Wendy; Do You Remember; Girls on the Beach; Drive-In; Our Favorite Recording Sessions; Don't Back Down

10/64 CHRISTMAS ALBUM — Capitol ST/T 2164 — Producer: Brian Wilson
Little Saint Nick; The Man with All the Toys; Santa's Beard; Merry Christmas, Baby; Christmas Day; Frosty the Snowman/We Three Kings of Orient Are; Blue Christmas; Santa Claus Is Comin' to Town; White Christmas; I'll Be Home for Christmas; Auld Lang Syne

10/64 CONCERT — Capitol STAO TAO 2198 — Producer: Brian Wilson
Fun, Fun, Fun; Little Old Lady From Pasadena; Little Deuce Coupe; Long, Tall Texan; In My Room; Monster Mash; Let's Go Trippin'/Papa-Ooo-Mow-Mow; The Wanderer; Hawaii; Graduation Day; I Get Around; Johnny B. Goode

BEACH BOYS JOURNALS PART 2

Date	Album	Catalog	Producer
3/65	TODAY	Capitol DT/T 2269	Producer: Brian Wilson

Do You Wanna Dance; Good To My Baby; Don't Hurt My Little Sister; When I Grow Up; Help Me Rhonda; Dance, Dance, Dance! Please Let Me Wonder; I'm So Young; Kiss Me Baby; She Knows Me Too Well; In the Back of My Mind; Bull Session With "Big Daddy"

7/65 — SUMMER DAYS (AND SUMMER NIGHTS) — Capitol DD/T 2354 — Producer: Brian Wilson

The Girl From New York City; Amusement Parks U.S.A.; Then I Kissed Her; Salt Lake City; Girl Don't Tell Me; Help Me Rhonda/California Girls; Let Him Run Wild; You're So Good To Me; Summer Means New Love; I'm Bugged at My Old Man; and Your Dream Comes True

10/65 — PARTY — Capitol DMAS/MAS 2398 — Producer: Brian Wilson

Hully Gully; I Should Have Known Better; Tell Me Why; Papa-Ooo-Mow-Mow; Mountain of Love; You've Got to Hide Your Love Away; Devoted to You/Alley Ooop; There's No Other (Like My Baby); Medley: I Get Around, Little Deuce Coupe, The Times They Are A-Changing; Barbara Ann

5/66 — PET SOUNDS — Capitol DT/T 2458 — Producer: Brian Wilson

Wouldn't It Be Nice; You Still Believe in Me; That's Not Me; Don't Talk (Put Your Head On My Shoulder); I'm Waiting for the Day; Let's Go Away for a While; Sloop John B.; God Only Knows

SMILE — Capitol 2580 (unreleased) — Producer: Brian Wilson

Partially or fully produced cuts: Heroes and Villains/Barnyard/The Elemental Suite: My Vega-Tables (Earth), I Love To Say Da-Da (Water), Mrs. O'Leary's Cow (Fire), untitled piano instrumental (Air)/Wind Chimes/Wonderful/Old Master Painter/Our Prayer/Cabin-Essence (Home on the Range)/Have you Seen) The Grand Coolee Dam/Who Run) The Iron Horse/Bicycle Rider/You Are My Sunshine/Do You Like Worms/Child Is Father to the Man/Good Vibrations/Surf's Up/Can't Wait Too Long
unscreened rumored cuts: Holidays; I'm In Great Shape; Red Run

9/67 — SMILEY SMILE — Brother ST 9001 (Capitol) — Producer: Beach Boys

Heroes and Villains; Vega-Tables; Fall Breaks and Back to Winter (W. Woodpecker Symphony); She's Goin' Bald; Little Pad; Good Vibrations; With Me Tonight; Wind Chimes; Gettin' Hungry; Wonderful; Whistle In

12/67 — WILD HONEY — Capitol ST 2859 — Producer: Beach Boys

Wild Honey; Aren't You Glad; I Was Made to Love Her; Country Air; A Thing or Two Darlin'; I'd Love Just Once to See You; Here Comes the Night; Let the Wind Blow; How She Boogalooed It; Mama Says

5/68 — FRIENDS — Capitol ST 2895 — Producer: Beach Boys

Meant For You; Friends; Wake the World; Be Here in the Mornin'; When a Man Needs a Woman; Passing By; Anna Lee the Healer; Little Bird; Be Still; Busy Doin' Nothin'; Diamond Head; Transcendental Meditation

1/69 — 20/20 — Capitol SKAO 133 — Producer: Beach Boys

Do It Again; I Can Hear Music; Bluebirds Over the Mountain; Be With Me; All I Want to Do (Dennis); The Nearest Faraway Place; Cottonfields; I Went to Sleep; Time to Get Alone; Never Learn Not to Love; Our Prayer; Cabinessence

8/70 — SUNFLOWER — Brother-Reprise RS 6382 — Producer: Beach Boys

Slip on Through; This Whole World; Add Some Music to Your Day; Got to Know the Woman; Deirdre; It's About Time; Tears in the Morning; All I Wanna Do; Forever; Our Sweet Love; At My Window; Cool, Cool Water

5/72 — SURF'S UP — Brother-Reprise RS 6454 — Producer: Beach Boys

Don't Go Near the Water; Long Promised Road; Take a Load Off Your Feet; Disney Girls (1957); Student Demonstration Time; Feel Flows; Lookin' at Tomorrow (A Welfare Song); A Day in the Life of a Tree; Till I Die; Surf's Up

5/72 — CARL AND THE PASSIONS, SO TOUGH — Brother-Reprise 2MS 2083 — Producer: Beach Boys

You Need a Mess of Help to Stand Alone; Here She Comes; He Come Down; Marcella; Hold On Dear Brother; Make It Good; All This Is That; Cuddle Up

1/73 — HOLLAND — Brother-Reprise MS 2118 — Producer: Beach Boys

Sail On Sailor; Steamboat; California Saga; Big Sur; The Beaks of Eagles; California; The Trader; Leaving This Town; Only With You; Funky Pretty; Mount Vernon and Fairways (A Fairy Tale); Mt. Vernon and Fairway—Theme; I'm the Pied Piper; Better Get Back in Bed; Magic Transistor Radio; I'm the Pied Piper; Radio King Dom

11/73 — IN CONCERT — Brother-Reprise 2RS 6484 — Producer: Beach Boys

Sail On Sailor; Sloop John B.; The Trader; You Still Believe in Me; California Girls; Darlin'; Marcella; Caroline, No; Leaving This Town; Heroes and Villains; Funky Pretty; Let the Wind Blow; Help Me Rhonda; Surfer Girl; Wouldn't It Be Nice; We Got Love; Don't Worry Baby; Surfin' U.S.A.; Good Vibrations; Fun, Fun, Fun

7/76 — FIFTEEN BIG ONES — Brother-Reprise MS 2251 — Producer: Brian Wilson

Rock and Roll Music; It's OK; Had to Phone Ya; Chapel of Love; Everyone's in Love With You; Talk to Me; That Same Song; TM Song; Palisades Park; Susie Cincinnati; A Casual Look; Blueberry Hill; Back Home; In the Still of the Night; Just Once in My Life

11/76 — '69 (LIVE IN LONDON) — Capitol ST 11584 — Producer: Beach Boys

Darlin'; Wouldn't It Be Nice; Sloop John B.; California Girls; Do It Again; Wake the World; Aren't You Glad; Bluebirds Over the Mountain; Their Hearts Were Full of Spring; Good Vibrations; God Only Knows; Barbara Ann

BEACH BOYS JOURNALS PART 2

....	ADULT CHILD	.........(Unreleased)	.........Producer: Brian Wilson

Life Is for the Living; Hey Little Tomboy; Deep Purple; H.E.L.P.; It's Over Now; Everyone Wants to Live; Shortenin' Bread; Lines; On Broadway; Two Can Play; It's Trying to Say; Still I Dream of It

| 4/77 | THE BEACH BOYS LOVE YOU | Brother-Reprise MSK 2258 | Producer: Brian Wilson |

Let Us Go on This Way; Roller Skating Child; Mona; Johnny Carson; Good Time; Honkin' Down the Highway; Ding Dang Solar System; The Night Was So Young; I'll Bet He's Nice; Let's Put Our Hearts Together; I Wanna Pick You Up; Airplane; Love Is a Woman

| | MERRY CHRISTMAS FROM THE BEACH BOYS | (Unreleased) | Producer: Brian Wilson |

Christmas Time Is Here Again/Child of Winter/Winter Symphony/Michael Row the Boat/Seasons in the Sun/Holy Evening/Christmas Day/Go and Get That Girl/Santa's Got an Airplane/I Saw Mommy Kissing Santa (original)

| 9/78 | MIU ALBUM | Brother-Reprise MSK 2268 (A) | Executive Producer: Brian Wilson. Producers: Al Jardine and Ron Altbach |

She's Got Rhythm; Come Go With Me; Hey Little Tomboy; Kona Coast; Peggy Sue; Wontcha Come Out Tonight; Sunday Kind of Love; Belles of Paris; Pitter Patter; Diane; Matchpoint of Our Love; Winds of Change

| 3/79 | L.A. (LIGHT ALBUM) | Caribou J235752 | Producers: Bruce Johnston, Beach Boys, Jim Guercio |

Good Timin'/Lady Lynda/Full Sail/Angel Come Home/Love Surrounds Me/Sumahama/Here Comes the Night/Baby Blue/Goin' South/Shortenin' Bread*

*Produced by Bruce Johnston and Curt Becher

| 3/80 | KEEPIN' THE SUMMER ALIVE | Caribou F236283 | Producer: Bruce Johnston |

Keepin' the Summer Alive/Oh Darlin'/Some of Your Love/Livin' With a Heartache/School Day/Goin' On/Sunshine/When Girls Get Together/Santa Ana Winds/Endless Harmony

ALBUMS PRODUCED BY OR PROMINENTLY FEATURING THE BEACH BOYS

| 1/71 | THE FLAME | Brother LP 2500 | Producer: Carl Wilson |

See the Light/Make It Easy/Hey Lord/Lady/Don't Worry Bill/Get Your Mind Made Up/Highs and Lows/I'm So Happy/Dove/Another Day Like Heaven/See the Light (Reprise)

| 5/72 | SPRING | United Artists UAS 5571 | Executive Producer: Brian Wilson |

Tennessee Waltz●/Thinkin' 'Bout You Baby○/Mama Said○/Superstar○/Awake■/Sweet Mountain○/Everybody●/This Whole World○/Forever○/Good Time●/Now That Everything's Been Said☐/Down Home

Produced by ●Brian Wilson and Stephen Desper○Brian Wilson, Stephen Desper, and David Sandler■David Sandler☐Brian Wilson and David Sandler

| 5/77 | BRUCE JOHNSON/GOING PUBLIC | Columbia PC 34459 | Producer: Gary Usher |

I Write the Songs/Deirdre/Thank You Baby/Rendezvous/Won't Somebody Dance With Me/Disney Girls/Rock and Roll Survivor/Don't Be Scared/Pipeline

| 8/77 | DENNIS WILSON/PACIFIC OCEAN BLUE | Caribou PZ 34354 | Producers: Dennis Wilson and Gregg Jacobson |

River Song/What's Wrong/Moonshine/Friday Night/Dreamer/Thoughts of You/Time/You and I/Pacific Ocean Blue/Farewell My Friend/Rainbows/End of the Show

| 7/77 | RICCI MARTIN/BEACHED | Epic PE 34834 | Producers: Carl Wilson and Billy Hinsche |

Stop Look Around/Moonbeams/Belle of the Ball/Everybody Knows My Name/Streets of Love/Spark of Me/My Old Radio/Precious Love/I Don't Like It/I Had a Dream/Here I Go Again

| 5/78 | ALMOST SUMMER* | Original Soundtrack Album | Producer: Ron Altbach |

Almost Summer; Sad, Sad, Summer; Cruisin'; Lookin' Good; Summer in the City; It's OK; Football; Island Girl; Christine and Bobby; We Are the Future; She Was a Lady

*FEATURING CELEBRATION WITH MIKE LOVE

| 2/79 | CELEBRATION | Pacific Arts PAC 7-122 | Producer: Ron Altbach |

Sailo/Lovestruck/She's Just Out to Get You/I Don't Wanna Know/Starbaby/Go and Get That Girl/How's About a Little Bit/Song of Creation/Country Pie

| 8/79 | AMERICATHON—ORIGINAL SOUNDTRACK ALBUM | Lorimar JS 36174 | Producer: Bruce Johnston |

It's a Beautiful Day

BEACH BOYS JOURNALS PART 2

Date	Artist/Title	Label/Number	Producer
3/81	CARL WILSON	Caribou NJ2 37010	Producer: James William Guercio
	Hold Me/Bright Lights/What You Gonna Do About Me/The Right Lane/Hurry Love/Heaven/The Grammy/Seems So Long Ago		
10/81	MIKE LOVE/LOOKING BACK WITH LOVE	Boardwalk NB 1 33242	Producer: Curt Becher
	Looking Back With Love/On and On and On/Runnin' Around the World/Over and Over/Rockin the Man in the Boat/Calendar Girl/Be My Baby/One Good Reason/Touch Me Tonight/Paradise Found		
4/83	ROCK 'N' ROLL CITY**	Hitsound/Realistic 51-3000 (Cassette Only)	Executive Producer: Mike Love
	Mike and Dean—*Lightning Strikes/Her Boyfriend's Back*		
	Mike Love—*The Letter●/The Locomotion●/Sugar Shack●/Du Doo Run●*		
	Dean Torrence—*Baby Talk/Wild Thing*		
	Beach Boys—*California Dreaming■*		
	Produced by ●Daryl Dragon ■Bruce Johnstone, Al Jardine, Tony Melcher		
5/83	CARL WILSON/YOUNGBLOOD	Caribou BF2 37970	Producer: Jeff Baxter
	What More Can I Say/She's Mine/Givin' You Up/One More Night Alone/Rockin' All Over the World/What You Do to Me/Youngblood/Of the Times/Too Early to Tell/If I Could Talk to Love/Time		

BEACH BOYS Repackaging and Reissues

Date	Title	Label/Number	Notes
7/66	BEST OF THE BEACH BOYS	Capitol T DT 2445	
8/67	BEST OF THE BEACH BOYS VOL. 2	Capitol T DT 2706	
11/67	DELUXE SET	Capitol 2813	Today-Summer Days-Summer Nights-Pet Sounds
6/68	STACK-O-TRACKS	Capitol DKAO 2893	Beach Boy Songs with original Instrumental Tracks Without Vocals
8/68	BEST OF THE BEACH BOYS VOL. 3	Capitol DKAO 2945	
5/69	CLOSE-UP	Capitol 2LP 253	Songs From Surfin' U.S.A. & All Summer Long
5/69	BEACH BOYS BIGGEST BEACH HITS	ERA HTE 805	Pre-Capitol Sessions
2/70	GOOD VIBRATIONS	Capitol ST 442	
8/70	ALL SUMMER LONG/CALIFORNIA GIRLS	Capitol STBB 500	Songs from All Summer Long/Summer Days Summer Nights
	DANCE, DANCE, DANCE/FUN, FUN, FUN	Capitol STBB 701	Songs from Today & Shut Down Vol. 2
5/74	PET SOUNDS	Brother-Reprise MS 2197	
6/74	ENDLESS SUMMER	Capitol SUBB 11307	
7/74	WILD HONEY/20/20	Brother-Reprise 2MS 2166	
10/74	FRIENDS/SMILEY SMILE	Brother-Reprise 2MS 2167	
4/75	SPIRIT OF AMERICA	Capitol SUBB 11384	
	GOOD VIBRATIONS—BEST OF THE BEACH BOYS	Brother-Reprise MS 2223	
11/81	TEN YEARS OF HARMONY	Caribou Z2X37445	Includes unreleased San Miguel and Sea Cruise
6/82	SUNSHINE DREAM	Capitol SVBB 12220	Includes Beach Boys medley
6/82	BE TRUE TO YOUR SCHOOL	Capitol N-16273	
8/83	RARITIES	Capitol ST 12293	Includes unreleased material compiled by Brad Elliot

BEACH BOYS UNRELEASED

Title	Composer	Title	Composer
Ba Ba Black Sheep	Brian Wilson	Lonely Days	Brian Wilson
The Big Beat	Brian Wilson	Honey Get Home	Brian Wilson
That Special Feeling	Brian Wilson	Games Two Can Play	Brian Wilson
They're Marching Along	Brian Wilson	Mrs. O'Leary's Cow (*Elemental Suite*)	Brian Wilson
Bobby Left Me	Brian Wilson	Air (Untitled-*Elemental Suite*)	Brian Wilson
My Solution	Brian Wilson	Barnyard	Brian Wilson
Marilyn Rovell	Brian Wilson	Do You Like Worms	Brian Wilson
Burlesque	Brian Wilson	Can't Wait Too Long	Brian Wilson
Boys Will Be Boys	Brian Wilson	I'm in Great Shape	Brian Wilson
Sherry She Needs Me	Brian Wilson	Pattycake	Brian Wilson
Lazy Lizzie	Brian Wilson	Just an Imitation	Brian Wilson
Get a Chance with You	Brian Wilson	Life Is for the Living	Brian Wilson
Part of Me	Brian Wilson	It's Over Now	Brian Wilson
If It Can't Be You	Brian Wilson	Still/Dream of It	Brian Wilson
Funny Boy	Brian Wilson	Everybody Wants To Live	Brian Wilson
No Big Thing	Brian Wilson	It's Trying To Say	Brian Wilson
We Don't Know	Brian Wilson	Lines	Brian Wilson
Crack the Whip	Brian Wilson	Winter Symphony	Brian Wilson
When I Get Mad I Just Play My Drums	Brian Wilson	Basketball Rock	Brian Wilson
Teeter-Totter Love	Brian Wilson	I'm a Man	Brian Wilson

BEACH BOYS JOURNALS PART 2

Short Skirts	Brian Wilson	Stevie	Brian Wilson
Clangin'	Brian Wilson		
Fallin' in Love	Dennis Wilson	Wild Situation	Dennis Wilson
I've Got a Friend	Dennis Wilson	Barnyard Blues	Dennis Wilson
10,000 Years	Dennis Wilson	I Didn't Mean To Make You Worry	Dennis Wilson
Barbara	Dennis Wilson	I Don't Know	Dennis Wilson
Holy Man	Dennis Wilson	School Girl	Dennis Wilson
Slow Booze	Dennis Wilson	Taking Off	Dennis Wilson
Holy Evening	Dennis Wilson	Time for Bed	Dennis Wilson
He's a Bum	Dennis Wilson		
Our Life, Our Love, Our Land	Michael Love	Brian's Back	Michael Love
Lisa	Michael Love	Bucks	Michael Love
Glow Crescent Glow	Michael Love	Children of the Night	Michael Love
Shooting Star	Michael Love	Phoenix Dreams	Michael Love
Jail Bait	Michael Love		
Italia	Alan Jardine	Ride Arabian Ride	Alan Jardine
Pink Champagne	Alan Jardine	Song of the Whale	Alan Jardine
Dr. Tom	Alan Jardine	Monterey	Alan Jardine
Canyon Summer	Alan Jardine	Polly Peptide	Alan Jardine
Rubles	Alan Jardine	Earthquake Time	Alan Jardine
Rockin Roadster	Brian Wilson, Roger Christian	Who Ran the Iron Horse	Brian Wilson, Van Dyke Parks
Malibu Sunset	Brian Wilson, Roger Christian	Grand Coulee Dam	Brian Wilson, Van Dyke Parks
All Dressed Up for School	Brian Wilson, Roger Christian	Old Master Painter	Brian Wilson, Van Dyke Parks
California Feeling	Brian Wilson, Steve Kalinich	Bicycle Rider	Brian Wilson, Van Dyke Parks
Lucy Jones	Brian Wilson, Steve Kalinich	H.E.L.P. Is on the Way	Brian Wilson, Mike Love
You're Riding High on the Music	Brian Wilson, Steve Kalinich	Christmas Day	Brian Wilson, Mike Love
Snowflakes	Brian Wilson, David Sandler	Santa's Got an Airplane	Brian Wilson, Mike Love
Rock and Roll Bash	Brian Wilson, Bob Norberg	Goin' to the Beach	Brian Wilson, Mike Love
Cabinessence	Brian Wilson, Van Dyke Parks	Soulful Old Man Sunshine	Brian Wilson, Rick Hehn
Behold the Night	Dennis Wilson, Daryl Dragon	Tug of Love	Dennis Wilson, Greg Jakobsen
It's a New Day	Dennis Wilson, Daryl Dragon	Companion	Dennis Wilson, Carly Munoz
Don't Let Me Go	Carl Wilson, Mike Love	Then I'll Be Someone	Carl Wilson, Tandyn Almer
I Just Got My Pay	Alan Jardine, Mike Love	Skatetown, U.S.A.	Alan Jardine, Mike Love
Loop De Loop	Brian Wilson, Alan Jardine, Mike Love	Do Ya?	Brian Wilson, Diane Rovell, Marilyn Wilson
Our Team	Brian Wilson, Mike Love, Diane Rovell	Recreation	Brian Wilson, Bob Norman, C. Pomeroy

I Saw Mommy Kissing Santa Clause (Original)	I'm Going Your Way	I Ran
I Saw Mommy Kissing Santa Clause (Standard)	Where Is She	Friday Night
Our Happy Home	We're Together Again	Tones
Even Steven	Princess of the Rain	Good News
Walkin'	Live Again	Good Time Mama
Carnival	Why Don't You Try Me	
	Inspiration	

UNRELEASED COVER VERSIONS

You Are My Sunshine	Battle Hymn of the Republic	Let's Dance
I Can't Get No Satisfaction	Come to the Sunshine	Ruby Baby
Long Tall Sally	He's so Fine	You've Lost that Lovin' Feeling
Heart and Soul	Secret Love	Deep Purple
On Top of Old Smokey	Money, Money	Gimme Some Lovin'
Game of Love	On Broadway	Jamaica Farewell
Old Man River	Runnin' Bear	River Deep, Mountain High
Seasons in the Sun	Shake Rattle and Roll	
Honeycomb	Michael Row the Boat Ashore	

BEACH BOYS JOURNALS PART 2

Dennis played the mechanic in Two-Lane Blacktop, *a film that also starred James Taylor, Warren Oates, and Laurie Bird.*

Carl, Bruce, Mike, Brian, Alan, Dennis

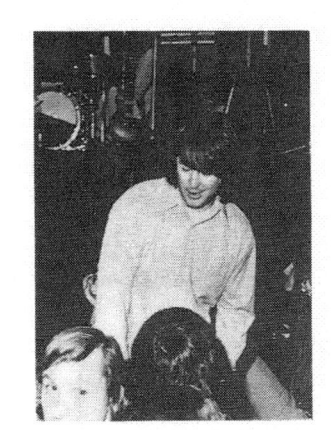

BEACH BOYS JOURNALS PART 2

THE BEACH BOYS
LOOKING BACK WITH LOVE?

AMERICAN JOURNALIST KEN SHARP PERSUADES VOCALIST MIKE LOVE TO SPILL THE BEANS ON 30 YEARS OF STRANGE VIBRATIONS

Mike Love has been the Beach Boys' frontman for the last three decades — the public face of the group whose strangely schizophrenic career has taken their image from squeaky-clean surf music to drug traumas, internal battles and record company conflicts.

Onstage, he's the rabble-rouser of the group — the party king who turns the Beach Boys' nostalgia act into a rock'n'roll circus, with Love as the lion-tamer. His nasal vocals have been aired on scores of hit singles, from "Surfin'" to more recent hits like "Kokomo", and now the group's latest U.S. album, "Summer In Paradise".

He's been responsible for maintaining the Beach Boys on a steady course of summer fun — sun, sea, surf, sand and schoolgirls — and keeping them away from the more ambitious paths they ventured along in the late Sixties and early Seventies. He's become the most controversial Beach Boy among fans, and over the last decade, diehard enthusiasts have filled Beach Boys fanzines with complaints about his stranglehold over the group's career. But it's safe to say that if Love hadn't been there to nag, cajole and drag them along, the Beach Boys would have disintegrated years ago. Love has kept them on the road, in the money, and in some kind of musical health during an era when the rest of the band would probably have opted for retirement homes.

A complex and outspoken figure, Love has presented conflicting personalities to the world in recent years. There's the combative showman, who stood up when the Beach Boys were being inducted into the Rock'n'Roll Hall Of Fame a few years back and publicly taunted Bruce Springsteen, the Rolling Stones and the Beatles that they couldn't match the Beach Boys. There's the peacemaker, the ambassador for the Maharishi's brand of meditation; the eternal teenager who has married a succession of barely post-adolescent brides; and, don't forget, the songwriter, credited as lyricist on scores of Beach Boys classics, and now involved in suing his former collaborator, Brian Wilson, for royalties on many of the songs for which he has never been credited.

A few months back, journalist Ken Sharp of Denny Somach Productions caught Mike Love on a day when he wanted to let rip — about the impending court case, his relationship with Brian Wilson and Brian's psychologist, Eugene Landy, his memories of the Beach Boys' past, and much more besides.

Originally printed in the U.S. magazine 'Goldmine', the interview caused something of a sensation. This month and next, you can see for yourselves why.

Q: Capitol's treatment of the Beach Boys' catalogue on CD has been fabulous. What was your impression of their 2-for-1 CDs?
Mike Love: I don't even know. I don't know.
Q: Have you seen them?
ML: No. You find that amusing?
Q: Yeah, it's hard to believe that being a Beach Boy, you haven't seen something like that.
ML: It is hard to believe. I find it hard to believe, too.
Q: Why is that?
ML: Why is that? Because I'm a Pisces, is that a good answer? (uproarious laughter) That's as good as I can come up with. There is nothing we can do to stop them merchandising them, so we're at their mercy. So if they've done something that, in the opinion of the caring public, is well done, then I'm glad to hear it.

For instance, they were going to do a "Best Of The Beach Boys Volume Three" in 19... whatever the hell it was, and I came in there and went, "Wait a second, call it 'Endless Summer'." And instead of being Volume Three, which sounds nauseating to me...
Q: The third rung of hits.
ML: Exactly. "Endless Summer" has a whole other vibe and it sold several million copies just with the switch of title. But then I'm a title guy anyway.
Q: The artwork on that album was strange. I could never tell who was who.
ML: Yeah, I know it was awful. I was on the roof of a little cottage in Rishikesh, India, when the Beatles and myself were there with Donovan and Mia Farrow. It was a teacher training course where you learn to become teachers of transcendental meditation. I was sitting on the roof one night talking to Paul McCartney and he was basically saying that we ought to take more care of our album covers. We really hadn't got into it that much — you take a photo or let the company come up with some horrible art like "Endless Summer".

So I said, "Paul, you know we always sort of cared what went inside the cover". Which I thought was a pretty cool answer, because Paul McCartney's very clever. He figures all kind of stuff out and he's good and he's prolific, but I sort of did a John Lennon "how do you sleep at night" without saying it in so many words. I got him, I thought. If you took an audio magnifier out and listened to the quality of harmonies on a Beatles project, and then listened to the quality on a Beach Boys project, there'd be a big difference, if I may say so egotistically and objectively. We just took a lot more care about that stuff. It doesn't mean we're more commercial or better or anything, but it was just our focus.

Q: What are your recollections of being with the Beatles in India?
ML: It was a Magical Mystery Tour. That was actually the highpoint of my life, being with the Maharishi in India. It was neat having the Beatles there too. It was very colourful. You couldn't be with anybody higher on the scale of celebrity at that time. And Mia Farrow had just left Frank Sinatra, and all the paparazzi said, "Gee, she left Frank for a guru!". So there was all that popular attention focused on that spot at that time.
Q: Do you meditate every day?
ML: Yeah. I have since December 1967. I do it in the morning and in the late afternoon or early evening. There's a distinctively different level of consciousness that goes beyond waking, dreaming and sleeping. Your metabolism goes to a level of rest twice as deep as sleep. It's very restful.
Q: The Beatles left midway into their teaching in India. Were you still there then?
ML: No, I'd actually gone before they left because I didn't block out enough time to be a teacher of TM. I went back a couple of years later and became a teacher.
Q: There's a Beatles bootleg out with a song on it recorded by the group while they were in India, called . . .
ML: "Happy Birthday Mike Love". It's cute. I have a copy of it. It was great. It was my birthday. George Harrison and I are both Pisces. Maharishi had fireworks and Indian musicians and magicians — all kinds of neat things going on — so they celebrated my birthday and his within a few days of each other, and the Beatles did that as a gift.

The other thing is that I was sitting at the breakfast table and McCartney came down with his acoustic guitar and he was playing "Back In The USSR", and I told him that what you ought to do is talk about the girls all round Russia, the Ukraine and Georgia. He was creative enough not to need any lyrical help from me, but I gave him the idea for that little section.
Q: Was there a rivalry in the Sixties between the Beach Boys and the Beatles?
ML: Yeah, I think so. There was no-one at the time who more profoundly impacted the industry than the Beatles, and there was no-one hotter at that point. But the Beach Boys were fortunate enough to be voted the No. 1

BEACH BOYS JOURNALS PART 2

The five surviving Beach Boys mustered a rare smile for this 1985 publicity picture.

group in England in the 'NME' right at the height of Beatlemania. "I Get Around" fared pretty well over there. The problem from our side wasn't the Beatles but the record company and our weak management. They had a big push going on and we were just relying on the momentum of our hits. We weren't handled with the promotional hootzpah that Brian Epstein had.

Q: Was McCartney there when you recorded "Vegetables"?
ML: Yeah. There were a couple of different sessions and he came to one. Definitely.

Q: Was he chomping celery with you guys?
ML: I'm not sure what he was chomping. He might have been chomping hashish! Some of those sessions were fairly foggy or smoggy.

Q: "Back In The USSR" was obviously a homage to the Beach Boys. What you did think of the song?
ML: My being in India influenced Paul to write that song, so it was kind of neat. I think it was fun of them to do that. It was lighthearted and humorous of them to do a take on the Beach Boys.

Q: Did you attend George Harrison's recent show in London?
ML: We went to the Royal Albert Hall — Alan, Bruce and myself flew over. Maharishi's people asked us if we would come over to do a show for the Natural Law Party, which we were ready, willing and able to do. But it didn't work out, because they asked us too late, and there wasn't time to get permits. But we decided to go over anyway, and the party was neat. I thought George sounded really good considering the fact that he hasn't toured very much.

Q: What were you trying to get across in your speech a few years back at the Rock And Roll Hall Of Fame?
ML: What I was trying to say was Bill Graham was in charge of running the show, he was stage managing. He had the band play real loud to drown me out. I was firing on a lot of people that night because I didn't like what that room represented, apart from the artists. I'm talking about the managers, the agents, the company heads, the accountants, all the people that don't mind that a guy is on drugs as long as he's touring and bringing in an income. They don't mind dividing a group if it's in the interest of billing them for their legal fees, like what happened with the Beatles.

Q: I was there, and was especially sad that the Beatles couldn't have dropped their differences that night.
ML: That was my point with respect to Paul McCartney not being there. And Diana Ross, if she didn't want to stand up there with the one surviving Supreme. So the thing is, I said that Mick Jagger was chickenshit to get onstage with the Beach Boys, and it's true, and I meant every word of it. I was saying that all this divisiveness and egos — with all the things going on in the world that need attention, and all the power in the industry, all they could come up with was this self-congratulatory Grammy-styled event. I call it the Rock And Roll Hall Of Shame. I felt that it would be neat if we could transcend management, agencies, record company affiliations and unify, try to encourage solutions for problems like starvation, homelessness, AIDS and the environment, to name four.

Q: Can you bring us up to date on the Eugene Landy situation?
ML: Brian Wilson surrendered to a conservatorship. My brother Stan started conservator proceedings, because he felt Landy was, and had been for several years, exercising undue influence on Brian, and taking his money in the process. So Carl Wilson got in there and engaged an expert attorney to get Brian out of Landy's hands and into a conservatorship. So now Landy is prohibited from any contact with Brian. He doesn't have the day-in, day-out grip on him he used to have.

Landy was supposed to be in Brian's life for a year or so, to put Brian through his 24-hour-a-day therapy, to get him into shape where Brian would fire him because he no longer needed him — maybe go once or twice a week for counselling or stuff. But Landy was an aspiring producer and writer, and he loved the business so much that he stepped into Brian's shoes, almost. He acted and behaved like a rock star. He and his wife wrote lyrics for Brian, and didn't think they were talented enough to bring it off.

Q: What did you think of Brian's book, "Wouldn't It Be Nice"?
ML: I never read it. However, excerpts were read to me which caused me to prepare a lawsuit against Brian. He's had the benefit of getting money from Al, Carl, Bruce and Mike's touring over the last nine years while he's supposedly been in therapy with Landy. In the meantime, Brian did two solo albums, and a book attacking me personally, plus other people. It's terrible stuff. Brian has delusions, but they're printed in his book as fact — and they're not, and I want him not only to apologise formally, but to retract them and set the record straight.

Then there's the little issue of me writing the lyrics for "California Girls". What isn't known is that I wrote many, many lyrics for a couple of dozen songs that I was not credited for. I have a huge list of them. It's unbelievable.

Q: Did you like Brian's first solo album?
ML: No.

Q: You didn't like it?
ML: Fuck, no.

Q: What didn't you like about it?
ML: First of all, the lyrics. Second, the arrangements weren't commercial enough. Third, he sounded like shit compared to what he could sound like.

Q: What are some of the songs you didn't get credit for?
ML: OK, "Little Saint Nick". Brian is credited with writing 100% of that. Well, guess who wrote the words? Mike Love, that's who. I wrote "Catch A Wave" and "Don't Back Down". He's credited 100%.

Q: How did that happen?
ML: Because he didn't put my name down. Murry Wilson was the publisher, and put all this stuff down. Interesting stuff. The same thing with "The Man With All The Toys", "Santa's Beard", "Merry Christmas Baby", "Good To My Baby". Guess who wrote the words? Doctor Love, that's who. "When I Grow Up", I participated in that and didn't get a stitch of recognition. "Help Me Rhonda": "Since you put me down I've been out doing in my head". That's my fucking line, thank you very much. Things like "Dance Dance Dance". I asked Carl if he wrote any lyrics and he said no. He just came up with the guitar line. Brian and Carl split 50/50 on that. I was the one who wrote the Chuck Berry-styled alliteration lyrics. That's my scene.

Q: Was this Murry or Brian Wilson?
ML: Either Murry, or else Brian didn't tell him. It's a bloodbath. It's millions and millions of dollars' worth of damage.

Q: Would you ever work with Brian again as a writer or producer?
ML: Sure I would, but I want him to .... "Be True To Your School", I wrote a lot of words to that and wasn't credited. It would have been nice if I was credited with "Catch A Wave". "South Bay Surfer". I wrote the words to "Hawaii". "Be True To Your School". "I Get Around", he put in for 100% of that. I came up ... I got witnesses, Al Jardine will testify in a court of law ... I came up with "Round, round, get around", and if that's not a hook I don't know what the fuck is. That was a chickenshit move to credit himself 100%. Virtually all the songs that were chart records, I had a hand in writing some, if not all, of the lyrics.

Q: How about "All Summer Long"?
ML: Yeah, I wrote that with him. "Remember when you spilled coke all over your blouse", I wrote that with him. To the best of my recollections, I wrote 50% of the words on that. In "I Get Around", Brian had "I get around from town to town/I'm a real cool head/I'm making real good bread". I wrote the verses, though, and the "round, round, get around" part.

There's interesting things like "409" where I came up with "She's real fine, my 409" and "giddy giddy up, 409", and was not credited, but Brian Wilson did give credit to Gary Usher for his contribution. So it was weird. It was like directly against me. He wouldn't fuck with anybody else, but he would with me.

I wasn't really even advised of my rights until just recently in the last few months when I consulted with a good litigation attorney. He's done incredible research on the rights of the songwriter that I've never even heard of from anybody until he started advising me of these things. I have a very good case. I hope we don't have to go to trial, because it's going to destroy Brian. He's going to be destroyed in depositions first of all, let along getting him into court.

Q: So what's your next move?
ML: Suing his ass to pieces, because he's hiding behind his lawyers and all that stuff.

Q: Have you started the suit?
ML: It's being prepared. It'll probably be pretty soon. You'll hear about it. *(The suit has now been filed — ed.)*

Q: Have you thought about writing your own book?
ML: I don't think my ego is that strong in that kind of department. I mean, I have a strong ego in terms of competition and creativity, and I'm proud of the contribution I made.

Q: That brings up that song "Hang On To Your Ego".
ML: That used to be "Hang On To Your Ego", and then it became "I Know There's An Answer". I changed the lyrics because I thought it was too acid for me.

Q: So there's no chance of a book?
ML: Who would want to fucking take the time to go through garbage like that just to rectify garbage? What I want is Brian to admit and say that half the stuff that he said in his book is outrageous bullshit. I just want it to be fair. That's the one thing that I'd like to have, a little bit of fairness, because he's been very unfair to the rest of the group over the years.

Now Brian is very ingenuous. You want to like him, you want to feel sorry for him because he's destroyed his life. I mean, who wouldn't feel sorry for a guy who is very gifted and who destroyed his life? But the untold story is that he's selfish, he's cheated his cousin and his group. He's been taking money and has not performed. The intent of his getting money to have therapy was not for him to do two solo albums and write a book defaming the group. The guy has mental problems. The thing is, he's crazy. He's a genius, but he's nuts, so a lot of the things he imagines, like the two-by-four his father was supposed to be beating him with, that's delusions.

Q: Was Brian's father Murry Wilson made out to be worse than he was?
ML: Murry was a prick. He was awful. I'm so glad he wasn't my father. He definitely did some damage. Carl's gotten a grip on life, but Dennis sure didn't. He kind of lost his grip.

Q: So he really was kind of a tyrant?
ML: Oh definitely. Very abusive and gruff and terrifying and intimidating and negative. Stuff like, "you guys don't know what you're doing". Those kind of remarks. Very unsupportive. However, he was an aspiring songwriter, and he knew that there was a value to songs. I didn't even know what

BEACH BOYS JOURNALS PART 2

LOOKING BACK WITH LOVE PART 2

THE SECOND PART OF KEN SHARP'S NO-HOLDS-BARRED INTERVIEW WITH THE CONTROVERSIAL BEACH BOYS FRONTMAN

Last month, Mike Love dealt with the most controversial subject in the Beach Boys' world these days — the nagging question of the writing credits and publishing royalties for some of their most famous songs.

In this second and final part of Ken Sharp's interview with the Beach Boys' frontman — commissioned for Denny Somach Productions and originally published in the U.S. magazine 'Goldmine' last year — Mike Love surveys the Beach Boys' work after "Pet Sounds", talks candidly about the band's recent internal problems, and explains the genesis of their latest album, "Summer In Paradise" — which remains unavailable in the U.K. outside the import shops.

Q: There's been talk about doing the entire "Pet Sounds" LP with an orchestra.
MIKE LOVE: That's been one of Bruce Johnston's biggest desires, I would say. It would be good. That and a symphonic album would be really good things to do. Several of the songs would lend themselves to it. The opening of "California Girls" is an overture kind of thing — and "Sloop John B", "Wouldn't It Be Nice", a lot of things.

Q: There are quite a few versions of "Good Vibrations". Did you write a few sets of lyrics for the song?
ML: No, I just wrote one set on the way to the session in Hollywood at Columbia Studios. I dictated it to my then-wife Suzanne on the Hollywood freeway on the way from Burbank to the studio. It was like a 15-minute drive. Just dictated the words.

Q: Did you have any input into the front cover of "Pet Sounds", which was shot at the San Diego Zoo?
ML: That was simply us going on location to shoot the cover — "Pet Sounds", a petting zoo. I suggested the title "Pet Sounds".

Q: Carl Wilson once described the "Smiley Smile" album as being a bunt instead of a grand slam, meaning it was a cheap substitute for "Smile". How do you look back on that LP?
ML: Too much acid. Brian got so wacked out by that time. He completely changed from being dynamic and competitive to being non-combative and non-dynamic. "Smile" was in the same direction as "Good Vibrations" and "Heroes & Villains", and then all of a sudden there was a grinding, screeching halt, a 180 degree turn, and it became "Smiley Smile".

Q: Will "Smile" ever be released?
ML: There are brilliant pieces of music but it's disjointed and fragmented and unfinished, so I don't see any real reason for it to come out, other than certain collectors would like to hear it — and they probably have it anyway (laughs).

Q: I'm not saying anything!
ML: You lousy bastard, that'll be $20 (laughs).

Q: Tell me about the song "Do It Again".
ML: I went surfing with my old high school buddy Bill Jackson in a place called Tressles in Southern California. It was a beautiful day, the waves were perfect. I just wrote that as a sort of diary of the day's events. It took no more than ten minutes to write.

Q: Many people cite "Sunflower" as the best collective Beach Boys LP.
ML: I liked it. Is that the one with "Add Some Music To Your Day"? I liked that song a lot. And what else is on there?

Q: "This Whole World".
ML: Yeah, I thought that was a great song. It's a philosophical kind of thing. See, Brian at that point was capable of a song or two but he wasn't capable of coherent thought for ten songs. Then it became more of Carl taking over the reins, or Bruce, or an outside producer — but I always took a laissez-faire attitude. I don't like recording, it's boring. Tedious. I like writing a song and singing it. But recording — I'd rather be outdoors, reading a good book, going to a movie. My favourite thing is not going into a room in Hollywood and living there for six months while you're making an album. Therefore I was never raring to get in there and be the producer on an album. Forget it. I'd rather write and let somebody else produce it and be done with it.

Q: I like "It's About Time" on "Sunflower".
ML: Yeah, but for me that's a little bit too guitary and rowdy. It's almost like we trying to be something we aren't. That ranks with "Student Demonstration Time" in that department. It's almost like we were trying to be an AOR band when we are really an AC (Adult Contemporary) band.

Q: Do you look back fondly on "Holland"?
ML: The experience of being in Holland was really neat. I thought it was cool to go outside the country and do something unusual. Unfortunately, we also shipped all our recording equipment over. It cost us an arm and a leg. But the "California Saga" trilogy was pretty cool, I thought.

---

publishing was when we started out. I wasn't from a showbusiness background. My dad was a sheet metal worker, and my mom was a housewife. All I knew was that I liked to sing and that I could make up words. I wrote my first song when I was maybe 10 years old.

Q: Then Murry Wilson had some good qualities?
ML: He was very good at promoting, getting radio stations to play our records. He was very smart and clever about it. He would have us go out and do hops and events where a DJ would make a couple hundred bucks and so would we. And since the DJ made some money, he'd be playing our records for the next six months until we did it again. So we built a real good foundation doing that kind of thing, not only in Southern California but all around the country until we got a momentum going.

Q: Have you been in touch with Brian?
ML: No, he's paranoid. We tried to have a board meeting and he was supposed to show up and he didn't come.

Q: Were you disappointed when Brian collaborated with other lyricists like Van Dyke Parks, Roger Christian and Tony Asher?
ML: I wasn't happy about it, but in the case of Roger Christian I wasn't as much into the terminology of car songs as he was. I wrote "I Get Around", which I guess is a cruising song but it's more generic. I wasn't into hot rods to the extent that Roger was, so he provided some lyrical content to support Brian's musical abilities, so that was good. But when I did come up with a hook or some lyrics, it's funny, 'cause it was almost like it was not recognised. It was definitely not legally recognised.

Q: How about the case of Tony Asher writing the lyrics for "Pet Sounds"?
ML: Now that was a different story. When it got to that period, that's when Brian started doing a lot of drugs. We were touring a lot, and we'd come back in and do an album like "Pet Sounds" — and some of the words were so totally offensive to me that I wouldn't even sing 'em, because I thought it was nauseating.

Q: Was that "Hang On To Your Ego"?
ML: Yeah. To me that was too much of a doper song. I just didn't want to have anything to do with it, therefore I didn't go down that road of acid and the things that destroyed Brian's brain. I'd still come to the sessions and I still wrote the words for "Good Vibrations", but I didn't participate in a lot of the stuff that was going on there, because I just didn't think the psychedelic route was the way to go.

Q: What was your initial reaction to the "Pet Sounds" material?
ML: Well, "Pet Sounds" was fine because he was still intact. "Good Vibrations" was great. That and "Heroes And Villains" was his highpoint and then from there it was into the toilet, because mentally he was incapacitated and emotionally he was destroyed by the acid. That's my opinion.

NEXT MONTH: The Beach Boys from "Good Vibrations" to "Kokomo", plus the story behind the group's new U.S. album, "Summer In Paradise".

BEACH BOYS JOURNALS PART 2

"Love You", issued when the Beach Boys were about to end their contract with Warners.

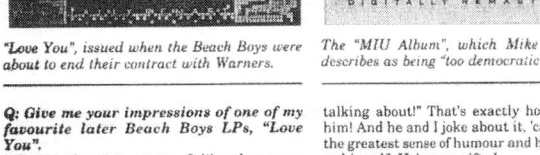

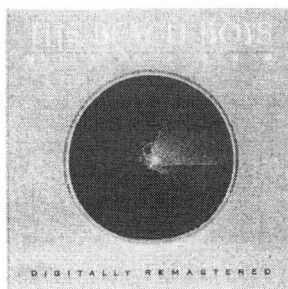

The *"MIU Album"*, which Mike Love now describes as being "too democratic".

"Keeping The Summer Alive", with what Mike Love calls "a pretty cool album cover".

"Summer In Paradise", the 1992 Beach Boys album which wasn't issued in Britain.

Q: Give me your impressions of one of my favourite later Beach Boys LPs, "Love You".
ML: "Airplane" is pretty, I like that song. I think there's cute things on it, but that was one of the last albums on Warners and they were in no mood to promote it. We were at the end of our contract. We had already signed with CBS and they were just like, forget it. They pressed up maybe 50,000 copies.

Q: So that's why the record never took off.
ML: That's right.

Q: How about the "MIU Album", which is one of your more controversial records?
ML: Well, a lot of those albums had some neat gems there, but there wasn't a coherence to them. It was too democratic. It's like, if you have an album and a hit song on it and it's very commercially viable, doesn't it make sense to have another song that would also be commercially viable? And a third and a fourth? I'm talking about trying to gain some sort of commercial recognition which gives you more power over your lives to do things that you want to do. In the Beach Boys' case, if you're not a success commercially, then all you are is a loveable anachronism.

Q: How about your view of 1980's "Keeping The Summer Alive"?
ML: I like the artwork. I thought that was a pretty cool album cover. But the title song could have been more commercial. "Goin' On" is great. That's Brian Wilson. See, Brian, I've said a lot of bad things about him, because he stole from me. That's history and that's a fact, and it will remain to be seen how it is resolved. But Brian in his worst moments is still Brian. He has a brilliant ability with music. I wouldn't say he's brilliant with words, and that's why he's always had co-writers, unfortunately in some cases. Not the best circumstances or people. Maybe they were kind of taking advantage of him.

Q: Did you like Van Dyke Parks' lyrics on songs like "Heroes & Villains"?
ML: I like Van Dyke Parks as a person. At the time, I thought his lyrics were alliterative prose, which is great if you appreciated his prose and his alliteration. He's brilliant. But as far as translating to mid-American commercial appeal, I don't think so. "Columnated ruins domino . . . over and over the crow flies uncover the cornfield". It's self-indulgent. Van Dyke Parks is on the new record, playing accordion. He's great. He's one of the nicest people in the world. And I tell him, "Hey, I thought your lyrics, Van Dyke, were brilliant, except who the fuck knows what you're talking about!" That's exactly how I talk to him! And he and I joke about it, 'cause he has the greatest sense of humour and he can laugh at himself. He's very gifted.

Q: How do you view the "Beach Boys" LP from 1985?
ML: As you remember, "Getcha Back" was the only chart record off that album, and that was clearly a case of fragmentation at its most ridiculous. For instance, Landy and Brian flew off to England to meet Steve Levine, who had done Boy George, and then Carl flew over to England too. Meanwhile, Mike Love and Terry Melcher write "Getcha Back". Terry let this guy (Levine) produce it where he shouldn't have. He should have done it himself because Terry wanted it to be more like the E-Street Band, which would have been a great crossover between the rock and adult contemporary markets.

Q: So Steve Levine was the wrong producer?
ML: For the Beach Boys. We cannot be successful just because he is a current hip groovy producer with some credits. It's way more complicated than that. Our vocal complexity alone is a daunting prospect for most producers. Most producers are engineers. They have the technical expertise and knowledge and maybe had the good fortune to have met the right people and become rich and made a successful album or two. What we needed was somebody to supply what Brian lacks today, which is perseverance and discipline — and the competitive spirit he used to have.

That's what we've done on the new album, basically by committee between myself, Bruce and Terry. Terry fashioning what he's strong at, Bruce helping with vocal arrangements, Mike Love with his hooks and his lyrics and saying what songs we should do, and where I believe Carl is most commercial. And I told Al . . . We had a rough time the last couple of years communicating. Al has this thing where he'll obsess on something that happened 20 years ago. It's hard for him to let go. So we've actually been having group meetings between Carl, myself and Al with the psychiatrist Howard Bloomfield, who's a good friend of mine — airing grievances and working things out. It's been very therapeutic for all of us individually and collectively. I think we've gotten to understand each other and see the other person's point of view and experience, and it's made the group better and stronger.

Q: That confirms a report I heard a little while back that Al Jardine had left the band.
ML: We got to the point where we didn't want to be in the same room or stage with him, because he was so negative about things. Once we were able to get into a forum where he could unload, we could empathise with some of it — not all of it — and air our points of view.

Q: Are you getting along better now?
ML: A lot. But the point is he wasn't even on the album until a couple of months ago when we finally resolved all the stuff.

Q: Tell me about the band's new restaurant, the Original Beach Boys Café.
ML: It's in Hermosa Beach, California, and it's a fun place. It's got all kinds of memorabilia and photos. There are some videos running. It's like the Hard Rock Café, only it's the Beach Boys.

Q: Have the Beach Boys considered issuing a set of unissued material like Bob Dylan's "Bootleg Series"?
ML: I think Al Jardine might be interested in getting involved in something like that, whereas my disposition is more like what can we do creatively now and in the future. I'm not so much into the past.

Q: It's been almost 10 years since your cousin and colleague Dennis Wilson passed away. What's your fondest memory of him?
ML: Dennis at the Sacremento Civic Auditorium, playing the drums and beating the hell out of them (laughs) and having screams that were at least as loud, if not louder, than the Beatles ever got, because he was so charismatic and so appealing to those young girls. He was like the sex symbol of the Beach Boys, very dynamic, very healthy, a powerful drummer — not finesse but raw power. And he was very generous to everybody and had a lot of spirit and energy.

Unfortunately, he got into drugs and alcohol and became addicted and it ruined his life, took his life, ultimately, and he was not enjoyable to be with in his last few years because of that. We had problems that arose from the alcoholism and its influence on his drumming. But as far as his essential nature, it was just a lot of raw energy and charisma — and he had a big heart.

Way back in the early days, we used to go fishing together, and that's when we first talked about doing a surfing song. We were on Redondo Beach breakwater, fishing. We went back to Brian and said, "Hey!". Then I wrote 90% of "Surfin'" and "Surfin' Safari" and "Surfin' USA", which I wasn't credited for.

Q: Next to Brian, I felt Dennis was the best songwriter in the band.
ML: His style of writing was so kind of subjective. I am more objective in relating to the masses. How do we take a concept like "Good Vibrations", which was ethereal and avant-garde in 1966, and make it accessible? Dennis didn't think that way, and I think he tried to emulate Brian's style. Brian did some changes which were very interesting and creative, but I thought Dennis's changes were more self-indulgent. But he definitely did come up with some good melodies and great moments. He had stuff in him. But he was not verbally facile. He was kind of in-between Brian and myself. He wasn't quite comfortable with words, he was more into feelings. Feelings were his strong suit, I think.

Q: Isn't Carl Wilson involved in a new project?
ML: He's been writing recently with Gerry Beckley (of America) and Bobby Lamm (Chicago), and they're doing a project together. I think they're going to start recording soon.

Q: "Summer In Paradise" was the first new Beach Boys album in over seven years. What took so long?
ML: What took so long is that the group has for the past several years been sort of coasting on the momentum of our success in the 60s. We got a little bit excited by "Kokomo" because it was the largest-selling single of our careers, and of that year. It was responsible for several million sales on the "Cocktail" album. It was the No. 1 video on VH-1 and Nickelodeon, and it also got the Jukebox Operators' Award.

Unfortunately, since Tracy Chapman and Anita Baker were on Elektra as well, the label didn't submit it for recognition as single of the year at the Grammys, because of politics. That's a flaw in the system.

The song was a collaboration with John Phillips, who came up with the verse and the verse-melody. I came up with the "Aruba Jamaica" chorus, and Terry Melcher wrote the "I want to take you down to Kokomo" part.

Q: Who produced your new record?
ML: Terry Melcher co-wrote and produced the whole record. His background is with the Byrds, Paul Revere & the Raiders, and at one time Bruce & Terry and the Ripchords. So he's most eminently qualified, of all the people I know, to position our group vocally.

BEACH BOYS JOURNALS PART 2

Q: What's the tone of the record?
ML: To tell you about the record, I think we should start with the concept, and for that I go back to "Beach Boys Party" and "Pet Sounds" — not qualitatively, but to draw a parallel. In 1966, Capitol Records was chomping at the bit for an album, and Brian Wilson wanted to spend a lot of time creating this piece of work which we know as "Pet Sounds". He was feeling the time constraints. He really wanted more time to develop it, and yet the label kept saying, "We want an album". So what we did was go in and record the "Beach Boys Party" session in just two back-to-back sessions.

On that album was "Barbara Ann", and we had no idea it was ever going to be a single. Al Cory, who was then the North-Eastern promo man for Capitol, actually chose it as the single. That bought us some time. Then "Pet Sounds" came out a few months later.

We wanted to get together and record something very masterful. In fact, I already have the title of the next album. We're going to call it "Masterpiece" — to make a real statement about life and all the issues that are important to us now, as opposed to 1962 and 1963. So we thought we needed some time, just like we did for "Pet Sounds" — and not just a year, but a couple of years, to develop the songs properly.

So what we did with this new album ("Summer In Paradise") was set out to do the definitive soundtrack for summer. Terry and I met and went over thirty songs. You've gotta understand that Terry for a while was a member of the Rotary (Club) — and middle-aged producers who happen to be in Rotary do not think romantically like a 17-year-old girl. I'd have to remind these guys that we are of an age when we remember in the remote history of our life that there was once a thing called romance. And girls love romance. They like a slow dance once in a while.

We settled upon what we felt were the most appropriate covers for the album. Through a process of elimination, the concept went from the definition of summer to take in a few other songs that would be appropriate at other times of the year. So we have a song called "Island Fever" which resonates well with the summer songs, but it's meant to come out in the winter. It's sort of like the cousin to "Kokomo", musically speaking. And we did "(Remember) Walking In The Sand", which I think is awesome. "Hot Fun In The Summertime" is the first single.

Q: You issued the album on your own label.
ML: The Beach Boys have been on Capitol, Warners, CBS, back to Capitol and in the case of "Kokomo", Elektra. So we've been distributing our records through major labels all our lives except for our first record. "Surfin'", which was on a label called Candix, which went bankrupt. We got a total of $900 royalties on that one, and then we signed to Capitol in 1962.

The problem with a major is — when we did the "Still Cruisin'" album, we went to radio with a song called "Somewhere In Japan", which was getting really good airplay. And that same week, our label, Capitol, were going to stations with eight other records to compete with ours.

The theme of "Still Cruisin'" was to have songs that had been in movies. It was basically a repackage. But then it got watered down by politics, meaning Brian's Dr. Landy forcing on a song called "In My Car" and a song by Jardine called "Island Girl", which were never in a movie. So to me the concept was a little bit diluted. I wasn't happy that the album was half repackage and half politics, though that's what happens if you're in a group and you divide it by five members and you get two songs each.

So this time I got approval from the group to take a hand in the project. Every song and producer we would use would have to be okayed by me and I would have the authority to exercise what I felt was the most commercial and creative strengths of all the guys. I was objective enough with Terry Melcher to create "Kokomo" — that was one where I took a real strong hand in the co-writing and then got it placed in the movie.

The idea of a thematic summer album really appealed to me. "Hot Fun In The Summertime" by the Beach Boys is phenomenal. On "(Remember) Walking In The Sand", Carl sounds so good, and the arrangement is so hot. It's just a mindblower. We did another one called "Under The Boardwalk" which is a mindblower. Everybody that hears it loves it.

Q: And you covered one of your own songs, "Surfin'".
ML: That was fun. In fact, playing it back blows my mind, because we approached it from the standpoint of what it would be like if we'd started out in the 90s. So it's got the hip-hop drums, the metallish guitar and our sound. It's not quite rap, but it's urbanised. And we have the most up-to-date technology. We're recording it right onto a hard disc using this pro-tools equipment. It's not even on tape.

Q: Who's putting out the record?
ML: We've created a new label. It's being distributed by a company called Navarre which is a national independent distributor, located in Minneapolis. I met a fellow at the airport that I knew from the CBS days, called Ron Alexenburg, and he's heading up the promotion for us. I just met him at Burbank Airport, and it was karmic. I told him I was thinking of taking the album over to Al Cory at Geffen because he's an old friend, but Ron said, "Why don't you go to a company where they need you?" And he introduced us to this guy Eric Paulsen who runs Navarre.

The thing about this deal is the margin we'll make by not being with a major. We won't have to sue a record company for the accounting because we can sue ourselves. It's much more direct. Just economically, if we went to a major and got a million dollars advance, then the record would come out, and by the time you calculated the money from overseas and here and there, it would be a good year before you got any accounting. They always try to cheat you. Every major company tries to use your money and pay you as little as possible and charge you all kinds of deductions. You know you're never going to be a priority to them, except when you're in a meeting, and even then they're thinking about their next meeting or their last meeting. Or they just gave so-and-so a ten-million-dollar deal, so your one-million-dollar deal doesn't mean shit.

In this situation, with Navarre, every 60 days we'll get our money. If you're actually signed to a label, then you're both their lifeblood and an expense. So they treat you as a predator, almost, not as a real partner.

Mike Love during the Beach Boys' 1969 tour of Britain and Europe.

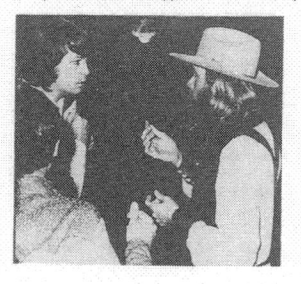

Most fans agree that the Beach Boys were at their peak as a live band in the early 70s — the only time when they were fully capable of tackling both their surfin' and hot rod oldies, and the complex material from their mid-60s LPs. Mike Love acted as their on-stage cheerleader.

BEACH BOYS JOURNALS PART 2

BEACH BOYS JOURNALS PART 2

BEACH BOYS JOURNALS PART 2

CLOSE ENCOUNTERS OF THE SURF KIND

Close Encounter of the first kind: sighting of the Beach Boys

THE day of the first Melbourne Beach Boys concert, I decided to declare war on the Victorian Railways, following the death of some poor young woman, a train that refused to go, and one that refused to stop.

There I was, trying to get myself into the city to (hopefully!) meet with Dennis Wilson and big brother Brian to discuss the meaning of life itself and other small fry.

The prospect of speaking to Brian Wilson, even if he was only the shell-shocked remainder of an over-indulgent love affair with certain chemical and/or vegetable substances, was a possibility deeply cherished, such was my respect for the man's profound contribution to the evolution of rock'n'roll.

Leaving for the Hilton Hotel in plenty of time, I tried catching a train, only problem was that a train passing through two minutes earlier, had travelled 200 metres beyond my station where a young woman had decided to take the hard way out by stepping in front of the train and having her body smashed into tiny pieces.

It took about 50 minutes for the Railways to get us a train around the accident scene and when I hit the city, I then tried to catch another, only to be told after sitting there for 20 minutes, it was defective.

By this stage, my cool was also becoming defective as I was now running 15 minutes late. I was cheered up by the announcement that we should all catch the train on the adjoining platform which I dutifully did. Only when it eventually moved, instead of stopping one station away opposite the Hilton, as I expected it to, it went express for five stations.

By the time I beat it back to the Hilton, I was 50 minutes late and the interview had been blown out for that day because the promoter's publicity lady, Patti Moyston, had already seen Beach Boy Dennis Wilson struggle manfully through two boring interviews and the prospect of a third could turn Dennis off all further Australian "conversations".

So the third interview and mine, which followed it, were cancelled. Thanks Vic Rail!

However, Ms Moyston, sympathising with my harrowing experiences, arranged for me to speak to Dennis the following day and she would see if Brian could be persuaded to also talk, something he had done only once since landing in Australia when Pat Bowring from the Melbourne Sun, had scooped everybody else with five minutes of Brian's time.

As things turned out, I got to talk to Dennis next day as planned and the following day, after it was obvious, Dennis hadn't died of boredom talking to JUKE, it was arranged for Brian to consent to be interviewed.

Hopefully for more than five minutes, although no-one could even guarantee it would last longer than 30 seconds, and after meeting and speaking to Brian Wilson, I knew what they meant.

As it was, it lasted for a bit over 15 minutes, which I suppose for Brian is sufficiently long enough to be interviewed by anybody.

I eventually spoke to Dennis after the first Melbourne concert which I enjoyed thoroughly with the exception of what I thought was valid criticism but which was to prove nevertheless irritating to Dennis, an intense man, fiercely independent, and very much on this tour the high profile of the three Wilson brothers.

Brian, on the other hand, was an enigma of sorts and such was his detachment or seeming remoteness during conversation, that this combined with his ability to answer even the most complicated questions with a simple "yes", "no", "I guess", "that's possible", made him an impossibly difficult interview subject.

But we tried, and just when it got very interesting (it seemed Brian was suddenly imparting some difficult truths), the answers seemed to frighten him and he decided to do a runner and end the interview.

Without seeming to sound enigmatic, Brian Wilson and reality seem to have a rather loose relationship, whether due to Brian's previous drug taking, particularly LSD, or some other reason which escapes my logic. Some of his answers never really had a lot to do with the question asked, while often, other answers which professed ignorance at certain situations, were either the answers of a fool or a liar.

Talking to Dennis Wilson it was soon obvious that the previous night's concert was a sore point with him, as I unreeled some criticisms. After listening patiently for a while to what he called my song-by-song criticism with what was wrong, he struck back.

"Look, is there anything else you want to talk about? You see, I get tired of doing interviews with guys like you who pick apart the show and it's as irritating as shit.

"It would be nice to talk about something else instead of 20 minutes song-by-song of how bad it was."

Actually Dennis, who turned out to be a really sweet guy, was a little over-sensitive to my general comments on the show, because overall I thoroughly enjoyed it, unlike some people, most notably Ian Meldrum.

Dennis Wilson made no secret of the fact the band was not happy with their performance simply because they had had to suffer equipment problems (the breakdown of their stage monitors which made it difficult for each musician to hear what the others were singing and playing) while also having to contend with colds which they believe they picked up on their flight to Australia.

Whatever the causes, Dennis Wilson felt sufficiently upset about it to express his discontent at their performance, yet sufficiently defensive to pounce on me when I made general criticisms of the show.

"Another factor which the audience don't realise because they are ignorant when it comes to electronics, is that we rehearsed at the Myer Music Bowl on the day of the show with the bowl empty and we didn't compensate for it because when it was full of people, the sound was completely different.

Close Encounter of the second kind: hearing the Beach Boys

"Generally, a lot of empty halls will be completely the same when full. Combine that with our problems with the monitors and the sound just wasn't loud enough."

He promised the second Melbourne concert would be 500 per cent better though and when we said a few words the day after, he assured me the second concert was far more satisfactory.

However, a couple of friends who saw both nights, said they thought the second show was not as good as the first night, so how can you win?

Although it goes back a long time, the most fascinating snippet of information to surface since the Beach Boys began their tour of Oz, was the report that just prior to this tour, Dennis Wilson had "discovered" the previously lost "SMILE" tapes.

As popular legend has it, "Smile" was to be Brian Wilson's knockout reply to the Beatles rocketing popularity at the time in 1967.

But Wilson was supposed to have destroyed at least the vocal tracks after "Sgt. Pepper's" was released, supposedly realising that he could only finish second best in any Pepper-Smile critical showdown.

"Brian didn't destroy the tapes at all," Dennis reassured me.

"What happened was that he discarded them by accident in the library at Brothers recording studio (owned by the Beach Boys). They were simply misplaced with no labelling on them and I found them purely by accident."

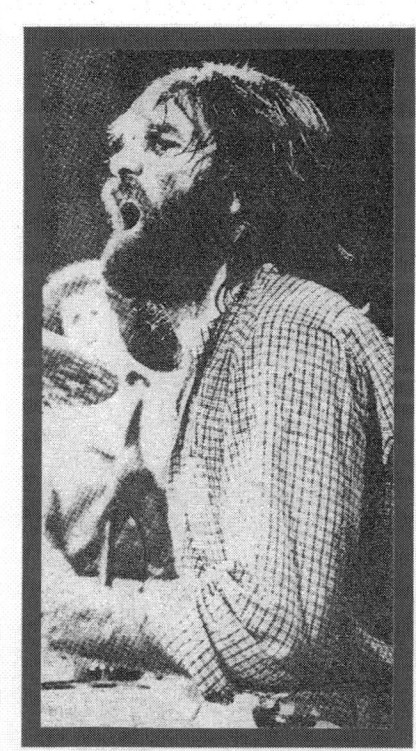

BEACH BOYS JOURNALS PART 2

Brian simply described "Adult Child" as having a lot of "serious adult-type songs".

Were there any surprises that veer away from what the Beach Boys have recorded before? "No, not really. Some of it's new, but yeah, there are some surprises. It's very adult new stuff, both vocally and instrumentally."

Dennis, on the other hand, was refreshingly honest about the album Warners is not sitting on.

"I think I like "Beach Boys Love You" (the previous album) a bit more," he said. Considering that album was a major disappointment, Dennis isn't exactly giving the new album a rave review.

He revealed that as soon as the Oz tour is completed, it's back to America to start working on the first CBS release, while he also finishes off his second solo album.

I was intrigued at how Dennis, at one point during the concert, departed the stage for a couple of numbers.

What seemed like a harmless enough question, produced a most surprising response.

"I left because I don't like the songs themselves (one of them was a Mike Love T.M. song 'Everybody's In Love With You').

I'm not an advocate of meditation, so I don't think I want to sing about it. I don't think it's right to promote something during certain parts of the show because you are a Beach Boy.

"I just feel that people come to see Beach Boys music and I think we should just do that. Mind you, I'm not slamming meditation," he added reasonably.

After further questioning about him being the most independent of the Beach Boys, the only one to ever surf, release a solo album, etc., he said his exit over meditation was not a question of making any big stand.

"I'm not against reform but I just don't meditate. I am sure, there are several members of the band who feel the same way."

This could perhaps be identified as a minor conflict within the band, a band that Mike Love told the obnoxious Paul Makin on Willesee (who, incidentally, got back some of his own treatment from Love and Alan Jardine and didn't like it a bit), was "split into two factions", whatever that means.

Close Encounter of the surf kind: talking to the Beach Boys

Dennis said they had just been stuck away in the library through the years since Brian misplaced them, and since he runs the studio, he makes it his business to go through all the tapes all the time because he's interested, and suddenly one day, he found himself face-to-face with the long-lost "Smile" master tapes.

"I ran across the Fire tapes, things like Worms, all the good ones," he said. When I asked him if the version of the title track of "Surf's Up" which originally formed part of "Smile" is the same one, he replied: "It's from the same era but it's not Surf's Up.

"The song just forms part of The Elements (supposedly a series of interconnecting Brian Wilson compositions). I don't know how long "Elements" lasts, but some of "Smile" has already been released, such as "Cabinessence" which appears on the "Sunflower" album."

While the band doesn't know what to do with "Smile", it's obvious that the incredible interest which will now result from the knowledge of the alleged "missing masterpiece's" existence, might influence the band to eventually release it as a curio in much the same way that Bob Dylan and The Band's "Basement Tapes" was belatedly released.

Contrary to a report that Brian Wilson has been played the tapes since their discovery, he says he hasn't.

"Dennis has told me he has the tapes but I don't know where they are and I haven't heard them yet," he informed me.

When Brian was asked if he would like to see the album released, he replied: "I don't think they would be right for now. That kind of stuff just isn't right now."

What sort of "stuff" is it?

"Oh they're just very sporadic tapes. They weren't done as well as Pet Sounds or had as much put into them. They were not as elaborate."

What about "Elements"?

"That I don't know about. It was such a jumbled mess that I don't even know. It wasn't organised. It wasn't completed. It was so ugh . . . we didn't even like it."

Well, would he like to see "Smile" eventually released then? Strangely enough, he said yes.

If Brian sounded slightly puzzled about his aborted "Smile" album, he was just as cryptic with what he didn't say about the "Adult Child" album Warners now have, which fulfills the Beach Boys recording contract with the label. Future releases will be released on Caribou Records, through CBS worldwide.

"Yeah, there have always been conflicts in the band," Dennis confirmed, "but they're just the conflicts that everyone experiences."

Didn't "Pet Sounds", Brian Wilson's masterwork, account for a lot of conflict in the Beach Boys at the time of its recording in 1966, one wondered? Popular legend has always been that the rest of the band were most displeased with the new direction of musical experiment upon which their resident genius was embarking.

"You read that?" Dennis asked in genuine amazement. "We were all involved in that record. We were involved on it almost every day and we were profoundly excited at participating."

As if to convince me of his sincerity, when we tackled the subject of the next CBS album, Dennis said he thought it would be more in the vein of a "Pet Sounds" album than their recent albums.

"I don't mean it will be a concept album, but it will be more involved in that we will spend more time on recording each track."

He said it would be a co-production by the group including Brian.

One song, which may be included on that album, is supposedly one of Brian's finest compositions in years, "California Feeling", which he has been sitting on now for about two years.

"I love that song very, very much," Brian readily concedes to me as he looks sheepishly away at some secret object invisibly floating in the air several feet away.

"I don't know when it will be released, but I love that song so very much. I suppose it is very possible it could be on the next album we record."

Frequently, in reading old articles on the Beach Boys, Brian Wilson's lack of self-confidence is very noticeable. Self-doubt and even paranoia were as much a part of his personality as warmth and, strangely enough, a very funny sense of humour.

While the only quirk of his personality that impressed itself upon me, was his difficulty in being able to convey his feelings frequently, Dennis made it clear that Brian's decision to quit touring with the band back in 1965 had nothing to do with self-doubt. Various versions cover such ground as a nervous breakdown while flying to a gig at Houston in Texas, to the loss of hearing in his right ear.

"Brian just decided to stop touring for a while." (More than ten years is a while?). Dennis went on to also explain Brian's gradual withdrawal as the band's producer and composer of the bulk of their material.

"He's always been with us but he just stopped in the sense of being the one producer who told everybody what to do and how it was to be done, and now, I guess, he realises that the group is no longer musically himself."

BEACH BOYS JOURNALS PART 2

Brian agreed he found it very strange at first to again be involved in producing the Beach Boys when he returned to the console for "15 Big Ones". His last full production involvement prior to that was in 1971, when he produced his wife, Marylyn and her sister as Spring. In fact, he told me, he's hoping to get around to completing the second Spring album some time in the future as most of it has already been recorded. The first one was notable for the extensive and elaborate Wilson arranging and production on such oldies as "Tennessee Waltz".

He's been finding the time to listen to American and British new-wave music and whether he was simply being diplomatic or not, I don't know, but he said he's heard quite a lot of it.

"I like nearly all of what I've heard, but there's no one I can name to you that I particularly like."

Last year, the Beach Boys got a lashing from the British music press when they cancelled their European tour at the 11th hour. But when you ask Brian why it was cancelled, he seemed unbelievably ignorant when he answered: "I don't know why it was cancelled. I don't really know what happened at all." Dennis said, it was simply a case of not enough time.

But the tour was booked and they must have known well in advance it was coming up? "Oh sure, but it wasn't just possible to have a very successful tour and we felt it would be wise to wait."

Brian was guarded on the possibility of going on the re-scheduled European tour this year around June.

"I hope to tour if I can, yes. If I'm up to it and my health is fine," Brian said.

What was his main health worry at the moment? "I don't know. I don't really know if I'm unhealthy and if I am, where. I haven't really had a good checkup. I'm feeling good on this tour. Feeling great every day, and last night, I felt this surge of energy and I really did feel good," he added.

Although outwardly Brian seems as healthy as the next person, as he sits beside you staring uncomfortably into space, there is a disquieting feeling which tells you that, although you are readily convinced he may have produced a classic Beach Boys song-like "California Feeling", I drew the inescapable conclusion that they will be very much the exception from now on.

Whatever the creative spark was which ignited Wilson's genius in the early to middle sixties, it now seems destined to flicker both faintly and infrequently.

As if to confirm your worst fears, he says enough himself to provide you with the answer you really don't want to hear. What was his approach to writing songs now? "I don't now. I haven't . . . I'm not writing anymore. I've stopped doing it," he says with quiet resignation, the sudden memory of which seems to momentarily pain him before he braces himself for what he now knows is the inevitable question to come.

Have the ideas stopped? "Yeah." How many songs would he have written in the last year? "About 20, I guess."

I told him some people would be more than satisfied with that as an annual output.

But Brian's not listening anymore.

It's as if the realisation that the ideas have dried up, has only suddenly occurred to him and its crushing meaning fills him with a panic need to get away.

"I've got to stop now, I'll talk to you later," he says as he rises from our poolside table and makes off in search of his bodyguard.

He knows he won't, but he felt he had to say it, and I felt I had to go along with him, while at the same time I felt an instinctive urge to say, "Brian, things are not what they seem, you'll see". But when I can't even be too sure what Brian seems to be, such advice becomes redundant.

Depressing as my conclusions about Brian seem personally to me, this is after all about the Beach Boys, and we all know they stand for fun, fun, fun, so to take us out on a happier note, the continuation of a favorite theme.

The cretinous mentality of your average Australian media interviewer when dealing with visiting rock personalities.

"You know some of the TV people in this country, phew!" and Dennis Wilson whistles in disbelief. "You know, you're my favorite person who's interviewed me in Australia so far. I've been getting questions like 'what is your private life like' and yeah, well, I replied 'the thing I like about it is that it's private'."

An elderly man who looks like he belongs to the Beach Boys American management, suddenly entered the conversation to recount how he had been watching Sammy Davis Jnr. being interviewed on Australian television a few nights previously.

"They asked him how was his sex life. If that had been me, I would have punched that interviewer," he said, and we all shook our heads knowingly.

"Yeah, I was asked a question like that," Dennis contributed. "I was asked if my father didn't like groupies (his father Murray is dead) and I said 'boys or girls?'."

Alan, Brian, Mike, Dennis, Carl

BEACH BOYS JOURNALS PART 2

BEACH BOYS JOURNALS PART 2

BEACH BOYS JOURNALS PART 2

BEACH BOYS JOURNALS PART 2

BEACH BOYS JOURNALS PART 2

With the light fading and the drizzle creeping down, Richard Digance had a tough task keeping the fans entertained while the Beach Boys prepared for their set. Earlier they came up to the House and we set out a cold buffet and drinks for them. Brian Wilson looked sadly at the laden table and asked "Have you any cake?" I fetched a newly baked chocolate cake I had made for the children, which he greeted with a huge grin. He lay on the sofa, ate the whole cake, and then went to sleep with a cushion over his head. The other members of the group had a hard time waking him up to go down to the stage.

They arrived on stage half an hour early, hitherto unheard of at Knebworth concerts! Their new album 'Keeping The Summer Alive' somehow seemed very appropriate in the damp weather conditions. Brian Wilson sat at the piano still half asleep and the group tried to rally him by suggesting it was his birthday and shouting 'Happy Birthday' to him. (It had been his birthday the day before). Creator of all the great Beach Boys classics, Brian was now a sad and tragic piece of sixties wreckage. They are a great dance band and we were all on our feet dancing throughout. It was only through seeing them live that one realises how many marvellous songs they have produced.

BEACH BOYS JOURNALS PART 2

Pages from the
Knebworth House
visitors' book.

BEACH BOYS JOURNALS PART 2

BEACH BOYS JOURNALS PART 2

BEACH BOYS JOURNALS PART 2

BEACH BOYS JOURNALS PART 2

BRIAN WILSON SESSIONS

Brian WILSON

SESSIONS

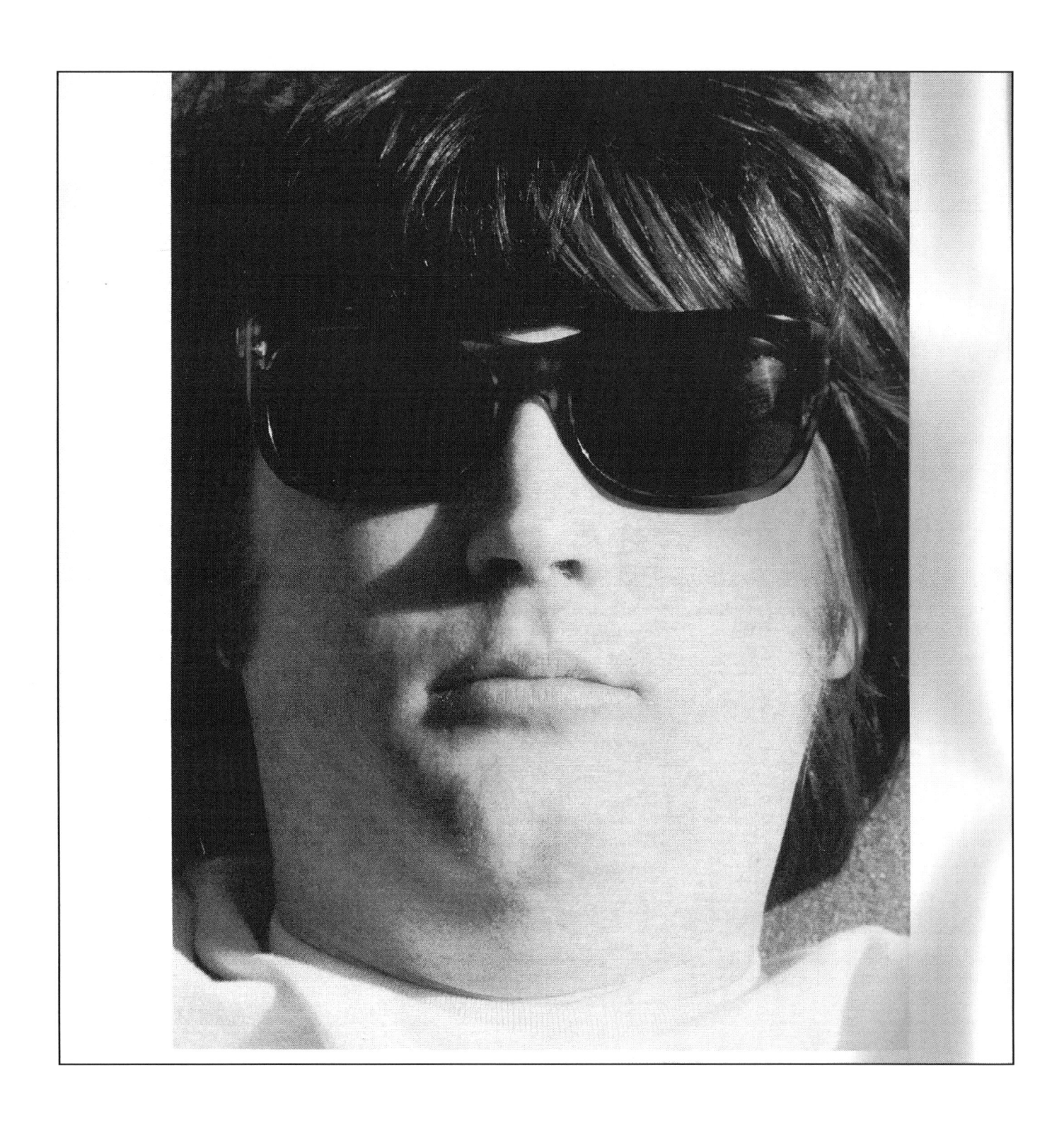

BRIAN WILSON SESSIONS

BRIAN WILSON SESSIONS

COMPUTER ENHANCED - DIGITALLY REMASTERED

Brian WILSON
SESSIONS VOL. 1 SWEET INSANITY

CD - 25

AFTER THE RELATIVE SUCCESS OF HIS FIRST EVER SOLO ALBUM 'BRIAN WILSON' (ON SIRE) IN 1988, BRIAN EMBARKED ON A SERIES OF SESSIONS WHICH RESULTED IN THE 'SWEET INSANITY' ALBUM WE HAVE PRESENTED HERE FOR YOUR PLEASURE. IT HAS A NUMBER OF STRONG SONGS, 3 OF WHICH SNEAKED OUT IN VARIOUS FORMS OVER A CONSIDERABLE PERIOD. 'SPIRIT OF ROCK 'N' ROLL' IS IN FACT QUITE 'OLD' (FROM 1966). 'COUNTRY FEELIN' **WAS** ISSUED AS PART OF A DISNEY CD COMPILATION IN 1991 AND 'SMART GIRLS' **WAS** ISSUED IN U.S.A. AS A CASSINGLE (ONLY).TO PROVIDE GOOD VALUE TO YOU, THE FAN, WE HAVE FILLED UP THE CD WITH THE VERY BEST OF THE HARD TO FIND RARITIES BRIAN HAS RECORDED OVER THE LAST 18 YEARS INCLUDING 'GOODNIGHT IRENE' IN SUPERB STEREO. THIS IS THE VERY BEST OF THE RAREST BRIAN WILSON, NOW CHECK OUT DEMO'S AND OUT TAKES IN THIS BOX SET FOR THE REST OF THE BEST OF......

#	SONGTITLE	TIME	SONGWRITERS	RECORDING DATE	COMMENTS
1.	CONCERT TONIGHT	0.16	(B.WILSON-E.LANDY)		TRACKS 1 - 13 FROM REJECTED FOLLOW-UP ALBUM TO 1988'S SELF TITLED 'BRIAN WILSON'. WAS TO BE TITLED 'SWEET INSANITY'
2.	SOMEONE TO LOVE	4.00	(B.WILSON-E.LANDY)		
3.	WATER BUILDS UP	3.20	(B.WILSON-E.LANDY)		
4.	DON'T LET HER KNOW (SHE'S AN ANGEL)	3.43	(B.WILSON-E.LANDY)		
5.	I DO	3.46	(B.WILSON-E.LANDY)		
6.	THANK YOU	3.23	(B.WILSON-E.LANDY)		
7.	HOTTER	3.51	(B.WILSON-E.LANDY)		
8.	SPIRIT OF ROCK 'N' ROLL	3.30	(B.WILSON-G.USHER-KELLY)		(W/BOB DYLAN) RECORDING ORIGINALLY COMMENCED AUG 19 '86 ORIGINALLY MIMED BY BRIAN (WITHOUT BOB DYLAN'S CONTRIBUTION)WITH THE BEACH BOYS AT THE END OF THE 25TH ANNIVERSARY T.V.SHOW PERFORMED IN HAWAII IN DECEMBER '86
9.	RAINBOW EYES	4.21	(B.WILSON-E.LANDY)		
10.	LOVE YA	3.08	(B.WILSON-E.LANDY)		
11.	MAKE A WISH	2.58	(B.WILSON-E.LANDY)		
12.	SMART GIRLS	4.12	(B.WILSON-E.LANDY)		ACTUALLY RELEASED IN USA ONLY AS A CASSINGLE CIRCA '89. BRIANS 1ST (& LAST) RAP SONG (W/BEACH BOYS SAMPLED SONGS THROUGHOUT)
13.	COUNTRY FEELIN'	2.45	(B.WILSON-E.LANDY-A.MORGAN)	1991	BRIANS CONTRIBUTION TO DISNEY'S 'FOR OUR CHILDREN' CD
	- BONUS TRACKS -				
14.	DADDY'S LITTLE GIRL	3.17	(B.WILSON-ALEXANDRA MORGAN-EUGENE E. LANDY)		FROM THE SOUNDTRACK FOR THE FILM 'SHE'S OUT OF CONTROL' STARRING TONY DANZA & AMI DOLENZ (MONKEE MICKEY'S DAUGHTER)
15.	HE COULDN'T GET HIS POOR OLD BODY TO MOVE	2.38	(B.WILSON-EUGENE E. LANDY-LINDSAY BUCKINGHAM)		RECORDING FIRST COMMENCED JUNE 28, 1988(ISSUED 1988) B-SIDE / BONUS CD SINGLE TRACKS FOR LOVE & MERCY (PROD. BY BRIAN & LINDSAY BUCKINGHAM)
16.	LIVING DOLL (A.K.A. 'BARBIE')	1.58	(B.WILSON-E.LANDY-A.MORGAN)	1987	ISSUED AS A BLUE MINI FLEXI DISC TO PROMOTE THE 'CALIFORNIA DREAM' BARBIE DOLL (& ACTUALLY CREDITED TO THE BEACH BOYS ON THE RECORDS' LABEL THOUGH DEFINITELY A BRIAN WILSON SOLO EFFORT.
17.	LET'S GO TO HEAVEN IN MY CAR	3.36	(B.WILSON-E.LANDY-G.USHER)	Mar'87	SOLO 45 FROM THE SOUNDTRACK ALBUM OF 'POLICE ACADEMY 4'
18.	TOO MUCH SUGAR	2.38	(B.WILSON-E.LANDY-A.MORGAN)	Mar'87	B-SIDE TO ABOVE (#17). ANOTHER LIFESTYLE ADVICE SONG (WHICH BORROWS HEAVILY FROM 'SHORTENIN' BREAD' ON THE VERSES)
19.	METAL BEACH	3.35	(B.WILSON-P.SHAFFER)	1989	(INSTR.) B-SIDE TO PAUL SHAFFER'S SOLO SINGLE 'WHEN THE RADIO IS ON'. PAUL IS DAVID LETTERMAN'S MUSIC ARRANGER / KEYBOARDIST WHO APPEARED IN 'SPINAL TAP' MOVIE & REGULARLY APPEARS IN TV/VIDEO SPECIALS (EG JERRY LEE LEWIS & FRIENDS ..... RON WOOD ETC & JOHN PHILLIPS / MAMA & PAPAS VIDEO 'STRAIGHT SHOOTER'
20.	BELLS OF MADNESS / FANTASY IS REALITY	4.09	(SAM PHILLIPS-ROB WASSERMAN-BRIAN WILSON)	1993	(ORGAN COURTESY OF AUDREY WILSON - B.BOYS MUM) COLLABORATION WITH DAUGHTER CARNIE ON ROB WASSERMAN'S 'TRIOS' CD. SAM PHILLIPS WROTE 'BELLS OF MADNESS' (CONTRARY TO WHAT ONE MIGHT THINK)WHILST 'FANTASY IS REALITY' PART(1.15 AND 1.32) WAS CO-WRITTEN BY BRIAN AND ROB WASSERMEN.
21.	STILL I DREAM OF IT	3.26	(B.WILSON)	Circa'76	ORIGINALLY THE FINAL TRACK ON BRIAN'S ILL-FATED SOLO ALBUM 'ADULT CHILD'. THIS SONG WAS OFFERED TO (BUT REJECTED BY) FRANK SINATRA.
22.	GOODNIGHT IRENE	2.38	(HUDDIE LEDBETTER)	1988	BRIANS CONTRIBUTION TO A LEDBETTER / GUTHRIE TRIBUTE CD. BRIAN SINGS ALL VOCAL PARTS, PLAYS KEYBOARDS & SYNTHESISERS, BANJO & SOUSAPHONE
23.	SPIRIT OF THE FOREST	2.43	(KENNY YOUNG)	1989	(RADIO EDIT) VIRGIN'S 45 FOR THE 'EARTH LOVE FUND' FEATURING MANY FAMOUS ARTISTS (EG CHRIS REA, KIM WILDE, KATE BUSH..... & RINGO STARR) BRIAN SINGS AT 0.36 SECS INTO SONG

TOTAL CD TIME - 74.10

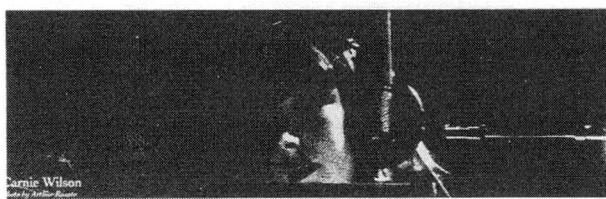

BRIAN WILSON SESSIONS

1. FANTASY IS REALITY/BELLS OF MADNESS 4:09
Sam Phillips, Rob Wasserman, Brian Wilson
(Eden Bristow Music ASCAP, Administered by Bug Music; Steev Music; Brother Bram Music/BMI)

This song was like a trip down to where we'd had *Fantasy is reality* in one key for years. Brian Wilson and my daughter Carnie had recorded together and she could sense very emotional. Carnie wanted to see that Brian had been working on the surface of his soul his entire life.

The song was written in collaboration with Brian, Sam Phillips, and myself. I asked Don Was to produce, as he is a fellow bass player/friend/admirer of Brian's work, and a great producer. Sam wrote the verses and choruses. Brian and I realized we had very similar views on the song's subject, so we decided to write a bridge based on our conversations about the nature of fantasy versus reality. When I asked Brian if he would like Carnie to sing the lead vocal, he said he had had the same idea! This session was like a family reunion—Brian's mother Audree entertained us with great stories of the old days of recording Beach Boys demos in the rec room studio. Rodney is Guitar... Just don't ...

BRIAN WILSON SESSIONS

COMPUTER ENHANCED - DIGITALLY REMASTERED

Brian WILSON — SESSIONS VOL.2 SWEET INSANITY OUTTAKES

CD - 26

AN INTRIGUING COLLECTION OF 5 INCREDIBLY STRONG (YET REJECTED !) SONGS FROM 'SWEET INSANITY' OPENS THIS CD. FANS WILL DEBATE FOREVER, BUT WE FEEL THAT TRACKS #2, #3 & #4 ARE AS STRONG AS **ANY** TRACKS ON 'SWEET INSANITY' & SHOULD HAVE BEEN INCLUDED IN THE FINAL TRACK SELECTION SINCE THE LATTER CD ONLY CLOCKS IN AT ABOUT 43 MINUTES - SHORT BY TODAY'S (CD) STANDARDS. NEVERMIND, THEY'RE **HERE** ANYWAY SO YOU THE FAN NEEDN'T MISS OUT. AS A MATTER OF INTEREST, TRACK # 11 IS THE ONE USED FOR THE BEACH BOYS' 25TH. ANNIVERSARY TV SHOW IN WAIKIKI DURING WHICH BRIAN MIMED TO THIS RECORDING.

#	SONGTITLE	TIME	SONGWRITERS	RECORDING DATE	COMMENTS
1.	CONCERT TONIGHT	4.51	(B.WILSON-E.LANDY)	Circa 90/91	FULL SONG. INTRO ONLY USED ON CD-25
2.	TURNING POINT	3.23	(B.WILSON-E.LANDY)	Circa 90/91	REJECTED FROM FINAL TRACK SELECTION
3.	HEAVENLY BODIES	3.19	(B.WILSON-E.LANDY)	Circa 90/91	" " "
4.	LET'S GET TONIGHT	3.38	(B.WILSON-E.LANDY)	Circa 90/91	" " "
5.	SAVE THE DAY (THE POWER OF LOVE)	5.21	(B.WILSON-E.LANDY)	Circa 90/91	
6.	SOMEONE TO LOVE	3.32	(B.WILSON-E.LANDY)	Circa 90/91	(ALTERNATE MIX) INCLUDES BRIAN'S 'RESPONSE' VOCALS
7.	WATER BUILDS UP	3.07	(B.WILSON-E.LANDY)	Circa 90/91	(ALTERNATE MIX)" " EXTRA TEAPOT NOISES
8.	DON'T LET HER KNOW (SHE'S AN ANGEL)	3.34	(B.WILSON-E.LANDY)	Circa 90/91	(ALTERNATE MIX) DIFFERENT LYRICS
9.	I DO	3.42	(B.WILSON-E.LANDY)	Circa 90/91	(ALTERNATE MIX)
10.	THANK YOU	3.18	(B.WILSON-E.LANDY)	Circa 90/91	(ALTERNATE MIX)
11.	THE SPIRIT OF ROCK 'N' ROLL	3.22	(WILSON-USHER-KELLY)	Dec '86	(ALTERNATE MIX) WITHOUT BOB DYLAN
12.	RAINBOW EYES	3.56	(B.WILSON-E.LANDY)	Circa 90/91	(ALTERNATE MIX)
13.	MAKE A WISH	2.47	(B.WILSON-E.LANDY)	Circa 90/91	(ALTERNATE MIX)
14.	SMART GIRLS	4.07	(B.WILSON-E.LANDY)	Circa 90/91	(ALTERNATE MIX)

TOTAL CD TIME - 52.40

BRIAN WILSON SESSIONS

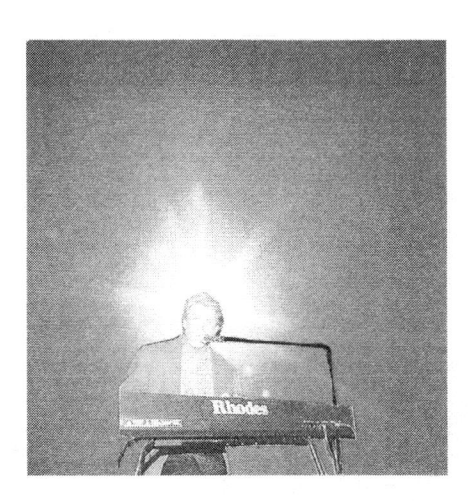

The massive lawsuit filed by Beach Boy Brian Wilson against A&M Records and its publishing subsidiary, Irving Music, is finally nearing the courtroom.

Filed at the Superior Court in Los Angeles, the suit sees the Sandbox Kid trying to reclaim vast publishing royalties – perhaps $50 million – and legal ownership of all his classic 1960s compositions. Charges specified include fraud, breach of contract and misrepresentation. He is claiming $100 million in damages.

His famous catalogue was sold to Irving Music in 1969 for a mere $700,000, by his father, Murry. Wilson claims the sale of his Sea Of Tunes publishing company was unbeknown to him and was made at a time when he was psychologically incapacitated.

Since that time, Wilson has received no publishing royalties from a pop catalogue perhaps second only to that amassed by Lennon and McCartney. Said royalties are esti-

Brian Wilson: still out to lunch

LOONY TUNES

mated to be worth up to $3m a year now, from songs such as 'Good Vibrations' and 'I Get Around'.

NME/VOX contributor David Swift was flown to Los Angeles last month to give a deposition to lawyers acting for both sides. Other journalists to give evidence to the attorneys included Beach Boys authors David Leaf and Steven Gaines, whose 1986 book *Heroes And Villains* revealed the contested sale for the first time to the public at large.

If Wilson succeeds, his pay-out could be the biggest in the history of royalties arrears.

Irving Music's defence is that Sea Of Tunes was bought in good faith and that a statue of limitations has now passed anyway. Attorneys for Wilson say that as he was not of sound mind at the time of the sale, no such argument exists. Indeed, his lawyers state that he "continues to suffer" from paranoid psychosis.

Co-defendant alongside Irving Music and A&M Records is an LA entertainment law firm which acted for the Beach Boys in the 1960's. The suit alleges that the law firm also worked for Irving Music during the sale of Sea Of Tunes, but did not declare a conflict of interest. Insiders say that the Californian legal profession is following the case with great interest, as, should Wilson win, some very big reputations could bite the dust.

An interesting side-issue is Murry's ill-treatment of Brian, documented in the damages suit. The one and a half inch thick court papers include the statement that "as punishment to plaintiff, Murry would remove his glass eye and force plaintiff to look at the scarred socket, all in an effort to frighten and terrify plaintiff".

BRIAN WILSON SESSIONS

COMPUTER ENHANCED - DIGITALLY REMASTERED

Brian WILSON — SESSIONS VOL.3 OUTTAKES

CD-27

WITH THIS CD, WE HAVE PACKAGED AS MANY 'FULLY PRODUCED' TRACKS TOGETHER IRRESPECTIVE OF VINTAGE. 3 SONGS (TRACKS 5 TO 7) OF THIS DISC WERE ORIGINALLY PLANNED FOR INCLUSION ON THE SOLO 'ADULT CHILD' ALBUM IN 76/77 BUT REMAIN UNRELEASED TO THIS DAY. OTHERS WERE SCRAPPED FROM BEACH BOY ALBUMS, LIKE 'RUBY BABY' FROM '15 BIG ONES'. FOR THE FIRST TIME ON CD, WE ALSO PRESENT UNRELEASED COLLABORATIONS BETWEEN BRIAN AND (JAN & DEAN'S) JAN BERRY AND 2 SONGS FOR 'SPRING'. THE ORIGINAL VERSION OF 'LIVING DOLL' (A.K.A. 'BARBIE') IS ALSO HERE AND A SELECTION OF ALTERNATE TAKES AND MIXES FROM HIS SELF TITLED 1ST ALBUM IN 1988.

#	SONGTITLE	TIME	SONGWRITERS	RECORDING DATE	COMMENTS
1.	MARILYN ROVELL	1.50	BRIAN WILSON	Circa '70's	ODE TO HIS (THEN) WIFE, A GREAT TRACK PERHAPS UNRELEASED DUE TO THE DIVORCE
2.	STEVIE	3.11	BRIAN WILSON	1980	(SEE ABOVE) SEEMS BRIAN ALSO HAD THE HOTS FOR FLEETWOOD MACS STEVIE NICKS
3.	LAZY LIZZIE	3.51	BRIAN WILSON	Circa Mid 70's	BASED ON 'BETTER GET BACK IN BED' FROM HOLLANDS 'MT. VERNON & FAIRWAY EP
4.	SHERRY SHE NEEDS ME	2.46	BRIAN WILSON	'65/'76	BACKING TRACK RECORDED IN 1965, VOCALS REDONE IN 1975
5.	STILL I DREAM OF IT	3.28	BRIAN WILSON	Circa '76/'77	SUBMITTED TO FRANK SINATRA FOR CONSIDERATION & REFUSED (NO REPLY).
6.	LIFE IS FOR LIVING	1.52	BRIAN WILSON	Circa '76/'77	A PERSONAL STATEMENT FROM BRIAN WITH SOME AMAZING LYRICS
7.	DEEP PURPLE	2.27	PARRISH-ROSE	Circa '76/'77	AS WITH TRACKS 5 & 6 ORCHESTRATION BY (XMAS LP'S) DICK REYNOLDS
8.	YOU'VE LOST THAT LOVIN' FEELING	3.51	MANN-WEILL-SPECTOR	Early '76	REJECTED FROM '15 BIG ONES' (ORIGINALLY PLANNED AS A DOUBLE ALBUM)
9.	RUBY BABY	2.20	LEIBER-STOLLER	Early '76	
10.	DON'T YOU JUST KNOW IT	2.52	BRIAN WILSON	Circa Late 70's	UNRELEASED DUET WITH JAN BERRY (FROM JAN AND DEAN), A GREAT SONG !
11.	WALLS	2.53	BRIAN WILSON	Circa Early 70's	2 UNRELEASED OUTTAKES WITH SPRING (TK 12 EVENTUALLY APPEARED ON THE EXCELLENT SPRING ALBUM. (WITHOUT BRIAN'S VOCALS)
12.	AWAKE	3.07	F.TUCKER	Circa '75	"
13.	CHRISTINE	2.50	BRIAN WILSON	Early 70's	THIS IS THE ORIGINAL VERSION OF THE 'BARBIE' ANTHEM (A.K.A. LIVING DOLL)
14.	ONE FOR THE BOYS	1.42	BRIAN WILSON	1988	DIFFERENT VOCAL ARRANGEMENT TO RELEASED VERSION
15.	THERE'S SO MANY (UP IN THE SKY)	2.05	B.WILSON-E.LANDY-A.MORGAN	1988	AT THE TIME THIS DEMO WAS DONE IT WAS CALLED 'UP IN THE SKY'
16.	MEET ME IN MY DREAMS TONIGHT	2.57	B.WILSON-A.PALEY-A.DEAN	1988	DIFFERENT LYRICS TO THE RELEASED VERSION
17.	BABY LET YOUR HAIR GROW LONG	3.24	BRIAN WILSON	1988	"
18.	HE COULDN'T GET HIS POOR OLD BODY TO MOVE	2.28	B.WILSON-E.LANDY-LINDSAY BUCKINGHAM	1988	"
	- BONUS TRACKS -				
19.	GEORGE FELL INTO HIS FRENCH HORN	9.11	BRIAN WILSON	Nov 7 '66	A BIT OF WIERDNESS RECORDED DURING THE 'SMILE' PERIOD
20.	WE LOVE YOU	4.59	JAGGER-RICHARDS	Early 90's	BRIAN SINGS ABOUT 3/4 OF THE VOCALS ON RYUICHI SAKAMOTO'S COVER OF THE ROLLING STONES' CLASSIC

TOTAL CD TIME - 63.40

BRIAN WILSON SESSIONS

Beach Boy on the beach.
Whatever happened to Brian Wilson?
Funny you should ask.
oui just happened to interview Brian and it seems Brian's spent the last four years in his bedroom. Alone.
Brian's been under doctor's care and...well, let him tell you all about it, in his very own words, in the December oui.

Brian Wilson, April, 1985

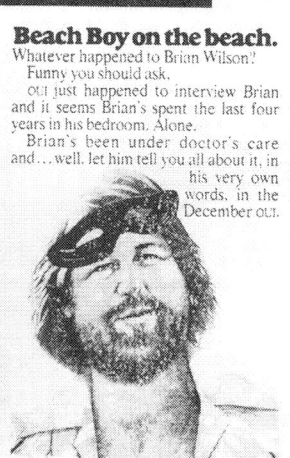

Brian Wilson, onstage at the third annual Malibu Emergency Room benefit concert, May, 1985

BRIAN WILSON SESSIONS

COMPUTER ENHANCED - DIGITALLY REMASTERED
Brian WILSON — SESSIONS VOL.4 DEMOS

CD - 28

WITH THIS CD, WE DECIDED TO COLLECT TOGETHER ALL THE PIANO DEMOS (TKS 1 - 10 & 13) AND PUT THESE TOGETHER WITH OTHERS WHICH ALSO FEATURE RHYTHM BOX (TKS 14-17), SO AS TO PROVIDE A UNIQUE COLLECTION OF RAW UNRELEASED SONGS IN THEIR MOST INFANT FORM WITH BRIAN (IN SOME CASES) RE-WRITING THE SONG MID-STREAM. TRULY A UNIQUE INSIGHT INTO HIS WRITING STYLE & PROWESS. WE'VE EVEN ADDED ON SOME BONUS TRACKS INCLUDING SOME UNIQUE TV APPEARANCES AND A FEW (SELDOM PERFORMED) SONGS BY BRIAN WITH THE BEACH BOYS LIVE IN CONCERT.

#	SONGTITLE	TIME	SONGWRITERS	RECORDING DATE	COMMENTS
1.	AIRPLANE	2.24	BRIAN WILSON	Early '70's	RECORDED BY THE BEACH BOYS ON THEIR 'LOVE YOU' ALBUM
2.	I'M BEGGING YOU PLEASE	1.40	BRIAN WILSON	Early '70's	'SOMETIMES THERE'S A FINE LINE BETWEEN BRIAN & WILD MAN FISHER
3.	I'LL BET HE'S NICE	2.27	BRIAN WILSON	Early '70's	ALSO RE-RECORDED BY THE BEACH BOYS FOR THEIR 'LOVE YOU' ALBUM
4.	IT'S OVER NOW	5.33	BRIAN WILSON	Early '70's	RE-DONE W/ CARL ON LEAD VOCALS-AVAILABLE ON 'JOURNALS VOL 2'
5.	LET'S PUT OUR HEARTS TOGETHER	2.37	BRIAN WILSON	Early '70's	RE-RECORDED BY THE BEACH BOYS FOR THEIR 'LOVE YOU' ALBUM
6.	LOVE IS A WOMAN	2.35	BRIAN WILSON	Early '70's	UNRELEASED VERSION
7.	LITTLE CHILDREN (A.K.A. 'MARCHING ALONG')	2.52	BRIAN WILSON	Early '70's	EVENTUALLY RELEASED ON 'BRIAN WILSON' HIS FIRST SOLO ALBUM
8.	MONA	1.51	BRIAN WILSON	Early '70's	RE-RECORDED BY THE BEACH BOYS FOR THEIR 'LOVE YOU' ALBUM
9.	STILL I DREAM OF IT	3.45	BRIAN WILSON	Early '70's	RE-RECORDED (TK #5 ON OUTTAKES CD)
10.	THAT SPECIAL FEELING	1.54	BRIAN WILSON	Early '70's	STILL REMAINS UNRELEASED IN ANY FORM
11.	SURF'S UP	2.33	B.WILSON-VAN DYKE PARKS	1966	FROM 'LEONARD BERNSTEIN' DOCUMENTARY ON CBS US TV
12.	I'M BUGGED AT MY OLD MAN	3.08	BRIAN WILSON	1976	FROM THE NBC US TV SPECIAL 'IT'S OK' (W/CARL & DENNIS) ORIGINALLY ON 'SUMMER DAYS' LP
13.	DON'T LET HER KNOW SHE'S AN ANGEL	2.26	BRIAN WILSON	Circa '90/'91	FULL PRODUCTION APPEARS ON 'SWEET INSANITY' CD
14.	BLACK WIDOW	2.34	BRIAN WILSON	Late '80's	EARLY INCARNATION OF 'MALE EGO'
15.	IN THE NIGHT TIME	2.11	BRIAN WILSON	Late '80's	NOT 'NIGHT TIME' BUT A TOTALLY DIFFERENT (UNRELATED) SONG
16.	LITTLE CHILDREN	2.01	BRIAN WILSON	Late '80's	DEMO WITH RHYTHM BOX (DIFFERENT TO SOLO PIANO VERSION, TK #7)
17.	WALKIN' THE LINE	2.50	B.WILSON-E.LANDY-A.MORGAN-N.LAIRD-CLOWES	Late '80's	MOST 'PRODUCED' OF ALL THESE DEMOS
	- BONUS LIVE TRACKS -				
18.	NIGHT TIME	2.56	B.WILSON-E.LANDY-A.MORGAN-A.PALEY	1988	LIVE VOCAL (CAN YOU TELL?) OVER BACKING TRACK ON US TV W / DICK CLARK
19.	THAT SAME SONG	3.19	B.WILSON-M.LOVE	1976	FROM 'IT'S OK' TV SPECIAL (W / THE DOUBLE ROCK BAPTIST CHURCH CHOIR)
20.	BACK HOME	3.32	B.WILSON-B.NORBERG	Jul30'77	W / THE BEACH BOYS (CBS CONVENTION, LONDON, ENGLAND)
21.	THE BOOGIES BACK IN TOWN	2.36	B.WILSON	Circa'78	
22.	INTRO - :	1.03		1985	THE 'MALIBU EMERGENCY ROOM BENEFIT CONCERT LOS ANGELES, CALIFORNIA, USA '85
23.	DA DOO RON RON	2.08	P.SPECTOR-E.GREENWICH-J.BARRY	1985	" " "
24.	INTRO - :	0.15		1985	" " "
25.	I'M SO LONELY	2.10	B.WILSON-E.LANDY	1985	" " "
26.	INTRO - :	0.25		1985	" " "
27.	MALE EGO	2.08	B.WILSON-M.LOVE-E.LANDY	1985	" " "
28.	INTRO - :	0.18		1985	" " "
29.	CALIFORNIA GIRLS	2.22	B.WILSON-M.LOVE	1985	" " "
30.	INTRO (FOR JOHN STEWART & STEPHEN STILLS)	0.49		1985	" " "
31	SLOOP JOHN B	3.44	TRAD. ARR. B.WILSON	1985	" " "

TOTAL CD TIME 72.00

BRIAN WILSON SESSIONS

BRIAN WILSON SESSIONS

COMPUTER ENHANCED - DIGITALLY REMASTERED

Brian WILSON
SESSIONS VOL.5 THE RARE WORKS OF BRIAN WILSON
CD - 29

THIS VOLUME PRESENTS A SELECTION OF SOME OF THE BEST OF BRIAN'S WRITING / CO-WRITING & PRODUCTION VENTURES DURING THE 1960'S. MANY OF THESE TRACKS (IN THEIR ORIGINAL 45 RPM VINYL FORMAT) CHANGE HANDS FOR HUNDREDS OF DOLLARS EACH, SO IF YOU'RE A TRUE BEACH BOYS / BRIAN WILSON FAN **THIS** DISC ALONE WILL MAKE THE BOX SET EXCELLENT VALUE FOR **MONEY**.

#	SONGTITLE	TIME	SONGWRITERS	RECORDING DATE	ARTIST
1.	BARBIE	2.15	(BRUCE MORGAN)		KENNY & THE CADETS
2.	WHAT IS A YOUNG GIRL MADE OF	2.08	(BRUCE MORGAN)		KENNY & THE CADETS
3.	THE REVO-LUTION	2.07	(B.WILSON-G.USHER)		RACHEL & THE REVOLVERS
4.	NUMBER ONE	2.11	(B.WILSON-G.USHER)		RACHEL & THE REVOLVERS
5.	THE SURFER MOON	2.22	(B.WILSON)		BOB & SHERI
6.	HUMPTY DUMPTY	1.32	(BOB NORBERG-CHERYL POMEREY)		BOB & SHERI
7.	NO GO SHOWBOAT	1.52	(B.WILSON-ROGER CHRISTIAN)		THE TIMERS
8.	RUN-AROUND LOVER	1.51	(B.WILSON-M.LOVE)		SHARON MARIE
9.	PAMELA JEAN	2.38	(B.WILSON)		THE SURVIVORS
10.	I DO	1.52	(B.WILSON-ROGER CHRISTIAN)		THE CASTELLS
11.	SHE RIDES WITH ME	1.52	(B.WILSON-ROGER CHRISTIAN)		PAUL PETERSON
12.	BEACH GIRL	1.54	(DAVID E. NOWLEN-B.WILSON)		THE NODAENS
13.	HE'S A DOLL	2.08	(B.WILSON)		THE HONEYS
14.	SACRAMENTO	1.59	(GARY USHER-B.WILSON)		GARY USHER
15.	THAT'S JUST THE WAY I FEEL	2.07	(GARY USHER)		GARY USHER
16.	THINKIN' 'BOUT YOU BABY	2.34	(B.WILSON-M.LOVE)		SHARON MARIE
17.	THE STORY OF MY LIFE	2.06	(B.WILSON-M.LOVE)		SHARON MARIE
18.	YES SIR, THAT'S MY BABY	2.32	(WALTER DONALDSON-GUS KAHN)		HALE & THE HUSHABYES
19.	FARMER'S DAUGHTER	1.57	(B.WILSON)		BASIL SWIFT & THE SEEGRAMS
20.	THE MONKEY'S UNCLE	2.35	(R.B. SHERMAN-R.M. SHERMAN)		ANNETTE (WITH THE BEACH BOYS)
21.	GUESS I'M DUMB	2.42	(B.WILSON-RUSS TITLEMAN)		GLEN CAMPBELL
22.	THINGS ARE CHANGING	2.51	(J.RICPELL-P.SPECTOR-B.WILSON)		THE BLOSSOMS
23.	TWELVE - O - FOUR	2.57	(BOB NORBERG)		BOB & BOBBY
24.	BABY WHAT YOU WANT ME TO DO	2.14	(JIMMY REED)		BOB & BOBBY
25.	VEGETABLES	2.19	(B.WILSON-VAN DYKE PARKS)		THE LAUGHING GRAVY
26.	I'LL KEEP ON LOVING YOU	2.23	(RON WILSON)		RON WILSON
27.	AS TEARS GO BY	2.29	(M.JAGGER/K.RICHARDS/A.LOOG-OLDHAM)		RON WILSON
28.	LADY LOVE	3.01	(B.WILSON-BILLY HINSCHE)		DINO, DESI & BILLY
	- BONUS TRACKS -				
29.	BARBIE (TAKE 2)	2.14	(BRUCE MORGAN)		KENNY & THE CADETS
30.	MISS AMERICA	2.17	(HERB ALPERT-VINCE CATALANO-DON DROWTY)		DANTE & HIS FRIENDS
31.	SHE RIDES WITH ME	2.03	(B.WILSON-ROGER CHRISTIAN)		JOEY & THE CONTINENTALS
32.	SURFIN' SAFARI (ARIOLA VERSION)	2.00	(B.WILSON-ROGER CHRISTIAN)		THE BEACH BOYS

TOTAL CD TIME - 72.49

BRIAN WILSON SESSIONS

THE BRIAN WILSON INTERVIEW

The Warner Bros. Words and Music Show for this month concerns one of the most anxiously awaited solo albums in twenty years—the self-titled solo debut from Brian Wilson.

As writer, arranger, producer and leader of the Beach Boys from 1962-1966, Brian led his brothers and bandmates to two dozen Top 40 singles (including three #1 hits) and an incredible twelve albums, before going into semi-retirement after the success of "Good Vibrations," arguably the best rock single of the 1960's.

After a chance meeting with Sire Records President Seymour Stein backstage at the Rock and Roll Hall of Fame Dinner last year, Brian returned to the studio to make this hallmark solo album, now out on Sire/Reprise Records.

In this half-hour interview with biographer David Leaf, Brian gives us some behind-the-scenes talk about seven of the tunes from the new record and some personal insight as to what it's like to be Brian Wilson in the 1980's. Insightful, informative and entertaining.

The program is divided into two quarter-hour segments (really 12:51 and 14:53, to be exact) with a break in the middle, leaving ample time for commercial announcements, PSA's or ID's. The show is ready for broadcast with voice-over intro's and outro's included (courtesy of Marc Graue).

The show was produced by Larry Butler for Warner Bros. Records and was engineered and edited by Marc Graue for Marc Graue Recording in Hollywood. The music is from the album *Brian Wilson* on Sire/Reprise Records, produced by Brian Wilson and Russ Titelman, Jeff Lynne, Lenny Waronker and Andy Paley. Executive Producer: Dr. Eugene E. Landy. The album is available on LP, Cassette and Compact Disc (1/4/2-25669).

BRIAN WILSON SESSIONS

COMPUTER ENHANCED - DIGITALLY REMASTERED CEDREM 13

Brian WILSON — SESSIONS VOL.6 — WRITING & PRODUCING

CD - 30 A

THIS CD IS **AMAZING** ! WE HEAR BRIAN'S FRANK ADMISSIONS IN REGARD TO HIS 'BEDROOM' PERIOD, EUGENE LANDY'S RELATIONSHIP WITH HIM, STUDIO TECHNIQUES, HOW THE BEACH BOYS REACTED TO HIM GOING SOLO, EVEN BRIAN'S FAVOURITE SINGLES OF ALL TIME. IF THIS WASN'T ENOUGH, THE DJ CONVINCES BRIAN TO USE A PIANO TO SHOW HOW HE CREATES A SONG (AND AMAZINGLY) BRIAN WRITES A SONG 'RADIO BLUES' ON THE SPOT, CERTAINLY A UNIQUE MOMENT. ADDED BONUS TRACKS INCLUDE MANY TRACKS FEATURING BRIAN'S SONGS, HIS PRODUCTION & EVEN BRIAN AS A GUEST VOCALIST ON OTHER RECORDS COLLECTED TOGETHER FOR THE FIRST TIME. FOR THOSE NOT FAMILIAR WITH (BRIAN'S EX-WIFE) MARILYN ROVELL'S GROUP 'SPRING' SHOULD CHECK OUT TRACKS #52 - #57 - THEN HUNT IT DOWN & BUY IT. CEDREM SOUNDLAB'S COMPUTERS WERE USED EXTENSIVELY ON TK #56 AS THIS WAS FROM A VINYL 45, THE RARE RHINO RE-ISSUE CONTAINING THIS SONG, HAS A LOT OF CLICKS & POPS (OBVIOUSLY OFF VINYL) & A FAULT DURING THE OPENING 5 SECS. SO CEDREM FIXED THE INTRO WHICH WOULD GO UNNOTICED IF NOT FOR THIS EXPLANATION, BUT REST ASSURED WE AT CEDREM ALWAYS AIM TO PLEASE THE TRUE FAN.

#	SONGTITLE	TIME	SONGWRITERS	RECORDING DATE	COMMENTS
1.	YOU'RE WELCOME	0.16		Aug20'88	W / NEW FM (NEW YORK) 'SATURDAY MORNING 60'S' W / PETE FORNATELE
2.	AMONG GIANTS	0.37		Aug20'88	BRIAN IS PROUD OF BEACH BOYS' HERITAGE
3.	'GOOD VIBRATIONS'	1.37		Aug20'88	DISCUSSING THE CLASSIC 45
4.	WHY DID IT TAKE SO LONG ?	0.26		Aug20'88	WHY A 22 YEAR GAP IN SOLO PROJECTS
5.	STUDIOS	0.40		Aug20'88	WHICH STUDIOS DID HE USE FOR THE ALBUM
6.	TAKING CONTROL	0.39		Aug20'88	HOW DID HE FEEL SHARING PRODUCTION DUTIES
7.	'SURFIN' SESSION'	0.21		Aug20'88	REMEMBERING HIS FIRST EVER RECORDING SESSION
8.	RECORDING TECHNOLOGY	0.45		Aug20'88	HOW HAVE RECORDING TECHNIQUES CHANGED OVER THE YEARS
9.	LEAKAGE	2.05		Aug20'88	SOUNDS 'BLEED' FROM GUITARS TO VOCAL MICROPHONES ETC.
10.	PET SOUNDS	0.21		Aug20'88	IS THE NEW ALBUM 'PET SOUNDS' PART 2
11.	LOVE AND MERCY	0.34		Aug20'88	INSPIRATION FOR WRITING FIRST SINGLE FOR ALBUM
12.	CAN'T HEAR STEREO	0.56		Aug20'88	BRIAN'S BAD EAR PREVENTS HIM FROM HEARING STEREO
13.	PEOPLES REACTION	0.34		Aug20'88	BRIAN PLEASED WITH PUBLIC ACCEPTANCE OF NEW ALBUM
14.	ENJOYING PROMOTION	0.52		Aug20'88	MAKING HIMSELF MORE AVAILABLE FOR INTERVIEWS
15.	SLUMP	1.07		Aug20'88	BRIAN TALKS ABOUT HIS 'BEDROOM YEARS'
16.	DRUGS	0.12		Aug20'88	BRIAN BRIEFLY RECALLS HIS (EX) DRUG HABIT
17.	MUSICAL GIFT	0.28		Aug20'88	IS HIS 'MUSE' GOD-GIVEN
18.	COERCING BRIAN TO PIANO	0.27		Aug20'88	DJ ENTICES BRIAN TO USE STEVE ALLEN'S (EX-) PIANO
19.	BRIAN PICKS 'MELT AWAY'	0.14		Aug20'88	BRIAN SELECTS A SONG TO PLAY ON AIR
20.	SURF CITY	0.52		Aug20'88	DISCUSSING THE WRITING OF JAN & DEAN'S BIG HIT 45
21.	'HELP ME RHONDA'	0.35		Aug20'88	NO MENTION OF THE 2 VERSIONS WHICH EXIST
22.	'I GET AROUND'	0.33		Aug20'88	BRIAN RECALLS THIS WAS WRITTEN VERY QUICKLY
23.	'CALIFORNIA GIRLS'	0.38		Aug20'88	KNOWING A HIT AT THE TIME OF THE ACTUAL RECORDING
24.	REALIZATION	1.10		Aug20'88	BRIAN SAYS HE FIRST KNEW THE BEACH BOYS WERE 'BIG' IN 1963
25.	NO NAMBY PAMBY	1.08		Aug20'88	MISCONCEPTIONS ABOUT BRIAN THE PERSON
26.	ANOTHER POCKET SYMPHONY	0.14		Aug20'88	DISCUSSING 'RIO GRANDE'
27.	BUTTERFLYS	0.51		Aug20'88	BRIAN & DJ BOTH NERVOUS & EXCITED ABOUT THE INTERVIEW
28.	EUGENE LANDY	1.59		Aug20'88	DISCUSSING THE CONTROVERSIAL DR. EUGENE LANDY & ACCUSATIONS AGAINST HIM
29.	CARL WILSON	0.33		Aug20'88	BRIAN'S RELATIONSHIP WITH BROTHER CARL
30.	BACK TO BASICS	0.31		Aug20'88	DIALOGUE CONFUSING
31.	A BUNCH OF HOO-EY (BRIAN AT PIANO)	0.27		Aug20'88	BRIAN CLEARLY MORE RELAXED AS THE INTERVIEW CONTINUES
32.	THE CREATIVE PROCESS	1.20		Aug20'88	DISCUSSING HOW HE STARTS TO WRITE A SONG
33.	CALIFORNIA GIRLS	0.56		Aug20'88	EXPLAINING THE INTRO & HOW HE WROTE IT
34.	'LOVE AND MERCY'	1.01		Aug20'88	BRIAN WROTE THIS ONE IN HIS 'PIANO ROOM'
35.	STILL A BEACH BOY	0.18		Aug20'88	BRIAN STILL CLASSES HIMSELF AS A BEACH BOY
36.	WON'T PLAY 'LOVE AND MERCY'	0.39		Aug20'88	THE DJ TRIES TO GET A SOLO VERSION OF 'LOVE & MERCY' & FAILS
37.	SURF'S UP	1.46		Aug20'88	BRIAN REMEMBERS THE TV VERSION OF 'SURF'S UP' ON NBC IN 1966
38.	CREATING A SONG	2.41		Aug20'88	ANALYSING THE WAY BRIAN COMPOSES A NEW SONG
39.	'RADIO BLUES'	0.54		Aug20'88	IMPROMPTU & TOTALLY UNREHEARSED SONG
40.	BRIAN'S JUKEBOX PICKS	1.35		Aug20'88	SOME OF BRIAN'S ALL-TIME FAVOURITE SINGERS
41.	HALL OF FAME	1.35		Aug20'88	BRIAN'S PROUDEST MOMENT OF ALL TIME
42.	LIVE PERFORMANCES	1.37		Aug20'88	WILL BRIAN BE TOURING & WHICH MUSICIANS WILL HE USE
43.	MISSING DENNIS	0.36		Aug20'88	WHAT DOES BRIAN MISS ABOUT DENNIS
44.	ONE FOR THE BOYS	0.42		Aug20'88	COMMENTS ON THE ALBUM'S BEACH BOY TRIBUTE SONG
45.	BRIAN'S HALL OF FAME SPEECH	1.49		1988	BRIAN'S ACTUAL SPEECH FROM THE AWARD NIGHT
	(BONUS TRACKS INVOLVING BRIAN)				
46.	LITTLE HONDA (THE 'HONDELLS')	2.01	BRIAN WILSON	Sep'64	BRIAN SINGS ON HIT VERSION
47.	SURF CITY (JAN & DEAN)	2.45	JAN BERRY-B.WILSON	1965	BRIAN ALSO SINGS HIGH HARMONIES
48.	RIDE THE WILD SURF (JAN & DEAN)	2.17	J.BERRY-B.WILSON-R.CHRISTIAN	1965	RARE EXTENDED VERSION
49.	SIDE WALK SURFIN' (JAN & DEAN)	2.17	B.WILSON-R.CHRISTIAN	1965	1963'S 'CATCH A WAVE W/ NEW LYRICS BY ROGER CHRISTIAN CREATED A 'NEW' TOP 30 HIT.
50.	TIME TO GET ALONE ('REDWOOD')	2.47	BRIAN WILSON	1968	BRIAN PRODUCTION OF 'REDWOOD' (W/ DANNY HUTTON LEAD VOCALS LATER OF '3 DOG NIGHT') BACKING TRACK RE-RECORDED FOR BEACH BOYS' OWN VERSION ON THE 20 / 20 ALBUM.
51.	SURFIN' DOWN THE SWANEE RIVER ('THE HONEYS' FEAT. MARILYN & DIANE ROVELL)	2.10	B.WILSON-STEPHEN FOSTER	1964	BRIAN'S AFFAIR WITH TRADITIONAL AMERICAN FOLK SONGS CONTINUES . FEATURES HIS EX-WIFE MARILYN. FLOP IN MOST COUNTRIES, BUT A #1 HIT IN COPENHAGEN (SWEDEN) & ILLINOIS (USA)
52.	IT'S LIKE HEAVEN (SPRING)	2.34	B.WILSON-D.ROVELL	1972	PROD. BY BRIAN 'SPRING' IS MARILYN & DIANE ROVELL'S GROUP, BRIAN'S (THEN) WIFE & SISTER-IN-LAW.
53.	GOOD TIME (SPRING)	2.48	B.WILSON-A.JARDINE	1972	CO-PRODUCED BY BRIAN (THIS UTILIZES THE SAME BACKING TRACK AS THE UNRELEASED LANDLOCKED ALBUM & FEATURES THE BEACH BOYS ON BACKING VOCALS)
54.	THIS WHOLE WORLD (SPRING)	3.05	BRIAN WILSON	1972	CO-PROD. BY BRIAN. (WITH VOCAL ARRANGEMENT BY BRIAN WILSON). RADICALLY DIFFERENT PRODUCTION TO BEACH BOYS' VERSION.
55.	FALLIN' IN LOVE (AKA 'LADY') (SPRING)	2.32	DENNIS WILSON	1972	CO-PROD. BY BRIAN
56.	FOREVER (SPRING)	3.12	DENNIS WILSON	1972	CO-PROD. BY BRIAN WITH VOCAL ARR. BY BRIAN BACKING VOCALS BY CARL WILSON)
57.	SWEET MOUNTAIN (SPRING)	4.19	B.WILSON-D.SANDLER	1972	CO-PROD. BY BRIAN (W./ VOCAL ARRANGEMENT BY BRIAN WILSON)
	TOTAL CD TIME 73.15				

BRIAN WILSON SESSIONS

Murry holds two-week old Brian.

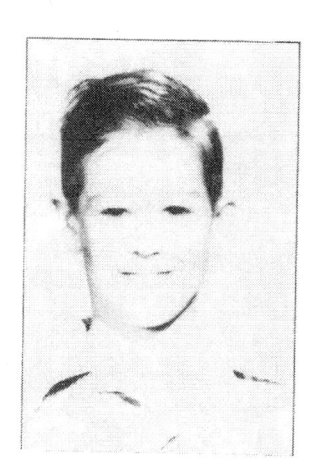

Brian, age 7

Eigth grade, 1956

Above, Brian is number fifty-one, fall 1957.

Brian in ninth grade, spring 1957.

Brian, spring 1959.

BRIAN WILSON SESSIONS

COMPUTER ENHANCED - DIGITALLY REMASTERED

Brian WILSON

SESSIONS VOL. 7 WORDS AND MUSIC

CD-30 B

KNOWING THAT A LOT OF FANS WOULD LIKE TO HEAR (& KEEP) THE RARE PROMOTIONAL CD 'WORDS & MUSIC', WE REPRODUCED IT HERE UNALTERED. AS IT IS UNDER 28 MINUTES LONG, HOWEVER, THIS GAVE US THE OPPORTUNITY TO ADD SOME OTHER EXCELLENT INTERVIEWS FROM BRIAN'S PROMOTIONAL 'ROUNDS' OF THE TV & RADIO SHOWS, TALKING ABOUT HIS FIRST SOLO ALBUM. ALSO WE HAVE STAN LOVE'S FAMOUS PRESS CONFERENCE (WHEN BRIAN ARRIVES) & VARIOUS NEWS STORIES & PRESS REPORTS IN ORDER TO PROVIDE YOU, THE FAN, WITH SOME OF THE MORE 'WARTS & ALL' CONVERSATIONS BRIAN HAD DURING THE PROMOTION OF HIS FIRST SOLO ALBUM & BIOGRAPHY.

#	SONGTITLE	TIME	SONGWRITERS	RECORDING DATE	COMMENTS
1.	'ONE FOR THE BOYS'	1.17		1988	'WORDS & MUSIC' PROMO CD - SEGMENT ONE -
2.	'LOVE & MERCY'	2.43		1988	
3.	'WALKIN' THE LINE'	2.28		1988	
4.	'MELT AWAY'	2.49		1988	
5.	'NIGHT TIME'	3.37		1988	
6.	'LET IT SHINE'	3.52		1988	- SEGMENT TWO -
7.	'MEET ME IN MY DREAMS TONIGHT'	2.53		1988	
8.	'RIO GRANDE'	8.11		1988	
9.	'LOVE AND MERCY'	0.33		1988	- TIMOTHY WHITE INTERVIEW (FOR WESTWOOD ONE) -
10.	AFRAID OF CRITICS	0.41		1988	
11.	JEFF LYNNE	0.58		1988	
12.	'CAROLINE NO'	1.22		1988	
13.	'PET SOUNDS'	1.13		1988	
14.	THE BEATLES	0.16		1988	
15.	'MELT AWAY' VOCALS	0.36		1988	
16.	THE FOUR FRESHMEN	1.52		1988	
17.	BRIAN'S FIRST SONG	0.22		1988	
18.	'BARBIE'	0.44		1988	
19.	CAR SONGS	0.55		1988	
20.	'DON'T WORRY BABY'	0.46		1988	
21.	'BARBARA ANN'	0.52		1988	
22.	'GOOD VIBRATIONS'	1.41		1988	
23.	'DO IT AGAIN'	1.21		1988	
24.	WRITING HITS	0.33		1988	
25.	'GOODNIGHT IRENE'	0.32		1988	
26.	MIKE LOVE	0.49		1988	
27.	CARL WILSON	1.03		1988	
28.	'BABY LET YOUR HAIR GROW LONG'	0.34		1988	
29.	'NIGHT TIME'	0.50		1988	
30.	BRIAN'S CONTRIBUTION TO MUSIC	0.22		1988	
31.	GETTING BACK	1.13		1988	- 'FRESH AIR' INTERVIEW ON US RADIO -
32.	HARMONIES	1.03		1988	
33.	THE BEACH BOYS RESPONSE	1.11		1988	
34.	SQUARE FRESHMEN	0.30		1988	
35.	FALSETTO	0.35		1988	
36.	SURF SONGS	0.39		1988	
37.	WATER	0.49		1988	
38.	CATCH A WAVE	0.52		1988	
39.	OLD RECORDS	0.48		1988	
40.	I DON'T WANT TO DIE	0.56		1988	
41.	FELT LIKE DYLAN	2.38		1988	
42.	DRUGS	1.33		1988	
43.	TURN IT DOWN	0.39		1988	
44.	PHIL SPECTOR	0.20		1988	
45.	EUGENE LANDY	3.04		1988	
46.	NO SMOKING	0.15		1988	
47.	ONE FOR THE BOYS	1.00		1988	
48.	WHY ARE YOU BACK ?	2.19		1988	- US TV REPORT #1 - TOUCHES ON BRIAN'S DRUG YEARS - US TV REPORT #2 -
49.	IDENTITY CRISIS	2.28		1988	BRIAN'S 'BEDROOM' YEARS
50.	LOVE & MERCY & ATTENTION	0.43		1988	BRIAN NEEDS ATTENTION & ACCEPTANCE
51.	HALL OF FAME	0.24		1988	COMMENTS ON THE PRESTIGIOUS AWARDS TO THE BEACH BOYS - US TV REPORT #3 -
52.	STAN LOVE'S PRESS CONFERENCE	1.08		1988	STAN LOVE (MIKE'S BROTHER & EX-MANAGER OF THE BEACH BOYS) IS CAUGHT OFF GUARD BY BRIAN WILSON WALKING INTO THE MIDDLE OF STAN OUTLINING HIS LEGAL ACTION TO SEPARATE EUGENE LANDY FROM BRIAN & FOR STAN TO TAKE CONTROL OF ALL OF BRIAN'S AFFAIRS. - 'WOULDN'T IT BE NICE' BOOK LAUNCH -
53.	MURRY THE BEAST	0.52		1988	THE BEST OF THE MANY INTERVIEWS BRIAN GAVE TO PROMOTE HIS BIOGRAPHY WHICH TOUCHES ON THE RELATIONSHIP BRIAN & HIS FATHER. THE ENCLOSED BOOK ALSO CONTAINS INTERVIEWS WITH MANY REFERENCES TO MURRY WILSON & HIS CRUEL TREATMENT OF BRIAN, DENNIS & CARL
54.	'THANK YOU'	1.20		1988	BRIAN PLAYS AN UNRELEASED SONG FROM 'SWEET INSANITY' & THE BEACH BOYS' HIT SLOOP JOHN B SOLO ON PIANO AT THE BOOK LAUNCH.
55.	'SLOOP JOHN B'	0.18		1988	

TOTAL CD TIME 74.09

BRIAN WILSON SESSIONS

Above, from the Hawthorne High 1960 yearbook, El Camino: According to Rich Sloan, "The Senate and the House sponsored this 'Club Charter' assembly, at which the famous quartet of (from left to right) Bob Barrows, Brian Wilson, Keith Lent, and Bruce Griffin made its first and last public appearance!"

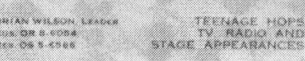

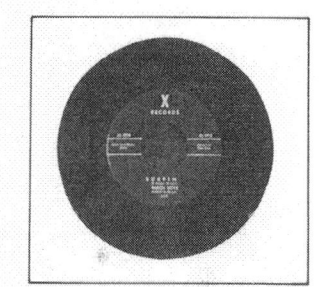

BRIAN WILSON SESSIONS

BRIAN WILSON SESSIONS

above: Brian with Roger Christian at NBC Studios in Burbank;

Dennis, Mike, Alan, Brian, Carl

BRIAN WILSON SESSIONS

BRIAN & MARILYN WILSON

BRIAN WILSON SESSIONS

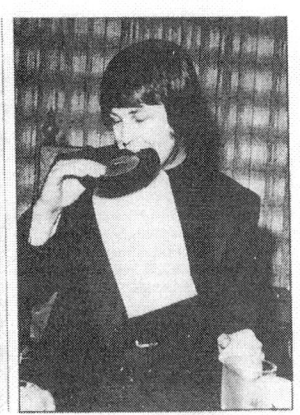

Marshall Berle: "I saw Brian one day in '66 in a cassette duplicating place about to go to Capitol to a big meeting. The Beach Boys loved to have meetings . . . they'd fight and scream and yell. Brian had eight loop tape cassettes made. One said, 'No comment.' Another said, 'I like that idea.' So every time during the meeting it came time for him to say something, he'd just put the right tape on; he wouldn't say a word. He had seven or eight tapes that said different things."

BRIAN WILSON SESSIONS

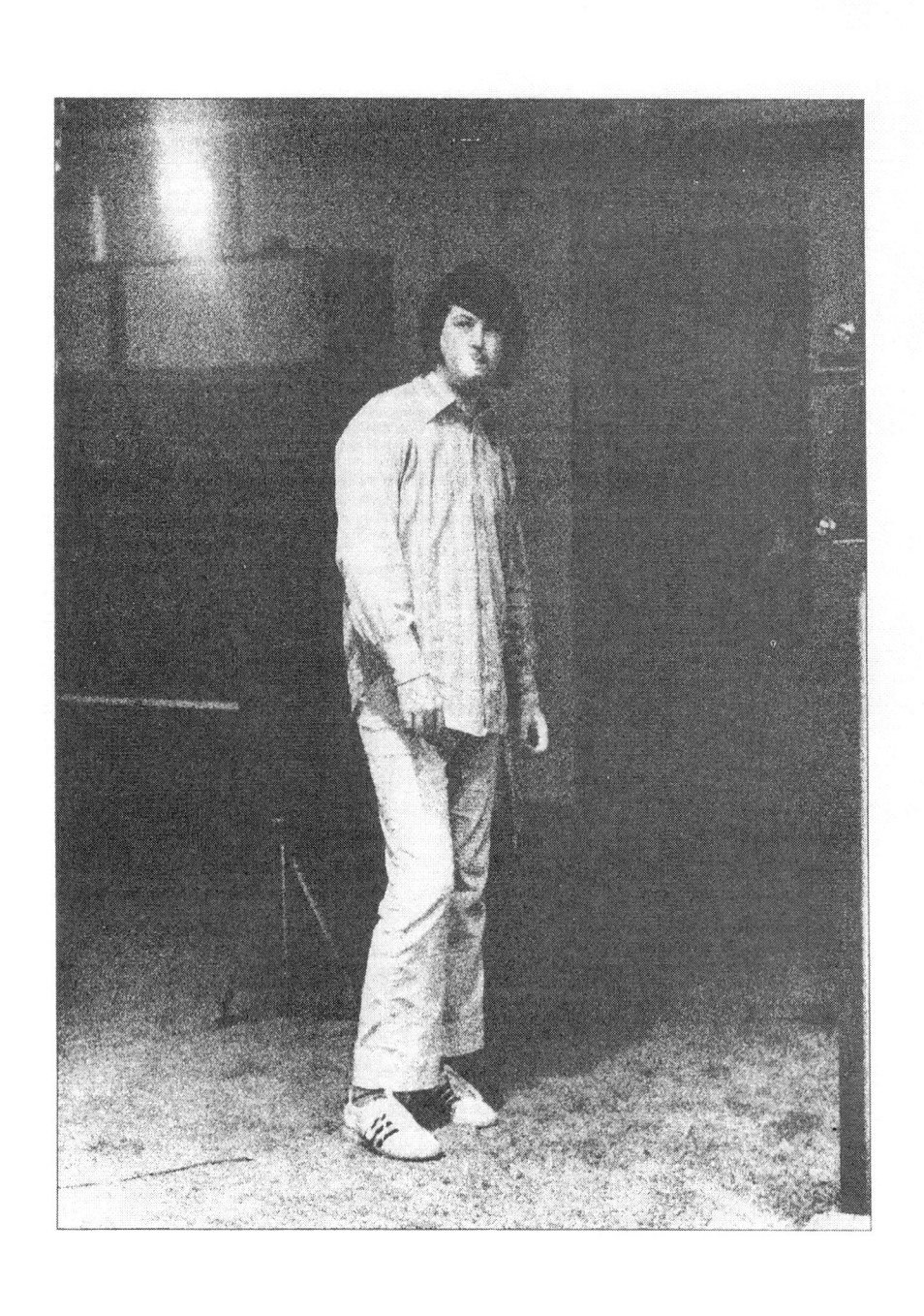

BRIAN WILSON SESSIONS

BRIAN WILSON SESSIONS

BRIAN WILSON SESSIONS

These pictures were taken in Brian's Bel-Air home studio.

Below, recording vocals. Pictured from left to right, Marilyn, Brian, Diane, and Dean Torrence.

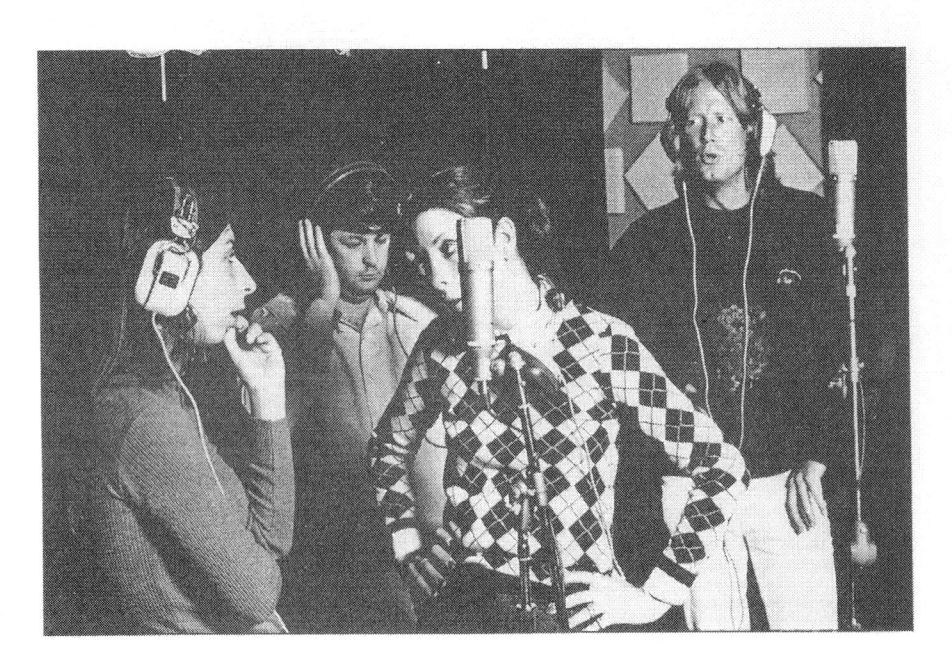

BRIAN WILSON SESSIONS

Right, Contract signing, July 1970. Back row (from left to right): Nick Grillo, publishing executive Rick Landy, and Carl Wilson. Front row, Brian and Mike. Below left, Jamming with the Flame at an L.A. club., 1970.
On the 20/20 album, the Beach Boys recorded a song called "Never Learn Not to Love." It is credited to Dennis Wilson, but it was, in fact, written by Charles Manson. It appears on Manson's album as "Cease to Exist."

BRIAN WILSON SESSIONS

Opposite and below right, Backstage at Anaheim Stadium, summer, 1975. Brian played volleyball and drove a golf cart (pictured with Marilyn and daughter Wendy) but did not go onstage. Above, Mike Love explains his stage routines: "Trying to draw a bridge betweeen the music and the audience and make it interesting is something that I've always been interested in doing. . . . There's one thing I do that's kind of a personal thing—I tell jokes sometimes which are corny, which are outright stupid and bomb. That, to me, is funny when nobody laughs."

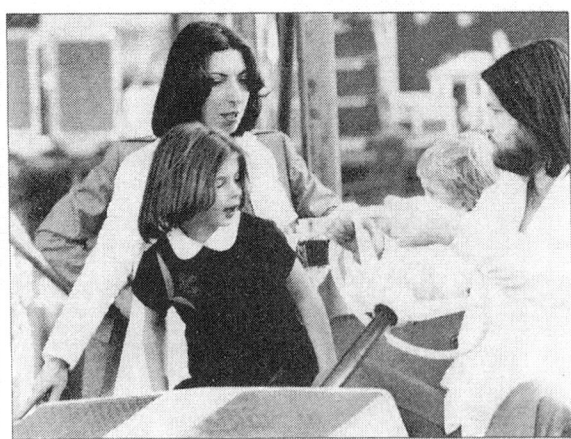

Brian at home, spring 1976. Above (from left to right): Diane, bodyguard Scott Steinberg, psychologist Eugene Landy.

BRIAN WILSON SESSIONS

L.A. FORUM 1977

BRIAN WILSON SESSIONS

Left to right, Marilyn, Brian, Dennis, Al & Carl at Brother Studio

BRIAN WILSON SESSIONS

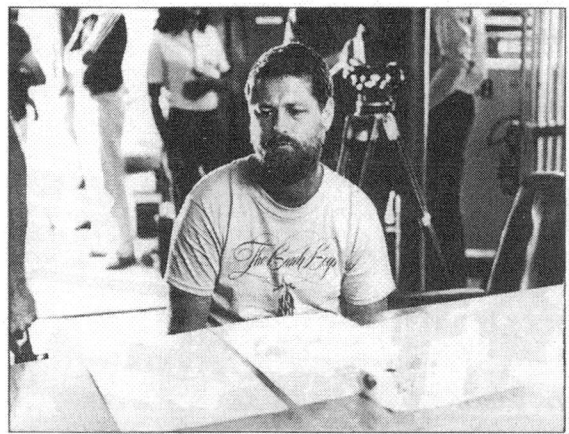

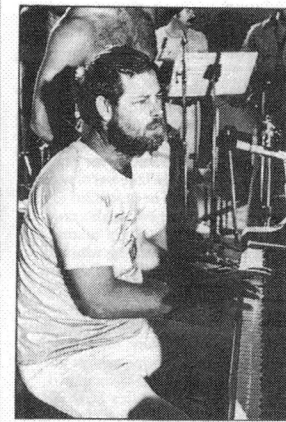

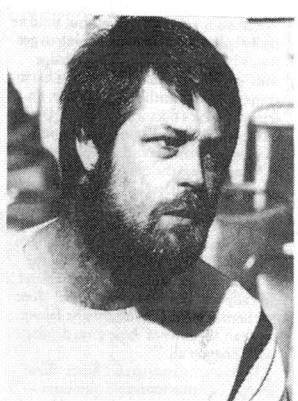

Brian Wilson, summer 1977.

The Beach Boys played for several hundred thousand people in a free concert at Central Park, September 1977.

Marilyn and Brian at the 1977 Rock Awards.

BRIAN WILSON SESSIONS

Onstage in Hawaii, March 1978.

BRIAN WILSON SESSIONS

BRIAN WILSON SESSIONS

BRIAN WILSON SESSIONS

THE HEALING OF BROTHER BRI

A MULTITRACK ROLLING STONE INTERVIEW with Beach Boys Brian, Dennis and Carl Wilson, Mike Love and Al Jardine...plus Brian's Wife, His Shrink, His Mom and His Dad, the Late Murry Wilson

BY DAVID FELTON

PHOTOGRAPHS BY ANNIE LEIBOVITZ

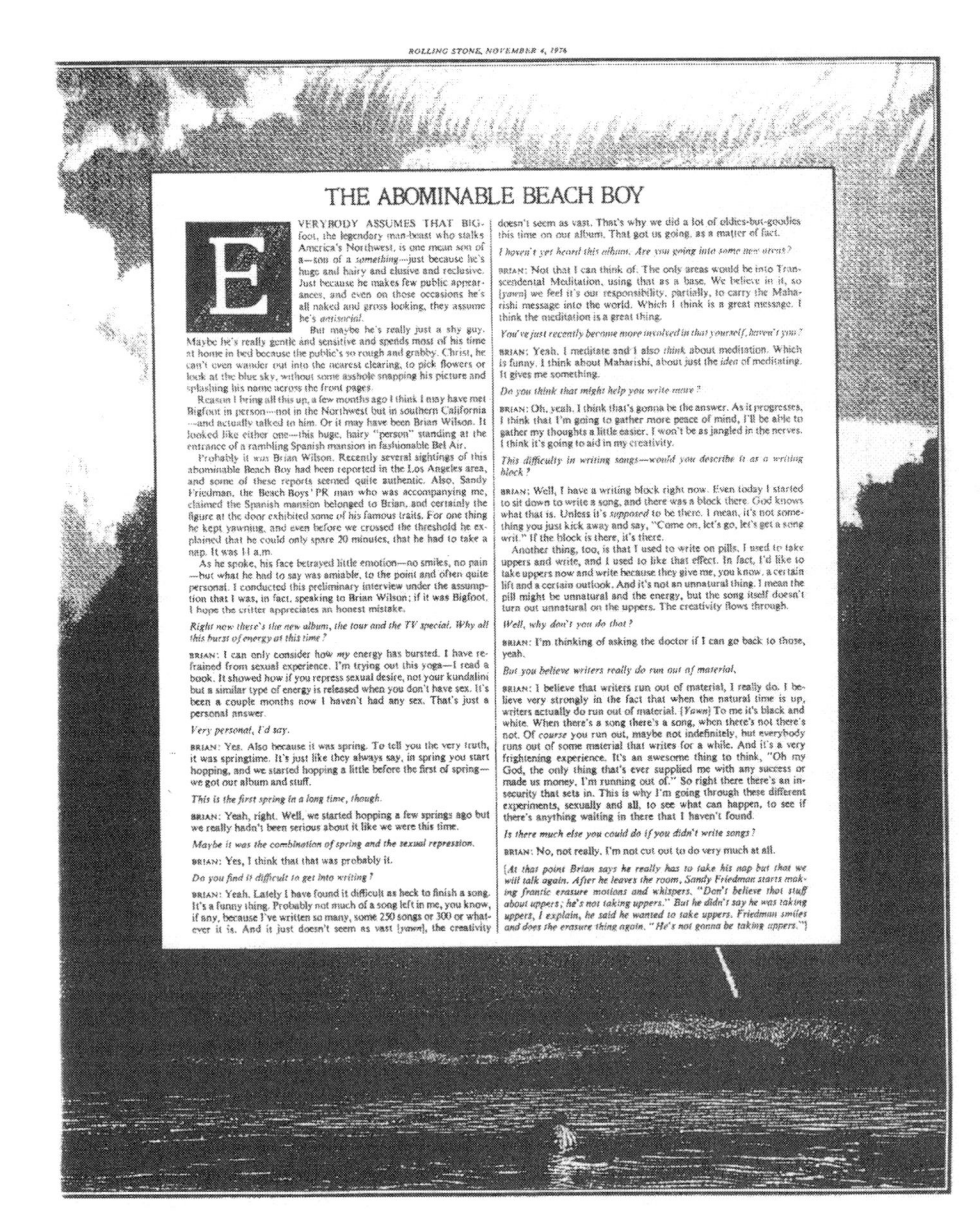

BRIAN WILSON SESSIONS

ROLLING STONE, NOVEMBER 4, 1976

THE ABOMINABLE BEACH BOY

EVERYBODY ASSUMES THAT BIGfoot, the legendary man-beast who stalks America's Northwest, is one mean son of a—son of a *something*—just because he's huge and hairy and elusive and reclusive. Just because he makes few public appearances, and even on those occasions he's all naked and gross looking, they assume he's *antisocial*.

But maybe he's really just a shy guy. Maybe he's really gentle and sensitive and spends most of his time at home in bed because the public's so rough and grabby. Christ, he can't even wander out into the nearest clearing, to pick flowers or look at the blue sky, without some asshole snapping his picture and splashing his name across the front pages.

Reason I bring all this up, a few months ago I think I may have met Bigfoot in person—not in the Northwest but in southern California—and actually talked to him. Or it may have been Brian Wilson. It looked like either one—this huge, hairy "person" standing at the entrance of a rambling Spanish mansion in fashionable Bel Air.

Probably it was Brian Wilson. Recently several sightings of this abominable Beach Boy had been reported in the Los Angeles area, and some of these reports seemed quite authentic. Also, Sandy Friedman, the Beach Boys' PR man who was accompanying me, claimed the Spanish mansion belonged to Brian, and certainly the figure at the door exhibited some of his famous traits. For one thing he kept yawning, and even before we crossed the threshold he explained that he could only spare 20 minutes, that he had to take a nap. It was 11 a.m.

As he spoke, his face betrayed little emotion—no smiles, no pain—but what he had to say was amiable, to the point and often quite personal. I conducted this preliminary interview under the assumption that I was, in fact, speaking to Brian Wilson; if it was Bigfoot, I hope the critter appreciates an honest mistake.

Right now there's the new album, the tour and the TV special. Why all this burst of energy at this time?

BRIAN: I can only consider how my energy has bursted. I have refrained from sexual experience. I'm trying out this yoga—I read a book. It showed how if you repress sexual desire, not your kundalini but a similar type of energy is released when you don't have sex. It's been a couple months now I haven't had any sex. That's just a personal answer.

Very personal, I'd say.

BRIAN: Yes. Also because it was spring. To tell you the very truth, it was springtime. It's just like they always say, in spring you start hopping, and we started hopping a little before the first of spring—we got our album and stuff.

This is the first spring in a long time, though.

BRIAN: Yeah, right. Well, we started hopping a few springs ago but we really hadn't been serious about it like we were this time.

Maybe it was the combination of spring and the sexual repression.

BRIAN: Yes, I think that was probably it.

Do you find it difficult to get into writing?

BRIAN: Yeah. Lately I have found it difficult as heck to finish a song. It's a funny thing. Probably not much of a song left in me, you know, if any, because I've written so many, some 250 songs or 300 or whatever it is. And it just doesn't seem as vast [yawn], the creativity doesn't seem as vast. That's why we did a lot of oldies-but-goodies this time on our album. That got us going, as a matter of fact.

I haven't yet heard this album. Are you going into some new areas?

BRIAN: Not that I can think of. The only areas would be into Transcendental Meditation, using that as a base. We believe in it, so [yawn] we feel it's our responsibility, partially, to carry the Maharishi message into the world. Which I think is a great message. I think the meditation is a great thing.

You've just recently become more involved in that yourself, haven't you?

BRIAN: Yeah, I meditate and I also *think* about meditation. Which is funny. I think about Maharishi, about just the *idea* of meditating. It gives me something.

Do you think that might help you write more?

BRIAN: Oh, yeah. I think that's gonna be the answer. As it progresses, I think that I'm going to gather more peace of mind, I'll be able to gather my thoughts a little easier. I won't be as jangled in the nerves. I think it's going to aid in my creativity.

This difficulty in writing songs—would you describe it as a writing block?

BRIAN: Well, I have a writing block right now. Even today I started to sit down to write a song, and there was a block there. God knows what that is. Unless it's *supposed* to be there. I mean, it's not something you just kick away and say, "Come on, let's go, let's get a song writ." If the block is there, it's there.

Another thing, too, is that I used to write on pills. I used to take uppers and write, and I used to like that effect. In fact, I'd like to take uppers now and write because they give me, you know, a certain lift and a certain outlook. And it's not an unnatural thing. I mean the pill might be unnatural and the energy, but the song itself doesn't turn out unnatural on the uppers. The creativity flows through.

Well, why don't you do that?

BRIAN: I'm thinking of asking the doctor if I can go back to those, yeah.

But you believe writers really do run out of material.

BRIAN: I believe that writers run out of material, I really do. I believe very strongly in the fact that when the natural time is up, writers actually do run out of material. [Yawn] To me it's black and white. When there's a song there's a song, when there's not there's not. Of course you run out, maybe not indefinitely, but everybody runs out of some material that writes for a while. And it's a very frightening experience. It's an awesome thing to think, "Oh my God, the only thing that's ever supplied me with any success or made us money, I'm running out of." So right there there's an insecurity that sets in. This is why I'm going through these different experiments, sexually and all, to see what can happen, to see if there's anything waiting in there that I haven't found.

Is there much else you could do if you didn't write songs?

BRIAN: No, not really. I'm not cut out to do very much at all.

[At that point Brian says he really has to take his nap but that we will talk again. After he leaves the room, Sandy Friedman starts making frantic erasure motions and whispers, "Don't believe that stuff about uppers; he's not taking uppers." But he didn't say he was taking uppers, I explain, he said he wanted to take uppers. Friedman smiles and does the erasure thing again. "He's not gonna be taking uppers."]

BRIAN WILSON SESSIONS

ROLLING STONE, NOVEMBER 4, 1976

Rising and shining: Brian Wilson (yawn) and bodyguard Scott Steinberg

SLEEPERS AWAKE

THIS MAY HAVE BEEN, AS the trades predicted, the bitchinest summer ever for the Beach Boys, what with their new album, their tour, and Brian Wilson finally getting out of bed. But as far as I'm concerned these last four months have been one endless bummer. I couldn't seem to come up with a new handle to their venerable rock legend. Let's face it, the Beach Boys are probably the most thoroughly written about, mythicized, analyzed, agonized over and deeply probed pop group in America. And this summer especially we've had Beach Boys up the ass: dozens of heavy feature articles in major magazines and newspapers; a dazzling, hour-long TV documentary; a three-month concert tour of stadiums and fairgrounds throughout the United States and Canada; release of *15 Big Ones*, the first album of new Beach Boys material in 42 months, in honor of the 15 years they've miraculously played, strayed, prayed and stayed together; and a scholarly sounding paperback entitled *The Beach Boys: Southern California Pastoral*, in which Cal State professor Bruce Golden puts the guys right up there with Dante, Cervantes, Shakespeare and Milton as masters of the pastoral form.

Well, why not, it's a great legend, and just like nearly everything the Beach Boys ever recorded, I can never stop listening to it. Mainly it's about Brian Wilson, the partially deaf boy wonder turned mad genius who tuned his one good ear into the drone of middle-class America and heard the lost chord of God. Until it drove him nuts, and finally silent.

So in June, when the word started spreading that Brian was ready to talk for the first time in half a decade, I flew down to Los Angeles to conduct an official ROLLING STONE interview. But it didn't work out exactly. Brian was ready to talk, all right, just as he was ready to walk or ready to start dressing himself; but there could be no definitive Brian Wilson interview because Brian Wilson was not yet definitively himself. Therefore I also talked to the other Beach Boys and to Brian's mother, his wife and his shrink. Plus in late 1971 I'd interviewed Brian's father Murry, while he was still alive, and I threw a little of that in somewhere.

The raw material, I think, is pretty good—some really touching stories, some laughs, hopefully some answers. But focusing it, as I mentioned, was a bitch. First I tried a musical analysis thing, portraying the Beach Boys as "primitivists" like contemporary composer Carl Orff. Both Orff and the Beach Boys ignored the virtuosic contrivances of established music and returned to the common, simple rhythms and harmonies of the people. They both orchestrated this folk element with layers of brilliant tonal color and ambiance to produce a music of incredible spiritual purity. I mentioned this to the Beach Boys and none of them had ever heard of Carl Orff. Which in a way, I thought, reinforced my theory but also sort of soured me on it.

Finally, in late September, I returned to Los Angeles at the suggestion of Brian's shrink, Dr. Eugene Landy. He wanted me to see Brian's progress since June. That day disturbed me a great deal, but it did provide an update and ultimately a focus for the story. For this in one sense is a story of gurus, of old and new methods of personal growth in the promised land called California. Brian's father was a guru of sorts, a frustrated songwriter and ruthlessly aggressive man who heard in his three sons the music he could never articulate himself, who as their manager drove them to such heights of success they eventually fired him. Then Brian took over as guru to the group, teaching the others his genius art of composing and producing, teaching them so well that when he eventually ascended to his bedroom, they could carry on his work with the public hardly noticing. Later came the Beach Boys' professional gurus—Maharishi Mahesh Yogi of TM and Dr. Landy of Dr. Landy.

I've no idea which method works best and I really don't care. But if you're seeking peace of mind and body, positive energy and a little spiritual glue, let me strongly recommend adding some Beach Boys music to your day, perhaps when you get up and just before dinner. It'll give you something.

MAMA SAYS

SHE'S SO GOSH DARN CUTE, the colorful clothes she wears and the way the sunlight plays upon her short platinum hair, you wish they all could be California girls like Audree Wilson, mother of Carl, Dennis and Brian and den mother to the Beach Boys since their first days in Hawthorne, California. More amazing, she was the wife of Murry Wilson, by all reports an extremely difficult man, as work-driven as she was playful, as rough as she was easy. A small, quiet, funny woman surrounded by fighting men, she spent much of her time and understanding bridging gaps and soothing wounds. Now the old man has died and the young ones have long since moved away to grow old themselves; so Audree sits alone these days in an elegant, hillside home above Hollywood, with the view and the pool and the shiny Jag in the driveway, and tries to adjust to the strange new peace that plagues her every hour.

BRIAN WILSON SESSIONS

AUDREE: The way it really started, Brian, he started singing when he was just a little bitty guy, three years old. He'd sing right on key. He loved to hear me play the piano, he loved the chords. And he'd say, "Play that chord again."

Brian just always had this incredibly marvelous talent. The other boys were a little slower, they were kinda like slow bloomers. Brian started writing arrangements when he was around 14. He loved the Four Freshmen—I know you've read that over and over—and he would make these incredible arrangements, sorta like them but he'd add what he wanted. And we'd sing the first two parts on the tape recorder, then play it back and sing the other two parts with it. That was great fun.

Did he ever take formal piano lessons or anything like that?

AUDREE: Brian took accordion lessons, on one of those little baby accordions, for six weeks. And the teacher said, "I don't think he's reading. He just hears it once and plays the whole thing through perfectly." Anyway, at the end of six weeks he was supposed to buy a large accordion, but we couldn't afford it. And that's all the training he ever had.

Brian is deaf in one ear. Was he born that way?

AUDREE: We don't really know. Brian thinks it happened when he was around ten. Some kid down the street really whacked him in the ear. However, it's a damaged ninth nerve, so he could have been born that way; it's called the ninth nerve and there's nothing they can do about that. I think it makes him more incredible.

The way he arranges, produces and records—the ambiance and total sound—is something that two ears can really appreciate. He's never heard that and I guess he never will.

AUDREE: Ah, he hears. [*Audree laughs in amazement.*] He doesn't maybe hear like we do, but he does.

So when did your sons start to record?

AUDREE: My husband was in the machinery business, big lathes from England, and the people from whom he imported them were here to visit us. And we took them to Mexico City. When we left, the refrigerator was completely stocked and we gave the boys enough money to buy whatever else they needed. We came back and here they had gone out and rented a bass, a big standup, as tall as Al for sure, and drums and a microphone. They had used every bit of their food money. And they said, "We want to play something for you." They were very excited about it, and I thought the song was darling—never dreaming anything would happen.

And that song was "Surfin'."

AUDREE: Right.

Well, then they signed with Capitol and they started making a lot of hits. How did that change your life at home?

AUDREE: Well, it was really very hectic. Telephones never ever stopped ringing. And I was doing all of the book work. I was making all the forms for the musicians' union and I was going to the bank and being so careful that all five of them got exactly the same amount to the penny. And I remember cooking dinner and we'd have to leave. I remember dinners not even being eaten because we had to fly out to wherever they had to appear.

How did they handle this success?

AUDREE: Well, being a mother, I thought they handled it so beautifully for being that young. But their father had a strong hand as far as . . . well, they didn't always listen to him. Later he'd say, "Why didn't you listen to me?" And they'd say, "Well, I guess we were punks."

There was a night during or after the Australia tour when they decided they didn't want their father to manage them.

AUDREE: It destroyed him.

Did you understand why they . . .

AUDREE: Oh, I understood perfectly. That was a horrible time for me. He was just destroyed by that and yet he wasn't really up to it. He'd already had an ulcer and it was really too much for him; but he loved them so much, he was so overly protective, really. He couldn't let them go. He couldn't stand seeing anyone else handling his kids.

Those were terrible days, frankly, and he was angry with me. You always take it out on the closest one. He was angry at the whole world.

What did he say at the time?

AUDREE: Not too much. He stayed in bed a lot.

YOU NEED A MESS OF HELP TO STAND ALONE

MEANWHILE, BACK AT THE Bel Air mansion, Brian had just gone upstairs for his noontime nap when Dennis Wilson bounded into the living room. Dennis is easily the most infectious Beach Boy, the prettiest, wittiest, most outgoing and independent, the most, say his family, like his father. Not surprisingly, it's gotten him into a lot of trouble over the years, with his dad, his schoolteachers and later with his notorious roommate Charles Manson, to whom he now, bearded and prancing impulsively, bore a striking resemblance. (According to *New Musical Express*, Dennis told a reporter for England's *Rave* magazine in 1968, "Fear is nothing but awareness, man. . . . Sometimes the 'Wizard' frightens me. The 'Wizard' is Charlie Manson, who is another friend of mine, who says he is God and the Devil. He sings, plays and writes poetry and may be another artist for Brother Records.")

As Dennis sat down, Sandy Friedman handed him a local trade paper with the Beach Boys on the cover. He glanced at it for a moment, then shrugged and said, "Come on, you can't read everything you believe." Then he stood up and walked to the center of the room for an important announcement.

DENNIS: I've just made a monumental decision. [*Dennis pauses dramatically.*] I'm not guilty about masturbation anymore! [*Then seriously, folks*] I just started my own record company. It's like, I've been in one group my whole life. I always thought if I wasn't a Beach Boy I would fail. [*Here Dennis sticks his arms straight out in mock agony.*] So I called up my attorney and said, "Hey, get me a record company." But my biggest piece of shit is, I'm gonna do a movie where I'm gonna be a flaming gay boy who wants to be a policeman.

So many positive things are happening in the Beach Boys' career right now. Let me tell you something about the Beach Boys . . . we had a very normal childhood. Our father beat the shit out of us; his punishments were outrageous. I never saw eye to eye with him, ever. In fact I used to lie to him when I was young. I learned at an early age to be very protective of myself, I played a great mind game.

But one thing about my father—beautiful music would always melt my father's heart. You always wanted to sing for him. Dad was a frustrated songwriter, and I think Brian wrote his music through him.

[*Dennis suggests we go to his VW camper in the driveway, where we listen to a cassette of two cuts from his planned solo album. They have kind of a Beach Boys sound to them, but rougher, more rock & roll, like Dennis's voice and temperament. Actually, they sound great. Finally I get up enough nerve to ask him a question that has intimidated me for some time.*]

I know this is an unpleasant subject, but it's been a number of years now, and I was wondering if we could discuss your experience with Charles Manson. . . .

[*But even before I finish, Dennis is shaking his head.*]

DENNIS: No. Never. As long as I live, I'll never talk about that. [*He gazes out the windshield of his camper.*] I don't know anything, you know? If I did, I would've been up on that witness stand.

[*Just then actress Karen Lamm Wilson, Dennis' new wife, drives up in a small sports car. "Gotta go, guys," yells Dennis, bolting from the camper and taking off.*]

❧❧❧

Inside, Carl, the youngest and most stable Wilson brother, had arrived, sporting, like all the Beach Boys these days, a full, rough beard, and like himself, a workmanlike jumpsuit. He owns a whole closetful of jumpsuits, in a spectrum of colors from gray to brown, and one suspects they are designed to ameliorate the last vestiges of a sweet baby chubbiness. Although he's occasionally made headlines in the past, resisting the draft for years before a federal court granted him C.O. status, his personality is basically shy and quiet. It was Carl who invariably kept his head while all about him were losing theirs, who took charge of stage performances after Brian left the road and who later took over record production when Brian could no longer handle that one.

Why was your father fired as manager?

CARL: My recollection could be kind of foggy on that. I just know it started in Australia—this was around '63 or '64. Brian, and Michael especially, wanted to not have my father involved because he screwed them up with chicks, you know? We'd want to find a girl to be with, the thing on the road, and he was really kind of prudish about it. Also, Brian really disagreed with the way my dad wanted things to sound. And I remember having a conversation with my dad in his bedroom at home. I said, "They really, you know, don't want you to manage the group anymore." When I think about it now, *Jesus*, that must have really crushed him. After all, he gave up his home and business for us, he was kind of crackers over us, you know?

Would your dad be more likely to confide in you?

CARL: Yeah, we had a great relationship. He was crazy about Brian, but he and Brian drove each other nuts. You know, here Brian is really growing massively musically, right? And his old man's telling him how the records should sound. My dad would say do it faster, and Brian would say no, it's gotta be more laid back, have more feel to it. But he was a great man, very sensitive. I really loved my dad a lot.

It about killed Brian when my dad died. He went to New York; my dad passed away. Brian split. He could not handle it.

He didn't go to the funeral?

CARL: No. That's how come he left, so he wouldn't have to be here and go. I think Brian hung onto that one for quite some time. I think he's okay with it now, maybe.

The area of questioning I find most difficult, it's so personal, is what we might call "Brian's problem."

CARL: Brian's behavior.

Yeah, well, you once said he went through hell.

Carl and Annie Wilson

BRIAN WILSON SESSIONS

Dennis and Karen Wilson

CARL: Well . . . a lot of anguish, a lot of anxiety, frustration, disillusionment. Brian worked really hard for the first seven years and he needed a break, I think he was pretty confused at the time by his environment. He just took a look and saw how fucked up the world was—he's not a dummy—and he said, "The world is so fucked up, I can't stand it; it's unspeakable how fucked up everything is." And I think it really broke his heart.

He's painfully conscious. When it hurts, it hurts; he can't bury it and grow. I mean, he's one of the nervyest people I've ever met. He does exactly what he wants to do. I remember [*sits back and laughs*]—this is so funny—when we did "Little Honda," Brian wanted me to get this real distorted guitar sound, real fuzzy. "This guitar sounds like shit," I said. "Brian, I hate this." And he goes, "Would you fucking do it? Just do it." When I heard it, I felt like an asshole. It sounded really hot. That was before fuzz became a big deal.

He's a true great, and his greatness has been a plague to him.

❦ ❦ ❦

That afternoon Lorne Michaels, producer of the TV special, held a scheduling meeting at Brian's house. Most of Michaels' crew was there, including director Gary Weis and writers Danny Aykroyd, John Belushi and Alan Zweibel. All the Beach Boys came too, except Brian left the room after a few minutes because he was "tired."

Actually he didn't miss that much—it was just a nice, friendly business meeting. The crew brought beer and pizza, and the Beach Boys played their new album. Michaels explained the shooting schedule for the next two weeks. Another meeting was announced for the following Monday.

Then an intense, tough-faced man who'd been sitting sort of off to the side suddenly assumed a peculiar authority. "Now, when you come back next Monday—no beer, no food, no anything," he announced sternly. "Today somebody was very naughty and brought beer. Brian's on a diet."

The scolding produced an awkward silence. Belushi shrugged and tried to explain the crew's transgression. "It was just a friendly gesture . . ."

"Yes, but Brian blew his diet. He had five beers," the man continued. "So next time you'll just have to drink coffee or nothing at all."

It seemed a bit embarrassing, this explicit discussion of Brian's personal indulgence. "Who is that guy?" I asked Carl as the meeting broke up. "Oh, that's Gene Landy," he said. "Brian's psychologist."

A few nights later I phoned Dr. Landy at his Hollywood home and asked if I could interview him. He was about to have dinner, but since he's one of those brusque, bustling, snap-snap-snap busy people who like to do at least two things at once, he told me to come right over.

We sat down in his newly converted garage library, I with my tape recorder, he with a large green salad, a glass of wine, a phone and an intercom. He wore green pants with white stripes, boots and a flappy-collared flower print shirt and looked really more like a record promoter than a shrink. In fact, years ago he did work as a promo man, for RCA, Coral, Decca, Mercury, and there still seemed to be a hard-sell, wisecracking, PR-bio feedback about him.

For instance, when I asked him, rather perfunctorily, who he was and what he did, Dr. Landy answered for 20 minutes, starting with the sixth grade. In short, he dropped out of sixth grade, unable to read, hit the streets, worked for the circus, fucked around a lot, worked for the record business, produced a radio show, went to night school and earned a bachelor's degree at the age of 30, went to med school but quit because of a liver disease, went to the University of Oklahoma and earned a doctorate in psychology, worked for the Peace Corps, Job Corps and VISTA, and finally, in the late Sixties, moved to southern California and immersed himself in group dynamics. Also he wrote a book of hippie slang, *The Underground Dictionary*, a copy of which he now pulled from a shelf, autographed and handed to me without charge.

"My background," Dr. Landy summarized, "is basically that of a hyperkinetic, perceptually disoriented, brain-damaged person. I'm also very bright, very intuitive, very sensitive, and I'm quite capable of reading what most people are thinking or doing."

I asked him how much he, a doctor, could talk about his patient Brian Wilson, and the question seemed to strike him for the first time. He immediately phoned a member of the California State Psychological Association's ethics committee, who advised him to phone Brian. He did, and Brian told him to do whatever he wanted.

Dr. Landy hung up the phone and laughed. "Brian would probably give me permission for anything."

How'd you get involved with Brian?

LANDY: They came to me. Marilyn, Mrs. Wilson, made an appointment, she came in and talked to me.

Then you must have had some kind of reputation.

LANDY: Right, I've treated a lot of people. [*He laughs*.]

Other celebrities?

LANDY: Yeah, yeah . . . the only one I can actually mention is the only one that went on television and said, "This is my shrink"—Richard Harris. But I've treated a tremendous number of people in show business; for some reason I seem to be able to relate to them. I think I have a nice reputation that says I'm unorthodox by orthodox standards but basically unique by unorthodox standards.

Well, you sound like a pretty heavy-duty Hollywood shrink.

LANDY: Yeah, I guess. [*Gleefully*] I'm *outrageously* expensive.

How much do you charge?

LANDY: How much do you think I charge?

I don't know, $40 is what I've been paying, so . . .

LANDY: I'm $90.

Ninety? An hour?

LANDY: Fifty minutes.

How can you charge so much and get away with it? You must be very good.

LANDY: I am. I do unusual—look at Brian, he's a two-year patient, two and a half at the most. Nobody else would have taken him on for under five. I do a thing that says you don't have to spend a lot of time.

What's that?

LANDY: Well, I'm using a team approach, a team of people who work for me in the general, overall supervision and treatment. Let's see . . . . I'm a clinical psychologist . . . there's a psychiatrist, Sol Samuels . . . there's Dr. David Gans, the physician . . . there's Joey, who's a shrink . . . Arnold Horowitz, another shrink who's working on another part of the situation . . . there's Scott Steinberg, that's six.

Who's Scott Steinberg?

LANDY: Another one of the boys . . . and the nutritionist is seven—I have a girl, Nancy, uh, whatever her name is, who does nutritional things.

Anyway, Marilyn called me in late September of last year because she just couldn't deal with the whole situation any longer. She has two kids that need to have their needs met. She has her own needs for her life. And, uh, Brian was basically withdrawn for a number of years.

What was he suffering from?

LANDY: Well, Brian was suffering from scared.

Scared of what?

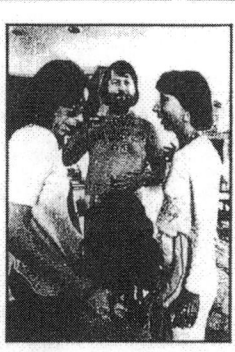

Brian, Marilyn (r) and sister Dianne

BRIAN WILSON SESSIONS

LANDY: Just generally frightened. He was not able to deal with frightened or even have a response to frightened and therefore lived in the area of fantasy for a while. He's in the process of returning from fantasy every day more and more.

What happened to him in fantasy?

LANDY: [*Shrugs*] . . . Nothing. [*He laughs impishly.*]

So why hire you? There must have been something that was bothering him.

LANDY: Well, it wasn't bothering *him*, it was bothering *her*. And the kids. I mean, when someone lives in fantasy, *they* don't mind—they're enjoying themselves.

He wasn't unhappy?

LANDY: No. Why should he be? It was the people around him.

Because he wasn't being a real person, or. . . .

LANDY: Because he wasn't relating on the level in the society where we have expectancies of what we expect people to do. When you pick the phone up, you expect it to say hello. If you do something different, depending on how different, you frighten people around you. And if you're frightened yourself, you simply withdraw.

But the point is, what you had to work with was a serious problem.

LANDY: It depends by whose definition—not by an eight-year-old's, by a 34-year-old's. We look at potential. When you stay at home and you can have the whole world if you want it, you're not living up to your potential. But who says you have to?

But he is a pretty weird guy.

LANDY: No, he's not a weird guy. Brian is absolutely one of the most charming people I've met. He only gets weird when he gets frightened. I see him as a really warm, loving, capable human being who when not frightened is a right-on dude.

I guess what I'm asking is, who are you working for? Are you working for Brian, or for the people who would like to see Brian better?

LANDY: I was hired by Marilyn on the condition that I can do my thing, whatever it is. And she took me at face value. And that face value process has paid off. I'm working for Brian Wilson to have something he has not had, and that's an alternative . . . that if he chooses to withdraw and be scared, that's as good as choosing not to, but to have the choice. And if Brian feels that he's better and likes better sitting in bed, then goddamnit, "Here's to you, Brian."

One thing that surprised me—when we were at that meeting with Lorne Michaels and the whole crew, you told them about not bringing beer next time. I expected a more traditional thing—you would have called Lorne aside, privately, and said, "Hey, look, don't have your guys bring it." But you said it right out in the open.

LANDY: Well, if I only tell Lorne, he's gotta tell the others, and I don't know if the message gets across.

But my first impulse was, gee, you're treating Brian like a child. The fact that a private matter was being brought out—wouldn't that have a humiliating effect?

LANDY: I don't feel humiliated when I make it very clear that I can't be in the same room with people that smoke.

But Brian wasn't making it clear. You were making it clear for Brian.

LANDY: That's right. But that's what I'm paid to do.

I understand that, but is that therapeutic?

LANDY: Well, the whole point is that Brian had enjoyed five beers, and that's not therapeutic. Now, I sometimes assist him in things that he's not happy I assist him in. "No more beer." [*Laughs*] Sometimes I overassist 'cause I compensate for his overindulgence.

He sort of has a rebellious nature to him.

LANDY: Naw, it's indulgent, not rebellious.

I was thinking of the way he sometimes puts people on.

LANDY: Brian doesn't put anybody on. Brian doesn't have that much of a sense of humor.

But Brian is extremely bright, astute, competent, capable and just eats up information. You don't have to fight to get it in him. He eats it all up, he's just hungry. That's why we're moving so quickly. He just hungers.

☙ ❧ ☙

It was high noon at Brother Studio in Santa Monica, and something of a showdown was about to disrupt the churchlike harmony of the place. The Beach Boys were there to record "I'm Bugged at My Old Man" for the TV special, but at the moment Brian Wilson was growing more and more bugged with Scott Steinberg. Scott, a short, thick young man with huge arms, stood guarding the entrance to a narrow corridor. He looked grim and unyielding. Brian faced him from about a foot away and looked absolutely ferocious.

"Where's my lunch?" Brian asked angrily.

"It's back there," said Scott, gesturing toward the corridor, "but you're not gettin' any."

Brian moved closer. Scott widened his stance and put his hands on his hips. "I want my lunch!" shouted Brian.

"No, Brian!"

"Why not?"

"You know goddamn well why not. You forfeited your lunch when you snuck upstairs and ate that hamburger."

"*But I'm hungry!*" bellowed Brian.

Scott cocked back his head. "You should have thought of that before you ate that hamburger."

After staring silently at this tough punk for another 30 seconds, Brian rotated his massive body and slowly lumbered back into the main recording studio. Then Scott relaxed, turned to an associate and snickered. "If he sings good, I'll give him the patty."

Scott is 19. Brian is 34.

WILD HONEY

WHEN BRIAN FIRST MET Marilyn Rovell, she was singing with an all-female group, the Honeys; later, with her sister Dianne, she formed a duo called Spring and recorded an album under Brian's direction. But the album bombed, as did several singles, and she's since devoted her time and energy to family affairs.

Mike Love has described her as "one of the most patient people in the world." And you can see why. As Brian's wife, Marilyn had to live with a man whose quirks, put-ons and indulgences were as celebrated as his pioneer writing and arranging talents. And that was when he was *healthy*. In recent years this small, resilient woman has had to manage a household of two young daughters and one sleeping giant pretty much alone.

MARILYN: Brian was always eccentric. From the day I met him I couldn't stop laughing. Just everything he did was funny. The way he lifted a fork was funny. [*Marilyn breaks up just thinking about it.*] He'd ride a motorcycle into Gold Star recording studios. I couldn't believe him!

Well, you know, he wanted a sandbox, so he got a sandbox. I mean, who am I to tell a creator what he can do? He said, "I want to play in the sand, I want to feel like a little kid. When I'm writing these songs, I want to feel what I'm writing, all the happiness." Brian wanted to experience it all. So he had this really good carpenter come up to the house—this was when we were living on Laurel Way—and in the dining room the guy built a gorgeous wood sandbox, around two and a half feet tall. And then they came with a dump truck and dumped eight tons of sand in it.

I have the funniest story, about the piano tuner—have you heard it? Okay, the piano tuner, who we still use, walks into the house . . . and the sandbox had been there awhile and I was very used to it. He says, "Okay, where's the piano?" I was busy in the house. I said, "Oh, it's over there in the sandbox," thinking nothing of it, right? There's this grand piano in the sandbox. He looks at me and goes, "Oh." All of a sudden he walks over to the sandbox and sits down, and he starts taking off his shoes and socks! That made me roar. He just took them off like, "Oh, sand, I got to take off my shoes and socks to go in the sand." And the sand, being that there is no sun, is freezing cold. By the way, the dogs had also used it—you know dogs and sand—and he puts up the hood thing, looks in the piano, and it was like he was going to have a nervous breakdown. "My God, this piano is filled with sand!" We had to vacuum it out.

I'll tell you another story about the piano tuner. One time after we first moved to this house, he came in and Brian sat down and hummed each note of the piano to the guy. Each note! It was Brian's tuning; he didn't want regular pitch, he wanted it tuned to his ears. He wanted the notes to ring a certain way—I could never explain it. But it was the greatest tuning job you ever heard.

Dr. Eugene Landy, Brian and Marilyn

BRIAN WILSON SESSIONS

How long have you two been married?

MARILYN: It'll be 12 years December. I got married when I was 16 and he was 22.

And how did all that come about?

MARILYN: Well, we were like girlfriend and boyfriend for a year and a half—I already was totally in love with him, you know—and yet he would never admit that there were feelings for me. And the time that he did do it . . . the guys were going to Australia, and I remember sitting in the airport with Brian and Mike, and Mike—Mike was, you know, Mr. Joker; still is—goes, "Wow, Brian, boy, we're sure going to have a good time in Australia." And Brian's kind of looking at me from the corner of his eye, and he's going, "Yeah . . . yeah, yeah, we are, aren't we." And I can't imagine why I said this, but I just went, "God, that's great, because I'm going to have a great time too." You know, the typical childish things. And Brian looked at me like—the first time I ever saw such an expression on his face—like, "What? What'd you say?" Anyway, they went on the airplane for 13 hours, and that night when they arrived in Australia I got the call from him. Two telegrams had come in the meantime. I got the call, and for the first time he called me "honey." It was, like, "Marilyn"—do you want to hear this?"

Sure.

MARILYN: I mean our love life?

I want to hear this story, anyway. I'm not sure about your love life.

MARILYN: "Marilyn, oh I couldn't wait to talk to you," he said. "I don't know what happened but on the plane it just hit me, it was like an arrow struck me in the heart, that I was going to lose you." He says, "I realize that, you know, that I need you and I have to have you as my wife, I've got to be with you, I can't stand the thought of ever losing you." And I mean, it was like four o'clock in the morning, and here I was just jumping like a rabbit. He called me three times a day, each day—$3000 worth of phone calls!

Actually there is one thing I'd like to ask you about your love life. Brian mentioned he was experimenting with celibacy, and I figured you would know if that's true.

MARILYN: Celibacy—what's that?

No sex.

MARILYN: No sex? Um . . . no, that's not true at all. I mean, I wouldn't say he was into it, you know, like a master. [*She giggles.*] But that definitely is not true.

He said he'd been refraining from sex for two months so that he would get more energy to do other things.

MARILYN: Let's put it this way—he refrains from coming.

Didn't Brian go through one of his most productive periods when you first got married?

MARILYN: Yeah . . . I remember him sitting in the sandbox when he was writing *Pet Sounds*. *Pet Sounds* was so heavy. He just told me one night, he says, "Marilyn, I'm gonna make the greatest album, the greatest rock album ever made." And he meant it. Boy, he worked his butt off when he was making *Pet Sounds*. And I'll never forget the night that he finally got the final disc, when they finished it, dubbing it down and all that, and he brought the disc home. And he prepared a moment. We went in the bedroom, we had a stereo in the bedroom, and he goes, "Okay, are you ready?" But he was really serious—this was his soul in there, you know? And we just lay there alone all night, you know, on the bed, and just listened and cried and did a whole thing. It was really, really heavy.

But *Pet Sounds* was not a big hit. That really hurt him badly, he couldn't understand it. It's like, why put your heart and soul into something? I think that had a lot to do with slowing him down.

But there you have a classic dilemma of popular art—the pressure to be creative versus the pressure to be commercial.

MARILYN: Brian has never . . . you can't pressure Brian.

Well, yes and no.

MARILYN: Well, you couldn't used to be able to pressure Brian. [*She laughs.*]

But isn't that sort of what's going on now with the new album and the tour—an answer to commercial demands?

MARILYN: It's that, but it's also something they need to do for themselves. You know, they're all just so happy to be back together. I mean, the thing that made me go to Dr. Landy was I couldn't stand to see Brian, whom I just love and adore, unhappy with himself and not really creating. Because music is his whole life, that's number one to him. So one of my girlfriends told me about Dr. Landy and I went and talked to him for an hour. I said, "I need someone who's gonna go to him, not where he has to go to you because he won't do it." And Dr. Landy said, "Yeah, I think I can do it." When I met Dr. Landy, I knew I'd met someone who could play Brian's game.

The game plan, as I understand it, was that you told Brian it was actually you who Dr. Landy was coming to see.

MARILYN: Well, it was my problem to begin with. So Dr. Landy was coming to see me for a while, and Brian kept peekin' his head in—"What are you doing with my wife?" you know? Then one day as I was talking to Dr. Landy, Brian just walked in the room and said, "Something's wrong with me, I need your help." And that started it all.

What was life like around then?

'Brian's greatness has been a plague to him.'

BRIAN WILSON SESSIONS

MARILYN: Well, it was a big drainer because of all the people coming around—too many weirdos coming over, drug people. And I've had it with drugs. Once we had our children I just said forget it, who needs it? You get all these drainers—that's my word for 'em—"Hey Brian, I gotta song, listen to this," you know? "Can you help me?" I didn't know how to get rid of all these people. Everyone just—"Oh, Marilyn's a bitch, she won't let anybody come in." It got to the point where I was just yelling and screaming at anybody that walked in the door.

I could kill the guy that gave him acid. Really, that was the worst experience for Brian to go through. Jesus, do you realize how sick that is for people to give people acid? How can people play with drugs like that? Wait a minute, don't get me wrong, I once tried a tiny bit of it years and years ago, like a quarter of a thing. That was enough for me. I wound up with cramps all night.

But Brian's trip happened to be a very outrageous one. It was a beautiful experience for him and yet being so naive and pure, I just don't think he was ready for it. And who knows if he ever would be?

Before you went to Dr. Landy, was Brian spending most of the time in his room, that sort of thing?

MARILYN: Yeah, he spent a lot of time in his room. But I would say through the last seven years it's been in spurts. Like one week he'd be real active and want to go out, and then he'd spend two weeks at home and not go anywhere. And then maybe he would spend a full day in bed or two days in bed and just say, "I don't feel good, I've got a sore throat," or something. It was difficult to find somebody who could help him 'cause I didn't know what needed to be helped. Sometimes I really thought to myself, is it me? Am I the one who's not seein' things right? And it was also difficult for the family to see it the same way, and the close friends, because everyone loved Brian and just said, "Oh, he'll get over it"—that kind of thing. But *I'm* the one who had to live with him.

It must have been very rough.

MARILYN: It was the worst, the absolute worst. But it just got to the point where I said, okay, this is it. The kids are getting too old; it's not that good they see their daddy in bed. I know that Brian wants to be a good father. He adores them. They adore him. And he didn't have an easy childhood, he really didn't. He once told me, he said, "Marilyn, I want you to discipline the kids. I'll do it wrong." Because he had it really rough. He didn't want to do the same thing to his kids, therefore he backed out of it totally. That makes me the mother and father both. And that's too hard, it's too hard. And so Dr. Landy assures me that I will have my 34-year-old husband soon, you know?

GETTIN' HUNGRY

THERE'S A DIRECTNESS about Brian Wilson that can be alarming. He doesn't mince words. Like he'll walk into this really posh Chinese restaurant, wave aside the niceties of cocktails or menus and simply ask, "Ya got any shrimp?" He's not being rude or childish, just getting the job done and the food there faster. And that's how he conducts interviews—dutiful, businesslike, wasting no time with small talk or unnecessary emotion, often prefacing his answers with the last words of your question, like some kind of oral exam. Sometimes you think he's joking because he says outrageous things from the corner of his mouth like Buddy Hackett. But usually he's quite serious, I think.

We were at the restaurant because Dr. Landy had set up a luncheon interview between me and Brian, which was nice of him except that he invited all these extra people—Marilyn, Audree, Dr. Landy's friend Alexandra and another shrink, Dr. Arnold Horowitz. Things looked bad for the interview, but Brian, in a remarkable act of quick thinking, solved the problem. Dr. Landy suggested we all move to a quieter table in the back. Everyone peeled off one by one, then Brian suddenly announced, "I think we'll stay right here." At first Landy was pissed. "Fine— you can pay your own bill," he snapped. Later, however, he told me on the phone, "That was tremendous, Brian really asserted himself. I thought that was marvelous."

At any rate, it allowed us to do the interview in relative privacy, away from family and shrinks and bodyguards. As it turned out, Brian may have had his own reasons for wanting to be alone.

Why don't we talk a bit about "Good Vibrations."

BRIAN: That would be a good place to begin. "Good Vibrations" took six months to make. We recorded the very first part of it at Gold Star Recording Studio, then we took it to a place called Western, then we went to Sunset Sound, then we went to Columbia.

So it took quite a while. There's a story behind this record that I tell everybody. My mother used to tell me about vibrations. I didn't really understand too much of what that meant when I was just a boy. It scared me, the word "vibrations." To think that invisible feelings, invisible vibrations existed, scared me to death. But she told about dogs that would bark at people and then not bark at others, that a dog would pick up vibrations from these people that you can't see, but you can feel. And the same existed with people.

And so it came to pass that we talked about good vibrations. We went ahead and experimented with the song and the idea, and we decided that on the one hand you could say, "I love the colorful clothes she wears and the way the sunlight plays upon her hair. I hear the sound of a gentle word on the wind that lifts her perfume through the air." Those are sensual things. And then you go, "I'm pickin' up good vibrations," which is a contrast against all the sensual—there's what you call the extrasensory perception which we have. And this is what we're really talking about.

But you also set out to do something new musically. Why this particular song?

BRIAN: Because we wanted to explain that concept, plus we wanted to do something that was R&B but had a taste of modern, avant-garde R&B to it. "Good Vibrations" was advanced rhythm and blues music.

You took a risk.

BRIAN: Oh yeah, we took a great risk. As a matter of fact, I don't think it was going to make it because of its complexity, but apparently people accepted it very well. They felt that it had a kind a naturalness to it, it flowed. It was a little pocket symphony.

How come you used four different studios?

BRIAN: Because we wanted to experiment with combining studio sounds. Every studio has its own marked sound. Using the four different studios had a lot to do with the way the final record sounded.

Did everybody support what you were trying to do?

BRIAN: No, not everybody. There was a lot of "oh you can't do this, that's too modern" or "that's going to be too long a record." I said no, it's not going to be too long a record, it's going to be just right.

Who resisted you? Your manager? The record company?

BRIAN: No, people in the group, but I can't tell ya who. We just had resisting ideas. They didn't quite understand what this jumping from studio to studio was all about. And they couldn't conceive of the record as I did. I saw the record as a totality piece.

Do you remember the time you realized you finally had it?

BRIAN: I remember the time that we had it. It was at Columbia. I remember I had it right in the sack. I could just feel it when I dubbed it down, made the final mix from the 16 track down to mono. It was a feeling of power, it was a rush. A feeling of exaltation. Artistic beauty. It was everything.

Do you remember saying anything?

BRIAN: I remember saying, "Oh my God. Sit back and listen to this!"

At that time did you feel it was your most important song? Did you think in terms like that—reaching a new plateau in music?

BRIAN: Yes, I felt that it was a plateau. First of all, it felt very arty and it sounded arty. Second of all, it was the first utilization of a cello in rock & roll music to that extent—using it as an up-front instrument, as a rock instrument.

Not to mention the theremin.

BRIAN: It was also the first use of a theremin in rock & roll.

By the time you did "Good Vibrations" you had matured your artistic concept far beyond the sort of thing you were doing, say, in "Surfin'." Was there any particular time period when you realized that you now were totally into creating music on your own terms?

BRIAN: Yes. *Pet Sounds* would be that period when I figured that I was into my own . . . via the Phil Spector approach. Now, the Phil Spector approach is utilizing many instruments to combine for a single form or a single sound. Like combining clarinets, trombones and saxophones to give you a certain sound, rather than hearing that arrangement as "oh, those are piccolos, oh, those are trombones."

How much was Spector an influence on you, artistically and competitively?

BRIAN: Well, I didn't feel I was competing as much as I was emulating, emulating the greatness of his style in my music. We have a high degree of art in our group. We've come to regard Phil Spector as the greatest, the most avant-garde producer in the business.

Yet he's not really a composer of songs.

BRIAN: Well, I'm a firm believer that he wrote those songs and gave the others credit. In order to produce them the way he did, he had to write them.

Mike Love mentioned the time you composed "The Warmth of the Sun" within hours of the John F. Kennedy assassination and how it illustrated that even during a very negative time you could come up with a very positive feeling.

BRIAN: Yeah, it's a strange thing, but I think we were always spiritually minded and we wrote music to give strength to people. I always feel holy when it comes to recording. Even during "Surfer Girl," even then I felt a bit spiritual.

What's the nature of your spiritual outlook today? Does it present you with a kind of attitude toward the world?

BRIAN: No, not really. I'm not as aware of the world as I could be.

Is that necessarily a bad thing?

Shaping up

BRIAN WILSON SESSIONS

'Many Happy Returns': Brian, Paul and Linda McCartney with daughters Heather and Mary

BRIAN: Yeah, because I think if I became more aware, I could structure my lyrics to be a little more in tune with people.

Are you working on that process right now?

BRIAN: Yes, I'm working on that right now, I'm working with people who I know know where it's at. Like Van Dyke Parks—he's a guy who's a link to where it's at for me. He keeps me very current on what's happening.

At one time you and he were working on a revolutionary album called 'Smile,' which you never released.

BRIAN: Yeah, we didn't finish it because we had a lot of problems, inner group problems. We had time commitments we couldn't keep. So we stopped. Plus, for instance, we did a thing called the "fire track." We cut a song called "Fire" and we used fire helmets on the musicians and we put a bucket with fire burning in it in the studio so we could smell smoke while we cut. And about a day later a building down the street burned down. We thought maybe it was witchcraft or something, we didn't know *what* we were into. So we decided not to finish it.

Plus I got into drugs and I began doing things that were over my head. It was too fancy for the public. I got too fancy and arty and was doing things that were just not Beach Boys at all. They were made for me.

Ever consider doing an album just on your own?

BRIAN: No, I haven't considered that because I didn't think it would be commercial if I did.

Well, so what?

BRIAN: Well, maybe I could do that then. I think I might.

What's this program with Dr. Landy and his team designed to do?

BRIAN: Well, it's basically designed to correct me from taking drugs.

You've had a problem with that?

BRIAN: Yeah, I had a problem taking drugs. Up until four months ago I was taking a lot of cocaine. And these doctors came in and showed me a way to stop doing it, which is having bodyguards with you all the time so you can't get to it.

What do you think of that approach?

BRIAN: That approach works because there's someone right there all the time—it keeps you on the spot. They catch you when you're ready to do something you shouldn't do. It works until you have finally reached the stage where you don't need it anymore.

Why did you consent to this program?

BRIAN: Because my wife called the doctors and legally she had the right to call them.

In addition to guarding you all the time, what else do Dr. Landy's people do for you?

BRIAN: They teach me socialization, how to socialize. They're just teaching me different social graces, like manners.

Didn't you at one time know those?

BRIAN: I did, but I lost them. Drugs took 'em away.

How could that be?

BRIAN: It just was. Drugs took 'em all away. I got real paranoid, I couldn't do anything.

Were you unhappy then?

BRIAN: I was unhappy as all heck. I knew I was screwing myself up, and I couldn't do anything about it. I was a useless little vegetable. I made everybody very angry at me because I wasn't able to work, to get off my butt. Coke every day. Goin' over to parties. Just havin' bags of snow around, just snortin' it down like crazy.

But aren't drugs just a symptom? There must be something else. Carl said that at some point you looked at the world and it was so messed up that you just couldn't take it.

BRIAN: I couldn't.

But the world is messed up. How do you deal with it?

BRIAN: The way I deal with it is I go jogging in the morning. I goddamn get out of bed and I jog, and I make sure I stay in shape. That's how I do it. And so far the only way I've been keeping from drugs is with those bodyguards, and the only way I've been going jogging is those bodyguards have been taking me jogging.

So in one sense you're not yet fully committed to the idea.

BRIAN: It's just that once you've had a taste of drugs, you like 'em and you want 'em. Do you take drugs yourself?

Yeah, I experiment.

BRIAN: Do ya? Do ya snort?

Sure.

BRIAN: That's what I thought. Do you have any with ya?

No.

BRIAN WILSON SESSIONS

BRIAN: That's the problem. Do you have any uppers?

I have nothin' on me.

BRIAN: Nothing? Not a thing, no uppers?

I wouldn't lie to you. I wish I had 'em, but I don't.

BRIAN: Do you have any at home? Do you know where you can get some?

See, now I guess you gotta get to the point in the program where you're not going to ask me questions like that.

BRIAN: That's right. You just saw my weakness coming out. Which I don't understand. I just do it anyway. I used to drink my head off too, that's another thing. They've been keeping me from drinkin', taking pills and taking coke. And I'm jogging every morning.

Had your wife not gone to see Dr. Landy and got him to work on you...

BRIAN: I'd have been a goner. I'd have been in the hospital by now.

THE OLD MAN

HOW DID YOU FIRST NOTICE something was wrong with Brian?

AUDREE: It was just that he'd stay in his room all the time. I would go over there, and there could be a houseful of people and he just wouldn't come down.

When you talked to him in his bedroom, would he make sense?

AUDREE: Oh, of course, perfectly. He just wanted to be alone. Sometimes he would say, "I'm really so tired," or, "I'll be down in a little while." And I'd think to myself, "You might or you might not, and if not, that's okay with me." I knew he was in trouble. I knew he had a problem.

Did he seem depressed?

AUDREE: Oh yes, I think so. He didn't show his depression to me that much because if I'd go upstairs to say hi or give him a kiss, he would always be sweet to me and say, "Hi, mom. How are you?" or, "I'm tired," or, "I have a cold," or, "My stomach is upset," or just anything. At that time I didn't believe it; I just thought, he wants to be alone. I would never—oh God—no way would I bug him. I figured if he wanted to talk to me he would tell me.

Do you think Brian's creativity began to be a burden to him?

AUDREE: I do. I think that he just went through a lot of pain. I think it was very painful for him to live up to this tremendous image that had happened just like that [*snaps her fingers*]. All of a sudden he felt he couldn't do it anymore, he felt like he had reached the pinnacle—and what was left?

And then for a number of years did he just sort of deteriorate?

AUDREE: Well, he went through stages. In fact, Marilyn would say, "Oh, Brian's so much better, we this or we that." I'd be happy to hear it. So it was kind of an up and down thing.

Carl says that he was the closest to his father, but that Brian and Dennis had a difficult time communicating with him.

AUDREE: Yes, they did. But in the later years, Dennis and his father had a great relationship. Well, they had something in common. They both loved to fish, they both loved boxing.

Dennis said when he was young his father used to beat the hell out of him sometimes.

AUDREE: Yeah, he really got the short end of the stick.

How did you feel when you heard about Dennis' involvement with Charles Manson?

AUDREE: Oh my God, absolutely horrified. Terrified. First of all, when Manson and his family, the girls, moved in with Dennis, Dennis had this beautiful, beautiful place —at Will Rogers State Park, right off Sunset. And he befriended them. They were just hippies and he thought Manson was the nicest person, a very gentle, nice guy. Murry had a fit. He knew there were a bunch of girls living there.

I went there one day. Dennis was at the recording studio in Brian's house, and he said, "Will you take me home?" And I was very hesitant because I thought, "Oh God, Murry's not going to like this." But I took him home, and he said, "Will you just come in and meet them? Come on, they're nice." And I said, "Dennis, promise me you won't tell Dad."

So I went in, and Charlie Manson was walking through this big yard with a long robe on, and Dennis introduced me. And we went into the house, and I think three girls were in the house, just darling young girls, I thought. I zipped through the house, got back in my car and left. And wouldn't you know that Dennis told his dad?

Did you get heck for that?

AUDREE: Yeah, he didn't like it. He was pissed.

How did Charlie strike you when you saw him?

AUDREE: I just thought he looked older than he supposedly is, like an older man, and I thought he had a kind face. That was the only impression I had. And I did think they were a bunch of leeches; Dennis had been through that before. He could never stand to see anyone who needed anything or anybody who had any kind of a problem... he was right there.

At that time nobody knew who Manson was.

AUDREE: No idea. In fact, when that horrible story came out about Manson's arrest for the Sharon Tate murder, Annie, Carl's wife, called me. And she said, "Ma, do you realize...?" I did not connect at all that that was the same person and the same family who had been with Dennis. When she told me, I just totally froze.

Well, it must have been a shock for Dennis as well.

AUDREE: Horrifying. I think the next day was his birthday, and he was at Carl and Annie's. I went there and we had dinner. And we were all very quiet. And somebody said something, and Carl said, "I don't think we should talk about it." So we just watched television and had a very quiet evening. We were totally terrified. I remember Carl saying, "Mom, let's all go back and stay at your house." And I said, "Carl, everybody knows where I live. What good would that do?" So I stayed at their house a couple of nights. And see, when they left Dennis' house, Manson or somebody stole Dennis' Ferrari, and they stole everything in the house that could be moved. Everything. Stripped. Dennis had kicked them out because they were into heavy drugs and he just wanted them out. And Manson, of course, had music he wanted published, and he wanted money, quite a sum, 10 or 15 thousand dollars. And Dennis turned him down. So Manson threatened Dennis, he said, "If you don't give it to me"—I'm paraphrasing—"something's going to happen to Scotty." Scotty was Dennis' first wife's son, and Dennis just adored him. He was really like his daddy.

But that was a terrible period.

You said that Dennis and his father later became much closer.

AUDREE: They were buddies. You know, it's the most amazing thing... the year that he died, Dennis called his father on Mother's Day and Murry told him, "I'm just going to live about a month." Which Dennis didn't tell me, thank God. I didn't need to know it. But he could tell Dennis that.

He'd had one heart attack.

AUDREE: He'd had a heart attack and he was just getting along famously. And six weeks later, it was in June, he just... well, it's weird the way that happened. I was waiting for him to wake up, thinking, "I wish he'd wake up. I wonder if he's really okay." I was standing in the kitchen, watching the clock, thinking I'll be so glad when he wakes up. And all of a sudden he woke up, and we had a great talk. He was in a good mood. He seemed to feel fine. And we talked for quite a while, about so many things. He said to me, "I'm so glad I've never had to take nitroglycerin." And I was glad, too, because I knew that would be frightening. That's for the pain. He said he wanted to take a walk—he'd been able to walk around the house but not outside yet. And I said, "Great, if you feel like it." So I was going to drive him down to Whittier Boulevard to walk. I went into the kitchen to make cereal for him, and all of a sudden I heard him yelling for me. I started dashing down this long hallway. He was in the bathroom sitting on the toilet. And he said, "Nitroglycerin," so I grabbed it and said, "Put it under your tongue." But he just sat there, very pale. And he said, "Cold water." So I got a cloth with real cold water on it and kept going like this on his forehead, and then

Audree (center) with Marilyn's parents, Mac and Irving Rovell

BRIAN WILSON SESSIONS

Al and Lynda Jardine, with sons Matthew and Adam

I held it on the back of his neck. And he still just sat there. I said, "Are you okay?" And he said, "I don't know."

I got up next to him to hold him—he was much bigger than I am—and he just toppled over. So I turned him over—I don't know how I did it, but I did it. And I realized he was really in bad trouble. In fact, I thought he was gone. By that time his face looked very flushed and his eyes . . . I knew he didn't like it at all. I went like this [*pats her cheek*] and said, "Baby, baby." All I said to him was, "Baby, baby, I love you." I ran into the bedroom and called the fire department. I never went back in that bathroom.

I locked the house, got in my car and went to the hospital . . . and sat there for quite a while. A doctor came out once and said, "We're doing everything we can." And I said, "I'm sure you are." And I knew that that was it.

Brian did not go to the funeral.

AUDREE: Nope. I understand that perfectly. You know, Carl was very angry that Brian didn't go to the funeral. And I said, "Carl, I understand perfectly." It didn't bother me. Brian couldn't face it. No way.

Do you think he'll go to yours?

AUDREE: I'd be surprised. You know, I don't know if he's ever been to one. To me, so what? I don't believe in funerals, frankly—the most barbaric, outmoded bunch of . . . [*censors herself and laughs*]. Anyway. . . .

In general you seem to have been much looser than your husband.

AUDREE: Oh yeah, a great deal more. He took life so seriously, really. It was hard for him to have fun. Once he said to me, "Sometimes you can be so mad or in some kind of mood, and somebody comes over and you can laugh and have a good time. Maybe I'm jealous of you." I used to think it would be so nice if he could just loosen up. But he was what he was, you know?

About ten years ago everyone started getting into drugs and marijuana, and I'm sure your boys did too. How did that affect you?

AUDREE: Well, I had a horrible problem with my husband about that. He was so, *sooo* against it, so mortified—I can't even think of a strong enough word. They all went and told him that they were smoking pot and, oh, he just thought that was the end of the world, the most horrible thing they could do. And of course he was angry with me. In fact, he was so angry he wouldn't allow them to come to our house for quite a while. And he told me I couldn't go see them.

But now, of course, dope is much better understood. Have you ever tried it?

AUDREE: Frankly, I did try it. In fact, I just zonked out. I was at Carl and Annie's house and I walked into the living room and I couldn't get up. I didn't like it at all. Then one other time, though, I tried it and I've never had more fun in my life. Laughed and laughed and laughed, just had a ball. This is since Murry's gone.

How old are you?

AUDREE: Thirty-seven. You know I'm lying. Should I tell the truth?

Let's see . . . you said you got married when you were 20 . . . and you had Brian after four years, and he just turned 34 . . . so you're about 58.

AUDREE: Exactly. Rats.

So what are you doing with your time?

AUDREE: Not as much as I should.

You mean not as much as you'd like?

AUDREE: Well, as I'd like and should for my own good, because I'm lonely a lot and that's ridiculous.

Do you still play music?

AUDREE: I don't like to play by myself. And I should because I just adore it. In fact, the other night some of my relatives were here and they were watching *Gone with the Wind*, and all of a sudden I just got bored and I went into the living room and I played the piano for a while. And I played the organ. And I was comfortable because I knew there was somebody here. But by myself I'm not comfortable. I just don't have anything in particular going for me.

❦ ❦ ❦

MURRY WILSON OBITUARY
Distributed by Warner Bros. Records in June 1973

Murry Wilson, father of Brian, Dennis and Carl, died Monday, June 4th, 1973. The Beach Boys have released the following statement:

"Murry Wilson was a hard, oyster shell of a man, aggressively masking a pushover softness which revealed itself at the sound of a beautiful chord or the thought of his wife and three sons. An unending source of high-powered energy, he could wear down the strongest souls just by explaining his thoughts in a telephone call. A jealous guardian of the incredible career he helped build for his sons, he was the enthusiastic champion of any who sought to help them, and the scourge of those who used the Wilson name for personal gain.

"He was a proud man, who wanted more than anything for his sons to be 'good boys.' In his eyes they remained 'boys' until the end, though Brian is now 30, Dennis 28, and Carl 26. They were not the 'tough' men he used to say he wanted them to be but, over his last years, Murry Wilson whittled down the generation gap through increased confidence in all three, despite their 'soft' ways.

"Although there were periods of storms too for Murry and his wife Audree, the last 18 months found them together nearly all the time. And, as if out of a gallant other-age, he almost always referred to her as 'Mrs. Wilson' when others were about.

"When it came to his machinery business, which fed the Wilsons until the Beach Boys were born, Murry worked harder than any man. The shop had to be absolutely clean and the demanding father shouted to his sons, 'Get in the cracks,' as they scoured the place on Saturday mornings. On the business side Murry said he wasn't a financial wizard, that he spent money too lavishly. But it was he who would first raise the alarm when his sons were about to embark on questionable business deals. Of one man who laid out a complex real estate scheme, Murry screamed, 'Sophisticated businessman? Hell no, he's just a son of a bitch and a crook. Get rid of him.'

"His continuing pleasure for years was music. He relished writing songs, anguished over lyrics and drove studio musicians like a construction foreman in his role as producer. His unbelievable energy could be applied equally to a studio session for the Beach Boys or a demonstration tape for a musical commercial he created. In a recent transatlantic telephone call, Murry devoted nearly a quarter of an hour to playing tapes of a tune he had written and was hoping the Beach Boys would record. As the tapes squeaked through the overseas connection, Murry enthused: 'Here's where Mike will come in . . . this part is a natural for Carl' . . . and on and on.

"Murry Wilson remained his sons' most enthusiastic adviser even in 1973, years after his formal managerial ties with the Beach Boys had ended. His compassion for their good fortune was enthusiastic, but critical when he saw them performing live about two months ago. After the concert Murry told someone: 'Tell the boys to sing out more, especially Carl—he's not projecting enough. They're getting good but people pay to see them great. And tell Dennis to keep his hands out of his pockets. But don't let him know the old man said it.'"

Mike Love and fiancé, Sue Oliver

A REALLY NEAT VISION

TALK ABOUT GOOD VIBRA-tions, Mike Love's seven-acre spread near Santa Barbara is positively infested with them. There on a bluff overlooking the blue Pacific and a tiny surfers' cove, Mike spends his few nonworking days of the year surrounded by jasmine, bougainvillea, wild strawberries, exotic chickens and a small community of serious transcendental meditators. These radiant, gracious people, most of whom help run the place when Mike's away, were heavy into abstinence abuse—no booze, no drugs, no tobacco, no meat.

Naturally I could only take it for about 24 hours, but I

BRIAN WILSON SESSIONS

understood why Mike would dig it. When you spend most of your time performing or recording in front of giant speakers turned up full blast, you need some refuge where the ringing stops. Also, Mike, of course, is a stone TM zealot, teaches it, preaches it, writes songs about it and has practiced it twice a day for the last quarter of his life. All the Beach Boys have practiced it off and on; Brian, in fact, was the first. But only Mike, in late 1967, flew to Rishikesh, India, where the Ganges leaves the Himalayas, to sit for a month at the feet of Maharishi (and at the side of the Beatles, Donovan and Mia Farrow). That experience convinced him that TM could not only change his life, it could change the life of the world.

"I didn't want to just come home 30 years later," he recalled, "sit down in front of the TV, pop the top off the beer can and sit there feeding my beer gut like so many millions of people were into."

Now, on a shimmering, starlit summer night, Mike sat down in his redwood hot tub in front of an infinite ocean, slurped the top off an organic fruit-juice fizz, and remembered a really neat vision he once had in Rishikesh.

MIKE: I was in my room and the mantra assumed a little melody. I was sort of singing it to myself, or singing it in my mind, and all of a sudden, from some other part of my mind, I was thinking, "Well, I'm in India, so there's a little sitarish impulse to the melody." And then I was thinking of the black kind of impulse—African, rhythmic drum impulses. Then the expression of the Latin kind of rhythm and sound, and the Chinese sort of singsong approach, and the Irish sort of hillbilly Appalachian music—all elements all around the world, Eastern, Oriental, Indian, African and Russian, that whole heavy, dramatic influence they have there, the Slovakian kind of thing. I mean, it was amazing; simultaneously this one little original melody was being played in different instruments and voice expressions and rhythms, until that one sound built to total cacophony, but it made sense.

The whole world, in other words, in its expressions of the same sound, was in harmony, although there was a difference in each one. And then once the whole world had attained that harmony, it became in harmony with the universe and the cosmos. And what I took it to be was a really far-out lesson that once everyone—starting with the individual—once all the nations and races became harmonious, even with their differences, only then will the world be in harmony with nature.

But anyway, it was neat to hear that melody building like that, like a symphony of nations. Like on the new album, "That Same Song"—the whole substance of that song is this:

"The rock of ages built that rockin' sound, till more and more people started to come around. They worshiped in church and built that great big choir, it grew and grew until it spread like fire."

FRIENDS

'D LIKE TO PERSONALLY thank the Beach Boys for breaking from their hectic schedule to put up with another crazy idea of mine—a group interview conducted in Brian's music room. We'd all had misgivings about the project. John Belushi, in town to film the TV special, had warned me, "Forget it. Group interviews never work." I suppose he was right. We'd hoped the group thing might put Brian more at ease, but it seemed to do just the opposite. We'd hoped to discuss the music, to get a *feel* of the music down on paper, but it became painfully apparent that that sort of thing is beyond words.

Yet there *is* a feeling here, of the warm brotherhood bond that has kept this gang together longer than any other white American band. That, and a sense of the good fart humor inspired years ago in the locker rooms of Hawthorne High.

First of all, let's test the mikes and see if all this stuff is working. We'll just go around the room, and you tell me your name and something about yourself.

CARL: Okay. This is Carl. I'm a really groovy guy.

DENNIS: This is Dennis, and I want to know if it's going on the radio . . . uh . . . I'm Dennis and—

BRIAN: This is Brian.

DENNIS: I'm not done, Brian. This is Dennis and I'm the cute one.

[*Everyone waits for Brian to speak again, but he simply stares ahead, his face expressionless.*]

MIKE: This is cousin Mike, checking in over here on 99.9.

Al is a little late, but he should be at his microphone shortly. What I'd like you to do this afternoon is sort of informally discuss your music, what songs or segments or devices you really are proud of.

DENNIS: There's a lot of things—how a record will fade out. I love the way Brian has faded out some of his records.

Yeah, there's a couple of songs— [Cont. on 50]

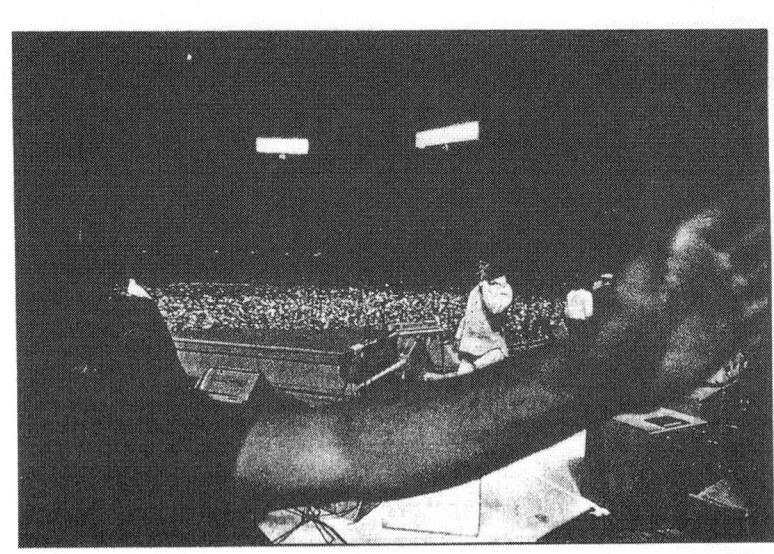

Brian with the Beach Boys at the Oakland Coliseum: 'They're all just so happy to be back together.'

BRIAN WILSON SESSIONS

[Cont. from 47] "Wind Chimes," I think, and "Little Bird"—where the part that delighted me the most was the fadeout.

CARL: "At My Window" is like that too, from *Sunflower*. I love the tag. We call fadeouts "tags"; we're big tag fans.

Do you remember when you started doing that sort of tag?

CARL: Oh golly—"Surfer Girl," "Surfin' U.S.A."—I think that's when Brian got the knack. Brian, would you like to comment?

[*Brian says nothing.*]

DENNIS: I think "Let Him Run Wild" was one of Brian's first tracks that he did a real stretch on. It was a real breakthrough.

CARL: That was on *Summer Days and Summer Nights*. The door starts to fly open on that album, musically speaking—the recording process and, you know, that whole total sound.

Brian, with these innovations, were they, like, planned ahead, or did you just try them in the studio?

BRIAN: We'd just try it, like spontaneous; whatever worked out spontaneously we'd usually go along with.

DENNIS: [*Whispers into Carl's mike*] Hi, this is Carl... and I wanna say that... I like pussy.

MIKE: Bomp-bomps, I guess, were the kind of little parts, the spontaneous inventions, Brian was talking about. We might have a song, a good pattern, a good chord structure, maybe a concept, maybe no lyrics, and the thing would come together in the studio.

CARL: I think one of the most unusual background parts Brian came up with is on "This Whole World."

MIKE: Oom bop didit.

DENNIS: Like the new one Brian's working on—mow mama...

MIKE: Mow mama yama...

DENNIS: Mow mama yama holy...

CARL: ...hallelujah.

MIKE: [*Sings*] Mow mama yama holy hallelujah.

What's that song, Brian?

BRIAN: That's from a song called "Clang." We haven't really got it together yet, so we can't talk about it. It's a spiritual sort of rock & roll song.

Some of your innovations in "Good Vibrations" must have struck people as a little unusual. Like taking six months to record it, and using four studios.

DENNIS: Actually, that's when Brian started losing his mind and he couldn't tell which studio was which [*much laughter*]. You know, so he'd go to Columbia, and he'd go, "Oh, jeez, wait a minute. I lost the tapes."

CARL: I remember Dad was worried about the bridge section. You know, the time change, "They can't dance to it."

DENNIS: [*Humbly proud*] It's still one of the all-time great standard rock & roll tunes. It was an honor to be able to take part in it. It was so superb. When there was all I could do to struggle to learn one line, one melodic line, Brian had eight or nine going. Brian had me in awe for a long time... till I figured out his secret.

Which was...

DENNIS: Shooting up acid.

[*Dennis' masterfully timed punch line, delivered with a sly pokerface, cracks up everyone.*]

MIKE: [*Embarrassed giggle*] Oh, God!

DENNIS: Naw, I was kidding.

[*Everyone, that is, except Brian, who continues to stare straight ahead as if he'd heard nothing. After a moment the doorbell rings and Al walks into the entrance hall. From the beginning of their career this smallest of Beach Boys, related neither by blood nor temperament, has stood apart from the others. Even today he readily admits that the Beach Boys are "not my whole life." For one thing he and*

his family live hundreds of miles up the coast in the remote Big Sur area of northern California. He is a "professional" rancher, dabbling in honeybees and Arabian horses on a 75-acre plot he owns near Monterey. And he's something of a politician, shaking hands with Governor Brown and supporting community action to preserve the Pacific coastline.

Yet his influence on the Beach Boys has been considerable. His early folk song background inspired the others to record, almost journalistically, their times and surroundings, in effect to write a new folk music for the Sixties, or at least the Sixties of Hawthorne. And to think he almost blew this profitable gig a year after it started, when he abruptly quit the group to enroll in dental school.

It took two semesters for Al to come to his senses, and when Brian phoned him in the summer of '63 and asked him to return, Al eagerly accepted. Brian explained that he didn't want to tour anymore, that he needed Al to replace him. And now as Al enters the music room, there is a curious sense of déjà vu. Brian suddenly stands up and leaves the room, allowing Al to again replace him in the group.]

CARL: [*To Brian*] You're not participating much in this.

BRIAN: I did a long interview the other day... let them go for a while. I'm just going to lay down. I got a little headache.

[*Brian heads upstairs as Al sits down in front of the sixth mike.*]

AL: This is Alan Jardine.

Did Brian tell you, Al, why he wanted to stop touring?

AL: I don't remember a reason. He just didn't enjoy going out there, and I think his weight had something to do with it even at that time. He was starting to get heavy, he didn't feel comfortable. At times he seemed to enjoy it, though. He always liked to hog the microphone, I remember that. If you were singing on the microphone with three people or even two people, he'd just move you right over [*laughter*]. He just wanted to make sure he got his part in, I guess. He's very aggressive in that way, and that's how he exhibited himself in the studio as a producer, with that very all-encompassing and very dominant personality.

[*Scott Steinberg enters the music room.*]

SCOTT: Do you need Brian?

Well, he said he had a headache.

SCOTT: [*Scornfully*] Bullshit. [*Twists and shouts*] Brian! Come on down!

BRIAN: [*From his room*] I'm tired, I'm lying down.

SCOTT: [*Bounds up the stairs*] No, you said you had a headache.

BRIAN: I... I said I had a headache to Felton.

SCOTT: No. We'll go downstairs now.

BRIAN: Well... I do have a little headache.

[*The group giggles affectionately at Brian's hasty excuses. Al continues.*]

AL: But eventually Brian became worn down and tired from all the work, the producing, from what I've been able to gather. And it was on our way to Houston, Texas, I was sitting next to him on the plane, and he just broke down and cried, he just crashed right there. This was at the end of '64, right after "When I Grow Up (To Be a Man)."

[*Scott leads Brian into the music room and directs him to resume his place behind the mike. Brian seems irritable and starts cracking his thick neck, twisting his head back and forth with his hands.*]

There's a couple of songs that I think illustrate the Beach Boys' sense of humor. Like, Al, you wrote "Take a Load off Your Feet."

BRIAN: [*Gruffly*] I think we should move faster. I don't think you're asking the questions fast enough.

AL: I was wearing Birkenstock sandals, and I read the instructions that came with them; it was inspiring to read about how important your feet are to the rest of your body. And so Brian and I got carried away. He'd come down at night and sit and play the bottles, these Sparklett's

bottles we had lying around. He walked around on the roof—there was this skipping sound on the end of the song, you know, and that was Brian on the asphalt roof of the garage, skipping around in a circle.

Another funny song is Mike's "She's Goin' Bald."

DENNIS: I took that song in a very strange way. I thought it was more or less about oral sex. [*Mike bursts out laughing.*] You know, [*sings*] "Get a job, sha na na na, sha na na na na. What a blow...." And I thought, Jesus, that's funny as shit—[*moronic voice*] "Hey, it's about getting a blow job, huh huh huh."

AL: Well, that's what it was, right?

MIKE: We were stoned out of our heads. We were laughing our asses off when we recorded that stuff.

CARL: Yeah, a little hash.

DENNIS: [*Gently ribbing*] Brian used to have a great sense of humor. [*He looks at Brian for some sort of reaction, but gets none.*] Michael, just tell me... what is the esoteric meaning behind a bald chick to you? [*To the others*] Michael once told me that if I ever had a dream about a toilet, I'd be bisexual. [*Mike starts shrieking with falsetto laughter.*] He said, "Dennis, you ever dream about a toilet?" I told him I had a dream that my grandmother, Grandma Betty, went down the toilet. He said, "Dennis, that means you're gay." [*The whole group cracks up.*] And I believed him. I went, "You're kidding! My God!" I went, [*moronic*] "Hey, Mom, am I gay?"

MIKE: [*Tries to regain his composure*] What... what about the time I told... [*but fails, explodes, spits, snorts, wheezes hysterically*]... I told my mom you had syphilis?

DENNIS: She wouldn't talk to me for three years. I'd go, "Hi," and she'd go [*gasps, shrinks back, wipes deadly scum off his clothes*]. One time I got Carl on television. And the guy was asking, "The group had a lull, didn't it? What was the cause of that lull?" And I said, "Carl was in the hospital for four years for junk!" [*Again the group breaks up.*] Carl goes, "What?"

[*Carl jerks backward in a fit, tears streaming from his eyes.*]

CARL: Oh God, we're so straight, it's beautiful. Really, we are so straight.

I DO... I SHOULD... I WILL

ON SATURDAY, SEPTEMBER 18th, Brian Wilson was nominated to the "Hall of Fame" on Don Kirshner's televised *Rock Music Awards* show. He didn't make it, but only because all the nominations in that category were ridiculously overdue and included other pioneers like Elvis, the Beatles, John Lennon and Bob Dylan. (The Beatles won.) But Brian did receive his own tribute on the show, a standing ovation when he made a guest appearance to announce the winners of the Best Single and Best Female Vocalist categories. And he looked stunning, with a new tuxedo, a new haircut and a new figure, down from 250 to 215 pounds. He handled his few routine lines with style and confidence, and as he left the stage, a friend of mine watching the show shouted, "He made it!"

Step by step, Brian is making it every day. He still seems a bit timid and programmed in, say, an interview situation, but when he's in front of a TV camera or a piano, his recovery seems nearly complete.

It's not, of course, and a few days later Annie Leibovitz and I returned to Los Angeles at the urging of Dr. Landy. "You gotta come down," he'd said, "it's been three months, and what you saw is not what you get. We got a new model... I think you'll be pleasantly impressed."

Well, it wasn't that pleasant, but in the end I was impressed. Bodyguard Scott Steinberg picked us up at the airport, and on the way to Dr. Landy's office he enthusiastically described Brian's progress in the four months he's been living with him. "When I first met Brian, God, he was very spacey," he said. "He was this big giant, he seemed like a gorilla to me." Scott, formerly a veterinary major at Los Angeles City College, knew about gorillas but at first knew absolutely nothing about Brian Wilson,

BRIAN WILSON SESSIONS

had never heard his music or his name. Which didn't really matter, his main job was to get him out of bed, take care of him and keep him clean.

"Basically he's a person now," said Scott. "Like even getting dressed for the *Rock Awards* show—he did it himself, he took his own shower."

At the office I asked Landy if there was any one time when Brian started to withdraw. "Yes, one time, one time in specific," he said. "It's all related to his use of acid. Acid attacks the limbic region of the brain, the part that affects one's whole emotional response. With someone like Brian, who had a predisposition toward psychosis, all it takes is one hit."

Landy's plan was for all of us to go to the same Chinese restaurant as before, affording a more scientific comparison, then to the Century West Club to watch Brian work out in the gym, then to his home to hear some new songs he'd written. At the restaurant I had a chance to ask Brian a few more questions, but this time he seemed slightly more tense, or, understandably, impatient.

One thing that puzzles me is why you consented to this interview at all. There've been so many stories about your personal life—doesn't that bother you?

BRIAN: No, that doesn't bother me.

Why not?

BRIAN: Any article's good. Long as it's publicity, I think that's all that matters. I think it's advancement for my career.

You went through two years of really intense withdrawal, but you started getting a reputation for being reclusive or eccentric long before that. You must have read all those reports of your being kind of nuts.

BRIAN: It bothered me, yeah, because I figured, "Why are they calling me nuts?" I didn't feel I was nuts.

Just weren't too active.

BRIAN: Right.

Last time we talked about the 'Smile' album, and you said you'd gotten too fancy for the public. I was wondering if perhaps today the public might not be ready for it, and if so, don't you have an obligation to find out by releasing it?

BRIAN: I do . . . I should . . . I will.

Do you know when?

BRIAN: I don't know, probably in a couple years.

There's been the conjecture that when you heard yourself being called a genius, it frightened you.

BRIAN: Yeah, it gave me a weird feeling, an eerie feeling.

But didn't you sort of agree with it, too?

BRIAN: Yeah, I did.

I think you must be fully aware of your contribution to music.

BRIAN: I am.

During lunch Brian committed an infraction, nothing big really, but it resulted in Landy yelling at Brian and Brian cringing back, his eyes smarting. Landy subsequently asked me not to write about the incident, that it was not typical of Brian's present behavior, that his reading about it might be harmful. When Landy left the room for a phone call, I asked Brian if such public admonishments didn't embarrass him. "That *is* embarrassing to me," he admitted. "Don't you object to that?" I asked, and he said, "I just feel brought down."

I felt brought down myself, and it occurred to me that Landy might be as concerned with his own image as he is with Brian's. (At one point Landy said, "Did you read the thing in *New West*? I don't want to appear like I did in that.") Later at the gym we were going up an escalator, Brian and Scott and Annie and me, and Scott asked, "So, what did you think of Brian today? Did he seem any different?" I couldn't answer him, I couldn't continue this game of dissecting Brian, mulling over Brian, in his presence, as if he wasn't there. Why do they have to do that? Why keep slamming him in public now that he's so much better? I mean, there's plenty of evidence Landy's method is working. I just hope that when Brian's fully healed, when he's finally in touch and he's learned all those good manners, I just hope he's strong enough to teach Dr. Landy a few.

Fortunately Brian had cheered up by the time we reached his home. He sat down at an old upright in his living room and whipped off three songs he'd written since June. He seemed amazingly confident, singing various parts, playing the piano, even smiling occasionally. One song was called "Hey, Little Tomboy" ("time you turned into a girl"). Another, "I Want to Pick You Up" ("'cause you're still a baby to me"). The third, the one I liked best, was a tribute to his wife and was entitled simply "Marilyn Rovell":

So glad I married a girl named Marilyn Rovell
So glad that I can say so far it's workin' out so well
She gets up at nine, while I'm sleepin' she's shopping
with Bobi or Dee
(That's short for Dianne)
If only she knew how happy it makes me to see her
carry my baby

Mary, oh Mary baby
Oh Mary, my Mary baby
Oh Mary, oh Mary baby
Oh Mary, oh Mary

And sometimes friends will ask us what the heck is
your secret
Part luck, part love, and we don't spend our money,
we keep it
And when I come home I say honey please fix me
somethin' good to eat
(She's right there cookin' it)
If only she knew how happy it makes me to see her
carry my baby

Mary, oh Mary baby
Oh Mary. . . .

Sure, the words are pretty homey, but then that's about the only input Brian's had in the last few years. And the music—pshew!—days later I was still humming it, it was so delicious. And that was just Brian and the piano; who knows how great it'll sound with the Beach Boys' voices and those funky instruments and the sound effects and echo and some kind of fantastic fadeout?

That is the miracle of his music. It just grabs you and follows you around like a little angel. It makes you feel good and gives you hope. It certainly gave me hope for Brian. In June he feared he was washed up as a writer, now here were three gems in three months—talk about progress! By the time I left his house I was convinced that, despite his sickness, despite his cure, Brian Wilson shall rise and shine again.

THE TAG

BRIAN STANDS BAREFOOT in the sand near Trances Beach, wearing a flowing bathrobe and carrying a surfboard that somehow looks like a tablet. It is June 20th, Father's Day, Brian's 34th birthday. He is there to film a spot for the TV special, a comic bit called "Brian's Nightmare" in which he's arrested and forced to surf. (Brian's fear of surfing and water is well known.)

Soberly he plods forward, accompanied by Danny Aykroyd and John Belushi in highway patrol uniforms. About 50 yards from the ocean they stop, and Aykroyd steps out to direct the breakers. Then he nods to Brian and says, "Okay, Mr. Wilson, here's your wave."

A small crowd of friends and crew people watches nervously, silently, as Brian carries out his sentence. His feet touch the surf but he plunges ahead, up to his waist, then dives in, his whalelike body atop the board and totally immersed in the cool, clear water. The crowd cheers like crazy.

Suddenly on the mind's horizon six giant figures appear, floating over the blue Pacific. They form a pyramid. At the base stand Carl, Brian and Dennis. On their shoulders stand Mike and Al. At the top stands Murry Wilson. He pulls a pipe from his jowly face, and as he begins to speak, the boys begin to chant in harmony with the universe.

BRIAN, DENNIS, CARL, MIKE, AL: *Mow mama yama holy hallelujah, mow mama yama holy hallelujah, mow mama yama holy hallelujah, mow mama yama holy hallelujah. . . .*

MURRY: I'm sure these guys didn't give you the facts right. The first record, called "Surfin'"—which I never did like and still don't like, it was so rude and crude, you know?—was the first song lyrically about surfing. It was just like a gold mine, waiting to be opened. And my boys were so hungry and thirsty to prove how good they were. My kids would whine, and I'd bawl them out. They were so exhausted I had to make them mad at me to get the best out of them. There's more than one way to give love to kids, you know? I drove them harder because they asked for it. They said, "Help us, make us famous, help us record. We need you, Dad."

I think the Beach Boys have been instrumental in changing the style of music to a great degree, not only with songwriters but also with band arrangements, with Negro artists, as well as the listening public. They're using Brian's *Pet Sounds* format, and his approach to bass root arrangements and his style of changing keys without any rhyme or reason. Without knowing it, he's created a monster—actually, he changed the concept of music.

BRIAN, DENNIS, CARL, MIKE, AL: *Papa oom mow mow, papa oom mow mow, papa oom mow mow, papa oom mow mow. . . .*

MURRY: We were driving in a car, going to a recording session, and I said to Brian, "I read in the *Times* that you experimented with LSD. Is that a put-on to the newspapers, or did you do it?" And he said, "Yes, Dad, I did." And I said, "Well, tell me Brian, do you think you're strong enough in your brain that you can experiment with a chemical that might drive you crazy later or maybe you might kill somebody or jump out of a window if it ricochets on you?" He said, "No, Dad, it made me understand a lot of things." I said, "Who're you trying to kid, Brian? What did you understand, except seeing like a nightmare in your brain, colors and things like that maybe?" And I said, "You know, Brian, one thing that God gave you was a brain. If you play with it and destroy it, you're dead, you're a vegetable. And we haven't heard the end of this. There are going to be people killed and people in sanitariums and insane asylums because they played with God."

BRIAN, DENNIS, CARL, MIKE, AL: *Mow mama yama holy hallelujah, mow mama yama holy hallelujah. . . .*

MURRY: I lost my left eye in an industrial accident at Goodyear, and I wear a plastic eye. But I'd like to add that it made me a better man. When I was 25 I thought the world owed me a living; when I lost my eye I tried harder, drove harder and did the work of two men in the company and got more raises. I put $2300 on my Hawthorne house, went into my own business and succeeded against millionaire dealers. Now you figure it out. Guts.

And that's what the Beach Boys have—guts. And talent. And I'm proud of them. I've been down on them a few times when they would make mistakes or not do what I figured was the best. And I never quit reminding them that they got a big break and "now get out there and earn your money. Don't whine to me, get up on that stage. So you're tired—you asked for it. Dennis, don't you miss a beat on the drum again. Quit looking at the girls and get on the ball." I drove 'em and I'm proud of it.

I don't know if you admire any of them or their accomplishments, but I think it's one of those success stories that can happen in America. And it isn't all talent—it's guts and promotion and just keeping at it even when you make mistakes. You can't be right all the time. But the ability to fight back, come back and create again is America. In other words, they're just Americans, they're like any one of you. Got it? Got the message?

BRIAN, DENNIS, CARL, MIKE, AL: *[Fading out as the sun begins to set] Oom bop didit, oom bop didit, mow mama yama holy hallelujah, papa oom mow mow, papa oom mow mow, mow mama yama holy hallelujah, papa oom mow mow, holy hallelujah, mow mama yama holy hallelujah, hallelujah, hallelujah, hallelujah, hallelujah. . . .*

BY BRIAN WILSON ©1976 NEW EXECUTIVE MUSIC

CONVERSATION WITH BRIAN WILSON

The poet laureate of surf and sand talks about the tribulations of being a genius, his ongoing struggle with things chemical and his monumental plans for the next great album

It would be difficult to overstate Brian Wilson's influence not only on the Beach Boys but on a whole generation of surf-music apostles from Hawaii to the shores of Peru. As the Beach Boys' leader, producer and chief songwriter, the bearlike 34-year-old Wilson is to California mythology what the Pope is to Catholicism. The sun-tanned, hedonistic minions of the West Coast are as much Wilson's children as the progeny of Greenwich Village are Dylan's.

From his first hit, "Surfin'," in 1961, to the artistically prophetic "Pet Sounds" (a concept album that predated "Sgt. Pepper" by 18 months), to "Good Vibrations" to "Sail On, Sailor," Wilson was responsible for the wide-open harmonies that became the Beach Boys' trademark. Even during an 11-year absence from live performances—and despite a nervous breakdown in 1964 and a hearing problem—Wilson remained the Beach Boys' undisputed spiritual leader.

"Brian Wilson *is* the Beach Boys," said brother and fellow Beach Boy Dennis Wilson. "He is the band and we're his fucking messengers!" In spite of their own enormous contributions over the past 15 years, brother Carl Wilson, cousin Mike Love and friend Alan Jardine enthusiastically agree that Brian Wilson was always very much the felt-if-not-seen presence that served to hold the group's sound *and* image together.

The term genius has often been applied to Wilson, and he's paid the price for it. After "Pet Sounds," Wilson embarked with lyricist Van Dyke Parks on an ambitious experiment in humor and song—the legendary but never-released "Smile" album. However, drugs plus Wilson's inability to deal with the mounting pressures of total adulation forced him to abandon the project.

Wilson stayed at the boards for another generation of Beach Boys' albums, but his life grew more and more erratic on the downhill slide. Wilson truly lived from moment to moment. He would arrive unexpectedly at friends' houses, often with a bizarre entourage in tow. Rumors circulated that he was drugged-out and insane; even that he had gone so far as to install a huge sandbox in the living room of his Bel Air home, where his piano sat. Eventually Wilson retired to his room, alone, vastly overweight, shrouded in enigma and mystery.

Today, Wilson is in the hands of a clinical psychologist who, through a physical-fitness program and stringent scheduling, is attempting to wrest Wilson from the hold of drugs and schizophrenia. But some of Wilson's oldest friends, recently declared persona non grata by the doctor, are suspicious of the doctor's methods. They also feel that Wilson will break down again before he can recover.

OUI sent free-lancer David Rensin to talk with Wilson. Rensin reports: "It's almost impossible to maintain a professional distance from Brian, simply because of his eyes. Often they are depthless and reflective; but sometimes you see in them a prisoner begging for help, a frightened child. Then Brian's calculating intelligence shows through and you feel used. It's hard to look, but harder to look away.

"Brian is a massive presence—like his rambling Bel Air estate, which was once owned by Edgar Rice Burroughs. His dining room is done with jungle-flora wallpaper and there are two framed pictures of est founder Werner Erhard on the wall. In the music room, there is a pool table on which Brian's daughters Carnie and Wendy carouse. During our talk, Brian perched on an overstuffed couch in the den. He seemed less nervous than I'd anticipated, but he has a short attention span and frequently got up to take a cigarette from a pack on the upright piano. Otherwise, despite the presence of one of his doctor-ordered attendants, he tried his best to answer directly, and he opened up even more when his watchdog left the room. Wilson, by his own admission, has tried to hide from the world these past few years. But even so, he was never really hard to find. His garbage cans are spray-painted with the family name.

"Nevertheless, we opened the interview with a discussion of his reclusiveness."

OUI: The newsmagazines and everyone else say that Brian's back. Where exactly have you been?
WILSON: In my room. I hid in my room for four years.
OUI: Why?
WILSON: A lot of reasons. One was drugs. I was taking a lot of cocaine, a lot of uppers, and I got my life all fucked up. They got me into such a paranoid state that I'd snort cocaine in my room and then it got to the point where I liked it there. Then, pretty soon, I didn't like it anymore, but I had no choice, because I'd gotten into the pattern of staying in my room.
OUI: Anything else keep you off of the streets?
WILSON: Pressure. People kept asking, "What's your next song going to be, Brian?" I didn't know, and it got so that I didn't want to know. And then I wasn't able to create because of the drugs. At first, I was creative on drugs and then I got to a point where I couldn't even go to the piano—I was too afraid.
OUI: But the Beach Boys depend on you, don't they?
WILSON: Yeah, they depend on me a lot,

BRIAN WILSON SESSIONS

BRIAN WILSON *Maybe I have a genius for arrangements and harmonics, but I don't think I'm a genius. I believe the word genius applies only to people who can do things that other people can't do.*

come to think of it. They couldn't function without me—they'd flounder. Their stage show is down pat, but they need me in the studio. The guys have always acted as though they look up to me—I don't know if they really do—but they've shown a lot of respect for my music and the stuff I've created for them.

OUI: For *them*?

WILSON: I approach it like that. I believe that what I'm doing is creating things for *them*. I do it for the group. Everything I do is for the group.

OUI: And your comeback was for *them*?

WILSON: Yeah. We hadn't been around for three or four years and I realized that we had to make some money, so I decided to make a go of it and to create some new music.

OUI: Isn't three or four years a long time between albums?

WILSON: I think our natural cycle is about three or four years. Not an album every six months.

OUI: You spoke of creating new music a moment ago, but a lot of the tracks on *15 Big Ones* are old songs.

WILSON: Well, we wanted to showcase some material that we thought was really good. I have a new attitude about oldies: Old songs are where it's at.

OUI: Are important things being written today?

WILSON: Sure, but not like those oldies. I think the oldies are greater, more original. The lyrics are more interesting. I even like the old Beach Boys songs better; *15 Big Ones* started out as an album of nothing but oldies, but then we ran out of them. Halfway through, Mike Love decided to make the record half old and half new. I didn't like the idea at first, but he literally forced us to do it his way. I resented that.

OUI: Some people say that Love's only interests are money and success. Is that true?

WILSON: He meditates. Michael is interested in both success and meditating equally. He used to be more interested in the money, but now he cares about the spirituality.

OUI: Mike has compared *15 Big Ones* to *The Beach Boys' Party*.

WILSON: Yes. They both have the same light feeling, but I don't think the new album is light artistically. The new album has much stronger, more elaborate tracks.

OUI: What do you think of the reaction you've gotten to it?

WILSON: Gerry Beckley from America says *Just Once in My Life* is one of the best cuts he's heard in a long time. But if the kids hadn't liked it, I would have been very hurt, because I put a lot into it. It would have wrecked me and I'd probably have hidden out again.

OUI: Do you think the industry or the kids would be unkind if you put out a bad album?

WILSON: No, I think they would be very understanding. They would realize that I was going through a bad period. I think they would simply expect a good album later.

OUI: When you were recording *15 Big Ones*, did you feel a lot of the old pressure you had been trying to avoid?

WILSON: Yeah. I felt a lot of pressure from the Beach Boys, because I told them that I'd produce an album for them and then I started to change my mind, and they said, "Come on, come on, Brian. You can't stop."

OUI: Why did you want to stop?

WILSON: Because I got tired of the job. I just didn't think we were getting anywhere at first, and I just wanted to go back in my room. But they pushed me and pushed me until it was done. I'm glad they did, now. I think it's a good album, and if you listen to it, you can see where all the work went.

OUI: Was it the album that got you out of your room?

WILSON: No, it was my doctor. My wife, Marilyn, called him and they decided to have me go on a health program of jogging and bowling and stuff like that.

OUI: Do you see your doctor a lot?

WILSON: He sees me a lot.

OUI: How do you like the new regimen?

WILSON: At first, I didn't have the balls for it. I didn't want to go out of my room. I didn't want to go anywhere. But now I see that it pays off to stay in shape. And it lessens my dependence on drugs. For sure.

OUI: Have you used drugs recently?

WILSON: No.

OUI: Do you miss them?

WILSON: Oh, no. I learned a lot about myself from them: I learned that I could put more into whatever I was doing; I learned about my energy levels; but now I maintain my physical stamina without them.

OUI: What got you into drugs?

WILSON: I don't know. Curiosity, friends. A lot of friends used them. They turned me on and started me on the road.

OUI: What are your views on marijuana?

WILSON: I think it should be legalized, because it's good for people. It helps them grow and see the light. There's a point where it becomes too much—just like drinking—but I think people can tell what their limits are.

OUI: What about acid?

WILSON: I didn't understand the effects of it at first. But later on, a couple of months after I first tried it, I started thinking about sounds and that's where *Pet Sounds* came from. Acid showed me combinations of sounds—how to combine different instruments to get a sound there's no instrument for. Infinite sounds. Forever sounds. Sounds that are combined and echoed so that they remind you of something you can't touch. Acid also taught me about color and showed me that it's more vivid than I ever imagined.

OUI: Would you take acid again?

WILSON: No. I don't think I need it now. I've had my big experience. Its usefulness has passed.

OUI: *Pet Sounds* is called a masterpiece and people say you're a genius because of it. Are you?

WILSON: Maybe I have a genius for arrangements and harmonics, but I don't think I'm a genius. I'm just a hard-working guy. I believe the word genius applies only to people who can do things that other people can't do. I can't do things others can't. I wasn't a genius in high school and I'm not now. But because of *Pet Sounds*, people thought I was a genius. You see, the album was a radical departure from what the Beach Boys had been doing previously. At first, the group thought it was a little too artistic, but I told them there was a need for this artistic kind of thing. This was in 1966. After they heard it for a while, they realized that I was right and they understood the validity of art records. Basically I think it just *scared* people into thinking that I was a genius. Maybe it overwhelmed them.

OUI: Did the album overwhelm you?

WILSON: Yes it did—while I was making it. When I played it back, it started me thinking that we hadn't had enough spirituality in our music until then. But in *Pet Sounds*, I think there was spirituality in the harmonics and in my voice. My voice carried a spiritual value that went very deep. Also it was the first time anyone had used the word God in a rock-'n'-roll song—in *God Only Knows*. The whole thing caused a big turn-around and made me more aware of spiritual love. I got a better grasp of it.

OUI: There's also a lot of Phil Spector—who is *(Continued on page 134)*

(Continued from page 114) considered the master record producer—in *Pet Sounds*.

WILSON: Yes. He's my idol.

OUI: Does he know that?

WILSON: Yes. I really respect him as a producer—so I just copied him. The music had an original feeling but it definitely copies his techniques. I thought that, using his style, his quality, his combining instruments into certain sounds, I could make impressive records with the Beach Boys. I enjoy copying.

OUI: Do you think you out-Spectored Phil Spector?

WILSON: Well, I don't know.

OUI: What about the famous rivalry between you two?

WILSON: It isn't a real rivalry. I think he bitterly resented the fact that we copied him, but he never called me on it.

OUI: Is there anyone else you'd like to copy?

WILSON: Sure. Three Dog Night. Elton John. Paul McCartney.

OUI: Do you really mean copy?

WILSON: Really copy. I mean really copy.

OUI: Same sound, same tunes?

WILSON: Yeah. Same sound, tunes, everything.

OUI: Why would people buy your record instead of the original?

WILSON: I don't know. We'd soon see. Maybe they would.

OUI: But what would the purpose be in copying?

WILSON: I think it would be funny. Yes, I think people would go, "Hah, hah, hah. They copied him."

OUI: Not for $4.95.

WILSON: Well, this is the chance we take.

OUI: You'd put your money into that kind of record rather than into land?

WILSON: Oh, yeah. Yes.

OUI: Have you seen Paul McCartney lately?

WILSON: Yes. The other night. I was scared of him when we had met earlier. He had said that *God Only Knows* was the greatest song ever written, and when he came to visit, I wouldn't come out of the pool house. I was frightened. If it was the best song, what was there left for me to do? This time, though, he played a lot of piano for me.

OUI: Is there a rivalry between the Beatles and the Beach Boys?

WILSON: Yes. It was set up long ago and I think it's just now peaking. I think the Beatles are going to get back together and have a big jam session with us.

OUI: Have you and Paul discussed this?

WILSON: No, but I just know it's going to happen. They're going to get back together, because I can tell they want to do an album like *15 Big Ones*. The

BRIAN WILSON SESSIONS

BRIAN WILSON *With doctors on your ass, it's impossible to make a move. I can write when I want, but I can't go to the studio unless they tell me I can.*

rivalry exists today and it's one that's going to go on and on and on. It's something you wouldn't believe. But the Beatles and the Beach Boys are going to be playing on the same bill pretty soon. And who knows who's going to close the show?

OUI: Have you met Dylan?
WILSON: No. But I'd like to.
OUI: What would you and he talk about?
WILSON: I don't know. That's difficult to determine. I think it would be up to him.
OUI: Why would it be up to him?
WILSON: I don't know. Maybe it would be up to me. I think we'd talk about something—and end up talking about something. Do we have enough material for the interview?
OUI: No, but do you want to stop for today?
WILSON: I'm just a little uncomfortable today. No, let's just go ahead.
OUI: How about rumors you're not often left by yourself?
WILSON: I have bodyguards. I have two people working for me per doctor's orders and they haven't left me alone for six months. They don't allow me to go where I want or anything like that.
OUI: Do you resent them?
WILSON: Yes. Very much.
OUI: The bodyguards aren't really part of the physical-fitness program, are they?
WILSON: Yes, they are. But they're also bodyguards. Some people aren't allowed to visit me unless they go with me.
OUI: Why?
WILSON: Because some of my friends use coke and the doctor doesn't want me to be around them.
OUI: If cocaine were offered to you, would you use it again?
WILSON: Oh, I would use it if I were around it, yes.
OUI: Doesn't that imply a lack of self-discipline?
WILSON: Yes, it does, but I would go back to it in a minute.
OUI: Are you comfortable with your contradictions? A while ago you said you were off drugs.
WILSON: Yes, I'm comfortable with myself—about my lack of self-discipline. I go through periods where I think, "God, I'm so thankful that I have a doctor," you know? Then I go through periods where I think, "Goddamn, he's doing nothing but restricting my fucking mind!" It's paradoxical, I know, and I feel an inner battle. Today I want to go places. I want to go to Danny Hutton's house, but I can't because of the doctor. I feel like a prisoner, and I don't know when it's going to end.

OUI: Do you think that you'll eventually be allowed your freedom?
WILSON: Yes.
OUI: How can the doctor stop you from just leaving?
WILSON: Well, I haven't got a driver's license and besides, he'd put the police on me if I took off.
OUI: The police?
WILSON: Sure, and he'd put me on the funny farm.
OUI: You mean he threatens to have you institutionalized?
WILSON: Yes, all the time. He's always got that threat of putting me on the funny farm.
OUI: So what are you doing about it?
WILSON: Waiting it out. Playing along. That's what I'm doing.
OUI: You're said to be good at that. One of the best.
WILSON: Yes, I am.
OUI: Van Dyke Parks says you're the greatest poker face there is.
WILSON: Yeah, I have a pretty good poker face. Van Dyke's too much. Do you have any uppers?
OUI: No.
WILSON: Could you find me some?
OUI: You aren't supposed to do drugs.
WILSON: But I'd appreciate it 100 percent. It would help me write; I want to write today. If you could get me an upper, I'd really——
OUI: Can't we finish the interview first? You say you've decided to wait your captivity out?
WILSON: Yes. I've decided to wait it out because, with doctors on your ass, it's impossible to make a move. I can write when I want, but I can't go to the studio unless they tell me I can. I can't record with the guys unless they say I can. It's kind of hard, you know?
OUI: Do you feel that the doctors are trying to change your thinking?
WILSON: Yes. They're making me think in terms of a schedule. Now you do this and now you do that. That's not the way I used to think at all, and it's very hard to get used to.
OUI: How did you use to think?
WILSON: I used to think sporadically. I never, ever had a schedule. I got used to the idea of being a night person. I'd think all night long but not at all during the day. I'd come to life at night.
OUI: That must have affected your health.
WILSON: Yes. It got me very fat and very lazy.
OUI: Did you know that people thought you were eccentric—maybe even crazy, sitting in your room for years?
WILSON: No. *(Continued on page 168)*

(Continued from page 134) I wasn't aware of that. I wasn't on a self-consciousness kick.
OUI: Have the doctors been successful in changing your thinking?
WILSON: Not really. I still think the old way, although that goes against the grain of the scheduling. I think I'm going to emerge victorious and combine the health benefits with my real personality.
OUI: Didn't your real personality like to surprise people by acting strange?
WILSON: Yes. I used to like to surprise people with a lot of very strange things—very strange ideas. I think that has an effect. It creates an atmosphere. People are surprised and off-guard. It creates a moody mood.
OUI: Why did you start trying to surprise people that way?
WILSON: Uppers. But I don't believe in it much anymore. I'm not into effects the way I used to be. I liked to surprise my brothers with strange recording ideas—like giving fire hats to the musicians.
OUI: When did you give fire hats?
WILSON: During the sessions for a song called *Fire*. It was going to be on the *Smile* album that we never released. I gave little toy fire hats to all the musicians, and we had a bucket of fire in the studio, too. The song had a lot of weird effects on it, like lots of screeching violins. Then a building down the street from the studio burned down, and I felt we were responsible for it spiritually. I got kind of scared, so we junked the tape.
OUI: The rumor says you burned the tape.
WILSON: We just erased it.
OUI: What happened to the rest of *Smile*? It's supposed to have been destroyed, too.
WILSON: A lot of it appeared on an album called *20/20*. I don't like to talk about it.
OUI: It's said that you also used to indulge in verbal practical jokes.
WILSON: Yes. I used to do a lot of that with Danny Hutton and Van Dyke. I'd get on coke and start acting real strange—very strange. But I always knew what I was doing.
OUI: Do you feel misunderstood?
WILSON: Yes, but they always knew I was doing a lot of coke and so they were anticipating that I was going to be acting kind of funny. After a few times, they'd just start thinking, "Aw, he's just on a program of practical jokes."
OUI: And were you?
WILSON: Yeah. I was acting that way because I was a drughead.
OUI: Do you remember, during the writing of *Sail On, Sailor*, telling Van Dyke

to convince you that you weren't insane?
WILSON: Yes.
OUI: Was that a joke?
WILSON: No. I was serious. I used to think I was insane. I'm a lot saner since I've had my doctor.
OUI: You seem to have mixed feelings about your doctor.
WILSON: I can't help it. That's the way I am. I think it's people's expectations of my behavior that create the problems. That definitely applies to people's expectations about my creativity.
OUI: Do you feel you were never encouraged to get help for your problems because people thought it would damage your creativity?
WILSON: I was always allowed to do whatever I wanted to do. All of a sudden I realized I had all that freedom, and it was hard to deal with it. I had money and success and everyone was scared of me. Then all of a sudden I got zapped. The freedom got taken away like that! But I think the doctor is trying to rehabilitate me in order to bring out some of my talent that's been buried.
OUI: Do you have anyone to talk to frankly about yourself?
WILSON: No, I don't. I don't.
OUI: Do you feel out of place?
WILSON: I used to. Now I've gotten in tune with people more and I'm more swinging. My life's more swinging.
OUI: The feeling of being out of place was expressed in *I Just Wasn't Made for These Times* on *Pet Sounds*, wasn't it?
WILSON: Yes. That song reflects my life. It was about a guy who was crying because he thought he was too advanced—that his ideas were too advanced and that he'd eventually have to leave people behind.
OUI: Isn't that, in fact, what happened to you?
WILSON: Yes, it did happen to me. I did *Pet Sounds* and all my friends thought I was crazy to do it.
OUI: What other songs reveal things about you?
WILSON: Well, let's see: *Till I Die, Caroline, No* and *California Girls*. *Caroline, No* represents the sweetness, the child in me, the gentle side. There is that side, you know. And *Till I Die*—"I'm a cork on the ocean, rolling over the raging sea"—represents the lack of ego in me. Yeah, I feel that humbleness toward life. I do. Whereas *California Girls* is an example of ego. I love girls, and I get on those trips every once in a while. They're so young, innocent.
OUI: Do you want to do a solo album?
WILSON: Yes. I consider *Pet Sounds* my

BRIAN WILSON SESSIONS

BRIAN WILSON *Records aren't as good as they used to be. There're too many producers and artists and they're all out for money. Business has gotten totally mercenary. There's very little art left.*

first solo album and *Friends* my second. I think I'm ready to do another.
OUI: So why haven't you done it already?
WILSON: I've always thought it best to keep the material for the Beach Boys rather than to do it on my own.
OUI: Haven't your brothers encouraged you to do a solo project?
WILSON: No. They want to keep the material for the Beach Boys, too: a solo album would take away from Beach Boys sales. It would split the group up too much—and I don't think that would be good.
OUI: Are they afraid of your going on your own?
WILSON: Yes, I think so. That's basically what the problem is. Sometimes I really feel like a commodity in a stock market.
OUI: But isn't your brother, Dennis, doing a solo album?
WILSON: Yes, he's going to, but I'm not.
OUI: Wouldn't a solo album by him have the same effect?
WILSON: It might. I don't think he should do it. Dennis has written some very good songs recently and I hope he uses them for the Beach Boys.
OUI: Have you told him your feelings?
WILSON: No, I haven't said a thing.
OUI: Has this situation ever made you want to leave the Beach Boys?
WILSON: I've wanted to leave them lots of times. In fact, I left them last week and then I came back.
OUI: Why did you want to leave the Beach Boys last week?
WILSON: Well, because I want freedom and I want to do my own album. I think if I stay with the Beach Boys and I do my own album, it's going to take away from the band. So I've got to make a decision: Either I'm going to stay with the Beach Boys and produce only their stuff or I'm going to go on my own and do an album by myself. I haven't decided which to do yet.
OUI: Couldn't you stay and make a solo album? It's been done.
WILSON: No, I don't think so. It would cause too much conflict.
OUI: Do you still have a studio at your house?
WILSON: No, we took it out years ago. But I'd like one again. I'd build a much more elaborate setup to experiment with instruments I've never used before. But I don't think I'll get one.
OUI: Why?
WILSON: My wife wanted it out in the first place. She said she had no privacy. People just kept coming up and making lunch and dinner and things like that. I didn't mind, but Marilyn couldn't stand it.
OUI: Can you work at Brother Studio?
WILSON: I don't like the atmosphere in Santa Monica as much as the atmosphere at a home recording studio. Home is better.
OUI: Will you ever tour with the Beach Boys again?
WILSON: No, I won't.
OUI: Had you ever planned to?
WILSON: Yes, but I changed my mind, because I really don't like touring. I don't like playing dates. I don't miss sweating onstage or being away from my wife. And I'm not cut out for touring. Besides, I'm just not made for the stage. I'm overweight and my voice isn't as powerful as it used to be.
OUI: If you don't tour, what will you do while the band's away?
WILSON: I'll write songs, work out, jog and stuff. I'll also probably go to the studio to make background tracks for the next album.
OUI: What's the next album going to be like?
WILSON: We haven't discussed the format of it yet.
OUI: With the group away and you tinkering in the studio, wouldn't you have the same situation that *Pet Sounds* came out of?
WILSON: Yes. I could come up with another *Pet Sounds*, and I very well may.
OUI: Do you feel it's necessary to prove yourself?
WILSON: Not as much as it used to be. I used to think I had to prove I was a singer or a good producer or whatever. But now I don't really need to do that at all. I don't have very much to prove.
OUI: What changed your mind?
WILSON: Well, a lot of the great talents of our time have really boggled my mind and have really got me to a point where I don't think I have as much to offer as I used to. So I think of myself as secondary in the talent department.
OUI: Do you really think you're secondary or is it——
WILSON: Just easier to say that? Yeah, it's probably easier. Yeah, I think you're right. I would like to record again, I really would, but I would like to do some simple tunes that explain where the group's at.
OUI: Who are the great talents in the music business now?
WILSON: I think they are Danny Hutton as a singer, Berry Gordy as a record executive and Phil Spector as a producer.
OUI: Danny's a close friend of yours, isn't he?
WILSON: Yes. I like him. I think he's a good singer. He quit Three Dog Night, and he's going on his own. I think it's a good move for him. It means freedom from touring. It will make it easier on his life. And his health.
OUI: *Pet Sounds* symbolized innocence becoming worldly and it appeared at a time when everyone was losing his innocence. What do you think is a comparable perception for now?
WILSON: I think possibly utilizing similar *Pet Sounds* concepts and changing the lyrics. Finding a new lyrics writer, the right guy for the new perception. I think Van Dyke's the man.
OUI: So you want to work with him again.
WILSON: Yes, I want to very much. We talk about it a lot.
OUI: Was it thought at one time that his lyrics were a bit too esoteric for some of the other Beach Boys?
WILSON: No.
OUI: Probably there are a lot of people who would like to team up with you.
WILSON: Yes. Do the boys at OUI write lyrics?
OUI: Some of them do.
WILSON: Do they want to work with me? Maybe we can, sometime. Are we almost through?
OUI: Almost. But what would the attitude, the tone, of the new *Pet Sounds* be?
WILSON: I think it would take on an attitude of freedom; an attitude of saying something and not caring what you're saying. Also a little bit of the country spirit. A little bit for democracy. There should be some American spirit in the lyrics. Something to pull everyone back together.
OUI: *Pet Sounds* had a considerable effect both on your life and the world of music. Would you do it all over again if it meant you had to spend the next 11 years in your room?
WILSON: I sure *would* do it, man. I mean, *I* wouldn't resist. If I had the chance to go in and really create another *Pet Sounds*, I'd do it. Shit, yes, I would.
OUI: Even knowing it might repeat the problems of the past ten years?
WILSON: That's right!
OUI: What do you see as your next big thing?
WILSON: My next big thing is probably going to be writing about meditation.
OUI: Capitalizing on the new-consciousness wave?
WILSON: Yes.
OUI: Like est? Has it helped your brother Carl?
WILSON: Oh, immensely. It's opened him up. My wife's taken it, too, and it's opened her up. It was a really great experience for them.
OUI: They talk a lot about it?
WILSON: Yeah.
OUI: But you haven't taken it?
WILSON: No.
OUI: Would you consider est?
WILSON: No, I wouldn't, because I have meditation and that's all I need. But I think est is good. Anything that opens you to life is good.
OUI: Does that include drugs?
WILSON: Yes, they open you to life to a point and then they close you. So you've got to be careful to find that point where it starts to close and then stop taking them. Transcendental Meditation is working well for me. I'm more energetic.
OUI: How long have you been doing it?
WILSON: Since 1968, but then I stopped. I came back to it about a half year ago.
OUI: Why did you stop?
WILSON: Because I got tired of it. I was getting to the point where there was no peace. You need a quiet environment for TM; you need almost absolute quiet to get it done. I couldn't do it around here, because there was just too much noise: kids, family, telephones ringing and everything. Just too many distractions.
OUI: You also devoured a lot of reading material while searching for the answer.
WILSON: Yes. A friend turned me on to books at Pickwick Bookshops. He thought Pickwick was the answer. It taught me a lot, but was ultimately confusing, because I started reading too many books. If I'd stuck with just a few, I'd have been all right, but I read so many authors it got crazy. So I stopped reading. I went through a thing of having too many paths to choose from and of wanting to do everything and not being able to do it all.
OUI: What about your dabblings in astrology?
WILSON: Astrology is a science. I think it works. I've seen instances where people have done my chart and they told me, "You're going to have conflict with this person" and it turns out to be true every time. I've seen predictions come true too many times.
OUI: Are you still into it?
WILSON: No. I don't follow it myself.
OUI: What do you think of the music business today? Is it better or worse than it used to be?
WILSON: I think it's gotten worse. I think the quality of records has gotten worse. The records aren't as good as they used to be. There're too many producers and artists and they're all out for money. Business has gotten totally mercenary. There's very little art left.
OUI: What can you do to change that?
WILSON: I think I can still make art records. I have an obligation to make art records. I know that's what started

BRIAN WILSON *"I Just Wasn't Made for These Times" reflects my life. It was about a guy who was crying because he thought he was too advanced and he'd eventually have to leave people behind.*

BRIAN WILSON SESSIONS

BRIAN WILSON *I'm going to make records my way. I'm in control and can handle things better. I'm going to grow from this album and take it right into the next, which will be another "Pet Sounds."*

people thinking that I was an eccentric genius and all, but I think more good art records would help the industry immensely.

OUI: Can you handle the pressure?

WILSON: Sure I can handle it. I'm going to make records my way. I'm more in control and can handle things better. Obviously the new album is an indication that I'm back. I'm going to grow from this album and take it right into the next, which will be another *Pet Sounds*.

OUI: What about the rest of the Beach Boys? How do you feel about them?

WILSON: Each has a different thing to offer. For instance, Al Jardine has a country sort of thing to offer. Mike Love has a white-pop kind of voice. Carl is R&B and Dennis is blues. I'm white pop. I think the key to our success is the rotation of the leads.

OUI: How about a personal observation?

WILSON: OK. Love has a lot of ego and plans a lot for the group. He's a planner, and I'm amazed at his ability to plan. And I'm amazed at Carl's ability to sing. Dennis' ability to sing is amazing, too. And Al Jardine is, uh, fantastic as an entertainer!

OUI: How do you think your brothers have handled things over the past ten years?

WILSON: I think they did it very awkwardly for a while. But then they smoothed out when they got into meditation. See, meditation smooths everything out. It smooths out your life.

OUI: Do you think you understand yourself?

WILSON: No. I don't understand myself. That's why I have a doctor.

OUI: What is understanding oneself to you?

WILSON: Understanding yourself is being able to accept yourself for what you're doing and not going through the hassles every time you make a decision by saying to yourself, "I shouldn't have made that decision." Understanding yourself is being able to give yourself a pat on the back and I'm not able to do that yet. But I want to be able to.

OUI: Are interviews part of the doctor's program?

WILSON: Yes.

OUI: Did you want to do them?

WILSON: No. I resisted at first, but now I think they're very provocative and stimulating. And each one is different.

OUI: Many artists feel they're best represented by their music and that interviewers often probe too deeply into their personal lives. Do you agree?

WILSON: What interviewers ask is perfect. Interviews are for publicity.

OUI: Do you ever find yourself just saying what people want to hear?

WILSON: Yes. I think so.

OUI: You finally surfed after all these years.

WILSON: Yes, it was during the shooting of our television special. Some cops arrested me for not surfing and then took me into the water with my surfboard.

OUI: Did you like it?

WILSON: Well, it was frightening and I fell off twice, but I'm going to go out soon and try it again.

OUI: Was it anything like the stories Dennis used to tell you?

WILSON: Oh, yes. I've sort of got a feel for it now. It's like what I thought: a raucous motion of the waves and the board bobbing up and down. Motion.

OUI: Will any songs come out of it?

WILSON: Mmmm. Maybe.

OUI: What do you want to do in life now?

WILSON: I want to become an athlete of great stature. My father was a very dynamic person and he created the winner attitude in me.

OUI: What sport?

WILSON: Baseball. And, I used to be a quarterback, once.

OUI: Do you think it's really possible for you to become a great athlete?

WILSON: Very possible and I'm going to pursue it. I just may go out for sports. I'm going to practice.

OUI: Pro?

WILSON: Yes.

OUI: At 34 aren't you a little old? And what about the music?

WILSON: I don't think I'm too old, and I'd have time for the music, too.

OUI: Good luck!

WILSON: Can you get me some uppers now?

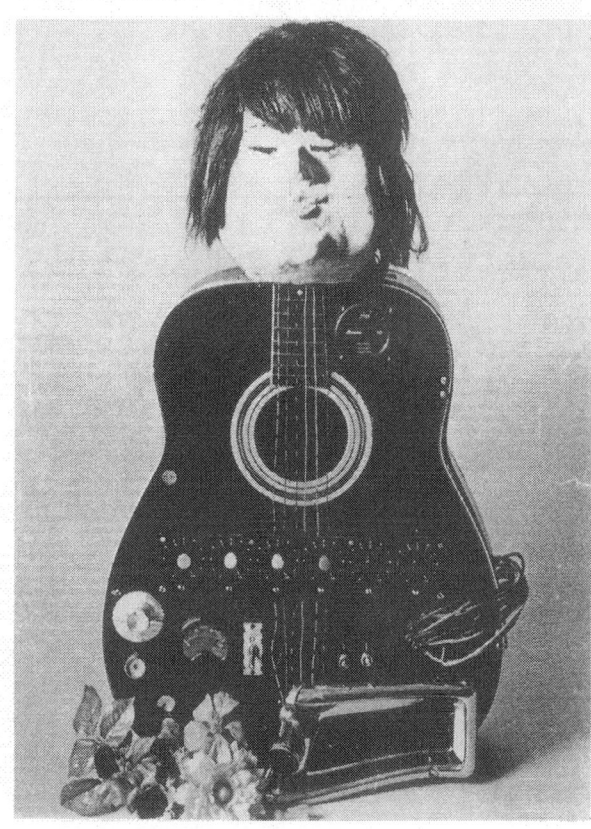

oui

BRIAN WILSON SESSIONS

SURF MOVIES ALWAYS MAKE ME CRY

NICK KENT chronicles the rise, fall and rise of BRIAN WILSON of the BEACH BOYS. He gave you surf music. He gave you the Californian sound. He gave you some of rock 'n' roll's most beautiful symphonies. And along the way, he went mad!

The incident occured in 1974. Paul McCartney, complete with the inevitable Linda, had just flown into Los Angeles — for business talks and the like — and already he was trying to get in touch with Brian Wilson.

McCartney and Wilson were no strangers. Derek Taylor, back in 1966 when he was The Beach Boys' publicist, had introduced the two composers.

Conversation had been easy and verbal bouquets had constantly changed hands throughout an evening that had reached its peak when Wilson had played back the final mix of a new composition of his — a song called *Good Vibrations*. McCartney of course had been mightily impressed.

But that was all some eight years ago, and times and personalities change.

Now there was no Beatles to contend with. Instead, McCartney was married, domesticated, a father.

Brian Wilson, however, hadn't seemed to have stood the rigours of the period as buoyantly. His personality, always as fitful as it was fanatical was weighed down by brooding hermetic traits, and he was often erratic, paranoid, crazed — cursed by a weight problem that had ultimately got out of all proportion.

Wilson soon enough got the message that McCartney was trying to contact him, and he just froze up, became terrified. Apparently he'd been informed of a quote attributed to McCartney to the effect that the latter considered *God Only Knows* to be the highest achievement in composition. Something like that.

Anyway Brian couldn't handle it. What was originally meant as just another verbal bouquet from one of his peers became twisted in the Wilson psyche. If he'd created the greatest song ever...I mean, now...what was there left to achieve? He just couldn't.

Paul and Linda stood for maybe an hour (who knows?) that night knocking on the door, trying to lure him out. "Brian...Brian it's alright. Really!"

An eye-witness states that they could hear him crying quietly to himself.

It's like Derek Taylor says. "Brian — one day he's coherent...bright, and then the next he can be just so damn illogical...strange...scarey."

We first got...no, well...uh...my brother Dennis came home from school one day and he said...um... Listen you guys...it looks like surfin's gonna be the next big craze and...uh...you guys oughta write a song about it. "Cos at that time we were writing songs for friends and...um...school assemblies.

"So it happened we wrote a song just to Dennis' suggestion and from there we just got on the surf wagon 'cos we figured...y'know...it'd be a hot craze. It's all because of my brother though.

"And he didn't know...he didn't...

"It just happened by chance."

The basic FACTS are pretty straightforward: Brian Douglas Wilson was born on June 20, 1942, the first of three sons to be brought into the world by parents Murray and Audrey Wilson.

The three brothers were brought up in the post-war stucco community of Hawthorne, one of those utterly characterless Californian suburbs positioned some thirty miles from the Pacific Ocean.

At Christmas time, for example, the shops would be stocked up with postcards of the community, artificial snow on the roofs, reindeer gamboling across the lawns (similarly layered in artificial snow). That sort of thing.

Anyway, the Wilson family was an acutely tight-knit unit, due mostly to Murray, a domineering father who adhered stolidly to all the arch-American maxims.

In his younger days, Murray Wilson would have been referred to as a "pistol", an extrovert boisterous sort who never got out of the habit of cracking terrible jokes and anticipating the response by slapping listeners on the back.

The whole family lived comfortably due to his moderately successful self-invested business dealing in heavy machinery, but Murray's hankering was towards making inroads into the music biz.

If his prowess as a composer was pretty dismal, his lack of success as a father is rather more significant. Strict to the point of being a bully at times, his rapport with his sons was fairly one-dimensional.

Derek Taylor: "Murray was always out of his depth. There was no malice in him whatsoever, mind. He was just a hot-shot from the suburbs...rather like someone who I heard being referred to as 'being heavier the nearer he gets to Manchester'.

"He knocked them about emotionally to the point where they became the image he'd set up for them. Carl had to take so much weight, be so calm. Dennis had to be such a crack-shot son.

"A daft man, really. He really scared the hell out of his boys. Mike (Love) had some great stories about him. I was always trying to get them out of him. Tell me more about Murray, Mike'." (Laughs)

Stories like the one about Murray's two glass eyes — one for normal use and a special blood-shot model for when he was hung over. Dennis once stole the bloodshot model, after Murray had spent the evening drinking somewhat to excess, and took it to school. He was soundly beaten.

Or the now legendary tale about the time Brian took his father's plate just before Murray had seated himself at the dinner table, went to the bathroom and excreted two large turds onto it. He returned to the table, replaced the plate, and waited. He too was soundly beaten.

But that was Brian. Wiggy, sure. But not mad. Not at that point anyway.

He was conscientious, hard-working, though a none-too brilliant scholar — as his report-books from both El Camino Junior High and El Camino College (Fall 1960-Winter '62) testified.

Music was his thing. Most of all he loved The Four Freshmen, a clean-cut close harmony team who specialised in 'respectable' pop, and would sit for hours by the record player singing along...testing his vocal range until he could reach an effortless, impressive falsetto pitch.

And he wrote songs.

It all picks up from here. The high-school bands. First there was Carl And The Passions, then they became Kenny And The Cadets, Brian was Kenny.

Finally there was The Beach Boys and a record called *Surfin'* on Candix records. It hit.

From Candix to mighty Capitol and producer Nick Venet who — in an era of tired chinless record executives — was sharp, into hip slogans and camel-hair coats. He and Murray didn't see eye to eye though.

The Beach Boys, see — this high-school band which featured the three Wilson brothers, a slightly older cousin called Mike Love and a weedy-looking local boy soprano named David Marks — had struck oil and Murray Wilson, their father, was determined to make up for lost time.

Photos of the band at the very outset of their career — before the weedy Marks was ousted, and the equally weedy Al Jardine, rescued from a tentative future as a dentist, was brought in — are still pretty hilarious. They all smiled like rabbits, had big ears and over-sized lumberjack shirts.

Carl the archetypal fat boy, Mike Love, even then with a receding forehead, and Dennis, his features not developed enough for him to be described as in any way good-looking.

Only Brian showed any visual promise: tall and at that time almost lean, he instinctively showed himself to be the leader.

Which he was, though Murray called the shots in most respects. As their manager, he stood for heavy discipline. Work, work, work. The guys just seemed to comply willingly.

Especially Brian whose songwriting was really the key to it all. Wilson was not merely a visionary as far as trends were concerned — he could almost calculate the longevity of each so that, by the time any given fad had burned itself out, The Beach Boys were inevitably long long gone — his instinct for pure rock expression was as impressive as it was seemingly effortless.

Indeed, Wilson's talents were such that from the sparsest of influences he created a whole California sound — a tonal feel complemented by lyrics that exploded Chuck Berry's more incisive observations in *The Promised Land* into a full-blown utterly irresistible myth.

As Nik Cohn observed in his *Awopbopaloobop* book:

"He (Wilson) worked a loose-limbed group sound and added his own falsetto. Then he stuck in some lazy twang guitar and rounded it all out with jumped-up Four Freshmen harmonies. No sweat, he'd created a bonafide surf music out of nothing. More, he had invented California."

Brian had the whole surfing-beach craze cased all by himself.

In 1962, he took Chuck Berry's *Sweet Little Sixteen* and transformed it into *Surfin' U.S.A.*, again in Cohn's words — "the great surf anthem, the clincher: a hymn of unlimited praise."

In 1963 he even eclipsed his own fantasies for The Beach Boys when, with Jan Berry of Jan & Dean fame he created *Surf City* — a virile all-American sun-kissed Valhalla where the ratio was strictly "two girls for every boy."

And who really cared if such fantasies were basically as dumb as hell — their very naivety only compounded the appeal. When The Beach Boys sang "*The girls on the beach/Are all within reach/And one waits there for you*" they were giving hope to every clumsy adolescent dreamer struggling through his awkward years. And that's all that really mattered.

Cohn again:

"There was by now no subject too soap-opera for him to take on. He churned out *A Young Man Is Gone*, an ode to the departed James Dean, and *Spirit Of America* and *Be True To Your School*. At the same time, he did some fine rejoicings, full of energy and inspiration — *Shut Down, 409, Little Deuce Coupe*. Fine rock 'n' roll music but brought up to date, kept moving and not left to atrophy. Best of all was *I Get Around*."

It's nigh impossible to affix a date, or a direct incident to explain the transformation from Brian

Brian Wilson (Pic: Michael Putland/LFI)

Wilson, Californian lad-visionary, to Brian Wilson the self-conscious 'creative artist' of *Pet Sounds*.

Nonetheless, December 23rd, 1964, remains symbolically an important date for The Beach Boys and Wilson in particular.

It was the day that Brian Wilson finally cracked up on a plane winging from L.A. to Houston where The Beach Boys were set to play a Christmas show.

The "wig-out" was a fairly obvious precursor to a complete nervous breadkown brought about by the hefty build-up of innumerable pressures and by sheer overwork. In fact, Brian's "condition" was so ragged at this point he went on to suffer two more similar breakdowns in quick succession.

The traumas, though, were providential in that they extricated Wilson from all his touring commitments with The Beach Boys and set him aside to concentrate almost solely on composing and recording. Brian could now concentrate on what he did best and moreover be allowed the creative elbow-room to experiment a little more, develop new formulae to

They all smiled like rabbits, had big ears and over-sized lumberjack shirts...

combat the likes of The Beatles (who had swiped The Beach Boys' teen titan throne that very year).

Brian Wilson, left to his own devices, could settle that score easily enough. The other guys knew that. At that time, they trusted Brian implicitly.

Off the road and away from all those pressures that must have undermined his personality and basically flattened his whole character, Brian Wilson started getting wise to a few things.

Ego, for one — the unfettered dynamic pitting of one's talents against all the other bands. This new band for example — The Rolling Stones. They weren't so damn hot!

The Beatles — now The Beatles were different. Brian dug the hell out of those albums. And that Paul? Boy what a talented guy!

And Bob Dylan...Well actually Dylan scared Brian a little, made him uneasy.

And then again, Brian was getting this...uh thing from Dylan's whole sound...his feel, y'know. He confided with friends that he honestly believed Bob Dylan was out to destroy music with his genius.

Very quickly, Brian Wilson was becoming besotted with 'Art'.

People would tell him the most common-place facts about such-and-such a composer or painter and Brian would just flip right out.

You mean to say Beethoven wrote some of these works when he was completely deaf? Boy, I bet...I bet this whole painting thing has been going on for thousands of years, right?

A visitor would read a fragment from a volume of Omar Khayyam and Brian Wilson would get up right there and then, his head positively swimming with all this magical dumb inspiration and just *know* that this guy had *all* the answers.

All these quasi-revelations were to start making tentative infringements on Wilson's music itself — but not for a while yet. The first post-touring album for example, was *The Beach Boys — Today* and it found Wilson both taking care of "business" with teen-beat retreads like *Dance, Dance, Dance,* and high-school romance rock (*Good To My Baby*) while exploring more adventurous aspects of both production and composition.

Wilson's dream lovers were suddenly no longer simple happy souls harmonising their sunkissed innocence and undying devotion over a muted halcyon backdrop of surf and sand. They were vulnerable, insecure, at times almost neurotic.

Brian's whole approach to romance was becoming more and more personalised, more honest in a distinctly autobiographical way.

The innocence was still there, for sure — God it had to be...it was the absolute deciding factor, the master plan that dictated to almost every aspect of his creativity — but it was becoming more worldly now. The rigours of experience were impinging themselves upon the very nature of his muse and Brian Wilson could no longer comfortably dream on like before.

For starters, he was married now.

His wife's name was Marilyn and she was the elder daughter of the Rovelles, a good Jewish family, comfortable enough to allow their younger offspring the benefits of a good nose-job.

Brian Wilson's penchant for "the great all-American teen Anthem" hadn't deserted him yet awhile. In 1965 he composed arguably his greatest work in that field.

California Girls at once took all that was best in Wilson's heroic myth-weaving patriotism stand and combined it with his new melodic and arranging sophistication. The results created an even more irresistible myth than the ones that had gone before.

'Well, East Coast girls are hip — I really dig the style they wear
And the Southern girls with the way they talk, they knock me out when I'm down there.
The Midwest farmers' daughters really make you feel alright
And the Northern girls with the way they kiss — they keep their boyfriends warm at night.'

Diplomatic, sure, but Brian and the guys were adamant:

'I wish they all could be California/I wish they all could be California/I WISH THEY ALL COULD BE CALIFORNIA GURLS'

That was the thing, see, with The Beach Boys. The were always "gurls".

So anyway it was 1965 and The Beach Boys were still on the beach. Only this time there was a new West Coast "sound" coming up — a "sound" which had nothing to do with sun and surfing and though it concentrated on harmonies in part, used the little jangling of a 12-string Rickenbacker guitar for a musical back-drop as opposed to the fat twang of the surf guitar.

The Byrds hailed from Los Angeles too but they were almost the complete antithesis of The Beach Boys.

For a start, they were more into a very defined "bohemian" thing — very cerebral in contrast to the Beach Boys' more physical predilections. Ostensibly they were around to electrically 'interpret' Dylan — spread the word on the new Messiah. Whatever, it was new and it caught on. Fast.

There were two more Beach Boys albums before the advent of *Pet Sounds* and both were, in their own way, cop-outs or, more to the point, "manufactured" product put out to satisfy Capitol. Both *Summer Days (And Summer Nights)* and *Beach Boys Party* were easy-formula fare, no real surprises. The latter seems almost symbolic in retrospect: a supposedly informal 'live' recording of a Beach Boys Beach Party (it was of course done in the studio): it featured lotsa accapella singing, acoustic guitars strumming over the crackling of weenies, bongoes, the girls joining in on the chorus, everybody making merry.

The whole album was very American and very dumb. You could almost hear Brian thinking to himself: O.K. that's it now, you guys.

From then on, fun — good, clean or otherwise — was very definitely strictly out of season.

At the very end of 1965 Tony Asher had more or less settled into the routine at the office he was working at.

The building housed a strictly nine-to-five breed who concentrated their efforts on coming up with "jingles", catch-phrases and the like for various advertising campaigns.

Asher had been allocated about five products, and was making quite a moderate success of his job as a copy-writer. The bosses thought his jingle for Gallo Wines, for example was particularly promising.

Asher was fairly contented anyway; the job itself wasn't taxing — although neither was it particularly inspiring. But it was secure.

So imagine Tony Asher's shock when, out of the blue, Brian Wilson of The Beach Boys — the leader of America's No. 1 hit group itself — phoned him with this proposition.

Wilson had a problem. Capitol were on his back, breathing heavily and threatening to possibly even sue due to the non appearance of a new Beach Boys album. Capitol had a right to be concerned, mind.

There were in fact just two unfinished tracks in existence at that point.

Wilson, in short, needed collaborative aid fast, though why he enlisted Asher's aid to this day remains a mystery — not the least to Asher himself.

Tony Asher had known Wilson vaguely from a few chance meetings when in his younger days, infatuated by recording studios and the music biz big-time, he used to hang out at sessions attempting to peddle songs he'd written. Now Asher was pretty intelligent — not so much 'hip' as *mature* — and Brian Wilson had struck him as an out-and-out hick, very dumb, hardly able to express himself verbally in company at all.

He seemed however to be very conscientious...hard working. Asher had found him agreeable, if overall, rather insipid.

So, anyway, here was Brian Wilson offering Tony Asher the chance to pick up on a potential gold-mine in royalties — Asher told his boss he desperately needed three months vacation and one day later he was setting down to work with his new-found collaborator in the living room of the latter's mansion in Bellagio.

Unbeknown to both of them *Pet Sounds* was to be Brian's great musical "breakthrough" and Asher's role — though the credits on the album suggest a strict division between lyrics and music — was soon to make itself obvious.

Wilson knew what he wanted lyrically. Each song, each melody and arrangement stated a mood and Tony Asher's job was to simply express that mood as eloquently as possible.

"It's fair to say that the general tenor of the lyrics was always his and the actual *choice* of words was usually mine. I was really just his interpreter."

There were exceptions to the rule, of course. Asher claims to have inspired *God Only Knows* for example:

"I can remember a discussion I had with Brian over that song because he was terribly worried that incorporating the word 'God' into a song — into the title itself — might be considered blasphemous." (Laughs) "No, but it's true. He loved the idea but was terrified that all the radio stations would ban the song just because of the word 'God'. It took a lot of persuading...

"Brian was constantly looking for topics that kids could relate to. Even though he was dealing in the most advanced score-charts and arrangements, he was still incredibly conscious of this commercial thing...this absolute need to relate."

At this point, Brian Wilson was out to move the very soul of teenage America. To create music so passionate, so majestic that when you turned on your radio — shazam — Instant Epiphany.

And Inspiration was everywhere.

Asher: "*Wouldn't It Be Nice* was... oh definitely Brian's idea. The innocence of the situation — being too young to get married — seemed to be immensely appealing to him. I can remember being in restaurants with him and some young girl would inevitably walk in and he'd almost...melt, y'know. He'd get all misty-eyed and just stare at her, muttering on and on about, 'Oh wow, she's just so-o beautiful. Don't you think...'

"Also then there was his sister-in-law Diane and I don't...I don't think I'd be wrong in saying that he was definitely infatuated by her. He was obsessed with, again, this innocent aura she seemed to possess. Brian was really just *so* naive."

Wilson's particular naivety, though creatively-speaking immensely stimulating, was personally far from appealing to Asher who now claims he loathed listening to Brian's gooey confessions. In fact, he remembers his three-month collaborative stint with Brian Wilson as something of a misery *outside* of the recording studio.

"The only times I actually enjoyed myself or even got comfortable with Brian was when I was standing by the piano working with him. Otherwise I felt hideous!

"Firstly, there were the physical surroundings which exhibited the worst taste *imaginable!* I came over one time and he'd bought...God, my powers to describe these are just inadequate, but...They were two clockwork parrots sitting on a perch made out of feathers. And every feather was dyed some disgusting synthetic colour, right.

"These monstrosities cost him apparently something like 700 dollars and he thought they were just *the greatest* (laughs)"... "But the thing was, Brian Wilson has to be the single most irresponsible person I've ever met in my life. You just wouldn't believe the extent of... this just total lack of responsibility he maintained.

"I mean, there were always documents to be signed, appointments that were never kept...Christ, Capitol would phone me as kind of a last resort and say 'Listen we hear you're seeing a lot of Brian... um would it be possible...could you get him to sign this'...

"I mean, I can even remember seeing this 125,000 dollar cheque that he needed to endorse...y'know, just laying around the house."

Instead, Brian Wilson was starting to indulge himself in what would ultimately become a disturbingly large-scale assortment of eccentricities.

Asher again: "He had this obsession with sleeping, for example. He'd sleep all through the day-time — only get up when it was dark. He was smoking an awful lot of dope then too. He just used to get these incredibly intense depressions. He'd just started taking acid too."

Asher recalls spending evenings with Brian where he's lose all control, fall into uncontrollable laughing jags, then burst into tears. The initial observation that he was just some conscientious dumb-bell from the sticks became the sudden awareness that Brian Wilson was really a totally unstable personality, incapable of self-discipline — except when he was seated at the piano or in the recording studio.

Then — and only then — would he pull himself

"Personally I could never understand why he'd married her in the first place. I don't know... maybe he loved her."

together and exhibit this almost awesome ability at controlling any given situation.

"You asked me if he ever showed flashes of lunacy, right? I'd have to say...well he had fits of this just *uncontrollable* anger. Then he'd fall apart and start crying during play-backs of certain tracks.

"It was like...he was constantly being buffeted between these two emotional extremes — from elation to depression and back again. He didn't go after people with knives if that's what you mean, though.

"It's like...yeah you could say he was doomed in a way. He was just so damn self-destructive! It wasn't the acid, so much. It was more things like the way he seemed to surround himself constantly with bad people and bad situations.

"That whole claustrophobic scene with his family for example, all was so blatantly obvious to me. It was like this dumb guy saying to himself: 'Aw gee, I don't deserve all this success. I'd better surround myself with all these jerks to make up for my good fortune.'"

First there was the weird relationship he maintained with Marilyn, his wife.

Asher: "It was this constant interplay of Brian just acting in this utterly belittling way toward her and Marilyn retaliating by storming off into another room yelling back something quite inane. It was very caveman-like. Personally, I could never understand why he'd married her in the first place. I don't know... maybe he loved her."

And then there were all the problems caused by Murray and "the guys".

The Beach Boys had been out on an extensive tour of foreign parts while Wilson and Asher were working on the music for *Pet Sounds*, and they'd just returned from a highly successful sojourn in Japan when they were allowed to hear what Big Brother had been up to in their absence.

Frankly, they were worried.

They just couldn't understand this new stuff at all — I mean you couldn't even dance to it, for Chrissakes.

Here they were back from a very lucrative conquest of all these exotic countries and Brian had been back home all along wasting his time with this Asher guy — whom no-one knew (he wasn't 'kin', that's for sure).

Asher gauges their reaction and personalities perfectly:

"Well, I always thought Al Jardine was kind of an underrated force in that band. I mean, I felt he was genuinely impressed by some of the music we were making. He'd take me aside sometimes and tell me how good it was.

"But Dennis...oh God, Dennis wasn't bewildered by anything! He just wanted to get the hell out of the studio and get back on the beach." (Laughs)

"And Carl...well, I always felt Carl was playing a part, y'know. He wasn't so much a hypocrite as...well, he seemed to be totally into promoting this role of him as real calm, loving, serene...he was always stroking his wife's hair, for example. Acting at being the Fat Buddha."

Finally, there was Mike Love who was definitely pissed off by the whole set-up. Love's main concerns were success and money; art and self-expression did not appeal to his set of values in any way whatsoever. So he acted morose and wouldn't say much in front of Asher or Brian except to throw in the occasional barked "Well, it sure sounds different to the old stuff" line.

And then again there was always good old Murray Wilson, by now completely out of his depth, but still determined enough to make his presence felt somehow.

Asher again:

"Murray was so strange...I've got to say that he came across to me as a really sick man. Pathetically so, in fact, but sick nonetheless. There were times for example, when he'd be saying to me 'Oh, all I'm trying to do is to help Brian. He hates me, he hates me.' Or 'Why are the other guys giving Brian such a hard time? Can't you talk to them, make them see...'

"And then, behind Brian's back, he'd be talking to the other guys...in the bathroom, say, just stirring it up. His whole thing it seemed to me was to get the guys at each other's throats constantly so he could establish himself as the one solid figure. He wasn't the leader though — Brian was — and Christ, you wouldn't believe how Murray resented him for that. His own father!

"And the other guys...listen. The Beach Boys would have gladly ganged up on Brian, if they conceivably could've but they were powerless. No-one really challenged...no-one could challenge Brian, for Chrissakes, because they weren't talented enough to take over. God knows, they've proved that since then...

"I mean, even then they were trying to do things off their own bat and it was just pathetic really. A pale reflection."

So you think that The Beach Boys had become absolutely expendable — almost desirably so, in fact — to Brian Wilson's music?

"Absolutely yes. No question about it.

"I mean, they were getting to be an impediment to him even in the areas they should have helped. There used to be incredible rows — fist-fights, everything.

"They were all allocated certain vocal parts, right, and they wouldn't be doing 'em right so Brian would just explode and start screaming 'Goddam it, you assholes, we've been here for three hours and you can't even do this simple thing!'

"Brian could have done it all by himself. The Beach Boys didn't play a single note on the album, by the way. It was all session musicians."

By this time, Capitol had gone far beyond simply demanding and stipulating ultimatums that fell on deaf ears. They took Brian Wilson's masterpiece just before it had reached its completion and released it immediately.

A cover shot was taken at some zoo in the L.A. area just prior to the band being banned from the place for "mistreating the animals" (the incident made the small columns of the *L.A. Times*; Dennis had apparently been the ringleader).

The Beach Boys singles — *God Only Knows* and *Wouldn't It Be Nice* — were issued and both sold in spectacular quantities, but the album itself was, ironically, to live up to the barbed prophecies of the "guys", Murray and Capitol itself.

It bombed.

1966 was evidently not just a good year for "quality product" taking off in the Americas. Even Phil Spector's orgasmic *River Deep, Mountain High* nose-dived away from the US charts almost as spectacularly as it was taken into the hearts and homes of the British consumer.

The Beach Boys' new-found mass audience in Britain — presumably the very same breed that had again, ironically enough, discovered the group via *Barbara Ann*, their first large-scale hit in the country some months earlier — bought the album in droves.

Brian's own *Caroline No*, arguably the most beautiful song he has ever written, however, failed to activate sales *anywhere*. Even though dear old Murray had allocated himself the final say by commandeering the final track and resolutely speeding it up from the key of G to the key of A "in order to make Brian sound younger".

Tony Asher meanwhile had disappeared back to his secure post at the advertising department — "for three reasons basically. First, that was the nature of my personality then...to be able to depend on a regular income. Second, I found Brian's lifestyle so damn repugnant. I mean, for say, every four hours we'd spend writing songs, there'd be about 48 hours of these dopey conversations about some dumb book he'd just read.

"Or else he'd just go on and on about girls...his feelings about this girl or that girl...it was just embarrassing as well as exhibiting this...just awful taste. His choice of movies, say, was invariably terrible. TV programmes...everything.

"Plus he was starting to get pretty weird."

Also, there was that other factor to bear in mind: *Pet Sounds'* comparative failure commercially (although Asher was still to make a respectable financial killing from his collaborative work on the album — approximately 40,000 dollars in royalty statements so far).

Asher still doesn't regret his disassociating himself from Wilson and The Beach Boys.

"I do believe Brian is a musical genius. Absolutely. Whatever I thought about him personally was almost always overridden by my feelings of awe at what he was creating. I mean, he was able to create melodies...

"God knows where he discovered those chords, those ideas for arranging a certain song. Maybe he'd had some formal training, though I doubt it actually.

"I can vividly remember for example the first time he played me his finished track for *Don't Talk (Put Your Head On My Shoulder)*. I was just literally speechless...Let's just say it was a great joy making music with him but that any other relationship with Brian was a great chore.

"I just felt, see, that the guy was going to go..."

Over the top, so to speak?

"Yeah, but that there was nothing I could do. That whatever was causing his problems had been pre-destined inside him from the age of nine, say. I'd try to talk with him about it and every time...it just fell on deaf ears. He'd say 'Oh, I can't handle this' or use some other catch phrases."

And now?

"The stories I've heard about his untogetherness these days would seem to figure. It could easily have happened, really; the irresponsibility...the inability to get himself together would ultimately just have had to affect his music. His occasional 'conditions' must have transformed themselves into a total life-style, I suppose.

"It's weird though y'know. I mean, you were talking just now about *Pet Sounds* being a masterpiece. Neither of us at the time thought that...at least, I...I don't know. I was more impressed by the production, really.

"To me it was just a great album, y'know...nothing more. It was like...I remember Brian was always saying during play-backs — 'Boy, for the first time ever Beach Boys songs are going to get lots of cover versions'.

"For me, see, it was just a chance to show some people — my parents, the guys at the advertising company — that rock music could be...uh, mature, y'know. And that's about as far as it went.

"Brian, though, was looking for acceptance. I mean *God Only Knows*...Mantovani could have easily made a cover version of that song. Lawrence Welk, too. But, before...well Andy Williams would never have covered something like *Little Deuce Coupe*.

"It's a shame really — what's happened since. I suppose I must hold the same view as most everyone else. I haven't heard anything particularly stirring from Brian or The Beach Boys. That track *Sail On Sailor* is just dandy, but otherwise it's been down to just isolated brilliant flashes.

"It's tragic actually — 'cos it's obviously still there but it's no longer in any usable form.

"But that's Brian maybe, for you.

"A genius musician but an amateur human being."

Pet Sounds was about to be released when Derek Taylor was taken on The Beach Boys' pay-roll, 750 dollars for dealing with the group's publicity.

Derek Taylor was at that time the single most prestigious L.A. figure with whom to have one's name allied in matters of business. Witty, very hip and a definite character to boot, plus, he knew The Beatles and had actually worked with and for Brian Epstein. There could be no grander recommendation.

Once enlisted into the ranks, Taylor worked fast. The candy-striped shirts that had for so long symbolised The Beach Boys were conveniently 'lost', whilst marriages — all the guys had been hitched for some time now unbeknown to their fans — were immediately made public knowledge.

Then there was the grand initiation ceremony afforded the release of *Pet Sounds*.

Taylor convened a reception in a suite at the London Hilton where England's most prestigious pop writers were given a preview of the album. Kim Fowley was unofficial master-of-ceremonies at the unveiling. Marianne Faithfull hovered fetchingly, while guests of honour Paul McCartney and John Lennon sat, their ears poised against the speakers, listening intently to a music that represented probably the most formidable threat to their own dictatorship of rock in the year 1966.

According to Fowley, after the record had finished Lennon and McCartney left the suite, returned immediately to the latter's home where, under the heady influence of Brian Wilson's 'new music' they supposedly went on to compose *Here There And Everywhere* that same evening.

As with most of Fowley's tall tales, that last tid-bit is afforded a dubious authenticity, but nonetheless The Beatles were among the very first to publicly acknowledge Brian Wilson's *Pet Sounds* as some kind of masterpiece.

Derek Taylor dutifully concurs with this view:

"But this time Brian had become very, very competitive, so much so that it was no longer that healthy sort of competitive spirit thing. It was a mad possessive battle against The Stones and particularly The Beatles.

"It was like this dumb guy saying to himself: Aw gee, I don't deserve all this success. I'd better surround myself with all these jerks to make up for my good fortune."

"An absurdly maniacal 'who's the fairest in the land' campaign, really. And I was in the middle of all this because...well firstly, he liked me because I was English and different. My life-style certainly seemed to appeal to him greatly.

"It's strange, too, because the fact that *Pet Sounds* hadn't sold at all well didn't affect him in the least. I doubt in fact, whether it even registered with him. He was only interested in these 'Who Is The Best?' heats.

"The Beatles...now, The Beatles were hot enough not to be over-concerned about anybody else, but they did think The Beach Boys were good...in fact, they'd arrived at that conclusion long before I had.

"Brian...of course, at that time Brian was very hot. He was always talking about a new plateau...all the time: 'The next record will create a new plateau for The Beach Boys in terms of creativity and acceptance.'

"Always these grand statements.

"He was constantly making changes with his collaborators too. Tony Asher had left the picture by that time and Van Dyke (Parks), who was also as hot as hell right then, was brought in to deal with the lyrics.

"Brian was taking acid, smoking a hell of a lot of grass and generally enjoying a new-found freedom that he would ultimately cut himself off from during one of those totally illogical frenzied brainstorms of his that would inevitably wreak havoc over everything.

"In terms of an 'era', this was all pretty much pre-acid, mind. I seem to recall only Brian and Dennis were turning on at this time. The rest certainly weren't. And even then, with Brian...it's weird actually, because Brian would only do it in fits and starts as if it had just been invented.

"He was definitely a man of whims. Fanatical...illogical whims at that! Religions were one thing. He'd been into Subud one minute, then onto something else without bothering to really absorb it all.

"God, he was so temporary, it was awful — and I'd dread the phone-call at 4 am demanding that I come over because I knew he needed me. We had a terrible falling-out that lasted about three weeks.

"I couldn't stand the fact that Brian didn't want me to like any artist but himself. I could never stand bands competing over me. It was never a problem with The Byrds, mind. But Brian...

"He was like another Brian, come to think of it... Epstein, another man of whims, surges, arrogance, manic depression and long periods of silence. Always demanding *too much*.

The other Beach Boys? Oh, it was always something of a pleasure touring with them because they were professional you know...good company. They were very concerned about Brian too.

All the time they'd be asking 'How is Brian? What does he think?' and so on. I never really heard a single disparaging word in all that time. Maybe a few jokes about his eccentricities, but always basically affectionate.

The final, and subsequently the most legendary, environmental innovation was the introduction of a sand-box into the music room.

Brian had a guy build a partition about four feet off the ground into a box shape. Then he put his grand piano in it and filled it with sand up to about two feet, so he could play piano with his shoes off in the sand.

And then he got into having meetings in the sand-box because you could roll around and cover yourself.

Probably the high-point of the whole *Smile* era was reached around November of 1966 when C.B.S. set about filming a TV documentary on Brian Wilson and his new music.

Everything about it seemed perfect. Here was everything Brian was striving for coming vividly to celluloid-enhanced realisation.

The main thing, first of all, was that this was not to be just another dumb pop show: the programme was to be introduced by Leonard Bernstein and, moreover, be directed by David Oppenheim, a middle-aged purveyor of high-brow documentaries who'd just come straight from his previous assignment — a documentary study of Stravinsky.

Brian naturally saw this as being "very heavy".

The show's actual peak occurred when our hero performed a live preview of *Surf's Up* — and it was perfect. So perfect in fact that Bernstein himself broke down afterwards and made some ecstatic claim on the air that the song was the most brilliant piece of contemporary music he'd heard since...blah,blah. Even the normally inscrutable Oppenheim was visibly moved by the performance.

But it was Bernstein's wild claim that really moved Brian. It horrified him.

It shouldn't have, of course.

A more sophisticated consciousness would have bowed graciously and maybe taken Bernstein's verbal bouquet with a pinch of salt.

Not Brian.

His reaction was bizarre...illogical and yes, ultimately very, very tragic. After all, was Bernstein's gushing testimonial not the very stuff upon which Brian Wilson's dreams had been formulated all along? And now here it all was: fulfilment — the very apex of acceptance.

It should have surely been the crowning hour. Instead, it may well have created the very undoing of all the brilliance that at one time had seemed so limitless...so optimistic.

It didn't take long for everything to fall apart. And yet again a key factor in the breakdown had to be The Beach Boys themselves, whose stubbornness twisted itself into a grim determination to undermine this 'new music' in order to get back to the old accepted, dumb formulas.

The guys — and in particular Mike Love — all hated and resented Van Dyke Parks and his 'weird' lyrics, and Parks was the first of Brian's new allies to be ousted from the Wilson camp.

In actual fact, Van Dyke himself called the shots on his own removal as soon as he had been given a taste of the other guys' resolve to thwart the project. He immediately distanced himself by getting involved in other work.

Van Dyke put his head back in to his own music again and became less and less available to Brian. And Brian suddenly became less and less sure of what he was doing with the album.

He'd have to go through a tremendous paranoia before he would get into the studio, knowing he was going to have to face an argument. He would come into the studio uptight, he would give a part to one of the group. And there would be instant resistance. And then, maybe after they left to go on tour, he would come back in and do it himself. All their parts.

The Beach Boys, of course, have a different story.

First of all, it would be totally unfair to attempt to gauge any overt malice from their collective intent. To them, it was very cut and dried. They didn't trust this new bunch that Big Brother had surrounded himself with at all — saw them all very simply as bad influences, filling *their leader* up with weird drugs, twisting his perspective, turning his brain inside out. Naturally, it just had to be stopped.

Van Dyke Parks had left and come back and would leave again, tired of being constantly dominated by Brian. Marilyn Wilson was having headaches and Dennis Wilson was leaving his wife. Session after session was cancelled.

One night a studio full of violinists waited while Brian tried to decide whether or not the vibrations were friendly or hostile. The answer was hostile and the session was cancelled at a cost of 3,000 dollars.

BRIAN WILSON SESSIONS

The stories that document Wilson's madness at this time tend to just reel on and on.

Another classic tale concerns one paranoid flash set off during the recordings of the *Fire* extract from the *Elementals* suite when a series of actual fires burnt down some buildings in the L.A. area.

Wilson, haunted by some concept of karma, actually believed that his music had caused the blazes and, frightened out of his wits by the seemingly God-like omnipotence of his own creativity, immediatedly set about destroying the tapes of his fire music.

The final absurd touch to the story is that Wilson tried for several hours to set fire to the tapes, but was unable to get them to catch alight.

Finally though, it was to be down to The Beatles to truly kick the whole *Smile* project in the head for reasons that aren't too hard to ascertain.

The late spring of 1967 saw the release of *Sgt. Pepper's Lonely Hearts Club Band* — so ecstatically received, so lauded as the last word in rock genius that it alone symbolically transformed that whole year into a closed shop for comparable coups.

Sgt. Pepper was such an achievement that nothing could possibly follow it, and Brian Wilson who desperately craved the same impact for his work, instinctively knew that however great *Smile* might be, its release on the heels of *Pepper* would place it as an also-ran by comparison.

As Derek Taylor recounts:

"By that time ...well, it was just all hell breaking loose. It was tapes being lost, ideas being junked — Brian thinking 'I'm no good' then 'I'm too good' — then 'I can't sing! I can't get those voices anymore'.

"There was even a time back then when there hardly seemed to be a Beach Boy at all."

Derek Taylor had, by this time, terminated his publicist job with the group.

Taylor had gone straight on to help organize the acts of the now legendary Monterey Pop Festival of 1967 and had immediately suggested that his former employees top the bill for the Saturday night portion of the weekend event. Initially The Beach Boys agreed to play willingly and then suddenly there was the 'Grand Reversal in Decision Making' which set up a mighty battalion of Beach Boys 'bad-raps' that were to indent themselves into the psyche of the whole blossoming West Coast acid culture. In very simple terms, The Beach Boys were deigned just *not cool* anymore.

Taylor again:

"The whole Monterey number did seem to set the band in a very bad light. They were certainly very heavily criticised at the time for their cancellation. It seemed in a way rather like an admission of defeat.

"And well, yes, I presume it had to be down to Brian. Those sorts of decisions were always his, really. I know for example, he's said, 'Yes' and I believe he must have said 'No' as well. It was certainly very much in keeping with his character at the time."

That actually figures because the album — certainly in comparison to what had been intended for the original *Smile* project — *was* a very humble proposition.

What had happened, it appears, was that Brian had taken three or four of the Van Dyke Parks collaborations, had quickly written some new songs either by himself or with the aid of Mike Love and, using minimal accompaniment, had recorded all of them in the make-shift studio in his living-room.

There were only three exceptions to this policy — both *Good Vibrations* and *Heroes & Villains* were simply presented on the album in their simple form while one track, the Parks/Wilson *Vegetables* had been produced by an uncredited Paul McCartney.

Otherwise the record was really just an exercise in...um, well how does "do-it-yourself acid casualty doo-wop" sound?

Smiley Smile, see, must still rate as about the all-time strangest album ever to be released by a major rock band; certainly no-one could begin to work out what it could possibly 'signify'.

Maybe the whole of *Smiley Smile* was really just one great cosmic 'put-on' instigated by Brian Wilson at the expense of all those who'd ever called him a genius.

Brian Wilson was in fact back with the "guys", committed once again to his family ties, going on outings with his mother Audrey and hanging out down at a local bowling alley with his in-laws.

Brian had always loved to go bowling with the guys — even when he was doing acid.

Van Dyke Parks had his own views of course. His contention was that *Smile* was lost. "It was lost, I think because of...there was a real Machiavellian piece of political manoeuvering that accompanied that album.

"It was good for me though as regards personal experience. In the intimacy of the whole thing, it was...there was an impressive innocence — before-guilt feeling. And nobody had the time or inclination [illegible] guilt."

"Mike Love by then was tough as hell and was taking care of things. A worldly fellow, Mike. Marriages and all that. There was no God in his life, then, I can tell you!!

"Then Al Jardine was...amusing. He possessed a very dry sense of humour did Al. Bruce (Johnston) was very business-like, very diplomatic.

"Dennis was...oh I could never make up my mind whether Dennis was actually *childish or child-like*. Maybe more of the former. He was pretty wild certainly. Irresponsible too. Though I didn't find him to be much of a problem.

"Carl was so sweet and young I found him difficult to relate to really. I just felt too damn worldly next to Carl's innocence. I was frightened I might taint him in some respect (laughs).

"I didn't really have too much contact with Murray which was probably just as well. I remember one half-hour when he rushed into my office. The first thing he said was 'Am I coming on too strong —' So I immediately said 'Yes'.

The final absurd touch to the story is that Wilson tried to set fire to the tapes, but was unable to get them to catch alight.

"Brian had hated him from time to time. And, of course, Murray hated the new music, which didn't help matters.

"I also recall having — oh God I still can't believe this one — a conversation with Brian and Dennis about The Beach Boys never having written surf music or songs about cars; that the Beach Boys had never been involved *in any way* with the surf and drag fads.

"I was told this one afternoon and I kept saying 'Listen, how can...I mean, how dare you give me this nonsense about you never having been involved in all this? I have the proof right here.'

"But no, they would not concede. I just felt it sad that they should be so determined to disown their past. The Beatles went through that — at about the same time, as it happens.

"The 'Brian Wilson is a Genius' thing? Yes, I started that off. It was my line: 'Brian Wilson is a genius, I think'. I seem to recall it all came about because Brian told me that he thought he was better than most other people believed him to be.

"So I put this idea to myself and went around town proposing the contention to people like Van Dyke and Danny Hutton and they all said 'Oh yes, definitely, Brian Wilson is a genius'.

"Then I thought, Well if that's so, why doesn't anyone outside think so? Then I started putting it around, måking almost a campaign out of it.

"And I still believe it. Absolutely. Brian Wilson is a genius. It was something that I felt should be established.

"Mind you, he *was* making some amazing music at that time. I mean, even when I couldn't face him, wher I couldn't handle his mad competitiveness or his temporary whims...he could manipulate people, could Brian. He was very cunning, very clever, even though there was a naivety there...this terribly shy young man whom you could tell the most mundane things to and he'd express just sheer amazement..."

Van Dyke Parks: Brian's latest lyricist was a *frail, aesthetic* figure of a man living in L.A., a city that had never heard of either word.

Originally from Mississippi, his family had moved to Hollywood when he was some thirteen years of age and the adolescent Parks had spent several years working as a child actor playing in movies opposite the likes of Bette Davis.

From there he had gone on to study classical piano and composition at the Carnegie Institute of Technology and having graduated, signed up with M.G.M. in the hope of being able to compose sound track music for Walt Disney films.

Instead, he'd ended up producing groups like the Mojo Men and Harper's Bizarre.

During this tenure he was eventually to be introduced to Brian. Parks had already collaborated on songs with Wilson's previous lyricist Tony Asher.

As is usual with most Van Dyke Parks rhetoric, the following recital tells one far more about the enigmatic Parks' dubious state of sanity than about the subject at hand!

"I vividly remember The Beach Boys appearing from out the West — basically because I recall my first reservations about their surfing abilities. I was a surfer, see — my brothers were both West Coast champions. I mean I *had* to surf.

"Anyway The Beach Boys were known to my set to be 'flat-landers' but then again, having by this time become fairly saturated with 'beach-life', I was suddenly impressed by their music for the first time.

"And I met Brian at this time...actually I met him during *Pet Sounds* when the inclusion of the cello — which I recall was my idea — was important to the development of that sound on the record. Brian generously did everything he could to help me along — so I became, as it were, an exercising lyricist. I just started writing the words for him.

Regarding the exact nature of his lyrics, Parks expresses dismay at the apparent incompatibilities often inherent in their mating with Brian's music.

"I thought, see...that one of the failures of the 'Smile period — our working together — was the fact that the words were maybe too important or something. Or were given unnecessary importance.

"And actually...the words *were* important to me. Rather than trying to make waves, I was really more interested in working with and for The Beach Boys and making the words innocuous.

"I was unsuccessful."

The whole nature of the Wilson-Parks compositional pairing remains, to this day, exceptionally bizarre on every level imaginable.

To begin with, Van Dyke Parks' expression was so diametrically opposed to Brian's. The lyrics to *Surf's Up*, for example, were a conscious attempt on Parks' part to transplant the wildly elusive baroque imagery that director Robbe-Grillet had achieved in visual terms for his film *L'Annee Derniere a Marienbad*.

Brian though...well, Brian loved Van Dyke's lyrics. For a while anyway.

They were full of big words that no other rock lyricist had ever used before — esoteric and very, very sophisticated, to his way of thinking.

This is how one Jules Siegal observed Brian in '67:
"It's a man at a concert," Brian said. "All around him there's the audience, playing their roles, dressed up in fancy clothes, looking through opera glasses, but so far away from the drama, from life. *Back through the opera glass you see the pit and the pendulum drawn*.
"The music begins to take over. *Columnated ruins domino*. Empires, ideas, lives, institutions — everything has to fall, tumbling like dominoes.
"He begins to awaken to the music; sees the pretentiousness of everything. *The music hall a costly bow*. Then even the music is gone, turned into a trumpeter swan, into what the music really is.
"*Canvas the town and brush the back-drop*. He's off in his vision, on a trip. Reality is gone; he's creating it like a dream. *Dove-nesting towers*. Europe a long time ago. *The laughs came hard in Auld Lang Syne*. The poor people in the cellar taverns, trying to make themselves happy by singing.
"Then there's the parties, the drinking, trying to forget the wars, the battles at sea. *While at port adieu or die*. Ships in the harbour, battling it out. A kind of Roman Empire thing.
"*A stroke of grief*. At his own sorrow and the emptiness of his life, because he can't even cry for the suffering in the world, for his own suffering.
And then hope. *Surf's Up! Come about hard and join the once and often spring you gave*. Go back to the kids, to the beach, to childhood.
"*I heard the word of God; wonderful thing* — the joy of enlightenment, of seeing God. And what is it? *A children's song!* And then there is the song itself; the song of children; the song of the universe rising and falling in wave after wave, the song of God, hiding the love from us, but always letting us find it again, like a mother singing to her children.
"So that's what I'm doing now, see. Spiritual music."
The record was over. Wilson went into the kitchen and squirted Reddi-Whip direct from the can into his

BRIAN WILSON SESSIONS

mouth; made himself a chocolate Great Shake and ate a couple of candy bars.

Italics are from the lyrics to Surf's Up)

Brian Wilson was out to shut down The Beatles at their own game and Van Dyke Parks' lyrics were much, much heavier than anything John Lennon's scathing Liverpudlian wit could whip out. Van Dyke's vivid parabolas of obtuse spirituality were Brian's very own secret weapon — his bid for a take-over of "pop."

An album laden with Parks/Wilson gems was "in the works" — by all accounts, a breathtaking masterpiece that would leave all competitors reeling in their tracks.

This album already had a title. At first it was supposed to be *Dumb Angel*, but that was quickly changed. Finally it was decided, the next Beach Boys album would be entitled — simply — *Smile*.

There have already been weighty accounts fully documenting every aspect of *Smile*'s creation through to the destruction at the hands of its very creator.

Smile, is probably the single most enigmatic rock recording project ever undertaken. The reasons that underlie this enigma are only too obvious. The album, even though it had approached a stage of completion, was never released.

It's when you start actually grasping for solid explanations that you get hopelessly enmeshed in hearsay — all of which only invites one to explore more thoroughly the psyche of Brian Douglas Wilson at the time.

"Oh well, that was because...the lyrics, Van Dyke Parks had written lyrics that were...it was all Van Dyke Parks and none of The Beach Boys. The lyrics were so poetic and symbolic, they were abstract, we couldn't."

"Oh no, wait, it was...no, really...I remember, this is it, this is why it didn't come out. Because, I'd bought a lot of hashish. It was really a large purchase...I mean, perhaps two thousand dollars worth..."

"We didn't realize, but the music was getting too influenced by it, the music had a really drugged feeling. I mean, we had to lay down on the floor with the microphones next to our mouths to do the vocals. We didn't have any energy. I mean, you come into a session and see the group laying on the floor of the studio doing vocals...you know..."

"You can't."

That was Brian Wilson himself explaining the reasons for *Smile*'s non-appearance — and, apart from the passage concerning Parks' creative incompatibility, it reads like a giant put-on, right? Right.

On the one hand, Wilson was about to expose his audience to the gargantuan heaviness of the Van Dyke Parks collaborations — 'Columnated ruins domino' et al — and on the other, he wanted the project to weigh in with this *new* concept: *Smile* as the great cosmic humour album.

The paradox was simply insurmountable. Then again there was Brian's healthfood fetish demanding to be eulogised (as on the quirkily brilliant *Vegetables*), plus the whole "health" kick which set Wilson building sauna baths and a gymnasium in the recording studio.

Following that, business meetings were to be held in the swimming pool — Brian's theory being, "If you take a bunch of businessmen and put them in a swimming pool with their heads bobbing out of the water, then they really get down to fundamentals. Because nobody can bullshit when they're in the water."

If they did Brian would 'dunk' them. And if it got boring, he would just start splashing about.

THE BEACH BOYS 1967 - 1981
Brian never came back, but the music did

Brian's mental, drug and health problems intensified. By 1968 despite a brief return of popularity with the *Wild Honey* and *Darlin'* singles, the band that were raised by Murray Wilson to represent all things Americana were sadly out of synch with events in the USA. The pitched battle of the 1968 Democratic convention, the assassinations of Martin Luther King and Bobby Kennedy, the intensification of hippie culture into radical off-shoots such as The Weathermen, set a backdrop against which the pristine harmonies and fun, fun, fun concept of the band's early hits now seemed cringingly immature.

The Beach Boys now found themselves playing to hostile crowds and, even worse, no crowds at all.

Things couldn't get worse it seemed. But they did. The group discovered Transcendental Meditation at least a year after it was hip to do so, and mounted a TM tour of America. They shared the stage with the Maharishi Yogi and the whole thing was a complete disaster. After suffering mass walk outs, then empty halls, the tour was abandoned.

"The Maharishi was talking about being able to increase the use of your conscious mind so it sounded pretty good to those of us who were in a profession that demanded creativity. He said you didn't have to give up the pursuit of material pleasures and that sounded real good to me," said Mike Love. Inadvertently he had summed up the internal crisis of America in the late '60s. A search for new spiritual values linked with a determination to hold onto the gains of Capitalism's most successful progeny.

Two more albums appeared on Capitol. *Friends* saw the whole group pitching in to write and produce. Brian's one solo effort was misleadingly titled *Busy Doin' Nothing*. He was, in fact, fully involved exploring his own downward spiral.

The last album on Capitol was *20/20*. It contained a collage of five pieces from the missing *Smile* album under the title of *Cabinessence*. A labyrinthian effort it enhanced the group's status as artists but the public gave *20/20* the cold shoulder. The group split acrimoniously with Capitol but their first effort for Warner Brothers, *Sunflower*, was not a success. Warner's put heavy pressure for the return of Brian into the group. Murray Wilson was ousted as the band's manager and replaced with an ex disc-jock, Jack Rieley.

Rieley masterminded a triumphant concert return for the group at the Los Angeles Whiskey A Go Go. Brian appeared, for one night only, on stage.

He was also reluctantly involved in the next two recording projects; *Surf's Up* and *Holland*. Both albums were critical successes but low sellers. Golden Oldies were the backbone of the group's now successful live shows. But inside the band, trauma was rampant. Jack Rieley was fired. Mike Love's brother, Steve, was brought in as manager. In 1973 Murray Wilson died.

But in 1974 The Beach Boys were America's most successful concert band — with very much the same repertoire they were playing in 1964. Capitol released *Endless Summer*, a double compilation of oldies. It climbed to the top of the charts in America, England and Australia. The group toured huge stadiums with Chicago and night after night, blew America's No. 1 band off stage with the infectious magic of their past.

Carl and Dennis Wilson were now heavily involved with studio experimentation and recording solo projects. Al Jardine was campaigning for ecology. Mike Love was making yet more money as a TM teacher. Brian's drug depression was reaching near fatal proportions.

In 1975 Warner's *insisted* Brian become a fully integrated recording member once again. A high priced specialist, Dr Landy, was hired and Brian was put under 24 hour bodyguard protection to keep him off junk food and junk drugs. The band recorded an oldies album, *15 Big Ones*, and despite Brian being only intermittently involved, a hugely expensive 'Brian's Back' campaign was mounted. He wasn't, but his sound was. The Beach Boys' rules of harmony and melody once again permeated America's popular culture. Children born years after *Surfin' USA* was first released were now responding to it as if it had just been written. "She was asking us to play our very first national hit which we recorded at least two years before she was born!" said the publicity conscious Mike Love, talking about a 10 year old girl at one concert.

The Beach Boys came to Australia in 1978 for a one million dollar guarantee, high-grossing, outdoor tour that hammered home both the enduring quality of their mid-'60s repertoire, and the cataclysmic disarray within the group. Brian was on tour. Sort of. The group was managed by Steve Love. Sort of. Behind the scenes, the Wilson clan and the Mike Love/Al Jardine axis were feuding with deadly intent. Brian on stage was a passenger but then, so were more than half of the players on stage. There were, for instance, *four* keyboard players simply because the Wilson/Love factions refused to agree to each other's choices. There was also a nasty fracas in Melbourne after Carl Wilson scored Brian some very much verbotten drug relief and was found out.

The Beach Boys today? In such total collapse they haven't toured for over two years now.

No other band so completely summarised the carefree spirit of American popular culture. No other group so completely sums up America's corruption and decline.

But their past is with us forever. All it needs is a hint of summer, a chance of a few lazy, carefree days and *Surfin USA, California Girls, Good Vibrations* et al will leap to the top of the charts once again. While the fragile humans who constructed them fade into ever deeper obscurity. As Dennis Wilson once said: "The Beach Boys is not a group, it's the music — the music is the star of this band."

BRIAN WILSON SESSIONS

page 24 SOUNDS July 31, 1976

STARSHIP • OYSTER CULT • KISS • SEX PISTOLS • QUO

ELTON, QUEEN dates

sounds

Brian Wilson
Making waves again
Exclusive interview

CAMBRIDGE FEST PAGE SPECIAL

BRIAN WILSON has never mentioned the sandbox before, and his psychiatrist, who explains that Brian tends to drop selected parts of the past from his memory, takes it as an encouraging sign. It comes up as Brian discusses the mystique that grew around him after his retirement as a performing Beach Boy, when he became a mysterious recluse and, some were saying, a mad genius.

"Well, I got behind that, because it's all true," says Wilson, adopting a sing-song lilt. His voice is high-pitched, like a teenager's. "I was a hermit, I was a musical hermit, I did stay alone, and it's true that I did have a sandbox, and the sandbox was in my house, it was the size of one room, and we had a piano in the sand, and all that's true. The idea of staying home and writing in a sandbox is all true, and it's pretty close to how I really am — I mean I'm that way.

"And the mystique grew, and I was getting fascinated with the fact that I was becoming famous and that there was interest in my style of life. I had a certain style of life, you know, a very eccentric person, and people began to take note of that."

Brian Wilson, a big, roly-poly bear of a man, is a lucid enough human being, even if some of his observations connect with reality at a decidedly individual angle. He appears tense, but is determined to carry through with this luncheon interview at a Beverley Hills Chinese restaurant, where he's surrounded by a party that includes his wife Marilyn, his psychiatrist, Gene Landy, his psychiatrist's young assistant and a Beach Boys publicist: just a part of the force that keeps Brian mobilized.

Brian's mouth, nose and eyes cluster tightly near the centre of his full-moon face, and as we talk small sparkles of perspiration form on the cheeks above his beard, like tiny tears coming out the wrong place. His pudgy fingers drum incessantly on the table, and underneath, his right leg jiggles up and down like a jackhammer (a few weeks later, at the Beach Boys' Anaheim Stadium concert, Landy will tell me it's been diagnosed as an organic, not a nervous, disorder.)

Brian converses directly and expansively, and when he warms up to a subject his enthusiasm makes him a downright campfire talker.

He usually looks straight ahead when he speaks, as if reading from the room's far wall. Sometimes he'll regard you with wary suspicion, then he'll take you in with a look that's both conspiratorial (as if to say, "I'm sure you understand what I mean") and challenging ("Don't you?!") Most of all, you're struck by his air of childlike vulnerability. When he unearths a feeling from the distant past it seems to hit him again with its original force, so he has to be a little careful.

The occasion, of course, is Brian Wilson's return to active duty as the Beach Boys' leader in the studio. He's back just in time to help them celebrate their 15th anniversary with their first album of new (or newly recycled anyway) material since '72's 'Holland'. "Well, it was my fault," he confesses. "In other words it was all banking on me if we were going to be creative, and it was my fault —"

"Not a *fault*, Brian," interrupts the vigilant Dr. Landy, who looks more like a record company promotion man than a psychiatrist.

"It was really my fault," continues Brian, undaunted, "because I was hiding in my bedroom from the world. Basically I had just been out of commission, I mean I was *out of* it. I was unhealthy, I was way overweight, I was totally a vegetable.

"In other words my life got all screwed up . . . It happened through my starting to take drugs. I started taking a lot of cocaine and a lot of drugs, and it threw me inward, I imploded, I withdrew from society, through drugs, and continued so for two, three, four years . . .

"Yeah, I was meditating, I took up meditation a couple of years ago, and that too turned me inward. It did increase my energy, although I wasn't using it for the purpose of recording records. The energy was devoted to seeing people partying, doing cocaine."

THE INTENSIVE program of physical and mental therapy began this spring. "He's learning," explains Landy's earnest young aide, seated to Brian's right, "how to develop a style of being able to take care of himself, to feel accepting and feel OK about who he is and what he can create." It's strange to hear that said about someone whose influence on pop music has been, to say the least, profound.

Besides swimming and running the perimeter of the large Rancho Park every morning with his bodyguard Stan Love (Mike's brother, a former professional basketball player with a good touch from the top of the key for a big man) and abstinence from drugs, the regimen includes Brian's separation from, well, bad influences, people like Van Dyke Parks and Danny Hutton, both of whom Brian holds in high regard.

It seems that the changes — and there certainly have been changes — haven't been worked way down deep yet (he's still known to ask interviewers for uppers, and certain friends question the reality of the whole "Brian is Back" campaign.) It still requires *enforcement*, and while Brian is grateful for his decreasing weight and his increasing ability to function, he must inevitably resent the fact that he is, in effect, a prisoner.

Brian's malfunctioning, Landy explains, was on the social level, not the creative, which explains how the fertile 'Pet Sounds/Smile' period could follow his first nervous breakdown. Brian remembers that day in December, 1964, his last day as a touring member of his band, very well.

"I was on tour with the Beach Boys, we were in Houston, Texas," he recounts cooly, keeping a distance from the live-wire memory. "Before I left, I told Marilyn, I said, 'Marilyn, you're in love with Mike.' She said, 'No I'm not.' I said, 'I know you are.' By the way she was looking at him at the airport and everything I thought she was in love with Michael. I had a nervous breakdown over it — over that plus other pressures.

"I just remember that I started to flip out, and Carl came to the hotel room and I slammed the door on him and said, 'Get out of here, I don't want to see anybody!' I told the stewardess, 'I don't want any food, get away from me,' like that, and I was crying on the plane and everything . . ."

BRIAN WILSON SESSIONS

Brian Wilson

"That was the start of the secluded period, but the secluded period ended with 'California Girls.' I started to get going back with that, then I had another nervous breakdown in 1972, which was after we went to Holland. I'd been away from home so long."

Those other pressures Brian mentioned were a grind of touring, compounded by his partial deafness: "The worst part of it is the sounds that come out on the stage, the loud sounds... I have twice as much sound going in one ear, and all that sounds drove me nuts. Between the audience and the amplified guitars, I couldn't take it, and that broke me down."

"15 Big Ones," Brian's first major studio endeavour since that second breakdown, started off, he says, "a little scary because we weren't as close. We drifted apart personality-wise. A lot of the guys had developed new personalities through meditation... It was a bit scary and shaky. But we socked into that studio with the attitude that we had to get it done. After a week or two in the studio we started to get the niche again.

"This time around, I thought, we had strictly commercial stuff — if you listen to our album you'll see that we were thinking about the public. We thought about songs, songs that were standards, that since they were already accepted once we figured would be accepted again, such as 'Blueberry Hill,' 'Palisades Park,' 'A Casual Look' — songs like that.

We figured it was a safe way to go.

If Brian eased back into activity via the less demanding oldies route, he's already looking ahead to more challenging tasks. "Oh yes," he says perkily, "we have some ambitions. We're thinking in terms of that right now. We've ordered some equipment, some of the most modern equipment you can get. We have the most modern studio that we could possibly have, so with the advent of these new instruments I think we can advance ourselves artistically."

THE ILL-FATED 'Smile' experience, though, has taught Brian about the dangers of indulgent ambition. "Well," he says, a little sheepishly, "we got a little arty about it, and it got to the point where we were too selfishly artistic and we weren't thinking about the public enough. It got to that level — partially because of drugs..."

The *public* is very much on Brian Wilson's mind, so much so that, asked about the individual Beach Boys, he doesn't detail their specific musical and spiritual contributions, but takes it from the demographic angle. "I see Mike Love as one of the best lead singers in that he sounds *young*," says Brian, picking up steam. He maintains that young, nasal sound. He's in tune with the teenagers, the 16 to 25.

"Carl is R&B. He keeps the group in tune with rhythm & blues music. Dennis, I would consider him hitting the 25 to 35 bracket. Al Jardine is also like Mike Love, he sounds young. So Al and Mike are responsible for our youth, Carl and Dennis are recognisible for 25 to 35, and I think I'm responsible for 25 to 45. So it's a careful blend of age groups we hit."

Brian inserts a straw into his mouth and slurps up a Coca-Cola like a big, soft vacuum cleaner. Yes, he says, grinding the ice cubes in his teeth, he often thinks in those terms: "Because I think music has become stereotyped and it's been bagged, and I think that if you spread your music around — where you make some of your cuts deliberately for the teenagers, and others, if you're artistic, you'll take in an older audience.

"But," he emphasizes, "I think you have to be constantly aware of the teenagers, because after all we are a young group of kids, so we still should be making music for the kids. I see no reason to desert them, you know what I mean? I see no reason to desert that audience."

That audience, though, abandoned the Beach Boys after the group left the surf music per se, and when the subject is broached, Brian drifts away for the first time. "Yes it did," he says softly, then clamps his mouth closed as if — there were moments when the group would all get tears in our eyes. Certain moods. That was probably when I learned emotional music, putting my heart into it.

"Those vocal parts... You can barely sing it, but then the guy giving it to you, you notice that he's giving four other guys different parts, and he's thinking them all at the same time. And then the rhythms involved, and then the layers and layers and layers..."

(Dennis' credibility, remember, is open to question, he did say, after all, of Brian's withdrawl: "I didn't see him any different than he's normally been. I don't know... It's very hard for me to accept the fact that my brother maybe did have a breakdown. I've always loved him and cared for him. Nothing changed. I saw nothing abnormal in wanting to be alone.")

Brian's version of the 'Pet Sounds' encounter: "I think they thought it was just for Brian Wilson only. I think the problem was that they knew that Brian Wilson was gonna be a separate entity, something that was a force of his own... So with 'Pet Sounds' there was resistance in that I was doing most of the artistic work on it, and for that reason there was a little bit of inter-group (sic) struggle....

"Well, it resolved in the fact that they figured, 'Well, sure, it's a showcase for Brian Wilson, but it's still the Beach Boys.' In other words —" here he flashes a cagey smile — "they gave in. They gave in to the fact that I had a little to say myself, so they let me have my stint.

"I explained to them, I told them that it was only a temporary rift where I had something to say, and I wanted to step out of the group a little bit, that's all. And sure enough I was able to. But we recovered with 'Wild Honey,' which was the album that Carl began to become the chief musician of the group."

Brian now anticipates no recurrence of that situation: "I don't see that anymore. I see a merging of the members of the group now, as we've done in our current album. I see a great merging of our talents again, and I hope it stays that way, because it's the only way to work. Group energy is much better, so we're into synergetics."

SINCE 1961, when he and Mike Love concocted the first surf song, everything Brian Wilson has touched has attained mythic proportions: The Beach. The California Consciousness. The Beach Boys, once again, and probably for good, an American Rock institution. And Brian Wilson himself, the enigmatic genius whose shrouded presence pervades popular music. The prodigious weight of those myths, you feel, is one of the adversaries in his silent struggle, but at the same time his pride in their creation is certainly one of the forces that accounts for his emergence.

"Well, it grows on," he reflects softly. "It grows on and on. At first it was the thing of surfing, where we were the only things coming up with this new Chuck Berry-orientated sound. And legends grew. Legends grew about 'Pet Sounds,' legends have grown about a lot of our music. 'Good Vibrations' was a legend. I'm proud that we have created several different legends... It's a unique quality we have, which I'm very proud of. The fact that we can be leaders at times — we have at least gone through periods where we're leaders.

"And of course," he adds, shifting into one of his peculiar tangents, "the group being a family is interesting. We're one of the only groups in the music business that has three members of a family in it. The Cowsills were similar. They were a big super group. From Providence, Rhode Island. I think they're from. But *families*! I think one of the reasons we're a legend is that we're a family. We've stayed together, my cousin, the three brothers, we've stayed together, and, you know, like that."

I ask Brian something about Phil Spector. "Well first," he answers, "he was probably more of an artist than most people knew." Suddenly he turns to Marilyn and asks her when she's leaving.

"Right now," she says, glancing at her watch.

"I'll go with you," Brian announces.

"Are you sure?"

"Yes."

Fearful of losing a hot Phil Spector anecdote, I ask pleadingly, "Are you going now?"

"Yeah."

"OK. Will I talk to you again?"

"OK."

"Alright," says Dr. Landy, "why don't we meet Monday so you can have lunch somewhere? Where do you want to meet?"

"Would it be possible to go up to the house?" I ask.

"I prefer to stay away from the house," Landy says quickly. He seems to know this is a sore point.

"I prefer to do it at the house." Brian sounds delighted at the idea.

"I know," says Landy, trying to dismiss it casually, "but I don't like to go to the house."

"Well I'm doing it, so don't worry about it. I'm doing the interview, you're not, so don't worry about it."

Landy turns to me, figuring I'm not about to tamper in the delicate relationship between a rock 'n' roll giant and his shrink. "Let's just stay away from the house," he says firmly. If the table were smaller he'd probably be kicking my shin.

I'm reduced to, "I don't care, whatever you want."

"Well," Marilyn cuts in, diplomatically but unconvincingly, "there's going to be some things happening at the house anyway."

Brian is still insistent, and he's almost whining now. "Well *I'd* like to have it at the house."

Landy doesn't want this public impasse to continue.

"Tell you what we'll do," he says, "we'll be in contact with you."

"Good talking to you," says Brian as he departs with his wife. His psychiatrist will take that too as an encouraging sign. Later in the afternoon, a secretary calls and tells me I'm to meet Brian Monday for lunch in the dining room at the Beverly Wilshire Hotel.

'I was unhealthy, I was overweight, I was totally a vegetable. In other words my life got all screwed up....'

The Beach Boys' main man climbs out of the soundbox and explains how he got off the Endless Bummer.

BRIAN WILSON SESSIONS

BRIAN WILSON SESSIONS

BRIAN WILSON SESSIONS

BRIAN WILSON SESSIONS

The last official picture of the six Beach Boys, taken in the summer of 1983, just months prior to Dennis's death. Clockwise from top left: Bruce, Carl, Al, Dennis, Mike, Brian.

BRIAN WILSON SESSIONS

The Beach Boys, 1984, without their surfing inspiration. They dedicated their 1985 album, The Beach Boys, *to the memory of Dennis.*

BRIAN WILSON SESSIONS

BRIAN, MARILYN, WENDY AND CARNIE WILSON

BRIAN WILSON SESSIONS

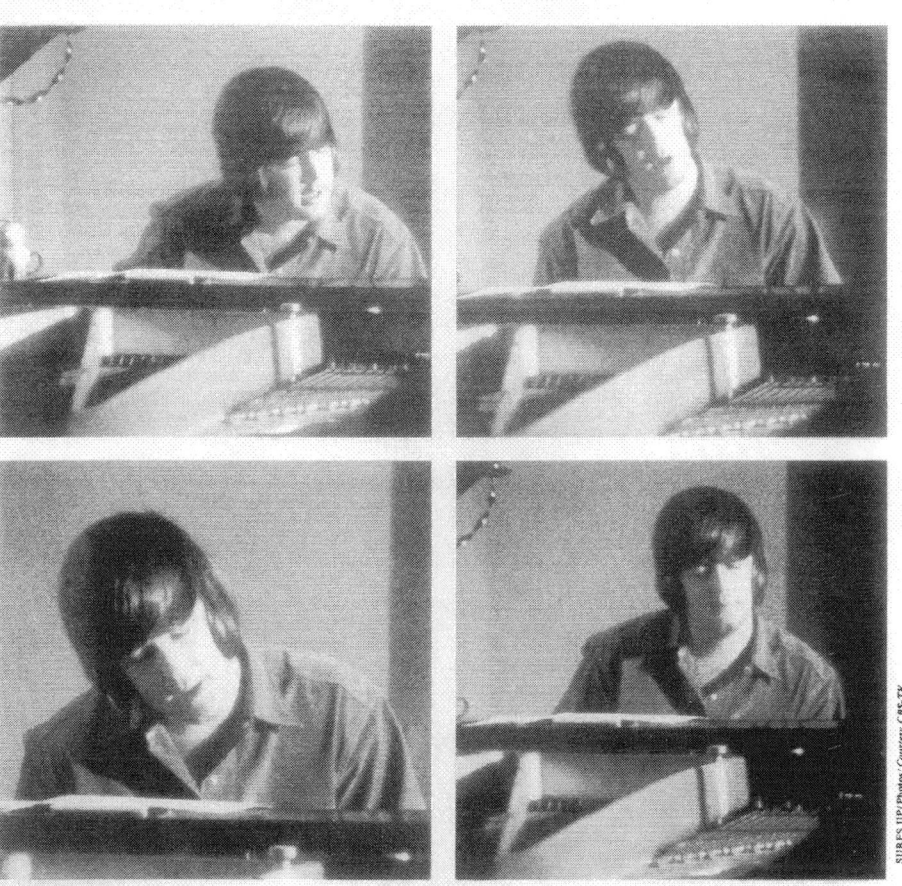

Brian performs "Surf's Up," 1966

BRIAN WILSON SESSIONS

COVER OF
ROLLING STONE
NOVEMBER 1976
(SEE ARTICLE
PAGES 30 - 44)

BRIAN WILSON SESSIONS

FROM OUI MAGAZINE
ARTICLE DEC 1976
(SEE PAGES 45 - 50)

BRIAN WILSON SESSIONS

A clean-cut Brian Wilson, the vastly gifted author of all the Beach Boys' classic hits, reads the dots in '64 (top) soon after the Californian group's first worldwide hit, Surfin' Safari. By '66 (centre) he was ingenuously testing the capabilities of the state-of-the-art recording equipment for the complex vocal symphonies on Pet Sounds. He was to return in '88 (left), after 20 years of creative torpor and crippling psychological illness, to finally release his first solo album.

Made in the USA
Columbia, SC
05 July 2025